THE ARCHIVAL AFTERLIVES OF PHILIPPINE CINEMA

A CAMERA OBSCURA BOOK

THE ARCHIVAL AFTERLIVES OF PHILIPPINE CINEMA

BLISS CUA LIM

DUKE UNIVERSITY PRESS *Durham & London* 2024

Project Editor: Lisa Lawley
Designed by Matthew Tauch
Typeset in Garamond Premier Pro by
Westchester Publising Services

Library of Congress Cataloging-in-Publication Data
Names: Lim, Bliss Cua, author.
Title: The archival afterlives of Philippine cinema / Bliss Cua Lim.
Other titles: Camera obscura book.
Description: Durham : Duke University Press, 2024. | Series: A camera obscura book | Includes bibliographical references and index.
Identifiers: LCCN 2023016215
ISBN 9781478025733 (paperback)
ISBN 9781478021001 (hardcover)
ISBN 9781478027867 (ebook)
Subjects: LCSH: Motion picture film—Preservation—Philippines. | Film archives—Philippines. | Digital preservation—Philippines.
Classification: LCC TR886.3 .L56 2024 | DDC 777/.5809559—dc23/eng/20230810
LC recordavailableathttps:// lccn.loc.gov/2023016215

Cover art: RJ Leyran (dir.), *Bugtong: Ang Sigaw ni Lalake*, 1989. Film still. Courtesy of Tata Nanding.

Duke University Press gratefully acknowledges the UCI Humanities Commons at the University of California, Irvine, which provided funds toward the publication of this book.

To Joya, Bella, Vallie, Alyssa, and Haru,

for their sustaining love

CONTENTS

ACRONYMS

ABS-CBN	A Philippine broadcast media conglomerate named for the 1957 merger of the Alto Broadcasting System (ABS) with the Chronicle Broadcasting Corporation (CBN)
BNFI	Bureau of National and Foreign Information
BRMPT	Board of Review for Motion Pictures and Television
CCP	Cultural Center of the Philippines
ECP	Experimental Cinema of the Philippines
FAP	Film Archives of the Philippines (1981–85)
FDCP	Film Development Council of the Philippines
FIP	Film Institute of the Philippines, founded in 1956 by Ben Pinga
LVN	Pictures, a major film studio founded in 1938
MIFF	Manila International Film Festival
MISD (or PIA-MISD)	Management Information System Division of the Philippine Information Agency
MOWELFUND	Movie Workers Welfare Foundation, Inc. (formerly Movie Workers Welfare Fund)
MPD (or PIA-MPD)	Motion Picture Division of the Philippine Information Agency
MTRCB	Movie and Television Review and Classification Board
NCCA	National Commission for Culture and the Arts
NFAP (or NFAP/PFA)	National Film Archives of the Philippines, established in 2011 and renamed the Philippine Film Archive in 2018
NFSA	National Film and Sound Archive of Australia
NMPC	National Media Production Center
PFA	Philippine Film Archive (see NFAP/PFA)
PIA	Philippine Information Agency
PMO	Privatization and Management Office
SEAPAVAA	South East Asia–Pacific Audio Visual Archives Association
SOFIA	Society of Filipino Archivists for Film (formerly Society of Film Archivists)
UP	University of the Philippines

ACKNOWLEDGMENTS

The generosity and candor of archivists are this book's foremost condition of possibility: wading into uncharted archival waters cannot be done alone.

Sometime in the mid-aughts, Vicky Belarmino and Mary del Pilar shared their personal papers with me, fading records of the dynamic vision of the Society of Filipino Archivists for Film in its founding years and its vital collaborations with the South East Asia–Pacific Audio Visual Archives Association and the National Film and Sound Archive of Australia. A chain of seemingly chance events ensued. Vicky gave me a copy of Doy del Mundo Jr.'s 2004 monograph, *Dreaming of a National Audio-Visual Archive*, opening my eyes to archival constraint as the largely unremarked enabling condition for scholarship on Philippine cinema. Years later, Doy introduced me to Bono Olgado, now a key interlocutor and dear friend.

With humility and appreciation, I acknowledge a profound debt of gratitude (*utang na loob*) to several archivists, librarians, collectors, scholars, advocates, and filmmakers: in addition to Vicky, Mary, Doy, and Bono, I am grateful to Bel Capul, Vicky Bejerano, Julie Galino, Simon Santos, Emely Serreng, Teddy Co, Marti Magsanoc, Ricky Orellana, Merv Espina, Shireen Seno, Keith Deligero, Erik Tuban, Gym Lumbera, Nanding Josef, Alfred Nemenzo, Rodel Valiente, Mhel Acurin, Eros Arbilon, Paul Grant, Misha Anissimov, J. B. Capino, Nick Deocampo, Leo Katigbak, J. R. Macatangay, Manet Dayrit, Regina Murillo, Wilma Azarcon, Mercy Servida, Josie Walters-Johnston, Rose Roque, Bernadette Patino, Kei Tan, Joel David, Martin Manalansan, Robert Diaz, Rolando Tolentino, and Patrick Campos. Bel Capul, Teddy Co, and Cesar Hernando passed away prior to the completion of this book; I am grateful to them for their early and impactful support of my research.

I acknowledge the invaluable institutional support of the Philippine Information Agency. At the University of California, Irvine, I benefited from various research, publication, and travel grants awarded by the Humanities Center, the Humanities Commons, and the Center for Asian

Studies. A Visiting Research Fellowship at Kyoto University's Center for Southeast Asian Studies in 2012–13 and a Fulbright Scholar Grant to the Philippines in 2017–18 allowed me to conceptualize this project. Amanda Swain, the University of California, Irvine's great enabler of humanities scholarship, gave me invaluable advice on grant applications. At Duke University Press, I am grateful to Ken Wissoker, my project editor, my copyeditor, and the anonymous readers who believed in this book.

I learned enormously from conversations with various colleagues, friends, and the graduate and undergraduate students in all my classes. I am deeply grateful to Carol Hau, Bono Olgado, Ray Edmondson, and Karen Redrobe for reading my earliest chapter drafts: their formative feedback helped to forge my understanding of scholarship as a kind of ethical risk-taking. I am humbled to be a part of the *Camera Obscura* book series and the journal's collective: profound thanks to Patty White, Sharon Willis, Connie Penley, and Bishnu Ghosh for their affirmation and guidance; and to Tess Takahashi, Lalitha Gopalan, Lynne Joyrich, and Homay King for support and inspiration. Ally Field taught me to see lost cinemas differently, while Amy Villarejo's reading of the final manuscript moved me to see it anew. At UCI, I am grateful to Dan Bustillo, Lucas Hilderbrand, and Mehra Gharibian for their incisive feedback on chapter drafts; to Fatimah Tobing Rony, Allison Perlman, and Kristen Hatch for long years of friendship; to Tyrus Miller, Desha Dauchan, Eric Hahn, Sharon Block, Sohail Daulatzai, Nikki Normandia, and Amy Fujitani for support and collegiality in the trenches; and to Cécile Whiting, Dan Bustillo, K. T. Wong, and Anirban Gupta-Nigam for crucial reading suggestions. In the face of daunting archive closures in the summer of 2020, Mehra remarked, "Most people say figuratively, 'The book is about the struggle,' but in your case, the fact that archives are closing or endangered is exactly what the book is about; these events have everything to do with your book." So encouraged, I went on to write about Sisyphean hope.

I moved frequently between the social, cultural, and academic worlds of Asia and North America across a decade of writing this book. This project slowly gestated in various talks for the Association for Southeast Asian Cinemas Conference in Singapore in 2012; the Philippine Cinema Heritage Summit, convened by the National Film Archives of the Philippines, in 2013; the South East Asia–Pacific Audio Visual Archives Association conference in Vientiane in 2014, and a Southeast Asian Cinemas Research Network Symposium in Glasgow in 2018, all of which opened doors to a larger Asian Pacific archive world. At these coordinates,

I am particularly grateful to Karen Chan, Jasmine Trice, Philippa Lovatt, Gaik Khoo, Mariam Lam, and Uwe Schmelter. Between 2017 and 2022, a number of invited talks—at the University of Southern California's Cinema and Media Studies Graduate Conference, the University of the Philippines' College of Mass Communication and Film Institute, Cornell University's Visual Culture Colloquium, the Los Angeles Asian Pacific Film Festival, Visual Communications, Cinema Sala, and the University of Toronto's Cinema Studies Institute and Centre for Culture and Technology—brought my keywords and investments into sharp focus, in large part due to the stimulating Q and A discussions they enabled. My thanks to Arnika Fuhrmann, Christine Balance, Patrick Campos, Marie Jamora, Jason McLagan, James Cahill, Michelle Cho, Patrick Keilty, Scott Richmond, and the engaged graduate and undergraduate students who responded to my work and organized these various events. I am especially grateful to Akira Lippit and Viola Lasmana for helping me to develop my arguments on amateurism by pointing me to the work of Roland Barthes and Edward Said. And I am deeply thankful to James Cahill, whose visionary efforts allowed my family to finally live together under one roof, at long last, in Toronto (though all three of us are tropical).

For me, writing and thinking would have been impossible without ample reserves of love, humor, and tenderness on both sides of the same ocean. My pathbreaking parents, the late Dr. Felicidad Cua-Lim (柯淑端) and Dr. Manuel G. Lim (林荣昌), came often to my thoughts and dreams. My mom was still alive when I began this book, and she listened patiently to my early trepidations. In Manila, my niece Alyssa Lim Jurado and nephew Adrian Lim Mombay were vacation buddies, Cinemalaya companions, and loyal supporters at public lectures; my brother-in-law, Don Jurado, helped with Cebuano translations. In Irvine, *lubos na pasasalamat* to Bono Olgado and Joey Dayrit for emboldening me to write the book I wanted to write and for tending to my affairs in California so I could be with my family in Manila. Across the years, Carol Hau, Rachael Ball, Chammy Uy, Jasmin Jamora, Priscilla Fernandez-Zaballero, Nappy Lustre, my late mother-in-law Dolores Orendain Escobar, and especially Nila Gregana smoothed multiverses whose forked paths connect Kyoto, Manila, and the East and West Coasts.

Portions of this book were published in previous forms. The epilogue's analysis of *Pepot Artista* draws on an earlier version in a different form, "Pepot and the Archive: Cinephilia and the Archive Crisis of Philippine Cinema," a short essay that appeared in *Flow* 12, no. 3 (July 2, 2010), https://www.flowjournal.org/. Chapter 1 is an expanded version of "A Tale of Three Buildings: The National Film Archive, Marcos Cultural Policy, and Anarchival Temporality," published in the anthology *Beauty and Brutality: Manila and Its Global Discontents*, edited by Martin F. Manalansan IV, Robert Diaz, and Rolando B. Tolentino (Temple University Press, 2023). Chapter 2 is a revised version of a prior article, "Fragility, Perseverance, and Survival in State-Run Philippine Archives," which first appeared in *Plaridel* 15, no. 2 (December 2018): 1–40. I am grateful to Temple University and the University of the Philippines College of Mass Communication for permission to publish these earlier pieces in their present form in this book.

I completed this book under the forms of loss and duress, banal and epic, personal and global, that the COVID-19 pandemic put us all through. In COVID's long wake, timespaces to breathe, think, create, and imagine—as well as to step away by living fully—were made possible by those closest to my heart. I am thankful to my beloved *kabiyak*, Joya, for more things than I can recount, but most recently for believing that a trickle can turn into a wave. I am grateful to our daughter, Nanabella, for teaching us so much by being so wonderfully different from ourselves. I am thankful to my sister Val, teacher extraordinaire and family savant, for emotional sustenance and for being my first best friend; to my remarkable niece Alyssa, for an abundance of intellectual curiosity and inspiring craftiness; and to our bunny, Haru, for being grumpy, therapeutic, loving, and beautiful by turns. Joya, Bella, Vallie, Alyssa, and Haru are my queer trinational family of choice; this book is lovingly dedicated to them.

INTRODUCTION

Keywords for Philippine Cinema's Archival Afterlives

I remember being told by a librarian at the Library of Congress's Motion Picture and Television Reading Room in 2012 that its collection included a preservation copy of Vicente Salumbides and Manuel Conde's *Ibong Adarna* (Adarna bird; 1941) on nitrate.[1] Discovering the whereabouts of the Philippines' last known nitrate film (in an American archive, not a domestic one), coupled with the realization that I would never be able to see it projected in its original format (preservation copies are unavailable for research access) confirmed film historian Clodualdo del Mundo Jr.'s painful insight concerning "the research difficulties that a scholar in Filipino cinema will have to face." He laments, "There are so many . . . films that are either irretrievably lost or totally inaccessible," either because the last print of a canonical film is in a foreign archive or because "the film no longer exists; the negatives are gone and no positive print remains." In the absence of available video copies, one must resort to studying lost films via production stills and secondary sources.[2]

Years later, when I emailed the Library of Congress to ask what nitrate elements of *Ibong Adarna* it held, an archivist responded that none of the library's databases showed a film print of that title.[3] Searching my records of that 2012 research visit, I found nothing to confirm my initial recollection. I must have conflated Filipino archivist Arnulfo "Mack" Junio's mention of a surviving nitrate copy of *Ibong Adarna* at the Film Archives of LVN Pictures, the Golden Age major studio that produced the film, with memories of seeing other nitrate titles in the catalog of the Library of

Congress.[4] Was it all just a false memory brought on by wishful thinking that a Filipino film still survived on nitrocellulose stock?[5]

I began reaching out to contacts in the Philippine archive world to ascertain whether the LVN copy Junio wrote about in 2003 still existed. This was one of many moments when my research for this book took on an investigative, almost "whodunit," quality, especially since the trail of many defunct institutional archives had gone cold. At the archives of the media conglomerate ABS-CBN (named for the 1957 merger of the Alto Broadcasting System with the Chronicle Broadcasting Corporation), I spoke at last with archivist Julie Galino.[6] Galino, a former Film Archives supervisor at LVN, recalled that although the nitrate dupe negative of *Ibong Adarna* was still in good condition at the end of its 2005 restoration, a safe storage facility could not be found for it: the LVN Pictures laboratory closed in 2005, the Philippine Information Agency's Motion Picture Division (PIA-MPD) had been abolished the previous year, and the ABS-CBN Film Archives declined to house (notoriously flammable) nitrate in its vaults, fearful of jeopardizing other holdings. *Ibong Adarna*'s dupe negative, the last Filipino nitrate film in existence, the very copy Junio mentioned in 2003, was disposed of shortly after the restoration two years later.[7] My belated discovery that the last copy of *Ibong Adarna* on nitrate was gone—fifteen years after the fact—hit me with full force, as though the film had just been destroyed. In hindsight, I understand this experience (of trickster memory and belated epiphany) as attesting to the unsettling latency, the delayed impact, of many of the historical events that move us.[8] This scene of wishful misremembering was my own unintended, personal response to archival precarity.[9] It resonates with Tina Takemoto's queer archival precept of "acknowledging how our precarious relationship to enigmatic materials may lead to projections, misperceptions, revelations," and "productive detours."[10] I reflect on the medial materiality of my own restored copy of *Ibong Adarna*—a digital movie file that originated in a VHS tape—in the postscript to this introduction.

Historically, advocates of audiovisual archiving have fought a losing battle to preserve what remains of Philippine cinema.[11] Of more than 350 films produced before the outbreak of World War II, only 5 complete films from the American colonial period survive, all feature-length films produced in Manila using the official national language, Tagalog-based Filipino.[12] The archival vacuum that surrounds vernacular filmmaking from regions outside the national capital is even more acute: to take only one example, the Visayan-language films of the Cebuano film industry are considered a "lost cinema," with only a handful of titles available, the earliest dating from 1969.[13] Most extant titles survive primarily in analog or digital video form, countless film reels having been melted for silver or sold by the ton for other uses.[14] That no nitrate elements of a domestically produced Filipino film are known to exist is an exceptionally bleak statistic—even by comparison to the dismal survival rates of nitrate cinema worldwide[15]—and functions as a kind of shorthand for the archival paucity that subtends Philippine cinema. Resisting the fetishization of lost filmic objects that such lacunae might provoke, historians of Philippine cinema—such as Nick Deocampo, Paul Grant, and Misha Anissimov—have drawn on paratextual sources and ephemera as crucial sources of archival knowledge.[16] Their approach resonates with Giuliana Bruno's elaboration of an "archeological intertextual" approach to archival lacunae. Paraphrasing Bruno, while the film might be lost, "the paratext can be found" in film magazines, publicity materials, and the paper trails of contractual agreements, censorship, and correspondence.[17]

AN ANARCHIVAL CONDITION

The dwindling number of surviving Filipino films has everything to do with the historically short-lived nature of the country's government-funded audiovisual archives, compounded by a dearth of funding, a lack of political will, and the inevitable deterioration of media formats and carriers.[18] The foremost example of the ephemerality of state film archiving initiatives is the first Film Archives of the Philippines (FAP), which lasted about five years, from 1981 to 1986.[19] Established by the Marcos dictatorship in 1981 and subsumed under the Cultural Center of the Philippines (CCP) and, later, the Experimental Cinema of the Philippines (ECP), the country's founding national Film Archives shuttered shortly after the regime's ouster by the People Power Revolution that took place along the Epifanio de los Santos Avenue (EDSA) in 1986. As elaborated in chapter 3, the 1986 EDSA uprising ushered in the presidency of Corazon "Cory" Cojuanco-Aquino and the withering of the FAP. This was followed by twenty-five years of state neglect that irreversibly damaged the majority of the Philippines' film holdings. In those gap years a nongovernmental organization, the Society for Film Archivists, founded in 1993 and later renamed the Society of Filipino Archivists for Film (SOFIA), spearheaded film preservation and restoration efforts and called for the establishment of a national audiovisual archive.[20]

In 2011, the National Film Archives of the Philippines (NFAP) was revived under the auspices of the Film Development Council of the Philippines (FDCP).[21] The archival mandate of this industry-focused state film agency consists of a single sentence.[22] Historically, the FDCP's weak archival mandate has meant that the degree to which the state film council pursues or neglects audiovisual archiving is at the discretion of the particular FDCP chair appointed by the sitting Philippine president. Upon President Rodrigo Duterte's election in 2016, the NFAP was deprioritized by the FDCP and rebranded the Philippine Film Archive (PFA) in 2018, its pace of restorations and activities slowing markedly.[23] The PFA remains on uncertain ground, the NFAP having been reestablished without the security of legislation to ensure ample funding, autonomous governance, and a permanent repository for the archive—all long-standing demands voiced by advocates and stakeholders. Bernadette Rose Alba Patino, a former archivist at the NFAP/PFA, offers this trenchant critique: "The lack of financial investment, consistent experienced and knowledgeable leadership, and sheer political will to establish a permanent archival facility to house FDCP's holdings—a crucial project that has languished for nearly a decade—continues to put all collections at risk. Such shortcomings render the vast majority of collections inaccessible to the public. Likewise, little has been done to address the idle progress in developing staff, infrastructure, and access points since the inception of FDCP's archiving program in 2011."[24]

As Patino and other critics have noted, plans to establish a permanent edifice for the national audiovisual collection have been floated by various state entities since at least the 1980s; as of this writing, none have come to fruition.[25] Lacking a permanent institutional space and a firm legislative mandate, the long-term prospects of the reinvented PFA (née NFAP), regardless of regime change and short-term presidential appointees to key film posts, are not assured.[26] Historically, permanence and sustainability are the most urgent and most enduring problems for state-funded Philippine film archives. The still-unfolding story of the first FAP's death and the uncertain afterlife of its successor, the NFAP/PFA, have broad parallels with the tragic dissolution of other key government media collections.[27]

I characterize this situation—the institutional precarity, scarcity, and circumscribed circulation of Philippine cinematic history—as an *anarchival condition*. Jacques Derrida's "archive fever" names the internal contradiction that burns at the heart of every archive and "threatens . . . every archival desire," underscoring the inevitable destruction, forgetfulness, and loss that "menace" the institutional drive to preserve and remember. Derrida's discussion of Freud's death drive reads: "The death drive is above all anarchivic. . . . It will always have been archive-destroying."[28] Archive fever both constitutes and consumes archival aspirations: "There would indeed be no archive desire without radical finitude, without the possibility of a forgetfulness which does not limit itself to repression."[29] Drawing on Derrida, Akira Mizuta Lippit defines the anarchive as the necessary complement to the archive, the inevitability of loss that shadows forms of historical survival. For Lippit, the prefix *cine* in *cinema* refers not only to movement but also to cinders, the ashes to which photochemical celluloid will inevitably be reduced. Deterioration, degeneration, and ruin constitute every archive's anarchival shadow.[30] The range of anarchival conditions with which all memory institutions necessarily contend include the ever-present possibility of loss, decay, or destruction; the scarcity of surviving works; the instability or unsustainability of institutional collections; and restricted access. Such challenges and constraints are anarchival in the sense of running contrary to notions of perpetual preservation and untrammeled retrieval. The Philippines' history of collapsed or endangered film archives directly contradicts the fantasy of archival permanence; I refer to this as an anarchival condition.

Even under the best possible storage conditions, with temperature and humidity regulated, the temporality of film preservation is one that continually defers an inevitable process of decay.[31] Paolo Cherchi Usai cautions that the fight against deterioration and obsolescence can never be won, whether on analog or digital media, while Ray Edmondson emphasizes that preservation is a perpetually unfinished endeavor that is meaningless without access: "Nothing has ever been preserved—it is only being preserved."[32]

THE POLITICS OF ARCHIVES

Constrained access to a severely attenuated corpus of Philippine cinema means that social subjectivity, cultural production, and historical knowledge are forged in the absence of a widely circulating reservoir of domestically produced films, that is, within a profoundly anarchival media horizon. The social subjectivities and political uses of cinema that might have arisen within the ambit of an abundant, readily available Philippine cinematic archive are a matter of conjecture. What worldings could have emerged if more Filipina/os and Filipinx,[33] both within the *bayan* [homeland] and without, understood themselves, in Dylan Rodríguez's words, as "both a direct descendant and vexed inheritor of the legacies of U.S. conquest, colonization, enslavement, and neoliberal ('multicultural') incorporation"?[34]

As Resil B. Mojares demonstrates, much of "traditional Filipino heritage" and even the Philippines' Anglicized name were inventions of American rule. We are confronted with the ineluctably colonial origins of Philippine memory institutions like the National Archives, the National Library, and the National Museum, all of which evolved from American entities founded between 1900 and 1901. Mojares's characterization of nationalism as the outgrowth of colonial state formation emphasizes agency and contingency alongside subjection and dependency: "Filipinism was actively crafted by Filipinos themselves, in ways and for purposes that did not always coincide with U.S. colonial aims," even as "it did not quite suffice for the time (nor does for ours.)"[35]

Like the elided colonial roots of Filipino archiving, Philippine cinema's anarchival situation, shot through with precarity and constrained circulation (ordinary Filipinos cannot readily access their own film history), is a political matter. As Ramon Lobato notes, "Questions of distribution are nothing if not political. If we understand politics as a struggle for power and resources, then distribution is politics at its purest."[36] Applied to media archiving, the necessarily political valence of circulation and the allocation of access can be read in different ways. Archival politics underwrite the official allocation of access; the selective prioritization of certain films for preservation and exhibition; and, conversely, the circumvention, via informal routes, of formal strictures maintained by government agencies, university and private libraries, or media industry archives.[37]

The politics of archives can be symptomatic, on the macro scale, of a dictator's attempts to instrumentalize the cinema or a post-dictatorship state's collusion with the interests of the local elite, leading to the corporate privatization of the (ideologically laden concept of a) "national film heritage." Anarchival politics abet a cultural amnesia about Philippine history that erodes sovereignty in favor of what Vicente L. Rafael calls "white love," contributing to a political nihilism that tolerates rather than resists contemporary forms of state violence.[38] Mike de Leon's short film *Kangkungan* (Summary execution; 2019) makes precisely this argument: forgetting the abuses enabled by Marcos era martial law (given that documentary footage of this period hardly circulates in the mainstream) fosters national complacency toward the extrajudicial killings normalized by Duterte's necropolitical war on drugs.[39] This critique can be extended to the regime's two-and-a-half-year imposition of martial law on Mindanao (from 2016 to 2019), the controversial Anti-Terrorism Act of 2020, and the 2021 abrogation of the defense agreement protecting the academic freedom of the University of the Philippines (UP).[40] Widespread cultural amnesia and revisionist histories regarding the Marcos dictatorship are among several precipitating conditions for the election of the late dictator's son, Ferdinand "Bongbong" Marcos Jr., to the Philippine presidency in May 2022, thirty-six years after his father's regime was ousted from power by a popular revolt of historic dimensions.[41] (Throughout this book, the "Marcos era" and "the dictatorship" refer to the administration of Ferdinand Marcos [senior], who was elected to the presidency in 1965 and who clung to power by declaring martial law in 1972, the beginning of the Marcos dictatorship.)

Over the course of this book, I touch on the fate of various state film archives and collections under the presidential administrations of Ferdinand Marcos (1965–86), Cory Aquino (1986–92), Joseph Estrada (1998–2001), Gloria Macapagal Arroyo (2001–10), Benigno "Noynoy" Aquino III (2010–16), and Rodrigo Duterte (2016–22). Audiovisual archiving is entangled with the country's political history because national film archives have been directly subordinated to the Philippine presidency, from the FAP in the 1980s to the present-day NFAP/PFA.

As chapter 3 demonstrates, the most significant difference between audiovisual archiving under the Marcos and post-EDSA governments is privatization: following the fall of the dictatorship, the media conglomerate ABS-CBN emerged as the country's dominant archival player. This conspicuous contrast, however, is counterbalanced by other significant continuities. One of the book's central arguments is that the Marcos era bequeathed an anarchival legacy in terms of the cultural policies, organizational structures, and political appointments that have proven so historically deleterious for audiovisual archives.

In the postdictatorship era, the FDCP has adopted the template of its predecessor in the Marcos era, the ECP, effectively corralling the film industry under the Office of the President.[42] In keeping with the so-called appointments clause of the Philippine Constitution, the executive officers of independent government agencies such as the FDCP and the Philippine Information Agency (PIA) are appointed by the president without need for approval from the Commission on Appointments and in the absence of congressional oversight.[43] Coterminous with the sitting president's period in office, the six-year term of presidential appointees to important state film and media entities promotes a shortsighted perspective on media archives. Historically, FDCP chairs prioritize splashy achievements during their own terms while deprioritizing projects launched by their predecessors, resulting in an erratic government approach to audiovisual archiving.

The deep continuities between the cinematic policies of the Marcos era and those of postdictatorship administrations mean that both audiovisual archiving and domestic film production and circulation remain severely curtailed. Excessive taxation (a 30 percent amusement tax on theatrical exhibition) and liberal film importation in the absence of protectionist policies (as stipulated by free trade agreements) stifle the competitiveness of domestic films vis-à-vis the avalanche of Hollywood product.[44] Since its creation in 2002 to foster "the development and growth of the local film industry," the FDCP has failed to ameliorate these deep-seated problems.[45] In recent years, archive advocates, myself included, have lobbied the Philippine Congress for legislation that ensures the institutional autonomy of a prospective national audiovisual archive and uncouples it from the FDCP.[46]

In his analysis of the relationship between Nollywood and the Nigerian state, Matthew Brown poses the question of the government's role in domestic filmmaking: "How . . . is the state economically and ideologically accountable for its film industry, and vice versa?" Both the presence and the absence of the state—especially in matters of cultural policy—have far-reaching consequences: "The first role is a role of presence, of recognizing, taking an interest in, and attempting to regulate the popular film industry, but doing so poorly. The second role is a role of absence, of possessing the mandate and even the resources to construct the national social economic infrastructures with which film could interact, but failing to do so."[47]

In the Philippine context, a historical analysis of the simultaneous presence and absence of the government in local cinema indicts cultural policy on several fronts: bureaucratic structures that put the film industry under direct presidential control; film importation policies that fail to protect local filmmaking in obeisance to free trade agreements; excessive taxation and censorship, reflecting the state's narrow interests in income extraction and the muzzling of cinematic dissidence; and the continuing ineffectiveness of government agencies in sustaining filmmaking and audiovisual archiving.

On the one hand, Brown recognizes that Nollywood—a primarily English-language video industry that cannot represent the geographic and ethnolinguistic diversity of Nigerian filmmaking—is a poor fit with reflectionist notions of national cinema. On the other hand, Brown argues that Nollywood can still be construed as a national cinema in the sense that its textual, aesthetic, and industrial characteristics "reflect the state of the state in which it is produced," a state "crippled" or debilitated by histories of colonial violence, authoritarianism, and corruption, all of which have a bearing on cinema.[48]

Extending the logic of Brown's analysis to the Philippine context, the anarchival situation of Philippine cinema reveals "the state of the state." That domestically produced films are perpetually disadvantaged in relation to Hollywood fare reflects the dominance of elite interests, whether in the form of benefices to oligarchically controlled media conglomerates (explored in chapter 3) or in allowing cartels to exert a chokehold over local film distribution and exhibition (resulting in local movies' perennial "audience problem," discussed in chapter 6 and the epilogue).[49]

THE PROJECT

This book explores the contours and consequences of Philippine cinema's anarchival condition. Rather than guaranteeing institutional permanence and establishing infrastructures of circulation, Philippine audiovisual archives are analogous to an ailing riverine system with dammed-up waterways rather than coursing channels of unimpeded flow (as elaborated in chapter 5). Whereas scholars across various disciplines often evoke the "politics of the archive" in a figurative sense, this book unpacks the politics and contexts of actual initiatives on the part of Philippine film archives, advocates, and informal players: to stay afloat; to achieve effective, autonomous governance; to rescue deteriorating feature-length titles; to migrate little-known experimental shorts; to bring peripheralized regional films to local audiences; and to address and thereby constitute an archivally conscious public. To this end, the book weaves together questions of institutional history, political context, cultural policy, and the agency of formal and informal players alongside medial materiality, film analyses, and production histories. Philippine film archives (formal, informal, or fictive-affective) are approached variously as institutional or private collections, as interpretively rich movies, and as people—resourceful social actors exercising archival power in profoundly anarchival, low- to no-budget circumstances. Archival memory is vested in material collections themselves and in the people who actualize remembered knowledge, institutional histories, ethical decisions, and creative work-arounds.[50] This book centers the undervalued labor of audiovisual archivists and advocates, as well as their self-theorizing, offering an on-the-ground analysis of cultural memory as it is made and unmade.[51]

Attempting to intervene in Philippine cinema's entrenched archival predicament, *Archival Afterlives* explores two parallel trajectories encompassing both formal and informal archival initiatives. First, this study recovers the history of key government film archives whose institutional demise led to the catastrophic loss of key collections and the rise of a powerful corporate archive. In the post-EDSA period, the failure of state audiovisual archives was followed by the privatization of a significant portion of the Philippines' remaining holdings by the media conglomerate ABS-CBN. The shutdown of ABS-CBN in July 2020 by the Philippine Congress was motivated in part by Duterte's suppression of news outlets critical of his regime.[52] The shutdown has destabilized the country's most extensive audiovisual collection, which del Mundo once called "the de facto national film archive."[53]

Alongside this first trajectory, which foregrounds cultural policy and the rise and fall of formal archives maintained by state and corporate institutions, hums a second trajectory consisting of decentralized, largely informal initiatives. The most obvious example is the tenacious advocacy movement led by SOFIA from the 1990s onward, a nongovernmental "coordinating body" advocating for a national audiovisual archive.[54] Spearheaded by professional archivists in charge of important formal collections, SOFIA's organized advocacy exists alongside more informal and ephemeral efforts.

The opening arc of the book traces the Marcosian state's halting attempts to centralize film archiving efforts and the subsequent ascendancy of a media conglomerate's preservation and restoration agenda following the ouster of the dictatorship and the turn to privatization. Framing Philippine cinema's anarchival situation as an interplay between state custodianship vis-à-vis corporate archives, however, apprehends only the formal dimension of Philippine film archiving. Informal players have also innovated vital alternative routes for archival access. Accordingly, the last two chapters and the epilogue pivot to understudied, but no less decisive, examples of informal archiving: Video 48, a legendary holdout video store that brings a private insider collection into public circulation; the Kalampag Tracking Agency, a microcuratorial screening program that recovers experimental shorts; and the historiographical and audience-building efforts of the Binisaya movement, which centers Visayan vernacular cinema and regional audiences beyond Manila.

How does an analysis of its anarchival situation change our understanding of Philippine cinema? The juxtaposition of formal institutional histories and informal minoritized practices exposes the fictive homogeneity of national cinema, uncovering the material messiness of media survival and decay; the cultural policies that underpin vagaries of institutional safekeeping and precarity; minor modes of archival collection and circulation beyond those promulgated by formal state or corporate archives; and the intertwined aspirations to constitute a supportive domestic audience for Philippine cinema and to rouse an engaged public for audiovisual archiving. The dominant historiographical understanding of Philippine cinema is exposed as partial in at least two senses. First, our grasp of Philippine cinema is partial in that it cedes disproportionate authority to a minute percentage of surviving films, despite their failure to represent a large but unrecognized corpus of nontheatrical, nonindustrial, and non-Tagalog films.[55] Second, what we think we know about Philippine national cinema is necessarily partial in the sense of being political, since archival agendas reflect dominant ideas of national culture and the cultural priorities enacted by state, corporate, and individual actors.

MEDIAL MATERIALITY, FEMINIST EPISTEMOLOGIES, AND AMATEURISM

With regard to the source documents for this study—published materials and legislative records circulating in the public sphere, the "gray literature" of unpublished internal reports and memoranda,[56] personal papers collected by insiders to these institutions, and oral histories—I adhere to the methodological principle that scholarship must be alive to the tension between "the institution as it wants to be seen," "the institution as others see it," "the unpublished record," and the "personal recollections of those involved." I take it as axiomatic that "memory resides not just in things, but in people."[57]

In addition, my study adopts the approach that media historian Lisa Gitelman describes as the process of "following documents," which traces "techniques of control" while also probing the various demands that social actors negotiate in institutional contexts.[58] Having pored over executive orders, legislative bills, government circulars, memoranda of agreements, and deeds of sale between the state and private companies, I concur with Gitelman that documents carry the cultural weight of bureaucratic authority, reflecting the power and control of state officials but also opening the door to accountability.[59]

In 2005 and 2007, well before I even conceived of this book, Mary del Pilar of ABS-CBN and Victoria "Vicky" Belarmino of the CCP shared paper files of the gray literature they had collected during their early years with SOFIA and the South East Asia–Pacific Audio Visual Archives Association (SEAPAVAA).[60] I vividly recall the brown manila envelopes and fraying folders they handed me, stuffed with unpublished conference reports, workshop handouts, and fragments of government correspondence. In the fading type of a 1990s dot matrix printer, I encountered the unindexed, uncatalogued traces of a long-simmering archival dream. I promptly photocopied these papers and cannot now remember whether and how many of those personal papers were published or unpublished "originals" or photocopies themselves. What Gitelman describes as the taken-for-granted concept of xerographic reproduction and the more recent ubiquity of digital scanning makes it hard for me to pinpoint exactly when, over the last decade, I scanned my photocopies into portable document format (PDF). The same goes for copies of documents from the MPD and the Management Information System Division (MISD) I accessed with the assistance of Belina "Bel" Capul and Maria Victoria "Vicky" Bejerano at the PIA from 2014 to 2016.[61] In working with such sources, I was participating in practices of documentary reproduction.[62] Paper is the documentary medium par excellence.[63] Thus, a materialist approach to media historiography recognizes that the institutional history of the film collections recounted here involves a plurality of media: film and video (multiply migrated via analog and digital formats and carriers), documented in and through another medium (paper), then remediated to PDFs and movie files on my laptop (digital formats encountered through software applications).

While sharing early drafts of my work, I was asked by two interlocutors why I so prominently acknowledge the names of the archivists I have encountered; one of these, an anonymous reader for a journal article, asked whether my analysis, in drawing on archivists' standpoints, might sacrifice objectivity. The answers to both questions are rooted in some of my deepest research commitments and the formative influence of both postcolonial historiography and feminist epistemologies (particularly the field-shaping conversations of the early 1990s) on my scholarly practice.

I adhere to those strands of feminist epistemologies that work toward no-nonsense, necessarily incomplete accounts of the worlds we live in that are nevertheless reliable because such situated knowledges can be held accountable for their claims. Sandra Harding insists, "It is a delusion . . . to think that human thought could completely erase the fingerprints that reveal its production process," arguing that we "acknowledge the social situatedness that is the inescapable lot of all knowledge-seeking projects."[64] Donna Haraway writes, "Feminist objectivity means, quite simply, situated knowledges."[65] It is "an argument for situated and embodied knowledges and against various forms of unlocatable, and so irresponsible, knowledge claims. Irresponsible means unable to be called into account."[66] I name various social actors in the Philippine audiovisual archive world, as well as the archives I've consulted, so that these power-differentiated sources (and my translations and interpretations) can be tracked.[67] Responsible scholarship is characterized by locatable assertions; it also candidly acknowledges "the critical and interpretive core of all knowledge."[68] In speaking frankly about situated knowledge and multiple standpoints, feminist epistemologies have emphatically *not* given up on objectivity in favor of relativism. (What good would a free-for-all descent into relativism, in which all claims are equivalent, be for feminism and other social movements interested in a critique of power and subjugation? Whose interests, after all, does the charge that all news is "fake news" serve?) What the feminist reconceptualization of objectivity gives up—illusory claims to innocence, totality, and universality, or what Haraway calls the "God-trick" of bogus transcendence—it gains in accountability. This is one of the advantages of feminist thinkers' attempt to forge "a usable, but not innocent, doctrine of objectivity."[69]

The impact of feminist epistemology on archival theory is evident in the work of Joan Schwartz and Terry Cook, who argue for the recognition that "archives . . . are not passive storehouses of old stuff, but active sites where social power is negotiated, contested, confirmed. The power of archives, records, and archivists should no longer remain naturalized or denied, but opened to vital debate and transparent accountability." In their challenge to the "professional myth of impartiality" in archival theory, Schwartz and Cook draw on Haraway to reflexively acknowledge the contexts and power dynamics shaping every memory professional's situated perspective.[70] While prime movers of the decentralized audiovisual archival advocacy movement in the Philippines have included both straight- and queer-identified men and women, my interactions with female middle managers and a female video clerk at both state and private audiovisual archives have been especially crucial for my research. The centrality of women archivists' efforts in the first two chapters and the historically feminized labor of archiving (imagined in Schellenbergian archival theory as a "handmaiden" to the masculine enterprise of history writing) make feminist analyses of knowledge production particularly germane for my work.[71] The women archivists central to this book may or may not identify as feminists or activists; nonetheless, their subjective capacity as women who watch over and speak for collections under anarchival duress has shaped the Philippine archive world.

Feminist epistemologies and postcolonial historiographies taught me that the claims, interests, and concerns of socially stratified historians, knowers, and doers are inherently situated, shaped by power relations and by historical and social contexts.[72] Over the course of my research, I came to realize that the standpoints of audiovisual archivists, curators, collectors, and video store clerks have been overlooked in my academic discipline, film and media studies, and undervalued in cultural policy decisions affecting the fate of Philippine film archives. This is likely due to a confluence of bureaucratic hierarchies (in which the administrative decisions of top officials take precedence over the recommendations of middle managers and staff) and the separateness of the disciplines of film and media scholarship from the world of archival collection management and preservation (a parochialism that is gradually being overcome).[73] Similarly, although the writings of Derrida and Michel Foucault have spurred an archival turn in philosophy and critical theory, such work has largely ignored the perspectives of professional archivists.[74] Audiovisual archivists are a relatively tiny class of memory professionals (globally, their number "barely reaches five figures"), but these undervalued cultural workers wield a great deal of power over our collective memory.[75] The belated revaluation and integration of archival knowledge into film and media studies are themselves historically emergent.[76] A way forward, a chance for the future of Philippine film archives, seems to me premised precisely on drawing from, translating, and interpreting (rather than claiming to transparently speak for) the experiences, knowledges, and advocacies of the heterogeneous individuals and communities who work with the nation's audiovisual archives.

Michel-Rolph Trouillot's analysis of the Haitian Revolution teaches me the impossibility of the "nonhistorical observer" fantasized by a positivist model that imagines an unmarked position for the historian. Trouillot calls on historians (whether professional or amateur) to "position themselves more clearly" in the controversies of their own unfolding present.[77] The term *global South* does not primarily refer to a geographical area but rather names an epistemic, historical, and political commitment that dwells in the undersides, antipodes, and peripheries of profoundly asymmetrical processes of globalization as a generative vantage point for a history of the present.[78] Yet it is risky to try to speak reliably about real-world crises while admitting that all knowledge is inevitably fragmentary and situated. Researchers can only take a stab at responsible accounts of real events by acknowledging the situatedness of our perspectives in hopes of creating what Haraway calls "a chance for a future."[79] The task, which demands laying my cards on the table as I have attempted to do here, intimidates me. I am neither a historian nor an audiovisual archivist by training. I am a film and media scholar who, by virtue of my dependence on archival materials—from analog to digital, from print to moving images—is a stakeholder in and advocate for Filipino audiovisual archives, writing in the wake of a decentralized archival advocacy movement that goes back to the 1950s.

In a word, I am an amateur. Amateurism can have unfavorable connotations—the "dilettante" or "dabbler" is the opposite of the academic professor. The valorization of professional expertise versus uncredentialed engagement is part of the taken-for-granted ideology of academia.[80] In contrast, Edward Said conceptualizes amateurism as a remedy for the constricting tendencies of professionalism. Professional specialization can result in a narrow disciplinarity that obstructs a historical appreciation of "real experiences" and "raw effort." Said enjoins intellectuals to "view knowledge and art as choices and decisions, commitments and alignments" irreducible to "impersonal theories or methodologies." Professional parochialism, Said suggests, can be counterbalanced by amateurism, "the desire to be moved not by profit or reward but by love for and unquenchable interest in the larger picture, in making connections across lines and barriers, in refusing to be tied down to a specialty, in caring for ideas and values despite the restrictions of a profession."[81]

I do not claim for myself the gamut of virtues with which Said invests the term, especially since commonplace understandings of the amateur are less idealized and range from the nonprofessional participant to the inept enthusiast. Across varied usage and valuation, however, the term's core semantic element is love: *amateur* derives from the Latin *amator*, or "lover." In dictionaries, an amateur has a love, fondness, or passion for something. For Said, it is a love that discovers, with excitement, the broader stakes of an issue; for Roland Barthes, it is constant renewal. Barthes writes that the "*amator*: one who loves and loves again" experiences the continually rekindled pleasure of engagement "without the spirit of mastery or competition."[82] In a letter to his partner, Nika Bohinc, published a year before their untimely deaths, Alexis Tioseco, a charismatic champion of Philippine cinema, declared: "The first impulse of any good film critic . . . must be of love."[83] Loving Philippine cinema and passionate about working toward sustainable audiovisual archives, I write as an amateur who—lacking the training of the professional archivist, historian, or ethnographer—tries to keep sight of the raw effort and the choices of those involved in the hopes of reconstructing reticulated histories without claiming to have mastered the complexity of the issues and fields I touch upon.

I learned to embrace my amateurism only gradually, emboldened by thinkers of both archives and historiography. My understanding of that near oxymoron, "amateur historian," is inspired by Trouillot, who emphasizes that history is told by a diversity of narrators and that historical production is not confined to professionals: "We are all amateur historians with various degrees of awareness about our production. We also learn history from similar amateurs."[84] In an era when ordinary people with access to digital devices generate huge quantities of records everyday—texts, images, and sounds across genres, carriers, formats, and platforms—many are already amateur archivists of their own lives. Glossing this reality, Cook writes, "The archives is thus transformed from source to subject." I take this to mean that archives no longer belong only to memory institutions and trained professionals. Rather, our "transformed archival landscape" demands inclusive forms of archiving awake to the diversity of in/formal archives' communities of users, creators, and researchers.[85]

Utopic visions of participatory archiving must, however, be tempered by a recognition of the market forces that permeate archival worlds, alongside the ebb tide of reduced privacy in an era of ever-accumulating records about everything and everyone. Our snowballing collections of selfies, text messages, videos, and voice recordings, our emails, apps, and cloud storage, all mean that we are becoming micro-level information managers while also being targeted as subjects of macro-level data mining through the "algorithmic unconscious of social media."[86] Jussi Parikka writes: "As every museum and archive knows (or should), the labor of how culture remembers and retrieves from memory is shifting from the official institutions to everyday media environments," from social media to cloud computing, with its "microtemporalities" and storage on enormous proprietary servers.[87] The public so often invoked as the inheritor of archival heritage is simultaneously an aggregate of private users, "mini-archivists" who are, in turn, assiduously being archived by private corporations and the state.

ARCHIVES AND ADVOCACIES

Carolyn Steedman usefully offers a "prosaic" definition of *archive* as a "name for the many places in which the past (which does not now exist, but which once did actually happen; which cannot be retrieved, but which may be represented) has deposited some traces and fragments, usually in written form. In these archives someone (usually from about 1870 onwards, across the Western world), has catalogued and indexed these traces."[88] In contrast to manuscript and document archives, the notion of the film archive is of far more recent coinage. In the United States and Europe, the first film archives were founded in the 1930s, though it took decades for them to be recognized as cultural institutions on par with museums and libraries.[89] The appropriation of the term *archive* in relation to film was a legitimizing tactic that pointed away from the profit-oriented movie industry by suggesting an "image of stability" and "safekeeping."[90] However, as the archival struggles of memory institutions in the Philippines and elsewhere painfully underscore, "There is no 'safe keep' or 'safe-keeping.'"[91]

Forming the very ground of scholarship and historiography, the archive is an enabling constraint.[92] Archives simultaneously facilitate and restrict the production of knowledge through what Derrida calls "consignation"—an archive's constitution of an archivable corpus, of objects of study under principles of unity (e.g., canon formation around auteurs and recognized masterworks).[93] As film scholars and historians have long known, archives are the ground for contested notions of national cinema; preservation priorities are often justified through homogenizing notions of national heritage.[94] By archival and anarchival condition, then, I allude to the duality of archives as a condition of knowledge: first, as an enabling constraint on historical production; and second, as the state or circumstance of actual archives and their vicissitudes.

Derrida traces the etymology of the archive to the Greek *arkheion*, the residence of the archons, those who wielded power over the law and were charged with the guardianship of official documents and the privilege of their interpretation. For Derrida, the archive is that place in which the "substrate," or material onto which documents have been inscribed (the "*topological*"), is traversed by the "authority" of the law (the "*nomological*").[95] Yet, in opposition to the state's active instrumentalization of archives in Derrida's writing, in the Philippines' underresourced archives one confronts the near absence of a *topo-nomological* investment in audiovisual archiving. Cinema-related legislation is scant, clustered primarily around censorship and taxation. Unsurprisingly, archiving is marginalized, since preservation and access correspond to neither the government's disciplinary (e.g., censorship) nor its revenue-generating (e.g., taxation) agendas.

Prompted by government inaction, a decentralized archival advocacy for film in the Philippines arose prior to the founding of the first national film archives and has outlived many state archival efforts, though many of its prime movers have worked for or with government agencies. Calls to establish a film archive date back to American rule.[96] An early articulation of archival consciousness in the postcolonial period was penned in 1952 by Vicente Salumbides, director of *Ibong Adarna*, who called for the establishment of a film library devoted to film preservation.[97] Four years later, Benedicto "Ben" Pinga founded the Film Institute of the Philippines (FIP), a nongovernmental, donation-based organization that espoused film conservation among its many goals.[98]

The Philippine government ignored these early appeals, and cinema was absent from pioneering cultural policies formulated in the 1960s.[99] This was the very decade when Pinga admitted that the FIP could not realize its aims in the absence of state subsidies.[100] Pinga spearheaded a 1977 conference entitled "Cataloguing and Preservation of Filipino Films," which called for a presidential decree to establish a national film archive.[101] Pinga's visionary efforts, which brought together state and nongovernmental participants to brainstorm on film preservation within a regional and international framework, are the first stirrings of an archival advocacy movement in the Philippines. These initial calls were renewed in 1975 by National Artist for Literature Bienvenido Lumbera, who advocated for a Filipino film museum: "Fires and careless prolonged use have destroyed most of the old films, so that invaluable information that could be obtained only from actual contact with early samples of Philippine filmmaking has been irretrievably lost." For Lumbera, the impossibility of a comprehensive historiographical discourse on Philippine cinema, rooted in the country's archival fragility, amounts to one thing: "the absence of a clear historical perspective in the evaluation of Filipino films."[102]

KEYWORDS, OR, A ROUTE PAST MOURNING

The conceptual scaffolding for this book endeavors to move past the framework of mourning that so frequently attends discussions of film's inevitable deterioration, analog media's material decay, or digital media's impending obsolescence.[103] Writing a book that centers activist hope rather than mourning means insisting that archival efforts are meaningful whether or not particular films or initiatives have survived. Rather than bewail the ephemerality of archival initiatives with little to no funding or institutional support, this book recognizes the agentive ingenuity and creative boldness called forth by anarchival conditions. In a Foucauldian movement, constraint is generative, spurring unlooked-for collaborations as social actors bypass blockages to archival access.

First, the term *archival silences* refers not only to "lost films" in the corpus of Philippine cinema but also to the absences that are constitutive of the production of historical narratives, from missing government records to nearly irrecoverable institutional histories. Second, *archival power* names dynamics of inclusion and exclusion in the production of historical narratives, not just practices of appraisal that value and institutionalize a minute percentage of extant records. Finally, activism, advocacy, and "making do"—creative work-arounds that have emerged to ensure the archival afterlives of Philippine cinema—are crucial expressions of archival power. Histories of prior state film archives' collapse caution against the costs of inaction; given this, perseverance and making do are striking traits of Philippine archiving cultures called forth by anarchival realities.

ARCHIVAL SILENCE

European and North American scholars writing on archives evoke images of kilometric proliferation. Ann Laura Stoler speaks of "kilometers of administrative archives" housed in "massive buildings," describing the Nationaal Archief in The Hague as having "ninety-three kilometers of documents in their holdings."[104] Giovanna Fossati writes that the Library of Congress, the British Film Institute, the Bundesarchiv, and the Nederlands Filmmuseum hold "film cans by the millions in their climate-controlled vaults." Noting that a 35mm feature film with a screen time of an hour and a half "takes about two and a half kilometers of film," she muses that the holdings of 370 European archives "makes for a fantastic length of film strip," corresponding to approximately "fifty times the earth's equatorial circumference."[105] The kilometric proliferation of moving image media archives in the global North contrasts strongly with the diminution and precarity that characterize state-run audiovisual archives in the Philippines. To be clear, this book does not regard Philippine film archives as failed approximations of better-funded, legislatively secure memory institutions in the global North. Wendy Willems enjoins media scholars to "acknowledge the agency of the Global South in the production, consumption, and circulation of a much richer spectrum of media culture that is not *a priori* defined in opposition to or in conjunction with media from the Global North."[106] In keeping with Franco Cassano's injunction "not to think of the South in light of modernity but rather to think of modernity in light of the South," I construe archival practices in the Philippines as provoking alternative modes of theorizing and historicizing cinema from a vantage point that centers the materiality of loss, the ephemerality of institutions, and the perseverance of cultural workers in inhospitable conditions.[107]

Archival silence is the ontological limit that belies the fantasy of a totalizing archive. Relative proliferation or scarcity notwithstanding, even the most abundant collections have absences. Trouillot maintains that silences are intrinsic to the production of historical knowledge: from the constitution of sources to the mustering of archives, the construction of narratives, and, through the assignation of "retrospective significance," the "making of history in the final instance." The crucial point is that "any historical narrative is a particular bundle of silences."[108] Reflecting on the "piecemeal partiality" of colonial state archives, Stoler contrasts the "unwritten" (the archival silence surrounding the tacitly known) with the "not yet articulated" (the silence of the forbidden and unsayable).[109] As Steedman observes, scholars in archives are often faced with "what is not actually there, with the dead who are not really present in the whispering galleries, with the past that does not, in fact, live in the record office, but is rather, gone."[110] The specter of the anarchival within the archive is a kind of revenant: a living remainder amid destruction, a trace of death. Even archives of the most plenitude are composed of fragments, the result of stewardship, whether careful or careless, and chance longevity. The deep silences, the negative spaces of archives are as constitutive of historical production as the positive presences that are actually there.[111]

A profound archival vacuum is the enabling constraint for Allyson Nadia Field's *Uplift Cinema*, given that none of the works of early African American cinema she analyzes have survived. Undeterred by archival lacunae, Field examines early films from the 1910s that epitomized Black uplift, a social, political, and philosophical movement that regarded individual achievement rather than systemic transformation as the key to African American advancement.[112] In "A Manifesto for Looking at Lost Film," Field challenges the discipline of film and media studies to push past "extant-centric film history," an untenable approach given that "more than 80 percent of [American] films made in the silent era [are] considered lost." Field declares, "For those of us who study nonextant films, absence is the archive." Paratextual ephemera—institutional discourse, publicity materials, and journalistic coverage—allow us to sift for "the presence in the absence," reconstructing the formal qualities as well as the production, exhibition, and reception of "nonextant films."[113]

When Salumbides describes his students' disappointment at being unable to screen his film *Florante at Laura* (1949) only three years after its initial release; when del Mundo and Lumbera write about a Filipino film being "irretrievably lost"; or when Deocampo's *Lost Films of Asia* teaches us to miss what we have never seen, these authors register the frustrating nothingness one sometimes confronts in archives.[114] In their study of Cebuano cinema, Paul Grant and Misha Anissimov ask: "How could those who undertake the writing of this history find anything to say about the films if they cannot be seen?" Confronted with the "rude fact" of a "missing cinema," they write of recovering "pieces in the archives," locating, "amongst the debris and ephemera, the para-cinematic elements" left behind. "From there we begin to construct (and here the purposeful nature is explicit) a narrative based on the most concrete evidence we can find."[115]

The point, then, is not to bemoan the silences, gaps, and losses that are the very condition of historiography, the editorial principle without which a coherent story about historical events could not be told.[116] This study of Philippine cinema's anarchival condition is a project of neither mourning nor nostalgia; rather, it attempts to offer a critical (though necessarily partial) analysis of how archival silences came into being and how they give meaning to what survives. In the first two chapters of this book, archival silences take many forms: not only the absence of lost films but also the deafening hush that surrounds the institutional histories of key memory institutions, huge swaths of whose past is forgotten.[117] Archival silence encompasses the paucity of documents concerning the tragic fate of important state collections like the FAP and the PIA-MPD film library as well as the lack of public outcry concerning their demise. In contexts where both politicians and ordinary citizens know little about the institutional custodianship of the national past and are thus indifferent toward archival crises, speaking about silence entails a certain amount of risk-taking and ethical troublemaking.[118] Working on Philippine moving image archives that struggle to endure, I am convinced of the eloquence of lost films and missing government records and the significance of the imperfect movie copies with which we make do.

ARCHIVAL POWER

While inevitable, archival silences are never entirely accidental; they are not given but produced (though not always deliberately). Silences reflect the uneven operation of archival power, defined by Trouillot as the exclusion or inclusion of people from direct participation in the production of historical narratives.[119] The Philippines' anarchival condition calls for a nimble understanding of archival power, one that scales from an individual's in/capacity to create or access records, to the collective level of in/formal archival efforts, to the sphere of the geopolitical (the national and international economic disparities that impact the archivally related affordances of different communities).[120]

In archival theory, the consideration of archival power centers on professional archivists' powers of appraisal, a term that refers to the evaluation of a record's "permanent value" to guide preservation priorities.[121] In an era characterized by "an avalanche of over-documentation in all media" amid restricted institutional resources, archivists' powers of appraisal decide who and what "will get full, partial, or no archival attention."[122] For Terry Cook, appraisal emerges as a central form of archival power through which archivists "co-create the archive" through practices of selection, acquisition, valuation, and their converse (silencing, disposal, or destruction of archival holdings), since the ever-accreting quantity of possible records must be winnowed down to the size of a manageable collection.[123]

Seven years before the revival of the NFAP, del Mundo wrote candidly about archival appraisal in these terms: "A ruthless form of selection must be done, simply because the resources will not allow for comprehensive archiving. The least that the country can do is preserve this canon of Philippine Cinema."[124] Del Mundo reflects, "In a country beset by poverty and pressured by economic and political problems, it may be a tall order to convince lawmakers that a national audiovisual archive should be in their list of priorities." He suggests a form of archival triage in which only canonical feature-length films would be prioritized for duplication, preservation, and restoration, at the expense of popular or unknown works in less valorized genres (documentaries, shorts, or experimental films). This admittedly "ruthless" exercise of archival power, urged with pragmatic resignation by a film historian and SOFIA past president, illustrates Derrida's principle of consignation at work.[125] While the logic of archival triage is an understandable response to an anarchival predicament, it raises the question of how to advocate for archives without reproducing the conservative, consecrating functions of memory institutions.

This book explores another form of archival power, one wielded not just by professional archivists but by various formal and informal players (technicians, collectors, curators, and filmmakers) who resourcefully devise low-cost means of ensuring the afterlives and circulation of lesser-known works of Philippine cinema. I am drawing here on Trouillot's notion of subjective capacity as central to the production of historical knowledge. He gives the example of a labor strike, which cannot be described as a historical event without recourse to the subjective capacities of the workers involved: "But peoples are also the subjects of history the way workers are subjects of a strike: they define the very terms under which some situations can be described. . . . There is no way we can describe a strike without making the subjective capacities of the workers a central part of the description." For Trouillot, the subjective capacities of the players involved in historical events are vital rather than incidental to our understanding of history: "A competent narrative of a strike needs to claim access to the workers as purposeful subjects aware of their own voices. . . . To put it most simply, a strike is a strike only if the workers think that they are striking. Their subjectivity is an integral part of the event and of any satisfactory description of that event."[126]

Similarly, there can be no adequate analysis of the archival afterlives of Philippine cinema—remaindered from prior institutional collapse and preserved-in-destruction via multiply migrated versions—without a consideration of the archivists and advocates whose purposeful actions made these afterlives possible. Archival power, I suggest, is instantiated in the subjective capacity of formal and informal actors to widen the ambit of circulation through practices of poor archiving and making do.

MAKING DO: PROPAGANDA FILMS OF THE FIRST QUARTER STORM

The ensuing discussion focuses on films from the posthumous collection of the PIA-MPD. I say "posthumous" because the MPD's internationally prominent Film Lab and Film Archive were shut down in 2004 on the grounds that government cost cutting and the shift to digital media made the maintenance of this unique film collection an ineffective use of state resources, as recounted in chapter 2.[127] During a visit to the PIA in 2014, I asked to screen four 16mm propaganda films that had been produced by the National Media Production Center (NMPC) in 1971 and 1972 to justify the Marcos regime's imposition of martial law. My research request would have come to naught had key figures of the Philippine audiovisual archive movement not stepped in, all of them women archivists who were middle managers at state film archives and members of SOFIA and SEAPAVAA: Vicky Belarmino of the CCP, and Bel Capul and Vicky Bejerano of the PIA.

The archival principle of "context linkage" demands that audiovisual archives maintain the skills and equipment appropriate to a work's original technological context.[128] While valuable, context linkage is an increasingly impossible preservation ideal for many chronically underfunded film archives in the Philippines and elsewhere in the global South. The PIA had been a premier film restoration lab in Southeast Asia in the 1990s; by 2014, it had one 16mm projector and one 35mm projector in working condition but lacked a film projectionist. The skills required by outdated technologies quickly become esoteric; a projectionist for our research screening had to be sourced through archival networks. Accordingly, the film inspection and technical equipment check were conducted with the assistance of Alfred Nemenzo of the CCP and Leonil Getes of the PIA. Nemenzo projected the four films. The NFAP's subsequent correspondence and inspection report describe three of the titles as in "good or fair condition"; however, one of the propaganda shorts, *From a Season of Strife*, was "actively decaying," with "heavy buckle and wave, faded color, and scratches."[129]

From a Season of Strife (NMPC, 1972) demonizes anti-Marcos dissent via a tendentious voice-over narration and unconvincing reenactments of student unrest. On January 26, 1970, student protesters outside Congress called for a nonpartisan constitutional convention. The previous year's fraud-ridden presidential elections had given Marcos a second presidential term while galvanizing a militant student movement. The propaganda film offers striking, unstaged glimpses of the size of the student protest movement (figures I.1–I.3) and the chaos that broke out on the evening of January 26, as President Ferdinand Marcos and First Lady Imelda Romualdez Marcos were leaving Congress, where the president had just delivered his State of the Nation address.

A suspenseful musical score accompanies an extreme long shot of the confused throng outside Congress. It is difficult to pick out the central action unfolding during one thirty-four-second take: Marcos and Imelda emerging from the building and moving through a crush of journalists, onlookers, and security forces to their awaiting vehicles (figures I.4 and I.5). They duck hurriedly into their car as police carrying riot shields enter the foreground, allowing the presidential convoy to drive away. A disembodied male voice-over intones: "These are the facts: on January 26, 1970, a reelected president, unprecedented in Philippine history, was stepping out of Congress after delivering his address. He was met by a hostile mob of demonstrators numbering more than fifty thousand. President Marcos had just been reelected by an overwhelming margin of over two million votes. . . . And yet, he was witness to demonstrations . . . mounted against his administration."

Portraying Marcos as a legitimate ruler harassed by a "hostile mob of demonstrators," the narration's tactical disinformation does not acknowledge that Marcos was the first president to be reelected to "an unprecedented second term" through what Talitha Espiritu calls "the staggering violence and fraud that attended the November 1969 elections."[130] The voice-over vilifies the protesters as "the enemy" whose growing menace provokes the imposition of martial law: "The suspension of the writ of habeas corpus did not deter nor contain the enemy that had gone underground, hiding behind various fronts and assuming different forms of dissent. Appearing legitimate on the surface, the enemy was using every available means, particularly the press, radio, and television, to implement its well-laid plans." What the narrational voice leaves out is that these protests marked the beginning of the First Quarter Storm. Marcos later claimed not to have seen the student activists' derisive placards and effigies,

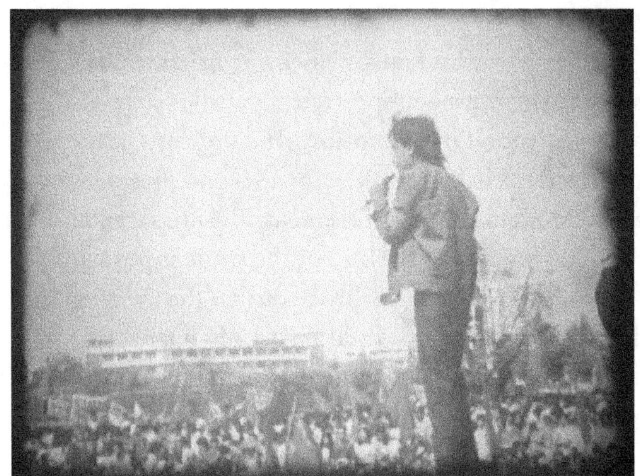

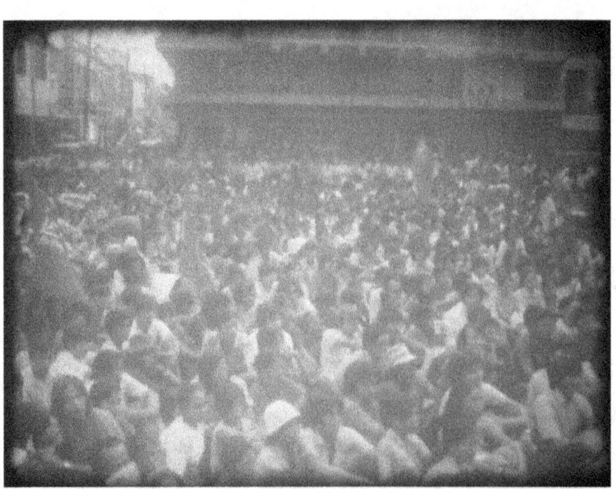

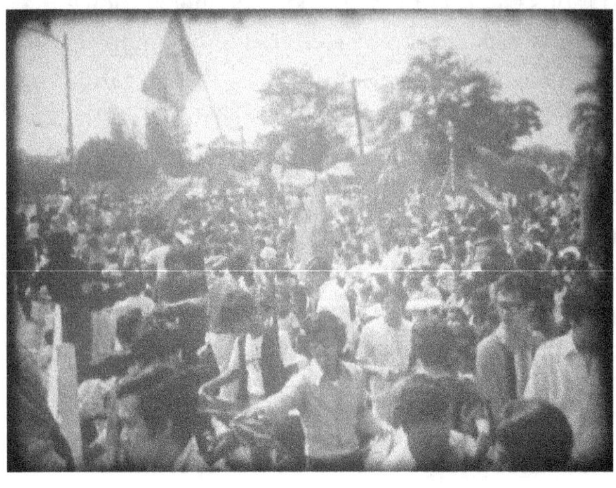

I.1–I.3 The militant student demonstrations of the First Quarter Storm documented in *From a Season of Strife* (National Media Production Center, 1972). Film stills.

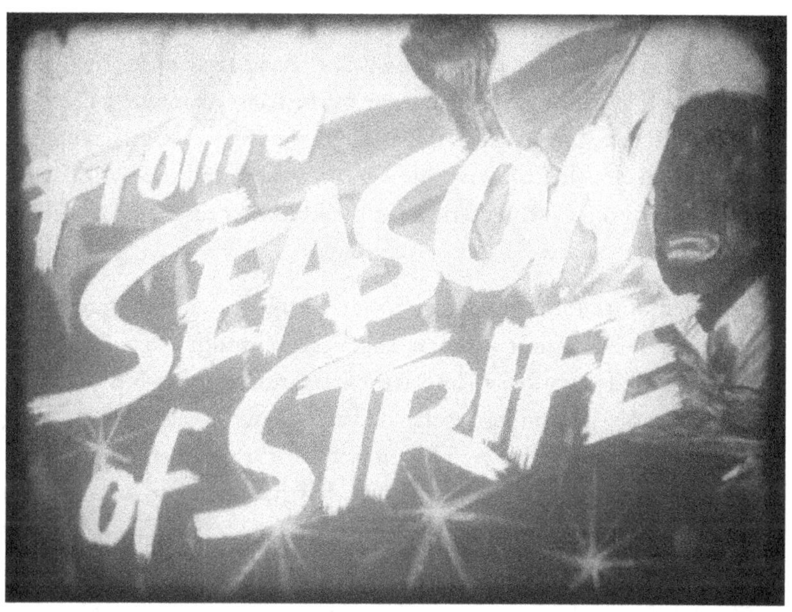

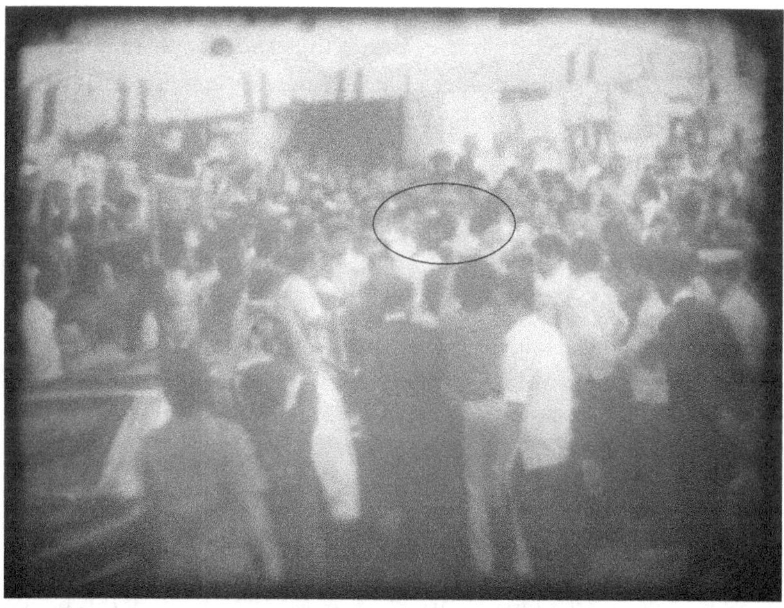

1.4 & 1.5 The benign visual track of the NMPC propaganda film *From a Season of Strife* offers a glimpse of Ferdinand and Imelda Marcos (*circled*) emerging from Congress on January 26, 1970, but leaves out the brutal dispersal of student demonstrators that sparked the beginning of the First Quarter Storm. Film stills.

which included a crocodile (*buwaya*) to signify his corruption. The benign visual track of a government convoy driving away omits the brutal crackdown that followed. The framing of the footage, intent on finding the First Couple in the melee, leaves the pivotal violence offscreen: the rocks and bottles the students threw in their ire[131] and the "truncheon-swinging riot police" who carried out the bloodiest dispersal of student demonstrators to date.[132] Vicente Rafael writes:

> The demonstrations of January 26 and 30, 1970, . . . precipitated what were till then the most violent clashes between youth and police. What set these confrontations apart was the extraordinary rage with which the police set on the demonstrators, moderates and radicals alike, resulting in the injury of at least a couple hundred and the death of four students. So significant were these events that they have come to be known in Philippine historiography as the First Quarter Storm. This storm set in motion a wave of marches and rallies protesting the "fascist" behavior of the state, many of which resulted in further violent clashes.[133]

My first glimpse of these images of the First Quarter Storm were at a small, collaborative research screening at the PIA on September 8, 2014. To my mind, that screening had a touch of the historic, instantiating the agile institutional collaboration that is the hallmark of the SOFIA-led advocacy movement. I remain amazed by what we unearthed that day: despite their bleached colors, distorted sound, and jumpy frames, these propaganda films' red scare rhetorics are vital to our understanding of history. The need to remember how the dictatorship strove to justify its repression of dissent is particularly urgent given the Duterte regime's reliance on extrajudicial killings and red-baiting tactics, which took their cue from Marcos era martial law and the defunding of cultural and historical state agencies under Bongbong Marcos's presidency.[134]

Like other Filipina/os of my generation—wryly referred to as "Martial Law Babies"—I experienced a childhood that took place entirely under the shadow of the dictatorship. In college, mentors in the student movement spoke with reverence for the activists who were killed or "disappeared" during the First Quarter Storm. My knowledge of this period accumulated gradually through various literary, historical, and journalistic sources, but I had never seen footage of those tumultuous years prior to that screening.[135] Even today, moving images of the First Quarter Storm remain scant.[136] In that cramped PIA office in 2014, I encountered an audiovisual record of the enormous student-led mass movement that rose up in resistance to state power. Practically announcing their own counterreading from within the frame of Marcosian propaganda, this filmic record—of the Diliman Commune's formidable barricade, of the sheer size of the protest rallies and the intensity of the students' faces—affected me deeply.[137] (Regrettably, the PIA's research contract restricts me from showing the films outside of a classroom or conference setting, or otherwise circulating them.)[138]

That same day, I wrote the PIA for permission to obtain digitized access copies of the propaganda films for research purposes and a special waiver of the PIA's footage fee (which would have amounted to over 300,000 Philippine pesos, or nearly US$7,000) on the grounds that I was requesting access for noncommercial scholarly and preservation uses and had already coordinated with the CCP to digitize the films and furnish the PIA with digital copies.[139] On paper, my request to digitize the films was approved the next day by the cabinet secretary for communications. In practice, the PIA secretary general, apparently feeling slighted by my request having gone above his office for approval, would delay access for over a year.[140] Meanwhile, the last surviving 16mm prints of these titles deteriorated further in a non–air-conditioned room for several months before finally being transferred to the NFAP's transitory storage facility.

On September 15 the following year, I was finally allowed to check out the PIA films from the NFAP for digitization by Rodel Valiente, a CCP technician. As the surviving quasi-archival arm of the PIA, the MISD was so underresourced and so undervalued by the PIA bureaucracy at the time of my request that projecting, much less digitizing or restoring, its own films was out of the question. To access these works, I arranged an interagency collaboration by which digital MPEG access copies of 16mm PIA films that had been turned over to the NFAP would be made for a nominal fee by another state institution, the CCP. In this exchange, all parties would be given complimentary copies of the digital files.

While the NFAP email correspondence referred to the CCP's analog-to-digital migration process as "kinescoping," that turned out to be a euphemism. According to a Wikipedia definition that CCP archivist Vicky Belarmino emailed to me, kinescoping is the duplication of broadcast television content onto film via lens-based capture: "a recording of a television program on motion picture film, directly through a lens focused on the screen of a video monitor."[141] Yet, as my photographs of the migration process attest and as Belarmino acknowledged, Valiente was not capturing a TV screen, but an image projected on an ordinary office wall (figures I.6 and I.7). Although the digitization resulted in undeniably "poor," imperfect images, the retention of a media artifact's original materiality and aesthetics is not the sole yardstick of archival value.[142] The resulting digital access copies are spatiotemporal palimpsests that capture not only the migrated content from the early seventies but also the walls of a cultural memory institution that had collaboratively enabled the film's digitization four decades later.[143] The CCP's dusty office wall becoming part of the filmic record is an imprint of anarchival conditions on the afterlife of an audiovisual work.

When I asked Belarmino how I should refer to this makeshift digitization process, she replied campily, in Taglish, "Nothing much. Kind of like a boy scout ploy. It's what Filipinos do in times of need" (*Wala lang*. Boy scout *paandar lang talaga*. It's what Pinoys do in times of need).[144] I read her allusion to Boy Scouts as implying skill and resourcefulness and have opted to translate the Tagalog slang term *paandar*, with its denotative meanings of starting (as with an engine) or moving forward (as with a vehicle) and its connotative associations with a clever joke or ruse, with the English term *ploy*, which is a cunning plan designed to turn a situation to one's own advantage.

As my research experience demonstrates, efforts to preserve and access films can be slowed by bureaucratic intrigues at state entities whose officials act as if the collections they administer are personal fiefdoms. Despite or likely because of this toxic political climate for research and archiving, committed archivists improvise workarounds to circumvent layers of red tape whenever rare opportunities to screen, rescue, migrate, restore, or lobby for endangered works of Philippine cinema arise. The outcome of our collaborative transfer process in 2015 was by no means a pristine restored digital copy. The rushed digitization of the PIA's martial law films yielded, in Hito Steyerl's sense, a "poor image," the diametric opposite of an expensive, high-profile digital restoration.[145] Flawed but vital digital copies are emblematic of archival practices of making do in the Philippines, the labor of tenacious audiovisual advocates improvising a path to digitization. (The imperfect digitization of Ferdinand Marcos's declaration of martial law in 1972 is explored in detail in chapter 2's manifesto for "poor archiving.")

Various aesthetic parallels to this concept of making do—in Latin America, South and Southeast Asia, and Africa—tell us that making do is a dimension of global South media cultures with analogs in multiple languages and contexts. Victor Goldgel-Carballo writes that "the informal economic practices referred to in Cuba as the '*invento*' ('invention'),

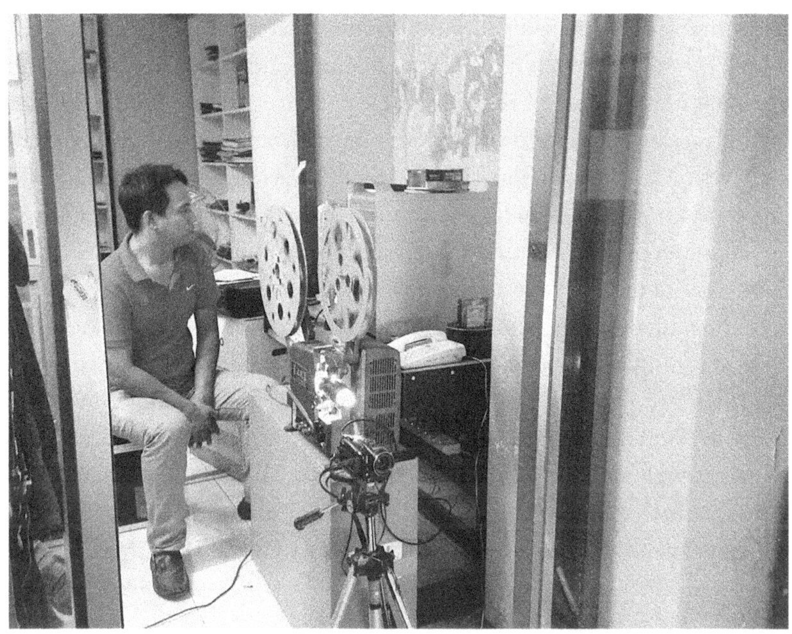

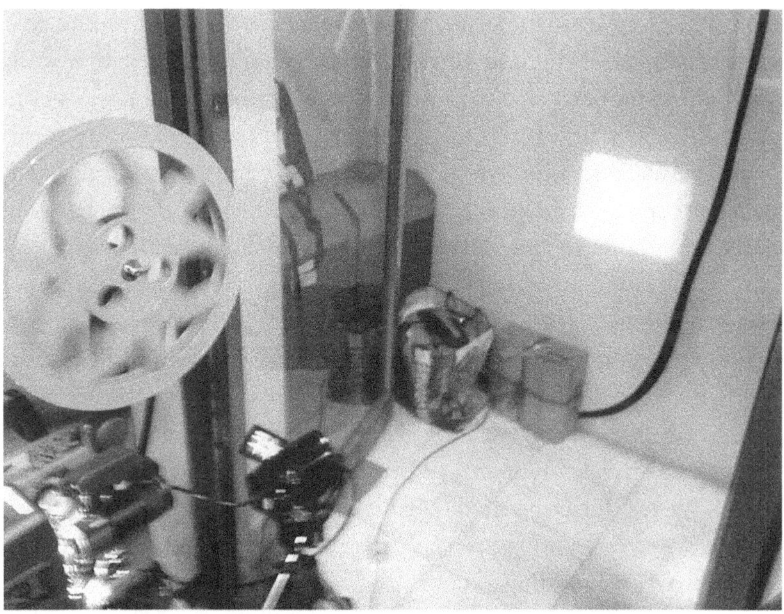

I.6 & I.7 Makeshift digitization of four martial law–era films from the PIA collection was conducted by CCP technician Rodel Valiente. The 16mm films were projected on an office wall and recorded on a digital camera. Photos by author, September 2015.

the more widely Spanish American '*viveza criolla*' ('creole cunning'), the Hindi '*jugaad*' (the ability to develop 'quick-and-dirty' solutions), and the imaginary article of the Congolese constitution, '*Débrouillez-vous*,' which exhorts citizens to sort things out by themselves—suggest potential for a global comparison."[146] Whereas Goldgel-Carballo explores making do as an Argentinean film aesthetic, I approach making do in light of broader material and institutional (an)archival conditions in the Philippines that underwrite the aesthetics of "poor images."[147]

The make-do migration technique I first witnessed at the CCP is a long-standing, widespread practice still employed by such institutions as the University of the Philippines Film Institute and the Movie Workers Welfare Foundation, Inc. (MOWELFUND), formerly known as the Movie Workers Welfare Fund.[148] Ricky Orellana of the MOWELFUND Film Institute recalls that one of the earliest uses of a similar method—projecting moving images from an analog film source to a wall and then recording these on a video camera—involved transferring Super 8mm films to U-matic videocassettes for the Independent Film and Video Festival in 1986.[149] Variously referred to as a quasi-kinescoping method (*pa-kino-kino*) or a "poor man's telecine transfer," such make-do transfers devise affordable work-arounds in restricted circumstances.[150] When discussing such improvisational tactics, those who employ them are not overly concerned about technical accuracy. The casual conflation of various forms of audiovisual migration, irrespective of formats and carriers (e.g., equating kinescoping with telecine transfers or flattening differences between older methods for the transfer of photochemical film to analog video tape and the current digitization of analog content), emphasizes continuities between durable, protean tactics of making do.[151]

The genealogy of make-do migrations goes back even further. In the 1980s, deteriorating studio era classics on 35mm film were transferred to Betamax by New Cinema auteur Mike de Leon, grandson of the LVN studio founder, Doña Narcisa "Sisang" de Leon. Del Mundo writes, "There was no budget for telecine transfer, so [Mike de Leon] merely projected the films and recorded them off the screen with a Betamax camera and recorder. The improvised recording was not able to get rid of the flickering effect."[152] In some cases, these flickering Betamax tapes are now the last extant copies of lost LVN films, themselves candidates for future digital restoration.

Rather than simply lament the shortcomings of archival efforts with little to no funding or institutional support, this book argues for a recognition of the creative ingenuity and resourcefulness engendered by anarchival scarcity. Many professional archivists in the Philippines have the requisite skill, training, and experience—but not the resources—to transfer and restore media titles to an internationally recognized archival standard. If they resort to a faulty approximation of kinescope or telecine transfers, such recourse is not the DIY (do-it-yourself) work of nonspecialists but rather a pragmatic work-around devised by trained professionals who are forced to work in ways that seem amateurish because they operate in contexts of pronounced constraint.[153] Recalling Barthes's *amator*, hard-pressed archivists, technicians, and filmmakers embrace versatile amateur tactics to secure the afterlives of movies they love.

THE ARCHIVAL AFTERLIVES OF PHILIPPINE CINEMA

This book proceeds from the premise that Filipino archival films in the hands of the state, private institutions, and individual collectors lead a posthumous existence. Extant older films are survivors of past archival crises and the closure or collapse of prior film collections previously maintained by motion picture studios or by government agencies.[154] The phrase "archival afterlives," used in this book's title, attempts to convey the uncanny texture of this unlooked-for, and in some cases literally postdiluvian, survival while also, I hope, being expansive enough to allude to other dimensions of the Philippines' archival condition.

Giuliana Bruno's book *Streetwalking on a Ruined Map* (1993), a feminist historiography of Italian silent films by director Elvira Notari, was forged in a context of extreme archival loss, given that only 5 percent of Italian silent cinema and three complete feature films by Notari remain.[155] Excavating this attenuated archive, Bruno argues for the "kinetic treatment of lacunae," an approach that prefigures my own. Bruno challenges us to relinquish fantasies of recovery and wrestle instead with cinematic afterlives: not what a film (or archive) once was, but "what it has become, following it through its 'sleep' to its present historicity."[156]

The *Merriam-Webster* online dictionary offers this remarkably apt entry for *afterlife*: "1: an existence after death; 2: a later period in one's life; 3: a period of continued or renewed use, existence, or popularity beyond what is normal, primary, or expected."[157] The notion of a subsequent, unexpected life after some turning point that might be considered a kind of death refers not just to extant film titles endangered by the institutional collapse of a major archive. It also refers to material processes of duplication, transfer, and migration across media formats, carriers, and platforms. Rather than usher in the supposed death of cinema, historical shifts from analog to digital eras proceed from the ontologically transitory quality of all media, whether old or new.[158]

In her farsighted book *From Grain to Pixel*, what Fossati calls "the archival life of film in transition" refers to the shift from photochemical celluloid cinema to digital film. Published in 2009 and written on the cusp of digital theatrical projection overtaking traditional analog projection worldwide, Fossati's book describes an era of "unprecedented change" affecting film production, distribution, exhibition, and archiving.[159] The audiovisual archival advocacy movement in the Philippines has lived through this very transition from photochemical cinema to digital media.

In the case of the film *Ibong Adarna*, the 2005 restoration that resulted in a new 35mm polyester print was also the occasion (or alibi) for the disposal of the nitrocellulose dupe negative on which the restoration was based. Such archival horror stories of survival in extremis, of a continued circulation that proceeds only from the point of death, are not confined to Philippine film history.[160] *Archival afterlives* pertains to such instances of medial migration and intensified loss. This is the painfully literal lesson of *Ibong Adarna* as a study in loss-as-survival: its transfer and restoration on polyester film was quickly followed by the disposal of the nitrate dupe negative, now seen as both dangerously outmoded (because of cellulose nitrate's notorious flammability) and superfluous, since a newer print was available. Given that access to such movies in contemporary formats or carriers follows from the death of prior incarnations, it is more accurate to speak of films like *Ibong Adarna* not in terms of their archival survival but in terms of their (an)archival afterlives, that is, cinema "preserved by the traces of its destruction."[161] Moreover, as chapter 2 illustrates, many archivists themselves persevere in a kind of archival afterlife, having lived through the decimation of collections they fought to preserve.

Chapter 1 considers the architectural propaganda of the Marcoses' conjugal rule, a subject with renewed relevance given that the revisionist social fantasies underpinning Bongbong Marcos's ascension to the presidency in 2022 have recast martial law as a supposed golden age of national development and architectural achievement.[162] The first chapter focuses on a trio of famous edifices that bookended the regime: first, the CCP Main Theater, completed in 1969; and second, the Manila Film Center, which collapsed during its construction in 1981, killing an unknown number of workers before opening to the public in 1982. Together with a third, never-built but repeatedly envisioned building—a permanent home for the national audiovisual collection—this architectural triad serves as my entry point into the cultural policy matrix of the Marcos dictatorship. Established amid the regime's highly politicized cultural interventions, the FAP atrophied in the immediate post-EDSA period. The first chapter closes by focusing on two problems bequeathed by the Marcos era Film Archives to the present day: first, the issue of presidential appointments for top film officials; and second, "anarchival temporality," the menace of loss that undermines promises of archival permanence.

The Philippine government has never regarded film archiving as central to the convergence between statecraft and cinema. Philippine cinema does not present a case in which the state, fearful of incriminating records, took steps to "sanitize" the archive, as with the South African government's attempts at records destruction in the early 1990s in order "to conceal violations of human rights," as Harris recounts.[163] Largely excluded from the dictatorship's political spectacle, the FAP was enmeshed in key cultural policies while remaining a "poor relation" to the regime's flashier cinematic initiatives.[164] The larger lesson of the first two chapters is that, far from ensuring archival permanency, Marcosian cultural policies amounted to an undoing of the dictatorship's own cinematic legacy, bequeathing an anarchival temporality.

Chapter 2 recovers the heretofore unwritten history of the PIA-MPD's dissolution in 2004, analyzing the implications of one film library's institutional death on three defunct collections it inherited: the state productions of the NMPC; a portion of the LVN Pictures collection; and the holdings of the Movie and Television Review and Classification Board (MTRCB), themselves remnants of the previous archival collapse of the FAP.[165] The archival afterlives of Philippine films are the work of archivists who persevere under inhospitable conditions they hope to change. In reflecting on the tactics that archivist-activists developed to cope with the decline of various state-run film archives, the second chapter conceptualizes survival and perseverance as a facet of the Philippines' enduring audiovisual archival advocacy.

Chapter 3 brings insights drawn from Philippine political history, media economics, and industry studies to bear on corporate privatization. The flip side of government indifference is that the largest state-of-the-art audiovisual archive in the Philippines is privately owned by ABS-CBN, a transnational media conglomerate controlled by a powerful oligarchic family. To approach the question of the Philippine state's indifference to audiovisual archiving critically means not just asking what the state has failed to do to preserve film and media but what this neglect says about the degree to which the Philippine state has served elite interests.

In the years following EDSA People Power, Cory Aquino's government chose to honor rather than repudiate the crippling external debt that the country had amassed under the dictatorship. The cash-strapped Aquino administration deprioritized culture, taking a hands-off approach to the film industry and film archiving while simultaneously restoring media outlets to oligarchic control and privatizing state assets to generate revenue. Analyzing the consequences of these decisions on Philippine film archiving, the third chapter tracks the institutional death of the FAP and the subsequent rise of the ABS-CBN Film Archives in the post-EDSA period. The chapter zeroes in on ABS-CBN's 2001 acquisition of the rights to ECP productions, widely regarded as the most significant films ever produced by the Philippine state. The Duterte administration shuttered ABS-CBN in 2020, enlisting anti-oligarchic rhetoric to veil its muzzling of press freedom.[166]

Restorations undertaken by the ABS-CBN Film Archives far outnumber those of the NFAP/PFA, which is unsurprising given that government archives rely on limited allocations and do not hold the rights to the majority of their collections. Offering a comparative analysis of state and conglomerate archives' restoration priorities, chapter 4 examines ABS-CBN's restoration and reissue of a 1982 star-studded lesbian classic *T-Bird at Ako* (T-bird and I, aka Lesbian love). Notable for its pairing of Philippine cinema's rival female superstars—Nora Aunor and Vilma Santos—within a same-sex romance, the box office hit represents a significant departure from the restoration priorities of the NFAP/PFA and the promotional rhetoric surrounding ABS-CBN's restoration catalog, both of which foreground auteurist masterworks. *T-Bird at Ako* elicits a lesbian cinephilia intensified by one of the stars' rumored affairs with women while showcasing the subcultural queer lexicon of early 1980s Manila. The film's rerelease addressed an archival public composed of lower-income fans and queer movie buffs, audience segments that are typically marginal to the marketing of high-profile restorations.

In her work on nineteenth-century colonial archives in India, Anjali Arondekar urges queer postcolonial studies to renounce the goal of "archival recovery," writing, "The critical challenge is to imagine a practice of archival reading that incites relationships between the seductions of recovery and the occlusions that such retrieval mandates."[167] How to take seriously

Arondekar's warning that every recovery of dissident sexual histories entails an answering occlusion of that very queerness for which we had hoped to secure incontrovertible proof? The fourth chapter answers that reflexive demand by thinking through the issue of anachronistic reception and the sometimes chronologically inappropriate terminology that is willfully wielded by queer, trans, and feminist analyses of older works. While *T-Bird at Ako* understandably may strike contemporary viewers as gender-normative, homophobic, and transphobic, the sex/gender categories of today's globalized LGBTQ+ vocabulary are alien to the time of the film's production and initial release. In grappling with these issues, I draw on both queer feminist theory's espousal of anachronism and queer and trans Asian studies' attentiveness to translation, vernacularization, and nonequivalence.[168]

The question of how archival films reach audiences animates the second arc of the book, which pivots from formal archives to informal collections and initiatives. Chapter 5 conceptualizes networks of archival circulation as a riverine system co-constituted by an admixture of formal and informal entities, social actors, and practices. The chapter juxtaposes Video 48, a legendary brick-and-mortar video store specializing in the Manila industry's Tagalog-language, feature-length fiction films, with the Kalampag Tracking Agency, a two-person microcuratorial initiative that recovers, migrates, and circulates experimental films and videos from Manila's alternative film scene. Both Video 48 (founded by collector Simon Santos) and Kalampag (helmed by Shireen Seno and Merv Espina) are crucial headwaters for Philippine cinema's archival currents, revaluing residual media from various historical eras and facilitating essential flows between private insider collections and a broader public.

The homogenizing canon-based rubrics that underpin institutional archiving priorities tend to conflate Tagalog feature-length films produced by the Manila industry with Philippine cinema writ large. Redressing the archival lacunae that surround vernacular cinemas is an archipelagic project that has been gaining momentum since the turn of the millennium. To unsettle the fictive homogeneity of Philippine cinema and explore alternative modes of archiving, chapter 6 focuses on the scholarly and filmmaking interventions of the Binisaya film movement, launched in 2009.

In a nutshell, indie cinema's "audience problem" is that popular domestic audiences have heard about these films but have never actually seen them. Despite being regarded as representative works of Philippine cinema in international film festivals, these films are largely inaccessible to most Filipino moviegoers owing to their limited distribution. Patrick Campos puts it thus: indie cinema's "nomenclature is 'Filipino'" yet its global circulation moves "farther and farther away from the local spaces of vernacular entertainment."[169] Given such a predicament, one critic enjoins filmmakers "to get involved in bringing their content [directly] to the audience . . . and hope that they are dreaming the same dream."[170] Visayan movie watching is a prominent motif of *Iskalawags* (Scalawags; dir. Keith Deligero, 2013), a film that metafictionally stages and archives the Binisaya movement's dream of creating a vernacular film audience in Cebu and beyond.

Chapter 6 and the epilogue conclude the book by analyzing two contemporary indie films as affective-cinephilic archives that nostalgically revisit Cebuano and Tagalog media consumption practices. Their archival value lies in chronicling abiding aspirations to cultivate both vernacular film audiences and a national public invested in audiovisual archives. Drawing a through line between the Binisaya movement's effort to bring Visayan films directly to local audiences and the archive advocacy's desire to bring a broad-based archival public into being, the epilogue centers on the 2005 independent film *Pepot Artista* (Pepot superstar), directed by film historian and SOFIA past president Clodualdo del Mundo Jr. My analysis of *Pepot Artista* construes the film's allusions and its remixing of archival footage as a tactical means of addressing (and thus bringing into being) an engaged public that advocates for audiovisual archives.

In approaching *Iskalawags* and *Pepot Artista* as affective archives that attempt to constitute publics beyond their representational content, I am influenced by Ann Cvetkovich's notion of affective archives as minoritarian "repositories of feelings and emotions . . . encoded not only in the texts themselves but in the practices that surround their production and reception." By fictively incorporating ephemeral experiences—like the Binisaya movement's "guerrilla" screenings to audiences in remote barrios—*Iskalawags* is analogous to an "archive of feelings" that "stands alongside the documents of the dominant culture in order to offer alternative modes of knowledge."[171] Whereas Cvetkovich was writing about the challenge to both heteronormativity and homonormativity posed by gay and lesbian activism and sexual cultures, *Iskalawags* archives minoritarian Visayan cinema's challenge to Tagalog cultural dominance in Philippine national culture. In arguing that small-budget indie movies directed by two filmmakers are affective archives, I echo Cvetkovich's reflexive admission that queer feminist scholars (myself included) are often "working as much to produce an archive as to analyze one."[172]

SISYPHEAN HOPE

In an illuminating conversation at the outset of my research, cinephile, curator, and archivist Teddy Co memorably characterized Philippine film archiving as a "Sisyphean history" of "fits and starts."[173] The *punctum* of Co's observation has stayed with me over the decade that it took to complete this book.[174] I began this project a year after the NFAP was reestablished, a period of heightened activity, visibility, and cautious optimism in the Philippine archive world. One presidential term later, the rebranded PFA, under FDCP leadership with little prior knowledge of archiving, was marked by high staff turnover, fewer film restorations, and still unrealized plans for a permanent repository. As I revise this introduction for the umpteenth time, I cannot shake off the feeling of being overtaken by events as I write. This must be common to anyone who attempts to craft, in however piecemeal a fashion, a partial history of the unfolding present.[175] Given the glacial pace of academic publishing in the humanities, scholarship is often outdated by the time it sees print. But historical contingency also renews the relevance of a past that initially seems distant. When I began my research into martial law propaganda films at the PIA, I could not have foreseen that Duterte's imposition of martial law in Mindanao, the passage of the Anti-Terrorism Act, the militarized encroachment on academic freedom, and Bongbong Marcos's presidential victory would cast new light on the archival traces of a prior authoritarian era.

The year 2020, already blighted by the global COVID-19 pandemic, ushered in profound, rapid transformations at many of the formal and informal archives I write about: a fire at Green Papaya, the art space where some of the Kalampag Tracking Agency's collection was stored; the closure of Video 48 in Quezon City; and the government shutdown of ABS-CBN, leaving the future of its vast archive uncertain. In the Philippine archive world, these unforeseen events evoked the familiar feeling of standing on the brink of an anarchival precipice. Reflecting on what had just occurred, Orellana commented: "Archiving in the Philippines is an evolving history. You think that the ABS-CBN Film Archives is standing on solid ground, and in the blink of an eye something completely unexpected happens. The history of archiving in the Philippines . . . never ceases to amaze you. It's sometimes frustrating, giving you an equal measure of hope and no hope as you go along."[176]

"Hope and no hope," effort and futility: the lifelong archivist's remarks return us to the scene of a Sisyphean history. In his famous essay on the

Greek legend, Albert Camus describes Sisyphus as an "absurd hero" who exerts his whole being only to accomplish nothing: "The gods had condemned Sisyphus to ceaselessly rolling a rock to the top of a mountain, whence the stone would fall back of its own weight. They had thought with some reason that there is no more dreadful punishment than futile and hopeless labor."[177] For Camus, the absurdity and futility of existence derive from one's self-awareness that, in reality, one's efforts are being constantly "undermined."[178] The inevitability of death underpins this sense of absurdity.[179] Death and futility have to do, of course, with consciousness of time and as such are (an)archival problems: "The absurd enlightens me on this point: there is no future."[180] The temporal consciousness of inevitable loss explored by Camus resonates with the uphill (existentially absurdist) defiance of time that lies at the core of the archival impulse. Nevertheless, Camus maintains that the myth of Sisyphus is not only about futility. Weariness is counterweighted with a refusal of despair, since "being deprived of hope is not despairing."[181] "Hope and no hope," as Orellana put it: even in Sisyphean, anarchival conditions, hope as revolt, as a refusal to give up, remains. This is a variant of what Elizabeth Povinelli calls enduring, and it resonates throughout this book.[182]

Insisting that the myth of Sisyphus is "a lucid invitation to live and to create, in the very midst of the desert," Camus offers two modern analogs to the ancient legend.[183] The first is from Franz Kafka's *The Castle*: a character, saddened to learn that K. persists in going to the Castle, regrets his "probably futile trip, that probably empty hope." Camus expounds: "'Probably'—on this implication Kafka gambles his entire work."[184] In clearly recognizing their almost certain failure while tenaciously maintaining that defeat is not assured, Sisyphean figures teach us that *probably* is an adverb of hope. The second of Camus's Sisyphean parables takes the form of a joke: "A crazy man . . . was fishing in a bathtub. A doctor with ideas as to psychiatric treatments asked him 'if they were biting,' to which he received the harsh reply: 'Of course not, you fool, since this is a bathtub.' . . . [The] man allows himself the tormenting luxury of fishing in a bathtub, knowing that nothing will come of it."[185]

Once encountered, Camus's joke is unforgettable, funny, and heartrending in the same breath. The joke's unblinking self-awareness about the limits of what one has chosen to do reminds me of the Philippine penchant for humor in times of crisis. The man who went fishing in a bathtub—fully aware that he would not be catching any fish—is probably making do. We may see the improvisational fisherman as a lunatic or as a Sisyphean figure of self-ironic perseverance. In the absence of more hospitable environs, such as a lake or a river, with lowered expectations but not without hope, he refuses to give up doing what he has chosen to do. A similar spirit animates those who love and advocate for Philippine cinema. Tioseco recalls his collaborative efforts to reform the controversial Metro Manila Film Festival: "I did it because part of me sincerely believed we could do things. A belief that, for a few moments, was infectious, for even those that knew in the back of their minds that nothing would come of it still chose to take part."[186]

At a Q & A for a talk I gave at Cornell University in 2019, the first question was posed by an undergraduate student: "Are you hopeful that there will be public outcry about this archival crisis?" I was taken aback by the query; I knew too much about the long-simmering, still-unfulfilled, historically Sisyphean archival dream to profess unbridled optimism. So I hedged, saying that I would not begin my answer with the predicate (am I *hopeful*?) but would start by unpacking the noun phrase (*public* outcry). Condensing the argument I elaborate in the epilogue, I explained that access creates public stakeholders for archives; in the absence of access, an engaged public cannot arise. At the same time, however, creating a public involves addressing a public as though it already existed, as Michael Warner suggests.[187] If I remain hopeful, then, it is because minor archival initiatives, informal circuits, and small films have created pathways to access, even if these efforts tend to be short-lived. But I should also have added that every activism and advocacy, however long-running or exhausted, is fueled at least in some part by hope. In that sense, this book is itself part of a long, unfolding history of hopeful attempts to co-imagine a public that uses film archives and wants them to thrive.

POSTSCRIPT: THE MEDIAL MATERIALITY OF *IBONG ADARNA*

The digital circulation of celluloid-born works foregrounds the thorny status of digital formats as untested preservation media, even as digitization dramatically improves the accessibility of archival holdings.[188] I am old enough and fortunate enough to have completed my graduate training at a time when 16mm and 35mm film prints were projected in our lecture halls; we watched film on film. Paolo Cherchi Usai rhapsodizes on the artifactual value of nitrate film: "Seen in a nitrate print projected on a big screen, the best work of the silent era can be an overwhelming artistic experience. Copy it, and at once the magic disappears. It is like copying a

Rembrandt with an Instamatic camera. The silver content of black-and-white film stock has been removed to such an extent that the glistening sheen of early cinematography often registers as an out-of-focus smear. The information is there. The art is gone."[189]

Having only ever screened silent cinema on acetate, videotape, or DVD, I belatedly realize that I have never really *seen* silent cinema and that, in Usai's sense, few of us have. Though far more accessible, digital versions of *Ibong Adarna* confuse the difference between content and carrier because the visible and audible decline of the nitrate source has become part of the migrated content, encouraging us to overlook the materiality of the digital file we consume. In retrospect, I cannot clearly recall the provenance of my analog-to-digital copy of *Ibong Adarna.* I surmise that I obtained a VHS access copy from the CCP that I subsequently burned to DVD, then ripped to a digital file years later. It was in that much-remediated form, multiply migrated from celluloid to magnetic tape to optical disc to M4V, that I encountered *Ibong Adarna*'s densely intertextual and national-colonial texture. In 2019, the ABS-CBN Film Archives completed "digital scanning and enhancement"—not a full restoration—of *Ibong Adarna.* Regrettably, I have not seen this version due to its limited circulation.[190]

Based on a *corrido*, a Philippine metrical romance that vernacularized Spanish narrative ballads, *Ibong Adarna* is a *moro-moro* movie drawn from the theatrical tradition of the Spanish *comedia*, a three-act drama in polymetric verse. Dating from the seventeenth century, the Tagalog dramatic genre of the *komedya* often involves a romantic conflict between Moorish and Christian protagonists. In keeping with this transcultural genealogy, *Ibong Adarna*'s politics of casting and costume are moralized and racialized.[191] The virtuous Prince Juan is played by Fred Cortes, a light-skinned mestizo Filipino actor with Euro-American features. He is characteristically clothed in white, as opposed to his older brothers, whose costumes and more Malay features are intended to convey their relative degrees of villainy. The diabolical eldest brother, Prince Pedro (Ben Rubio), is clad in dark colors that register as black on the monochromatic footage, while the middle sibling, Prince Diego (Vicente Oliver), is attired in a combination of black and white, an allusion to his moral ambiguity (figure I.8).[192]

Simultaneous with its Spanish influences, *Ibong Adarna*, an early studio era film produced by LVN Pictures during the American colonization of the Philippines, exhibits pronounced Hollywood influences. An overhead crane shot of dancers in an ornamental radial pattern is reminiscent of Busby Berkeley musicals.[193] The movie's Hollywood-style Orientalism,

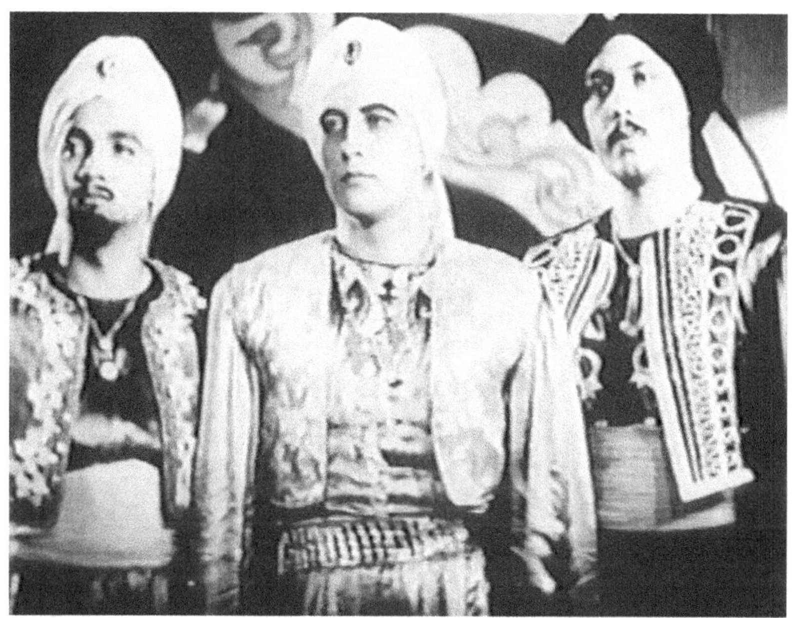

I.8 Costume and casting carry racialized, moralistic undertones in *Ibong Adarna* (Adarna bird; dir. Vicente Salumbides and Manuel Conde, 1941). Film still.

paired with the *komedya*'s Spanish Catholic influences, produces incongruous dissonances in the film's ethnoracial register: the title card that declares the film an adaptation of a Philippine legend uses a font reminiscent of Chinese calligraphy (figure I.9); in a later scene, a turbaned protagonist in a faux Middle East setting utters a penitent Christian prayer. Perhaps most shockingly, dark theatrical makeup reminiscent of blackface is used on minor actors playing an unnamed miniature couple (figure I.10). Imperiously interpellated by the film's fair-skinned mestiza heroine as *negrito* and *negrita*, the couple's depiction conflates popular names for an indigenous Philippine people, the Agta Negritos, with visual codes signifying racial primitivism drawn from American popular culture.[194]

The echo of blackface minstrelsy in *Ibong Adarna*, one of the few surviving Philippine films of the American colonial period, suggests that blackface as an "index of popular white racial feeling in the US" was imported into colonial Filipino cinema. The result is a merging of what Eric Lott calls white American culture's commodification of the "culture of the dispossessed" with Tagalog mainstream cinema's pejorative stance toward indigeneity.[195] *Ibong Adarna* thus affirms Deocampo's insight about the

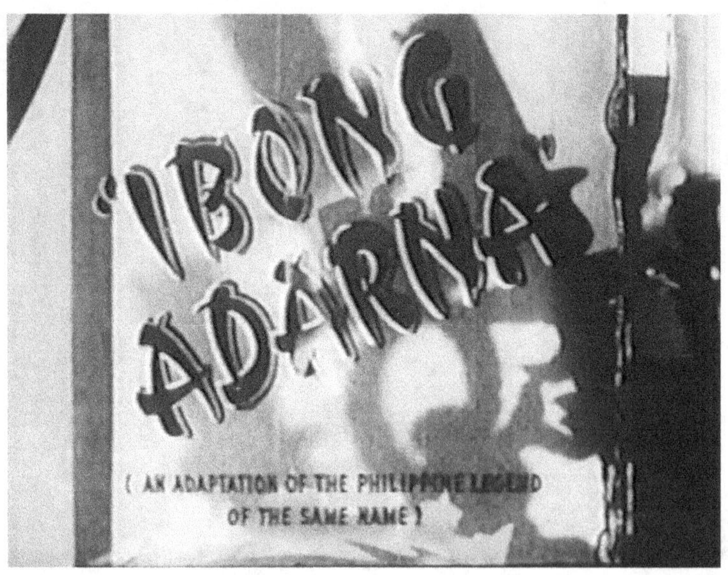

I.9 The title card of *Ibong Adarna* uses a font reminiscent of Chinese calligraphy, evoking Hollywood-style Orientalism. Film still.

confrontation between "hegemonic colonial cultures" in the first decades of Filipino filmmaking: "What constituted 'native' in [early] Philippine cinema was a complex combination—a hybrid—of cultural influences. . . . Hispanic and American (even later, Japanese, Tagalog, and other regional attributes) . . . combined to shape 'native' cinema into the 'national' cinema that it is today, or seeks to achieve in the future."[196]

The *ibong adarna* of the title is a magical bird whose beautiful nocturnal songs lure the two false princes to sleep, after which the bird's droppings turn them into stone. Only Prince Juan, whose kindness to a beggar is rewarded with the latter's sage advice, avoids his brothers' fate: armed with seven *dayap* (limes) and a *labaha* (razor) against the *adarna* bird's sleep-inducing songs, our hero slashes his arm and squeezes the citrus over his cuts whenever he is in danger of falling asleep. The two older brothers, who had been hard-hearted toward the beggar, are turned to stone, but the youngest prince emerges victorious in the film's most beautifully shot, carefully orchestrated scene.

At the peak of a mythical mountain, the prince marvels at the low-hanging, silver-leafed branches of a mystical tree (figures I.11–I.14). The scene's stark tonal contrasts between highlights and shadows, as well as

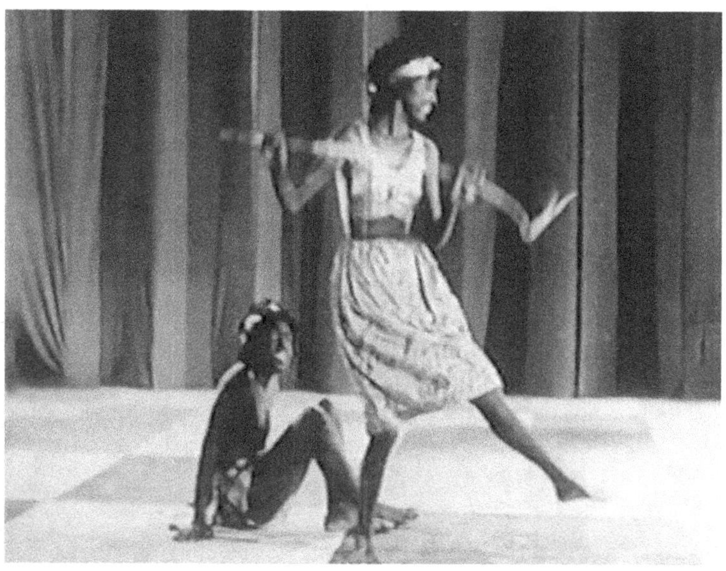

I.10 *Ibong Adarna*'s depiction of unnamed indigenous characters (referred to only as a "negrito" and "negrita" couple) rehearses visual codes signifying racial primitivism drawn from American popular culture. Film still.

the deft use of high- and low-angle framing, heighten our sense of anticipation for the film's visual and acoustic centerpiece: the sight of the *ibong adarna* and the diegetic sound of its evening song rising above the chirping of other birds, voiced by coloratura soprano Angeles Gayoso. Her warbling is accompanied by the trilling of a piccolo in alternation with a flute, together with subtle chimes and xylophone on the orchestral soundtrack composed by Francisco Buencamino Sr. The scene's alternation between pleasure and pain is embodied by the hero himself: a close-up of Prince Juan wincing as he squeezes citric acid over his self-inflicted wounds is followed by a long shot of him marveling at the enchanted bird he subsequently captures.

In 1995, a project proposal from the PIA to the National Commission for Culture and the Arts (NCCA) recommended the immediate retrieval and restoration of twenty Filipino film classics, including *Ibong Adarna*, "identified as [possessing] high heritage value."[197] Accordingly, the credits at the beginning of my copy of *Ibong Adarna* announce that the 2005 film restoration was funded by the NCCA, adding that "the soundtrack has been digitally restored and the image was printed from the existing 35mm nitrate dupe negative with sound."

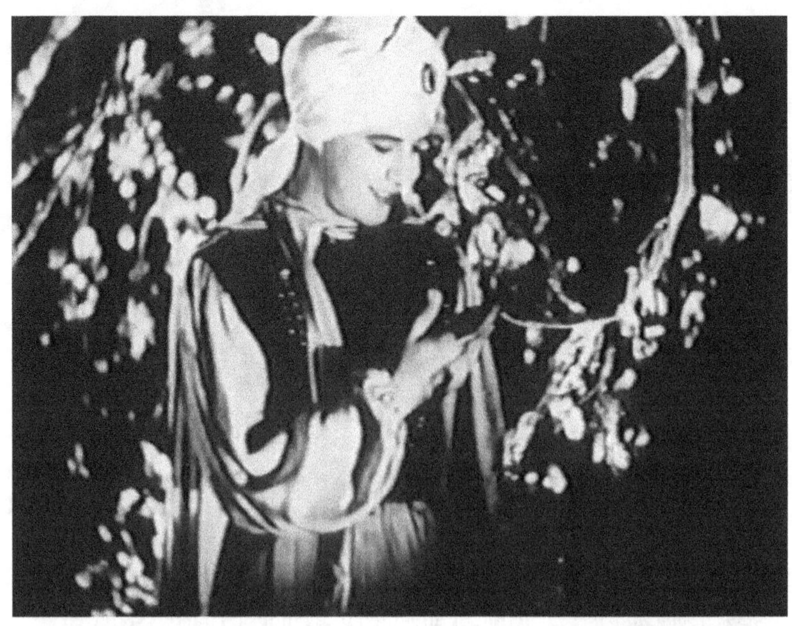

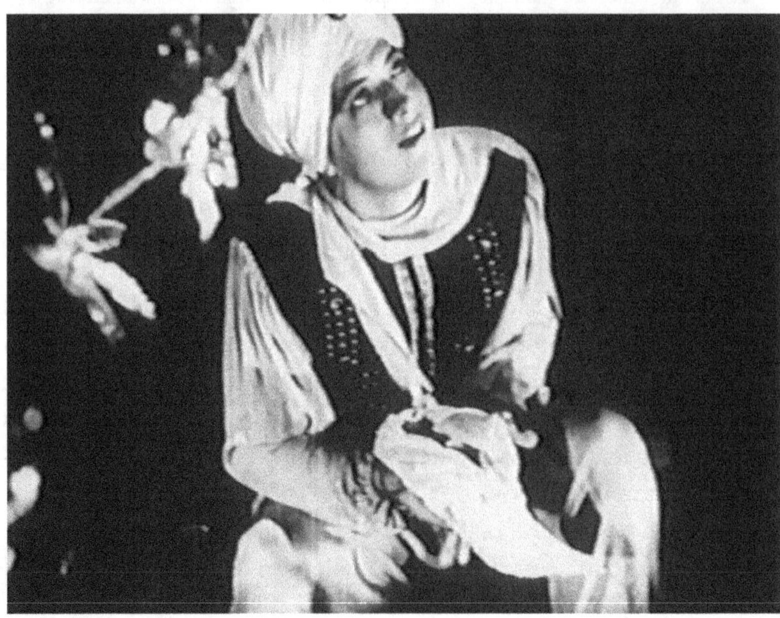

I.11–I.14 Prince Juan (Fred Cortes) encounters the *adarna* bird. Film stills, *Ibong Adarna*.

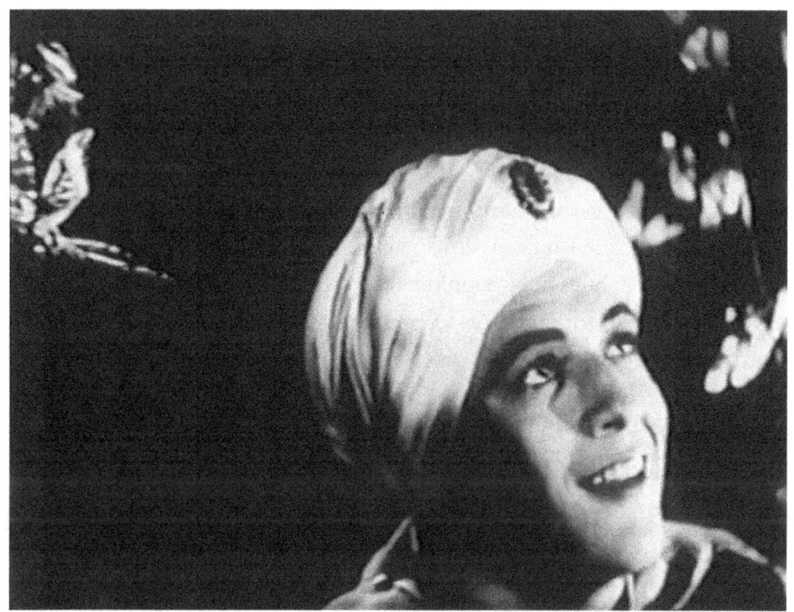

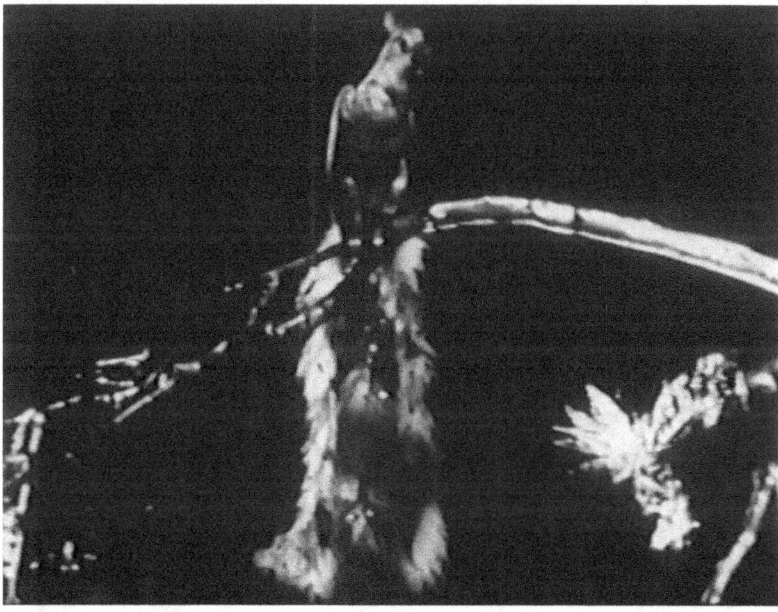

Del Mundo notes that spectacle is central to the *moro-moro* film, in both its sumptuous costumes and its overt reliance on special effects (glass shots, dissolves, stop-motion cinematography, and matte work). Upon the film's initial release in 1941, studio publicity touted the spectacle of the *adarna* bird's "multicolored plumage."[198] Such spectacles, however, are much diminished in the 2005 restoration's anarchival afterlife. In my multiply migrated copy, the bird's grayish body slowly dims and brightens, alerting us to moments when lost hues likely would have appeared. In lieu of colorful feathers at the center of the mise-en-scène, one sees a green or blue blotch at the bottom left edge of the frame. As scholars of video remind us, "The physical storage technology introduces some of its own artifacts and specificity into the [electronic] signal."[199] Archivist Benedict "Bono" Salazar Olgado speculates that such blotches in *Ibong Adarna* are likely to be video noise on the edges or borders of the frame that typically worsen with each successive generation of videotape duplication.[200] These unexpected colors in a black-and-white film suggest my copy's origins in a kinescope transfer intended for television broadcast. A vertical white scratch is prominent in the scene of Prince Juan's encounter with the bird; more noticeably, the vertical and diagonal white scratches that render Prince Juan's encounter with Princess Leonora nearly illegible were possibly caused by machine rollers during chemical processing of the celluloid footage (figure I.15).[201]

To note these material details is not to fault the restoration but, rather, to highlight this specific copy's journey from cellulose nitrate to VHS to digital file. Lucas Hilderbrand's redemptive reappraisal of the "inherent vice" of video decay construes the medial materiality of "distortion, degeneration, inferiority, and obsolescence" not as poverty or failure but as "indexical evidence of use and duration throughout time."[202] Like a dog-eared book, what Arjun Appadurai calls the "social life of the thing" becomes visible in the well-worn media commodity's "consumption, duration, and history."[203]

To speak of a "film" by naming its title is to speak of a false singularity: every film is actually a multiplicity of prints, copies, or versions of the "same" title, each having endured an internal history.[204] The "internal history of the copy" is impacted by the vagaries of each film print's circulation, exhibition, and preservation; the frequency of projections; the people who handled, safeguarded, or neglected it; the circumstances in which it was stored and screened; and by subsequent analog and digital transfers. While we may do our best to evoke the "original" experience of *Ibong Adarna* during its first theatrical run, there remains "a huge difference between the moving image we are allowed to see today and what audiences saw at the time of its

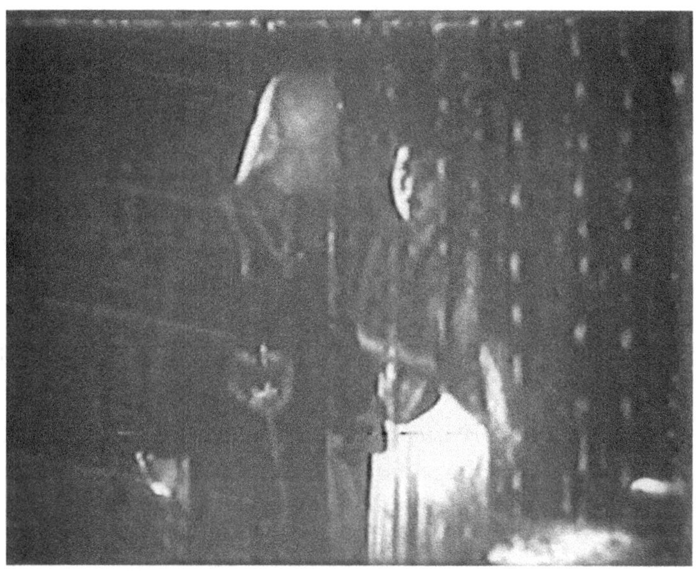

I.15 Border/edge video noise and scratches are evident in a multiply migrated analog-to-digital copy of *Ibong Adarna*. Film still.

initial release."[205] The clatter of a celluloid projector in a crowded public theater has given way to the whir of my laptop at home.

The migration of sonic or visual content to new carriers—from nitrate film reels to digital files on discs, drives, and servers—typifies archival preservation in an age when analog and digital entwine. Yet migration is neither neutral nor lossless. Unlike the content, the artifactual and material attributes of the carrier cannot be migrated.[206] In digitizing a vinyl record, one copies the song but loses the look and feel of the record and its album sleeve, the sound of the needle as it touches the groove. In digitizing nitrate cinema, one forfeits the luminous character of the films' "rich tones and high silver content,"[207] which lent them a "silky warmth" and "diaphanous glow."[208] In my imagination, Prince Juan's first encounter with the *adarna* bird comes closest to evoking the lost auratic experience of nitrocellulose film's velvety black-and-white beauty.[209]

For many archivists, nitrocellulose encapsulates the challenges posed by medium obsolescence, as distilled in the 1970s rallying cry of the American film preservation movement, "nitrate won't wait." Like all motion picture film stock, nitrocellulose begins its process of deterioration as soon as it is manufactured. Nitrate film emits chemical fumes that, reacting with moisture and air, produce acids that eventually "corrode the silver salts in the emulsion, destroying the image and the support that bears its traces, until the film is completely ruined."[210] While nitrocellulose can be long-lasting, it is also chemically unstable and highly flammable. By 1949, it began to be supplanted by motion picture films with another type of base: cellulose acetate. The popular term for acetate, *safety film*, is a misnomer since cellulose acetate is prone to "vinegar syndrome," a form of decomposition whose onset is signaled by the odor of vinegar. Polyester film, which was widely used from the mid-1990s until the transition to digital production, decomposes more slowly than its predecessors, though it is subject to problems like curling and delamination.[211] Regardless of base polymer, then, the life span of photographic film is marked by spontaneous, inevitable, and irreversible deterioration. In this material sense, archival collections are continually being preserved so as to stave off the anarchival possibility of an archive becoming a sepulcher for dead media.[212]

Archival decay belies André Bazin's claim that in capturing the profilmic, photography and photochemical cinema are an ontological "defense against the passage of time," aspiring to the "preservation of life by a representation of life."[213] For Philip Rosen, Bazin's preservative obsession, the desire to embalm time and maintain the past against decay, is an essentially defensive fantasy that seeks to disavow "time passing, duration, and change" because these "raise the problem of death."[214] Bazin was writing in 1945. Decades later, we know only too well that the physical carriers of photographic and cinematic images—whether celluloid film, analog tape, or digital discs and drives—are also subject to decline; the substrate suffers its own demise.

In *The Death of Cinema*, film preservationist Paolo Cherchi Usai asserts that "cinema is the art of moving image destruction," since the more we run a film through a projector, the more it is seen and handled, the more quickly it is destroyed. Declaring that film preservation is "futile," he writes, "preservation of the moving image is a necessary mistake."[215] Usai's polemical assertion and his book's postscript (a faux epistolary rant) are a type of reverse psychology, forcing us to articulate our investments in audiovisual archiving in the face of a lifelong preservationist's insistence on its simultaneous futility *and* necessity.[216] That Sisyphean recognition animates the rest of this book.

CHAPTER ONE

A Tale of Three Buildings

Marcos Cultural Policy and Anarchival Temporality

Alone among other Philippine presidential administrations, the conjugal dictatorship of Ferdinand and Imelda Marcos recognized the power of media. In the first fully mediatized presidential elections of 1965, the Marcos campaign cunningly wielded print journalism, radio, television, and film to achieve Marcos's first presidential victory. Broadcast media and the movies were central to the most expensive, bitterly fought, and media-saturated election the country had ever seen, made possible by electrification and radio penetration in both rural and urban households in the sixties (figure 1.1).[1]

The Marcoses soared to national popularity through a barrage of radio ads, televised commentaries, live broadcasts of political rallies, and a controversial propaganda film, *Iginuhit ng Tadhana* (Written by destiny; dir. Conrado Conde, Jose De Villa, and Mar S. Torres, 1965) (figure 1.2).[2] Countering accusations that Ferdinand Marcos had murdered his father's victorious congressional opponent, Julio Nalundasan, in 1935, the film gave the Nalundasan case a pro-Marcos spin.[3] Initially banned from exhibition by the incumbent Macapagal administration, the biopic was theatrically released shortly before the November 1965 election, the Supreme Court having lifted the ban in response to public outcry over the film's censorship.[4]

Politicians take to the air

by LORENZO J. CRUZ

1.1 Cartoon illustration by Lorenzo J. Cruz for the magazine article "Politicians Take to the Air," *Weekly Graphic*, July 28, 1965. The 1965 presidential election was the most media-intensive election the Philippines had seen to that point.

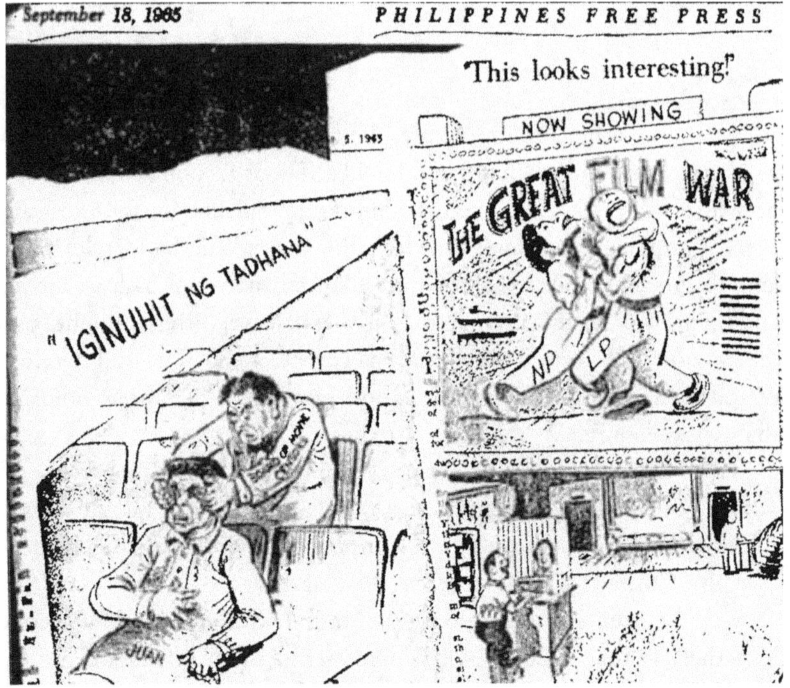

1.2 The cinema was critical to Ferdinand Marcos's first presidential victory, as evidenced in this cartoon depicting "The Great Film War" over the controversial Marcos biopic *Iginuhit ng Tadhana* (Written by destiny; dir. Conrado Conde, Jose De Villa, and Mar S. Torres, 1965). Cartoon illustration for the magazine article "The Press Discovers the Cinema" by Nick Joaquin (pseud. Quijano de Manila), *Philippines Free Press*, September 18, 1965.

The first Philippine political celebrities buoyed to success by print journalism, radio, television, and film, Ferdinand and Imelda Marcos went on to captivate enormous crowds of record-breaking size at the Nacionalista Party's rallies in 1965.[5] Ordinary voters marveled at the elocutionary brilliance of the presidential candidate and the glamorous beauty of his wife, Imelda, who regaled the crowd with a repertoire of songs in Tagalog, Visayan, Ilocano, and English.[6] Conflating "reel life" with "real life," *Iginuhit* blurs on-screen melodrama with the couple's off-screen political career. As a paradigmatic celebrity couple, Ferdinand and Imelda Marcos were a cinematic love team on the political stage.[7]

The decisive role of film and broadcast media in cementing their popular base, I surmise, laid the foundation for the couple's abiding interest in Philippine cinema. Film became a focus of the Marcoses' cultural policies and monopolistic takeovers of broadcast corporations and newspapers in decades to come.[8] At the twilight of the regime in the early 1980s, the Marcos administration generated a profusion of cultural policies concerning film. Eventually, the erratic and personalistic character of these policies undermined the Marcoses' pioneering cultural initiatives—such as the first FAP—thus endangering the dictatorship's own cinematic legacy (e.g., the deteriorating NMPC films explored in the introduction and chapter 2).

The media darling of the 1965 campaign season, Imelda Marcos established the CCP, falsely claiming that it was erected solely through 35 million pesos' worth of private donations raised during the Marcoses' first one hundred days in Malacañang Palace.[9] That is the beginning of the story, but we know what followed: the declaration of martial law and the abrogation of human rights in 1972, rampant cronyism and corruption, and a tragic construction accident at the Manila Film Center in 1981.

Following the deadly collapse of the Manila Film Center five months into its frenetic construction, strident anti-Marcos critic and former University of the Philippines president Salvador P. Lopez voiced the nation's diagnosis of the First Lady's mania for architectural construction: "There's no question about it: Mrs. Marcos is a compulsive builder. She has a bad case of the edifice complex, though fortunately non-Oedipal and non-fatal."[10] The term *edifice complex* was the pun-loving Filipino public's shorthand for the massive state-sponsored architectural reinvention of Manila during the twenty-year rule of Ferdinand and Imelda Marcos from December 1965 to February 1986.[11]

From the mid-1970s to the early 1980s, as state power, public funding, and cultural authority were increasingly concentrated in the First Lady's hands as governor of Metro Manila, representative to the Interim National Assembly, and minister of human settlements, Imelda Marcos promulgated a utopic vision of Metro Manila reborn as the City of Man, a humane city "able to bring out what is true, good and beautiful in man and his environment."[12] The dictatorship's urban vision attempted to reclaim the nation's capital from the alternative geography of student dissent that culminated in the First Quarter Storm of January through March 1970, when anti-Marcos youth protesters were violently suppressed by police and military forces.[13]

In contrast to student activists' "fearful geography" of street protest, the Marcosian edifice complex erected grandiose buildings that, as Gerard Lico argues, were propaganda realized in architectural form, asserting state power through megalithic "spectacles of legitimation."[14] The CCP complex, built on reclaimed coastal land along Roxas Boulevard, was the nucleus of the regime's ambitious architectural overhaul of Manila's urban space. In practice, the City of Man entailed the forcible displacement of sixty thousand slum dwellers as well as a beautification program that spray-painted parched foliage green and hid the capital's squatter colonies from the gaze of visiting foreign dignitaries.[15]

Weaving together strands of spatiality, temporality, and cultural legislation, this chapter suggests that the catastrophic effects of Marcos era cultural policy on Philippine film archiving can be apprehended as a tale of three buildings. Completed in 1969 during the early years of the Marcos regime, the first of these structures is the CCP Performing Arts Theater. Institutionally, the CCP functioned as the dictatorship's central implementing agency for cultural policy initiatives; the fledgling Film Archives of the Philippines was initially subsumed under its auspices.[16] Funding for the construction of the CCP Performing Arts Theater was riddled with fiscal malfeasance.[17] In addition, CCP practices exemplified a neocolonial politics of patronage that often devalued the Filipino artistic labor it claimed to celebrate.[18] Nonetheless, in hindsight, the CCP is not only the first but also the most enduring realization of dictatorship architecture and cultural policy. In contrast, the Manila Film Center, erected in the twilight of the dictatorship, exemplifies the failure and decay that haunt the Marcoses' edifice complex. Built to house several government film entities, the Manila Film Center—and, with it, the Film Archives situated on its premises—was the most memorable casualty of Imelda Marcos's characteristically rushed construction timetable, an *Imeldific temporality* that proved not only unrealistic but also lethal.

In the wee morning hours of November 17, 1981, the scaffolding of an upper floor of the Film Center collapsed under the weight of quick-drying cement, burying and killing the construction workers beneath who had been working around-the-clock to complete the building. Following the Film Center's completion in 1982, members of the First Family participated in numerous exorcisms in response to accounts of haunting.[19] Despite criticism that proximity to the sea air would harm its collection, the Film Archives was housed on the ground floor of this purportedly haunted Film Center until 1986, when the conjugal Marcos dictatorship was swept away by popular revolt. In the post-EDSA era, the Manila Film Center has alternated between periods of disuse and dereliction. From 2001 to 2020, it became the site of queer reoccupation and renewal by the performers, tourist audiences, behind-the-scenes workers, and organizers of the Korean-owned *The Amazing Show*, touted as "the 'largest transvestite show in Asia.'"[20]

The CCP Performing Arts Theater and the Manila Film Center—two emblematic edifices that bookend the dictatorship, both hailed as Philippine versions of the Athenian Parthenon by Imelda Marcos's characteristically overblown rhetoric—actualize Marcosian cultural policy in built form.[21] In addition to these two structures, I triangulate a third edifice that never was (or has not yet been): a permanent building to house an envisioned Philippine Audiovisual Archives under suitable archival conditions.[22] Though never built, this structure has been frequently envisioned by a tenacious advocacy movement. Since the 1990s, stakeholders and advocates of audiovisual archiving have collectively imagined and fervently anticipated a "place that does not yet exist."[23] Throughout this chapter, I invoke these three edifices not only as material structures of built space but also as institutions that emblematize and operationalize cultural policy.

Buildings and other repositories for historical records are core to received definitions of archives.[24] "Buildings are, by their nature, intimations of stability and survivability," writes Ray Edmondson, since buildings communicate the "permanence and continuity" of the institutions they house and epitomize.[25] For Derrida, the archive is that place, house, dwelling, or domicile where stored records pass from private to public hands.[26] In other words, the archive is that repository where access is brokered. In contrast to such notions of the archive, the Philippines faces the problem of audiovisual archiving in the absence of a permanent building.

In juxtaposing three edifices in this chapter, I reflect on the question, "How does architecture govern?"[27] Architecture is plaited with film's uneven place in Marcosian cultural policy in the long struggle to establish and sustain a national audiovisual archive. Since a building to permanently house such an institution has been repeatedly planned but never erected, this phantom edifice demands a notion of architectural governmentality open to instances of failure.[28] As of this writing, the NFAP/PFA building still belongs to the virtual genre of unrealized architecture, pointing to negotiated histories forged by state bureaucracy, cultural policy, and the heterogeneous players of a persistent audiovisual archive advocacy.

Ann Laura Stoler directs our attention to the "political content of archival forms," reminding us that archives are not only repositories of information but also "condensed sites of . . . political anxiety" that embody modes of "governance," "power relations," and "technologies of rule."[29] Infused with a "healthy and thoroughgoing suspicion of official state politics," as Jonathan Sterne puts it, cultural policy studies maintains that "the administration of culture is no small matter." This explains why much cultural policy research on the Philippines has centered on the Marcos regime: if cultural policy studies "understands culture itself as an object of administration," then it is cut to the measure of the Marcos dictatorship, which decisively politicized culture in general and film in particular.[30]

Triangulating these three buildings to explore the Film Archives of the Philippines' articulation within the dictatorship's cultural policy matrix, this chapter argues that the continued instability of the present-day NFAP/PFA has deep roots in the political culture of the Marcos era. The conjugal dictatorship of Ferdinand and Imelda Marcos demonstrated an unprecedented investment in culture, but cultural policies under the dictatorship sought to bring the film industry under direct presidential control rather than create the conditions for Philippine cinema to thrive. Despite having been historically excluded from founding state cultural policies, film suddenly occupied center stage through a succession of initiatives introduced in the twilight of the Marcos era, as the Philippine economy plummeted.[31] Forged in the context of economic, social, and political chaos, the first, short-lived Film Archives was subjected to multiple organizational reshufflings and mired in the patronage politics of the Marcos regime, what Doreen Fernandez has aptly called a cultural politics of "whim and memorandum."[32] Founded in 1981, the Film Archives withered by dispersal amid the dictatorship's presidential decrees, its fate and funding never having been secured by an act of Congress.

Excavating the ironic legacy of Marcos cultural policies and institutions, this chapter identifies two enduring problems bequeathed by the Marcos era Film Archives to the present day: first, the established but deeply problematic practice of presidential appointments to state film entities; second, the issue of *anarchival temporality*. Contravening the more conventional notion of archival temporality as (an impossible fantasy of) permanent preservation, the anarchival temporality of Philippine audiovisual archiving—a time of precarity, loss, and unsustainability—is the flip side of the Marcos dictatorship's frenetic pursuit of perpetuity.

ANARCHIVAL TEMPORALITY, CULTURAL POLICY, AND PRESIDENTIAL APPOINTMENTS

The particular form of anarchival temporality that shadows Philippine cinema, I argue, is historically rooted in Marcos era cultural policies and practices. Ferdinand Marcos, the first president to evince a keen interest in film, established the Philippines' first national film archive, the FAP, via Executive Order 640-A under the supervision of the CCP in 1981. Exemplifying the dictatorship's fickle approach to cultural policy, the FAP was reclassified under the newly created ECP the following year, 1982. Three years later, in August 1985, the ECP was dissolved and the FAP transferred to a censorship agency, the Board of Review for Motion Pictures and Television (BRMPT).[33] But the censorship board was itself unstable. Denounced by a vigorous anticensorship movement helmed by filmmaker Lino Brocka and the Concerned Artists of the Philippines, Marcos's censorship entities were subjected to numerous reshufflings, forced resignations, and rushed appointments.[34] In October 1985, a month after the Film Archives had been transferred to the censors, the censorship board was itself abolished by a dictator struggling to pacify the opposition.[35]

This chaotic timeline and the FAP's "unsettled organizational status" tell us that although the Marcos regime was the first administration to be seriously interested in Philippine cinema, its erratic and self-contradictory policies were ultimately deleterious for film archiving.[36] The FAP changed hands three times in four years and was defunct in five. The last organizational move was excoriated by critics who rightly noted that BRMPT censors who "cut and delete footage from pictures" are diametrically opposed to archivists, who painstakingly "collect and conserve every single part of motion pictures."[37] Those objections notwithstanding, the FAP was turned over to the censorship board a year before the Marcos regime itself collapsed, overthrown by the EDSA People Power Revolution. Lasting a mere five years (1981–86), the first Film Archives of the Philippines remains the grimmest example of the many ephemeral film archiving initiatives subsequently undertaken by the Philippine government.

Bernadette Patino highlights one of the most unfortunate consequences of the FAP's demise in 1986: the subsequent "hegemony of industrial narrative cinema in contemporary audiovisual discourse and archival practice." The first FAP bore the stamp of Philippine film archiving pioneers Ben Pinga and Ernie de Pedro, who were committed to archiving short films, documentaries, and early cinema. In the decades following the collapse of the FAP, their founding commitment to noncommercial, alternative filmmaking was supplanted by the industry-focused archival agenda of SOFIA, ABS-CBN, and the NFAP/PFA, which privileged the restoration and exhibition of "feature-length narrative cinema . . . as the ultimate archival priority, reflecting an embrace of a primarily industrial view of both Philippine cinema and audiovisual heritage."[38]

Following the dictatorship's demise in 1986, the five-year-old FAP eventually withered under the new government of Marcos's successor, President Cory Aquino, its collection subject to dispersal and attrition. Though FAP Director General de Pedro pleaded desperately for state funding and support, the Aquino government did not come to the Film Archives' aid.[39] Following the dissolution of the ECP and its replacement by the Film Development Foundation of the Philippines, the FAP collection was transferred to a censorship body, the BRMPT, renamed the Movie and Television Review and Classification Board (MTRCB) later that year.[40] Chapter 2 of this book retraces the itinerant and attenuated afterlives of the FAP's collection—transferred to the MTRCB in 1988, the MTRCB's film holdings were deposited in 1999 at the PIA-MPD, where they remained until the latter was abruptly dissolved in 2004. A decade later, between 2013 and 2015, the remainder of the FAP's severely diminished collection was turned over to the NFAP.

The year 1986 marked the beginning of a twenty-five-year gap between the demise of the first FAP and the long-awaited establishment of the NFAP in 2011, during the term of President Noynoy Aquino. In those gap years, much of Philippine film history was irretrievably lost. Uwe Schmelter, who served as head of the Goethe-Institut Manila in the 1980s, describes the appalling state of the FAP collection toward the end of the dictatorship in 1986: "Thousands and thousands of films . . . were starting to rot because there was no electricity and no air conditioning" at the Manila Film Center. As a result, films and documents "had gone lost due to missing conservatory conditions."[41] Both Schmelter and de Pedro recall that the FAP collection at the Manila Film Center had been flooded.[42] Patino summarizes the institutional dispersal that followed: "As the MTRCB lacked proper archival facilities, many of the FAP's audiovisual holdings were scattered among various government institutions, handed back to private collectors, or left in the basement of the abandoned Film Center."[43] The conditions that led to the FAP's demise in the Marcos era foreshadowed recurring patterns of institutional instability experienced by independent, academic, and government archives in the post-EDSA period.

As discussed in the introduction, key posts in government media entities that oversee audiovisual archiving, such as the FDCP and the PIA, are held by presidential appointees in the absence of oversight from Congress or other state entities. Putting culture and especially the film industry directly under presidential control did not begin with Ferdinand Marcos but was inherited from the first postwar censorship body established in 1961 by President C. P. Garcia.[44] It was the Marcoses, however, who shrewdly used film-related appointments to amplify authoritarian, personalistic control over the cinema. Historically, the problematic practice of presidential appointees for government positions—a practice that invites the exchange of political favors—stems from the Marcos regime's wholesale co-optation of the civil bureaucracy. Appointing candidates selected by the president to plum government posts effectively enmeshed state officials in the dictatorship's patronage politics. In his analysis of the political economy of the Marcos dictatorship, Albert Celoza writes: "All local officials . . . owed their positions to the president. Their appointments to government positions were highly regarded as favors and did not necessarily result from their qualifications. Those who were favored owed gratitude and returned the favors to the person responsible for their appointment."[45]

In the aftermath of Marcos's ouster in 1986, a position paper on the Aquino government's newly created Presidential Commission on Culture and the Arts notes a major problem with presidential appointments to key cultural positions: the danger that they might serve the cultural agenda of influential individuals, creating a nondemocratic culture of censorship or suppression.[46] Ignoring such critiques, all successive presidential administrations in the aftermath of the Marcos dictatorship have continued the fraught practice of presidential appointments for state agencies. The now naturalized practice of presidential appointments to the present-day FDCP (itself a contemporary version of the Marcos era ECP), based more on the appointees' ties to the sitting president than on their qualifications, is a vestige of Marcosian practices that has had pernicious effects on the NFAP/PFA, since few FDCP chairs have appreciated the significance of archiving, acknowledged its complexities, or been open to consultation and feedback from archivists and stakeholders.

THE CCP PERFORMING ARTS THEATER

Noting that the state has a vital stake in "preserving and promoting" all aspects of Philippine culture, Ferdinand Marcos created the Cultural Center of the Philippines by executive fiat in 1966, thus circumventing the need for congressional approval.[47] Designed by National Artist Leandro Locsin, the CCP Performing Arts Theater opened in 1969. (It was renamed the Tanghalang Nicanor Abelardo in the post-dictatorship era and is now popularly referred to as the CCP Main Theater.) Over the years, contradictory accounts emerged about the CCP's genesis.

In early interviews, the First Lady had publicly given the credit to her husband, in keeping with a gendered conception of national/familial labor emphasized in publicity surrounding the First Couple that emphasized the wife's submission to her husband's rule. In interviews with the Marcos-controlled media, Imelda projected herself as housewife and housekeeper to the nation: "While the President takes care of the major national programs like geothermal sources, etc., I take care of the house keeping of the country because human settlements is really housekeeping."[48] Although Imelda Marcos's early pronouncements associated culture and the arts with "women's work," this gendered submission to her husband's authority eventually eroded.[49] In later revisions of her previous accounts, she refused to cede the originating vision for the CCP to Ferdinand Marcos. As the CCP became a reality, state propaganda and Imelda Marcos herself vigorously asserted her sole authorship, claiming that the CCP was her brainchild.[50] Popular journalism dubbed the CCP Main Theater the "Imelda Project," unwittingly portending the Marcoses' extreme personalization of cultural policy in years to come.[51]

Leandro Locsin's vernacular architectural design for the CCP Main Theater was a unique departure from the cityscape of postwar Manila. While other Filipino architects internalized foreign architectural trends

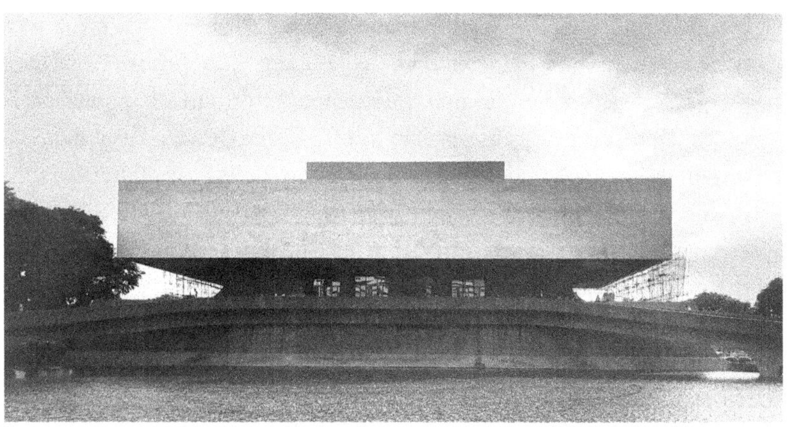

1.3 Performing Arts Theater, Cultural Center of the Philippines. Architect: Leandro Locsin, 1969. Photo by author, August 2017.

by working with steel and glass, Locsin embraced inexpensive concrete to create a dramatic structure of formidable scale based on the iconic Filipino rural house on stilts, the nipa hut. According to Nicholas Polites, the humble nipa hut's "raised floors" and "massive overhanging eaves" were approximated in "the massive cantilevered block . . . [that] serves as a protective eave over the balcony that surrounds the lobby" of the CCP Main Theater (figure 1.3).[52] Locsin's architectural achievement launched a fetish for indigeneity in Marcosian architecture; however, the conjugal dictatorship's exoticization of folk motifs, ethnic symbols, and vernacular iconography was belied by the regime's neocoloniality and land grabbing from indigenous minorities.[53]

Marcos propaganda alleged that the CCP Main Theater had been erected solely through the charismatic fundraising of Imelda Marcos.[54] In fact, CCP funding was sourced from US government funds and private loans and riddled with fiscal malfeasance. President Lyndon B. Johnson, on Imelda's urging, diverted a share of the US$28 million in war damage funds slated for Filipino veterans' education to the CCP as well as apportioned special Senate funds in exchange for Philippine support for the Vietnam War. In addition, a loan of between US$5 and $7 million was secured from the Chemical Bank of New York by the CCP Board of Trustees, for which a newly created subsidiary of the Philippine National Bank served as guarantor.[55] Thus, from the outset, an initiative whose declared objective was to foster and safeguard Filipino cultural heritage was mired in a highly politicized, questionable allocation of funds from US war damage payments and federal aid as well as loans from private American banks. Despite its corrupt origins and the Imeldific politics of patronage it emblematized in the Marcos years, in hindsight the CCP has turned out to be not only the first but also the most substantive example of dictatorship architecture and cultural policy.

The CCP's enduring relationship with Philippine cinema originated in the Marcos years, when it served as the dictatorship's primary cultural policy apparatus, though critics denounced the CCP as an elitist and neocolonial institution. In addition to functioning as a premier performing arts venue and a museum exhibition space for modern and contemporary art, it was also "endowed with authority and extra-legal powers" because the First Lady chaired its Board of Trustees.[56] As the principal cultural policy instrument of the Marcos state, the CCP had a seat at the table for all significant film-related state initiatives in the 1980s.[57] Nationalist historian Renato Constantino denounced the CCP as a "palace cultural revolution—for the elite."[58] Aiming to bring foreign artists to the Philippines to serve as an "inspiration" for local artists, the CCP subjected Filipino artists to inequitable, discriminatory compensation in comparison to international visitors who were paid far more. Financial outlays for the "royal treatment" of foreign artists accounted for 32 percent of CCP costs, dwarfing what the CCP spent on domestic arts programming.[59]

In the post-dictatorship period, as artists and intellectuals who had previously protested the CCP's cultural politics of patronage, elitism, and neocolonialism took the helm under Cory Aquino's administration, the CCP's cultural policy frameworks pivoted toward "Filipinization, democratization, [and] decentralization."[60] From the late 1980s onward, the considerably democratized, still monumental, though increasingly dilapidated CCP has become a vital hub for the arts community. In 2005, the CCP co-organized the annual Cinemalaya Independent Film Festival (later renamed the Cinemalaya Philippine Independent Film Festival), which, together with other key local film festivals, spearheaded a renaissance of the domestic film industry by providing production grants and a distribution and exhibition platform for talented indie digital filmmakers, though Cinemalaya has prompted its share of controversies and detractors.[61] In the long gap years between the demise of the FAP in 1986 and the NFAP's revival in 2011, film archivists and historians at the CCP worked collaboratively with SOFIA, the PIA, the UP Film Center, MOWELFUND, and the NCCA to pursue urgent film preservation and restoration projects and to call for the reestablishment of a national film archives.[62]

The two best-remembered architectural initiatives of the Marcos era are those that bookend the regime: in the euphoric early years of the Marcoses' popularity, the CCP Main Theater embodied the regime's cultural aspirations as the cornerstone of the City of Man; in the twilight and aftermath of the regime, the Manila Film Center exposed the deadly excesses of the dictatorship and the afterlives of its built spaces and anarchival policies. A critical consideration of both edifices exposes the hollowness of Marcosian revisionist histories that rebrand the martial law era as a golden age of development and infrastructural achievement.[63]

THE MANILA FILM CENTER

Described by one journalist as the "the ultimate symbol of Marcos decline," the Manila Film Center condenses the economic crises of its day.[64] From 1978 to 1983, the half decade leading up to the assassination of Benigno "Ninoy" Aquino Jr., underemployment tripled under the debt crisis.[65] At about the same time, from 1976 onward, capital outlays for government construction projects—such as those erected in the CCP complex under Imelda's Ministry of Human Settlements—increased fourfold.[66] Economists surmise that the Marcos regime might have survived the 1980s, "when world recession came and exports were hit hard," were it not for government overspending on lavish construction projects that helped the country's external debt balloon to US$15 billion—the steep cost of the Marcosian edifice complex.[67]

On the orders of Imelda Marcos, who also chaired the Filipino Motion Picture Development Board, the Film Center was built at breakneck speed in order to be completed in time for the opening of the Manila International Film Festival (MIFF) in January 1982. The project proved both massive in scale (costing an estimated 200 million pesos) and corruption-ridden (construction went forward in the absence of a building permit, qualified contractors, and government oversight of the blueprints).[68] Five months into the hurried construction, at 2:00 a.m. on November 17, 1981, the scaffolding that held up concrete slabs and beams on the sixth floor of the nine-level structure buckled under the weight of the quick-drying cement being poured over it, burying construction workers on the floors below; this catastrophe was the second fatal accident at the site.[69] The official cover-up that followed resulted in there being no accurate tally of the fatalities, although it was reported that, of 204 workers assigned to that overnight shift, 100 were still missing two days after the accident.[70] Philippine newspapers in the Marcos-controlled mediascape downplayed the death toll while foreign journalists painted a grisly portrait of the tragedy. Elliott Stein writes: "More than 200 persons were buried under fast-drying cement. A security blanket was immediately imposed; nothing could be done until an official statement, minimizing the accident, had been prepared. Ambulances were not permitted access to the scene of the disaster until nine hours after the cave-in. . . . Orders were given to slice in half those caught unconscious in the quick drying porous cement. Had they been dug out or drilled out whole, construction would have been further delayed. This graveyard shift claimed well over 100 lives."[71]

The first home for the FAP had caved in even before it had opened, boding ill for the long-term prospects of the country's first national film archives. Simultaneously attempting to mitigate the tragedy and defend the First Lady's vision, official statements enumerated various state film initiatives the Manila Film Center would house once completed; this gave Marcos-muzzled news coverage of the tragedy a surreal public relations cast.[72] The FAP was prominent in Imelda Marcos's vigorous defense of the Manila Film Center, as with all local journalistic reportage of the accident. The First Lady held a press conference to announce that the Film Center would be "finished on schedule," enumerating the benefits to the domestic film industry and to the national economy that the MIFF would generate.[73]

Rebuilt from the rubble of its deadly collapse, the completed Manila Film Center was to be a regenerated ruin (figure 1.4). In the final phase of the frantic construction—between Christmas Day in 1981 and the MIFF's opening night gala on January 18, 1982—seven thousand workers surged onto the construction site, laboring in nonstop shifts, an unforgettable sight variously described by journalists as a human "swarm" of workers[74] looking like "huge colonies of ants" at work on a mammoth undertaking.[75] In a sardonic piece titled "Who Says Rome Can't Be Built in a Day?," Salvador P. Lopez sketches an incredulous horizon of reception for both Imeldific temporality in general and the newly minted Manila Film Center in particular.[76] Though Rome wasn't built in a day, what journalists called the "instant film center" came awfully close.[77]

Although Imelda Marcos had touted the MIFF as a regional counterpart to the annual Cannes Film Festival that would establish the Philippines

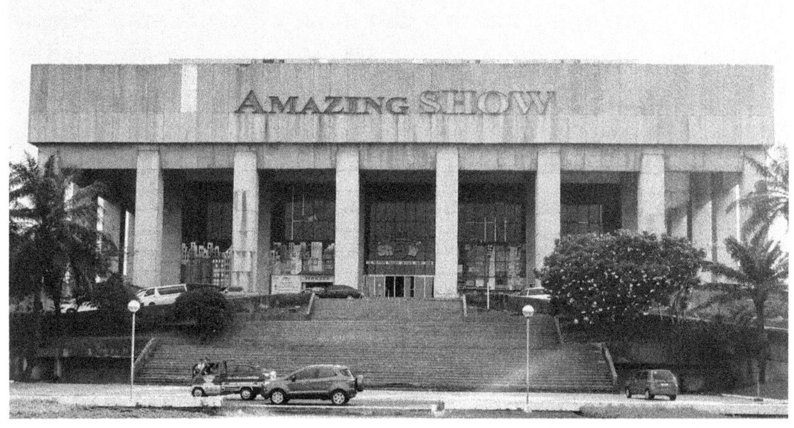

1.4 Manila Film Center. Architect: Froilan Hong, 1982. Photo by author, August 2017.

as the center of Asian filmmaking, the MIFF was held only twice before the festival permanently closed its doors.[78] The first MIFF in 1982 was, by some accounts, a letdown. The recent tragedy cast a pall over the festival; several international guests canceled, boycotted, or withdrew their films.[79] To Filipino moviegoers, however, the second MIFF in 1983 represented an appealing departure from a suffocating norm. In the context of strict state censorship over domestic film production and exhibition, the film festival (administered by the ECP) took advantage of its censorship exemption to screen uncut soft-core exploitation films.[80]

Known colloquially in the Philippines as *bomba* (explosive) or "bold" movies, the soft-core screenings at the second and final MIFF in 1983 were an attempt to recover the immense expenses incurred by the construction of the Manila Film Center. The festival's *bomba* films attracted record crowds and raised an estimated US$6 million. They also drew the ire of the Philippine Catholic Church and prominent New Cinema auteurs like Lino Brocka and Mike de Leon, who castigated the MIFF for its extravagance and hypocrisy.[81] Though the Marcoses' edifice complex had initially been bankrolled by foreign debt, by the early eighties the World Bank and the International Monetary Fund demanded that the Philippine government tighten its belt and abandon frivolous projects. When Prime Minister Cesar Virata cut government subsidies for the MIFF, Imelda Marcos turned to the lucrative exhibition of *bomba* films at the festival. However, in keeping with the fickle character of Marcos era cultural policies, *bomba* cinema's hiatus from censorship did not last. A few months after the close of the 1983 festival, police squads confiscated negatives and arrested the very producers whose profitable *bomba* films had saved the MIFF and the Manila Film Center from financial ruin. Ferdinand Marcos later widened the jurisdiction of the censorship board with yet another executive decree.[82] In the long run, public outcry against *bomba* at the Manila Film Center and the dictatorship's arbitrary censorship policies set in motion a chain of events that would lead to the dissolution of the Film Archives' umbrella agency, the ECP, and destabilize the FAP's eventual home at a censorship body, the BRMPT.[83]

In his fascinating firsthand account of having worked at the ECP during this tumultuous period, film scholar Joel David recalls that the dissolution of the ECP was a direct consequence of the destabilization of the Marcos regime following opposition leader Ninoy Aquino's assassination on August 21, 1983. The ECP, which oversaw both the FAP and the MIFF, was mired in Malacañang Palace intrigues, chiefly the animosity between Imelda Marcos and her eldest daughter, Maria Imelda Josefa Remedios "Imee" Marcos. In keeping with the personalistic nature of Marcos era cultural politics, the ECP was divided between the camp of Imelda (which administered the Film Archives and the Film Fund) and the camp of Imee (which oversaw the Film Ratings Board and the Alternative Cinema Department). Galvanized by the MIFF's exhibition of *bomba* films, ECP workers from Imee's camp participated in the anticensorship movement, creating an ironic situation in which "one government institution [was] agitating against another."[84]

The archival fragility of Philippine cinema hummed in the background of the controversial international film festival. Tucked away in an auxiliary theater at the second MIFF was a retrospective screening of Filipino film classics from 1951 to 1982 that the festival should have spotlighted, given the MIFF's declared goal of launching the Philippines as a hub for Asian filmmaking. Instead, what Stein called "by far the most interesting section of the festival" was sadly "the most poorly attended, most badly projected" part of the program. Several films were shown in the wrong aspect ratio, such that "heads and/or subtitles [were] lopped off." Film reels were projected out of order, and "some of the 16mm prints were so dupey that time spent watching them was as time spent watching a blank bedsheet." The abysmal condition of the archival screenings leads Stein to the heartbreaking conclusion that "the festival spent millions on fripperies but treated its own national cinema as a poor relation."[85] Despite technical consultations with UNESCO prior to the construction of the building's archival section, film archiving had clearly taken a back seat to the Manila Film Center's flashier divisions.[86]

In his discussion of the co-constitutive dynamic between *space* and *place*, Michel de Certeau characterizes place through the law of the "proper," that is, via notions of ordered, stable positionalities. In contrast, space is processual and brought into being by practice, "caught in the ambiguity of an actualization." Continually and discordantly transformed, space "has none of the univocity or stability of a 'proper.'" The apparent dichotomy between *place* and *space*, however, is continually undone by the push-and-pull dynamic between them: "*space is a practiced place.*" Spatial stories are powerful everyday practices that articulate place and space: "Stories . . . carry out a labor that constantly transforms places into spaces or spaces into places." While space is determined by "the actions of historical *subjects*," stories of the dead have, for Certeau, a place-making function, since places "are ultimately reducible to the *being-there* of something dead."[87]

The tragedy of November 17, 1981, the multiple exorcisms performed in its wake, and the Film Center's enduring tales of haunting are "spatial stories" in Certeau's sense, everyday practices that produce the Manila Film Center as place. "This Film Center is the only *palais du festival* which is also a mass mausoleum," writes Stein. At the MIFF's gala opening in 1982, the air "thick with thousands of flies" and the stench of putrefaction were tangible memento mori of the construction workers slain by Imeldific temporality, their bodies decomposing beneath the glitz of the film festival.[88] Within a year of the fatal accident, six exorcisms—variously observing Catholic, Chinese, and Igorot rites—had been held to rid the building of rumored ghosts and to halt the "freak fatal accidents" that plagued the Manila Film Center.[89]

First emerging in the wake of the 1981 collapse and continually retold and reinvented in the present day, ghost stories about the haunted Manila Film Center represent an enduring spatial narration that has been as formative to that regenerated ruin as the corpses of the unnamed workers buried in concrete beneath it. What we learn from Certeau's remarks on the place-making character of stories is that narratives about the haunted Manila Film Center make the space habitable but only on condition that we do not forget to remember its ghosts. Against the strenuous disavowals of the Marcos regime, ordinary Filipinos' spatial stories about the Manila Film Center insist on remembering that something dead is there, that the erstwhile film palace is a mass grave.

The undervalued workers who built the Film Center, only to be entombed within it, grimly attest to the layered materiality, the ineluctable archival dimension at work in all cities. If "a city is a memory machine," then the city-as-archive points to an accretion of historical events that gain significance in the collective memories of those who live there. Moreover, the "politics of urban naming" are key to the commemorative practices of all cities.[90] Imelda Marcos shrewdly realized this when, in the wake of the November 17 tragedy, the Manila Film Palace was more modestly renamed the Manila Film Center.[91]

On Imelda Marcos's orders, hastily completed architectural projects had transformed Manila in less than a decade, resulting in a spatiotemporal oxymoron: the *rushed monument* that is also a *regenerated ruin*. Rather than commemorate authoritarian accomplishment, however, Imeldific temporality leaves behind a legacy of hauntings that cannot be exorcised and the failure of two Marcos era initiatives, both bound up with the Manila Film Center from their inception—the MIFF and the first Film Archives of the Philippines.

THE PHILIPPINE AUDIOVISUAL ARCHIVES BUILDING-TO-BE (OR NOT TO BE)

Institutional dislocation engulfed the FAP upon the abolition of the ECP and the administrative transfer of the archive's office and personnel to the BRMPT in September 1985, less than five months before the conjugal dictatorship was itself deposed.[92] According to de Pedro, the Marcos government drafted, but never released, a "corrective Executive Order" that would have granted the FAP relative autonomy by placing it either under the Office of the President or within the jurisdiction of the CCP; this alternative organizational structure was explored in response to domestic and international criticism of Executive Order 1051's transfer of the Film Archives to a censorship body. A draft of the corrective executive order was circulated for consensus approval by the various parties involved—film industry representatives, the board of censors, and the president's legal office—but the forces of history overtook the slow-moving wheels of policymaking. The Marcos government was deposed before the orphaned

Film Archives found a secure institutional home. In his May 1986 report to the recently installed Aquino administration, FAP Director General Ernie de Pedro recounted that, under the jurisdiction of a newly reconstituted censorship body, the MTRCB, staff salaries for the FAP had gone unpaid since December 1985.[93] My research has uncovered no official response to de Pedro's urgent appeal for state support from the Aquino government.

The post-authoritarian state's silence, inaction, and neglect augured the beginning of a twenty-five-year gap between the demise of the first FAP and the long-awaited revival of the NFAP in 2011. In 1999, what remained of the FAP collection in the censors' hands was summarily returned to the films' rights holders; unclaimed films were "turned over to other archives who may be able to give better care and attention to the films."[94] Further deterioration and dispersal of the defunct FAP collection ensued.

In those gap years between the demise of the FAP in 1986 and the founding of the NFAP in 2011, SOFIA emerged as the lead nongovernmental coordinating body for an audiovisual archival advocacy movement that remains active today. Annella Mendoza, a founding member of SOFIA, recounts that in 1996, "A consensus was reached by various government and film related agencies to build a national storage facility to house our national collection. Within a span of one year, the national AV [audiovisual] storage site was identified and the technical design and construction specifications were drawn."[95] Mendoza is referring to a 1996 report conducted by Australian media preservationists Mark Nizette and Guy Petherbridge that proposed another Marcos edifice, the National Arts Center in Mount Makiling, as a possible site for a national audiovisual archive, citing its "lower average temperature" and "lowered pollution levels."[96] Nearly two decades later, in 2013, the reinvented NFAP commissioned architectural plans for a permanent archival compound, possibly to be located in Tagaytay City, which enjoys a cooler climate than Metro Manila.[97] In August 2020, the PFA announced that the FDCP's planned "construction of the Film Archive Heritage Building in Intramuros," a historic district in Manila, had been delayed due to the COVID-19 pandemic. As of this writing, none of these plans have come to fruition.

Nonetheless, this nonexistent building for a Philippine Audiovisual Archives has been the focus of long-standing collective imaginations about place and an anticipatory temporality of future outcomes in which not only the NFAP/PFA but also the wider community of stakeholders in the Philippines' and Southeast Asia's decentralized audiovisual archive movement are deeply invested. The discursive trail of this edifice-to-be is by now considerable: it dates from UNESCO consultant Christopher Road's technical specifications for the archival section of the Manila Film Center in 1981, to Nizette and Petherbridge's 1996 feasibility study, and the Leandro V. Locsin Partners' architectural design concept in 2013. As sociologist Michael Ian Borer notes, where "places that do not exist, yet" are concerned, "time, especially individuals' anticipation of potential and imagined future events, is of paramount importance for understanding perceptions of place."[98] As such, I understand the profound necessity for keeping alive the anticipatory collective demand for this spectral-building-to-be. At the same time, however, this expectant optimism is inevitably counterweighted by anarchival temporality, which forms the focus of this chapter's penultimate section.

TWO CURRENTS OF ARCHIVAL THEORY: TOWARD AN ANARCHIVAL ANALYSIS

The first Film Archives of the Philippines was an oxymoron: it was an archive that failed to last. And this is a sticking point, because the durative sustainability of archives goes to the heart of a state archive's promise to the public. Ray Edmondson explains: "Organisational continuity or 'perpetual succession' . . . are implicit in the idea of preservation. Archives which start up with lots of promise and then fail to survive organisationally or to perform competently destroy public confidence in the whole idea of preservation, and can do immense damage. Archives are inherently permanent entities . . . government instrumentalities come and go, but archives have to go on forever."[99]

Edmondson is here articulating an archival theory of institutional perpetuity, sustainability, and preservation culled from his on-the-ground experience as a preeminent audiovisual archivist. In opposition to a seductive but often loosely figurative evocation of "the archive" as a capacious theoretical metaphor, the theoretical and philosophical perspectives offered by professional archivists are alive to what Ann Stoler calls the ethnographic "disjuncture" between archival "prescription" and the actual day-to-day "practices" and power dynamics at work in real-world archives.[100] There is a blurred but still important distinction between "the archive" as a theoretical figure and actual archives embedded in particular institutional, national, historical, cultural, political, and economic contexts. Paul Grant emphasizes that speaking of *an* archive in its specificity (versus *the* archive in a larger figurative sense) centers the labor of memory professionals and the public's activation of archival collections: "To think of an archive in its singular[ity] as opposed to a common reference to 'the' archive is to strip away the implication that there is some transcendental archive which the public either chooses to use/access or not. The purposeful labor of memory professionals is in some sense pushed to the margins. . . . 'An' archive on the other hand, is constructed, can be demolished, is interpreted, and maintained; it can be useful or useless, ultimately assembled and not neutral."[101]

In contrast to the practical, experiential, and historically embedded archival theory offered by thinkers like Ray Edmondson, Terry Cook, Karen Gracy, Verne Harris, and Giovanna Fossati, there is what I would call an archival theory of the imagination that sets itself the philosophical task of inventing generative questions, devising the very parameters by which certain problems become answerable and recognizable. I owe this line of thinking to Gilles Deleuze's *Bergsonism*: "In philosophy and even elsewhere it is a question of finding the problem and consequently of positing it, even more than of solving it. For a speculative problem is solved as soon as it is properly stated. . . . But stating the problem is not simply uncovering, it is inventing."[102] As I have argued elsewhere, a key takeaway from Henri Bergson's work is that "the framing of one's questions always has a bearing on the answering knowledge produced."[103] Throughout this book, I have attempted to think both currents of archival theory together—the pragmatically grounded alongside the philosophically imaginative—in the hopes of unearthing their generative conjunctures and disjunctures rather than valorizing one type of archival theory over the other.

An imaginative archival theory is offered by Akira Mizuta Lippit's reading of Jorge Luis Borges's short story "The Library of Babel" (1941). The narrational voice in Borges begins by saying that some call the universe the Library and maintains—against the opinions of skeptics—that this Library is both eternal and infinite and that "the most ancient peoples" were "the first librarians."[104] In this "total" Library, "perfect, complete and whole," no two books are identical, and every expressible thought in every language, and in every time (from "the detailed history of the future" to "the true story of your death"), has been archived.[105] Yet initial euphoric hopes—of finding, somewhere in the Library, the solution to every problem, the justification for the universe itself, and the vindication of every person's life—eventually give way to despair. In the Library of Babel's enormity, the chances of finding a book of genuine epiphany are minuscule, though some "fanatics" persist in the belief that the "perfect compendium of all books" must exist, and that a librarian "analogous to a god" must know how to find it.[106]

Confronted with Borges's fantastic, total archive, Lippit conceives the problem of archiving differently. In Bergsonian fashion, Lippit invents a different question than the problem of infinite, enduring totality contemplated by the story's narrator:

> Does the universe that Borges envisions, the fantastic archive that contains every inscription and future inscription, also contain the record of all that is not only uninscribed, but uninscribable, every trace of the unrecordable and unrepresentable? . . . Does an archive of the uninscribable exist apart from the Library of Babel, or is it the basis of its possibility, a secret architectural condition of the universal archive? Is the archive of the uninscribable, unwritable, and unrepresentable possible only as the destruction of the archive? Is it necessary to found, always in the ruins of the archive, a shadow archive? Another archive that replaces the archive, that takes place in its ruin as an afterthought and effect of destruction?
>
> . . . This other archive takes place in the ruin of the archive, *an event of the ruin*.[107]

The questions posed by Lippit's imaginative philosophy go through another door than Borges's story: away from permanence and totality, toward ruin and destruction; toward what has been lost, repressed, or made secret; toward what was unrecorded, unrepresented, and uninscribable in the first place; that is, toward every archive's anarchival shadow. "To archive *otherwise—anarchivize*."[108]

To conceive of archives otherwise is to acknowledge the remaindered guise of their anarchival afterlives. An anarchival analysis construes Philippine film collections as past or ongoing events of ruin, in both philosophical but also profoundly pragmatic senses. This anarchival otherwise is the converse of the permanent enduring Edmondson incisively identified as the temporal fantasy of (idealized) archives, roughly corresponding to Borges's evocation of comprehensive totality as the spatial fantasy of the Library of Babel. Lippit asks, "Which archive survives in the end? Which one remains, the archive or its shadow?" In doing so, he proffers an opposite postulate to fantasies of permanence, recognizing that inevitable destruction, rather than total conservation, is *the* archival condition of possibility. If, as Lippit suggests, "this and all archives are realized in destruction, preserved by the traces of destruction," then the condition of being remaindered—of being the surviving trace of a prior archive's destruction—not only describes Philippine cinema's anarchival afterlives but also demands to be recognized as "the secret architectural condition" of all real-world archiving as such: the struggle to preserve and sustain a comprehensive collection in the face of the ever-present, foundational danger of loss, deterioration, or destruction.

Precarity is the converse of the fantasies of certainty, security, and permanence that archives stand for. The anarchival condition of collections being destroyed, remaindered, and remade more accurately describes actual Philippine audiovisual archives in their specificity than ideals of archival permanence. Thinking Derrida's archive fever through Lippit's reading, two meanings of the *anarchive* come into view: first, the anarchive as an event of ruin, of memory institutions emerging as much from destruction as from preservation; second, the anarchive as a virtual archive emerging from a feverish passion, a lovesick yearning for permanence that burns throughout the precarious afterlife of its destruction.[109] Both anarchival impulses underwrite the history of formal and informal archival initiatives in the Philippines: a fervent longing for a lasting audiovisual archive, despite the country's history of collapsed or endangered collections. Philippine cinema's archival afterlives, then, continually contend with anarchival temporality. Anarchival time is the converse of enduring sustainability, naming the threat of transience and ephemerality that shadows real archives' aspirations for permanence. In closing this chapter, I turn to anarchival time and explore its relationship to the temporalities of the Marcos dictatorship.

IMELDIFIC, MARTIAL, AND ANARCHIVAL TEMPORALITIES

Anarchival time is the flip side of Imeldific time, the dictatorship's frenetic pursuit of perpetuity through the rushed construction of urban monuments. In his 1969 profile of Imelda Marcos, National Artist Nick Joaquin describes the First Lady as a "beautiful dynamo" who was almost fatiguing to watch, so impelled was she by an overwhelming sense of temporal scarcity.[110] Hints of what Lico calls the "Imeldific timetable" of state architectural construction under the dictatorship emerged in 1974, when the Folk Arts Theater, "an arena-type ten thousand-seat theater," was completed in seventy-seven days to host the Miss Universe Pageant and to impress foreign dignitaries during their brief stay in the city. The now-defunct PhilTrade complex, composed of over 250 "vernacular-inspired pavilions" that served as kiosks and booths for a United Nations trade conference, was completed in a mind-boggling twelve days in 1979, anticipating the frenetic pace of construction on the Manila Film Center in 1981.[111]

Architect Froilan Hong's account of the final, frenzied days of the Manila Film Center's construction, which reads like a bizarre game of "beat the clock," remains the most vivid account of what Imeldific temporality was like for those who labored under its strictures. Three days before opening night, the lobby escalator and the facade's glass paneling had been installed, although there was not yet a main theater or a main lobby to speak of. A thousand workers toiled to "finish in 72 hours a lobby that would normally take six weeks, and a 1,400-seat theater that would usually take three months to complete." The rest of the interiors were completed at a likewise feverish pace: as soon as the soundproofing panels for the theater were nailed into place, another crew painted over them; as soon as cement slabs were laid on the floor, workers installed the tile and unrolled the precut carpet over the newly created aisles. Curtains were hung the prior evening, and on the frantic morning of the festival premiere, two enormous chandeliers were hoisted up to the ceilings, the granolithic floors polished, and the main film screen installed. By 2:00 p.m. the primary projector was in place; "at 7:00 p.m., 30 minutes before zero hour, they were still bolting down some 300 theater seats, even as tuxedoed guests were peeping in, befuddled by all the commotion."[112]

For the First Lady, time always seemed to be on the verge of running out; this emphasis on speed might have been fueled by an underlying defensive fantasy of staying one step ahead of the increasingly defiant anti-Marcos movement. Imeldific time was darkly implicated in the indefinite temporality of martial law, a bloodstained, simulated legitimacy that allowed Ferdinand Marcos to hold on to the presidency instead of relinquishing it at the end of his second term as the 1935 Constitution mandated.[113] First declared by Ferdinand Marcos in September 1972, martial law ushered in military-backed authoritarian rule without an end date in sight, as Ferdinand and Imelda attempted to extend their hold on power into perpetuity and become, in Benedict Anderson's memorable phrase, "Supreme Cacique[s] for Life."[114] The era of abusive martial power from 1972 to 1981 (formally) or to 1986 (in actuality) were years in which the Marcoses governed on stolen time.[115] This may partly explain the conjugal dictatorship's efforts to erect, as quickly as possible, a monumental—but ultimately haphazard—legacy. My hunch is that the anarchival time of government film archives is the penumbra of martial and Imeldific temporalities: a time of collapse and precarity directly linked to the conjugal dictatorship's longing to quickly yet perpetually personify state power.

The collapse of archival permanence under the Marcos dictatorship involves a temporal inversion: constitutionally, political power is curtailed by defined term limits, while the temporal fantasy of archival permanence imagines that archives can preserve collective memory by going on forever. In declaring martial law to bypass the constitutional term limits of the Philippine presidency, however, the Marcos regime created conditions under which archival longevity became its opposite: anarchival ephemerality. Ironically, the conjugal dictatorship's repressive pursuit of permanent power doomed many of its cultural policy initiatives, including the first Film Archives of the Philippines, to transience.

Derrida warns that the archive is far from an "assured" concept; it is emphatically not a "question of the past" or a concept that we already have unproblematically "at our disposal." Rather, archiving always raises the question of an undecided and radically open future: the "question of a response, of a promise and of a responsibility for tomorrow."[116] Indeterminacy shrouds the possibility of the NFAP/PFA ever having a permanent long-term home. On the one hand, uncertainty is common to all archives in their struggle against forgetting, obsolescence, and loss. On the other hand, as I hope to have shown, Philippine cinema's anarchival temporality has deep, historically specific roots in the cultural policies and practices of the Marcos era, subtended by the temporal rhythms of martial law and the Imeldific-Marcosian city.

CHAPTER TWO

Silence, Perseverance, and Survival in State-Run Philippine Film Archives

Decisions to preserve, neglect, or imperil remnants of the past are never neutral; power is at the crux of the social existence of archives. Archiving is an inherently political activity since it involves "an assertion of values and hence of a viewpoint" on how much of the past will be allowed to survive.[1] This political dimension of archiving demands high ethical standards for those charged with the care of cultural memory. Given that much of archival work is unmonitored and unvalidated, "the survival of the past is constantly at the mercy of the present."[2]

This chapter focuses on the dissolution of the PIA-MPD and the posthumous fate of its film collection. I refer to its posthumous fate because the MPD's internationally prominent film laboratory and film library were shut down in 2004 by order of Renato S. Velasco, the PIA director general appointed by President Gloria Macapagal-Arroyo, on the grounds that government cost cutting and the shift to digital media made the unit an ineffective use of state resources. Concurrent with the closure of the MPD was the creation of a new MISD, to which several former MPD personnel were redeployed.[3] The 2004 closure of the MPD amounts to a momentous yet little-known instance of heritage destruction conducted in the absence of a documented archival policy.[4] On my first research visits to the PIA Film Vault in August and September 2014—a decade after the MPD was dissolved—I encountered an extensive but derelict collection.[5] In the absence of temperature and humidity controls (the Film Vault was not even air-conditioned), several film cans leaked a black ooze (figures 2.1–2.5). The scent of vinegar, an index of deteriorating acetate film stock, hung heavy in the air.[6] The aim of the ensuing analysis is not to fault individual decisions but to underscore the historical significance of the Philippines' audiovisual past and to learn from the unintended consequences of the dissolution of the PIA-MPD.

To clarify, the PIA-MPD was never an official state film archive; the PIA's mandate centers on the dissemination of "development-oriented public information" through media and information/communications technology.[7] The absence of an explicit archival mandate for the PIA meant that its pioneering film preservation and restoration efforts were vulnerable to abrupt closure. During its heyday from the mid-1990s to the early 2000s, the PIA-MPD's film production, postproduction, and preservation capabilities were crucial to SOFIA's coordination of major collaborative restorations with international partners.[8] The abolition of the PIA-MPD effectively hobbled SOFIA's film restoration efforts and underscores the need for a firm legislative mandate for state agencies explicitly charged with audiovisual archiving.

This chapter begins by reconstructing the institutional histories of several film collections hard-hit by the closure of the PIA-MPD in 2004. What lessons should we take away from these state-institutional histories of Philippine cinema's archival fragility? The aftermath of the MPD's abolition underscores the drawbacks of a narrowly financial, profit-driven perspective on state film archiving that devalued analog cinema in relation to digital media while also ignoring the unique demands of audiovisual archiving by conflating it with paper-based librarianship. The demise of the PIA-MPD affirms audiovisual archive advocates' calls for legislation to safeguard the institutional continuity and autonomy of Philippine media archives from the vagaries of political whim.

As detailed in the introduction, the collaborative efforts of archivists at the PIA-MISD and the CCP, all prime movers of SOFIA and members of SEAPAVAA, enabled me to screen martial law propaganda films from the PIA collection in 2014. Excavated from the Film Vault of the defunct PIA-MPD, four 16mm propaganda films from 1971 to 1972 stood out: *PFM's Declaration of Martial Law*, *From a Season of Strife*, *The Threat . . . Communism*, and *The Enemy from Within*. The makeshift digitization of these titles at the CCP the following year was my first eye-opening encounter

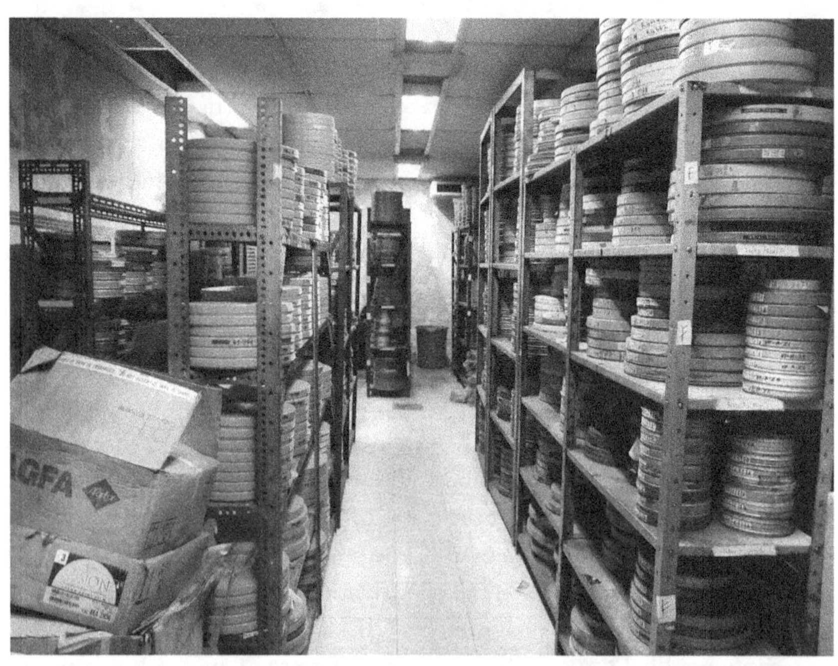

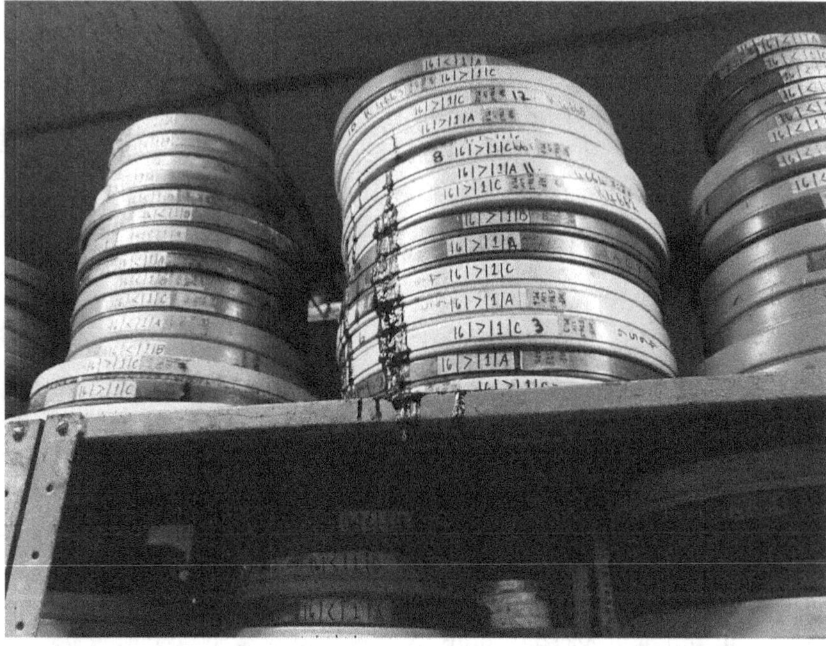

2.1–2.5 Deteriorating reels of film at the PIA Film Vault in 2014, a decade after the MPD was dissolved. Photos by author, August and September 2014.

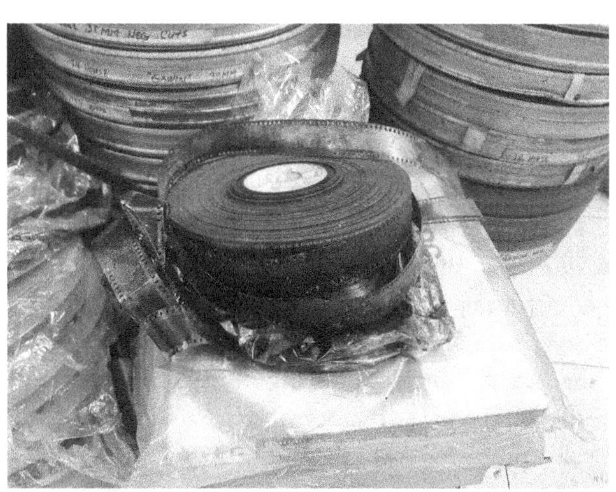

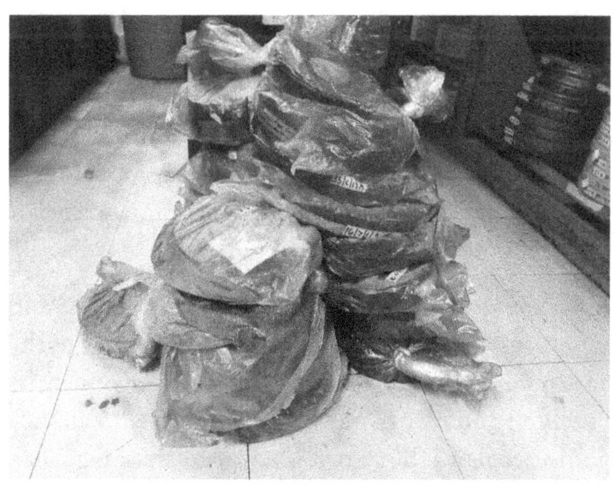

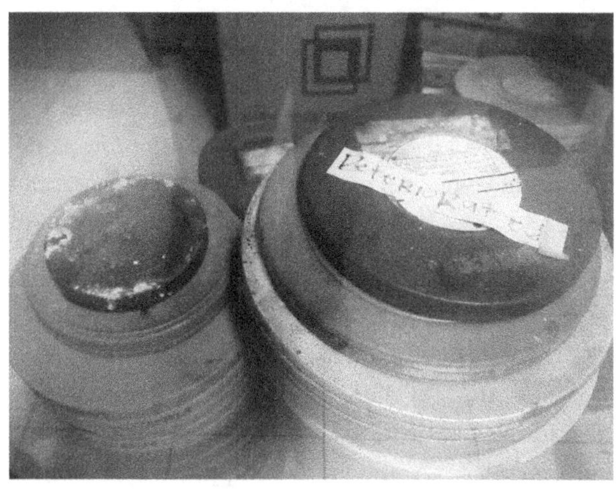

with Philippine archivists' resourceful tactics of making do despite institutional constraints. The penultimate section of this chapter offers a close reading of two different versions of Ferdinand Marcos's infamous declaration of martial law in 1972, imperfect yet vital copies of the dictatorship's deteriorating filmic legacy. The chapter concludes by conceptualizing archival survival as entailing exhaustion and perseverance on the part of film archivists who witnessed the painful deterioration of valuable film collections they had fought to preserve.

The Philippine experience of film archiving underscores the need for accountability on the part of "official guardians of the national heritage and its custodial institutions" and the value of vigilance among those who care about memory institutions devoted to cinema. At stake in this vigilance is the broader effort to transform what we do with and what we do about Philippine audiovisual archives. Ray Edmondson comes to a similar conclusion in his historiography of the NFSA's struggle to achieve legislative autonomy through the 2008 NFSA Act.[9] For Edmondson, the NFSA's decades-long struggle confirms the vulnerability of state film archives to the missteps of politicians and bureaucrats, and the importance of tenacious critical dissent in calling the questionable decisions of state officials into account:

> Eternal vigilance is the price of preservation. The bureaucratic and political landscape can change quickly. The official guardians of the national heritage and its custodial institutions cannot unfailingly be relied upon to fulfill their duty of care. Nor, when they fail, can they be easily brought to account. The system is not self-correcting. Ultimately, cultural institutions are public property and national treasures, and there is a wider duty of cultural stewardship shared among those who create the content of collections, those who curate and preserve them, and those who use them. The ways of expressing this stewardship will vary, but it will include the support and advice of professional and advocacy groups, and when necessary may require their open and persistent dissent.[10]

Heeding Kathryn Pyne Addelson's work on the relevance of feminist epistemologies to public policy, my scholarship endeavors to make Philippine film archiving's predicament visible as an urgent public problem and to intervene in the ensuing arena of conflict that my own work and that of many others before me have constituted, fully aware that it takes time for archival consciousness, advocacy, and political support to take hold.[11]

Edmondson emphasizes that every archive is a memory institution that needs to remember and preserve its own history. My critically reflexive historiography of Philippine state film archives proceeds from the conviction that "institutions . . . which are guardians of a nation's memory need to also preserve their own memory, to know how and why they have come to be what they are. . . . It is fundamental to their ethos, identity, and public accountability."[12] In the Philippines, historical knowledge about film-related state institutions is neither readily available nor easily reconstituted. The history of the PIA film collection—which is entangled with that of other undervalued and underfunded film archives in the Philippines—affirms Edmondson's insight that the vicissitudes memory institutions are subjected to end up defining the surviving "heritage" such institutions are mandated to preserve.[13]

The story of the PIA-MPD's demise is little known even within the Philippines' audiovisual advocacy movement. As Michel-Rolph Trouillot remarks of historiography, "Some facts are more recalled than others." The following account foregrounds facts that hardly circulate due to what Trouillot might call a low "frequency of retrieval."[14] The recovery of the PIA-MPD's nearly lost history underscores Verne Harris's proposition that "remembering and forgetting are not opposites"; sometimes, "forgetting can become a deferred remembering."[15] Hence, the missing government circulars and irrecoverable films that surround the PIA-MPD's closure may not be forms of forgetfulness. Rather, they delineate a deferred remembering whose time has come.

ARCHIVAL FRAGILITY: THE FATE OF SIGNIFICANT FILM COLLECTIONS AT THE PIA-MPD

The abolition of the PIA-MPD had wide-ranging consequences for its singular film collection, which included 2,373 titles that ranged from experimental cinema to award-winning works, government media productions, and films from donor countries and agencies.[16] Significantly, the MPD's dissolution had negative repercussions for three key collections entrusted to the PIA: films from the National Media Production Center (NMPC); the Movie and Television Review and Classification Board (MTRCB); and LVN Pictures, a major film studio established in 1938.[17]

Upon its creation in 1986 by President Cory Aquino's Executive Order No. 100, the PIA became the repository of Marcos era government productions not archived elsewhere by virtue of its having absorbed the functions, assets, and facilities of several of the dictatorship's media agencies.[18] Of particular historical value are the documentaries, propaganda films, short films, plugs, and stock footage produced by the NMPC, an agency charged with disseminating information about government programs to the public and implementing the state's development agenda through media.

In addition to the NMPC's audiovisual holdings, the PIA sheltered a second crucial film collection adversely affected by regime change: the imperiled remains of the first defunct Film Archives of the Philippines (FAP). Cory Aquino's administration failed to revive the FAP despite the ailing archive's appeal for state funding and support.[19] After the Marcos regime was deposed by the EDSA People Power Revolt in 1986, the holdings of the defunct FAP were caught in the uncertain transition between Marcos era cultural institutions and the new film entities created by Cory Aquino's administration. Dispersed among various state entities with little direct connection to film archiving (the Experimental Cinema of the Philippines, the Manila Film Center, and the MTRCB), the FAP's collection was whittled down by attrition and deterioration. According to a brief history of the MTRCB film collection prepared in 1999 and filed at the PIA-MISD, the defunct FAP's holdings were consigned to the MTRCB in 1988, two years after the Film Archives' demise. This transfer of jurisdiction notwithstanding, the remains of the FAP collection were stored at the Manila Film Center for four more years until they were moved to the MTRCB's Quezon City office in 1992.[20] In 1999, the MTRCB's own film holdings—214 titles composed of 1,583 reels of 16mm prints and 35mm prints and negatives—were deposited at the PIA-MPD for safekeeping.[21] Thus the PIA-MPD belatedly inherited surviving fragments of the former FAP collection (via the MTRCB) over a decade after the overthrow of the Marcos regime. In short, the PIA-MPD enabled the archival afterlives of multiple at-risk film collections until its own institutional death 2004.

In the Sisyphean history of Philippine film archiving, no rescued film is guaranteed a permanent safe harbor. This is the painful lesson gleaned from the intertwined histories of various endangered state film archives—the Marcos era FAP (which withered after 1986), the MTRCB's Film Archives and Library Division (turned over to the PIA-MPD in 1999), and the PIA-MPD itself, whose abrupt closure in 2004 resulted in the decay of films entrusted to its care. In 2004, citing "streamlining and cost-cutting measures," the PIA began the process of handing over the MTRCB Film

Collections in its custody to the CCP, MOWELFUND, and the UP Film Center.[22] The MTRCB holdings deposited in MOWELFUND were eventually transferred to the NFAP in 2012.[23]

A third significant film collection under the PIA's custodianship was decimated in the aftermath of the MPD's closure: a clutch of films previously held in the vaults of LVN Pictures, a once-powerful film studio. Established in 1938, LVN Pictures was among the Big Three studios that dominated Philippine film production from the 1950s through the early 1960s.[24] Film historian Clodualdo del Mundo Jr. recounts that in 1994, LVN decided to discard films by other production companies that had long remained unclaimed in its storage vaults. Only a handful of production outfits retrieved their films upon being notified of the purge; the rest of the films—over a thousand rusting cans of celluloid comprising seventy-two titles—were dumped in the studio's open basketball court, exposed to months of sun and rain. Led by another film historian, Agustin "Hammi" Sotto, SOFIA coordinated the rescue of these films. Archivists at SOFIA and PIA-MPD inspected the salvaged titles and identified twenty-five priority films for rescue; while some had completely printable and restorable elements, others were incomplete or unrestorable.[25] Through SOFIA's intervention, the PIA-MPD agreed to shelter the remains of LVN's discarded holdings in 1994.[26] When SOFIA and LVN approached the PIA in 1994, it was only to provide "temporary shelter" for the rescued films, many of which were already in an advanced state of decay. The PIA ended up housing these titles for more than a decade since a new NFAP was not established in the interim.

The abolition of the MPD and the subsequent underfunding of the PIA's film collection meant that, by 2007, almost all those rescued LVN films had degraded past the point of recovery. In 2004, Capul, then PIA-MISD staff director and a member of both SOFIA and SEAPAVAA, wrote SOFIA to inform them of the dissolution of the MPD and to update them on the condition of the LVN film collection at PIA: "Most of the 72 film titles (comprised of 1,471 reels of master negatives, sound negatives and prints) which were transferred to PIA in rusty old cans [in 1994] were irretrievably lost and already in different stages of deterioration at that time. Only about 3% of these transferred films have survived." Capul was writing to "request SOFIA to seek clearance from LVN to dispose [of] the lost films and [to arrange for] the transfer of the remaining 3% of the films to other archives who may be willing to temporarily host them pending the establishment of the national film archive."[27] I found no reply from either SOFIA or LVN among the PIA records I perused. Three years later, in 2007, Capul informed LVN that by that point 99 percent of the LVN films deposited at the PIA in 1994 had already deteriorated beyond repair. Capul was no longer asking for permission to transfer the surviving films to another archive; she was asking for clearance to discard nearly the entire LVN collection at the PIA. Unable to make other arrangements for its films (the revival of the NFAP was still several years away), LVN approved, in 2008, the PIA's disposal of most of the films SOFIA had rescued from its backlot in 1994.[28] The characteristically clipped, neutral tone of such institutional correspondence is profoundly at odds with the tragic content of these letters. Capul, who had been instrumental to the rescue of these films in the nineties, penned the very letters that asked LVN for permission to dispose of the salvaged reels thirteen years later.

The demise of the majority of the LVN collection stored at the PIA's film vault is a microcosm of Philippine cinema's anarchival fragility. Whether they survived the collapse of the first FAP in 1986 or were recovered from a heap of rusted film cans in 1994, few rescued Filipino films enjoy permanent institutional protection from the ravages of decay. In 2013, then NFAP head Bono Olgado identified key heritage films in the PIA collection and requested the immediate transfer of fifty-two titles (525 cans of 16mm and 35mm film) to the NFAP.[29] This was done in compliance with a presidential directive requiring government agencies to turn over their audiovisual collections to the NFAP.[30] The PIA film collection was subsequently turned over to the NFAP in four batches from 2013 to 2015.[31] The former MPD's holdings are now housed in transitory storage facilities since the NFAP/PFA still lacks a permanent institutional space to house its collection.

THE MISSING CIRCULAR: FROM MPD TO MISD

On the eve of its abolition in 2004, the MPD was the "PIA's largest division" and one of its most prestigious units. Its forty-two staff members accounted for 14 percent of the Central Office personnel, while its floor area (2,379 square meters) occupied 32 percent of the agency's total office space.[32] According to Capul, the PIA-MPD was a "one-stop shop for [everything from] production to postproduction. Our lab had the reputation for [film] processing of international standard."[33] The lab handled footage from such major Hollywood films as Francis Ford Coppola's

Apocalypse Now (1979) and Oliver Stone's *Platoon* (1986) and *Born on the Fourth of July* (1989).[34] The PIA was also the postproduction facility for the alternative film workshops collaboratively mounted by the MOWELFUND Film Institute and the Goethe-Institut in the eighties and nineties, discussed in chapter 5. Pioneering the art of archival film restoration in the Philippines, the MPD restored a total of twenty-two historic Philippine films in collaboration with the NCCA and SOFIA, the most prominent of which are two of the five surviving prewar films, *Tunay Na Ina* and *Giliw Ko* (both from 1938), and Gerardo de León's acclaimed *Noli Me Tangere* (Touch me not; 1961). Despite its exceptional track record, the PIA-MPD was dissolved on the grounds that its film production and restoration facilities were "difficult to sustain financially" and that MPD resources were "underutilized."[35] A PIA newsletter, *Tinig* (Voice), articulated the rationale for the cutbacks: "To cope with the hard times, the government had to resort to some measures, often radical. Cost cutting and streamlining were the measures employed by the government along with optimization of funds to favor high-impact projects. Indirectly, part of the process was the dissolution of the MPD."[36] The discourse of cost cutting promulgated by state entities during the Arroyo presidency (2001–10) belies the corruption and plunder allegations that implicated her administration in multiple political scandals.[37]

The closure of the MPD (centered on photochemical cinema) to make way for the creation of a new unit, the MISD (focused on digital information management), was rapidly accomplished across four PIA circulars issued from March 8 to April 29, 2004.[38] Director General Velasco's first circular, dated March 8 of that year, created a review committee that would "evaluate the functions of the Motion Picture Division and recommend measures to maximize the utilization of its existing resources."[39]

Notably, Velasco's second circular—which possibly announced and justified the dissolution of the MPD—could not be located by the PIA Records Section despite persistent search requests by MISD staff.[40] The missing circular confirms Trouillot's insight that every event enters the historical record with "some of its constituting parts missing"; "inborn absences" attend the production of facts. As Trouillot discerns, "Historical facts are not created equal. They reflect differential control of the means of historical production at the very first *engraving* that transforms an event into a fact."[41] Denotatively, engraving refers to the process of producing a design by carving out or cutting into an object; figuratively, the idiom "engraved in memory" evokes the fixing of something in recollection.

Trouillot's evocative metaphor recognizes the nonequivalence between what has transpired and its retrievable trace (the surviving record, eloquent with silence).

In lieu of this missing circular, I reconstruct the PIA bureaucracy's reasons for shutting down the MPD through other surviving circulars and an article titled "Fade Out: Motion Pictures Division, Fade In: Management Information System Division," from a 2004 issue of the PIA newsletter, *Tinig* (figure 2.6). Judging from its mode of address, the article aims to assuage the anxieties of PIA employees affected by the restructuring. *Tinig* is likely to have circulated internally within the PIA and possibly interorganizationally among other government agencies.

The *Tinig* article takes an upbeat view of the profound organizational overhaul of the PIA resulting from the dissolution of the MPD and the concomitant creation of the MISD. Laying responsibility for the dissolution at the feet of the review committee, the article reports that the MPD "will be dissolved as recommended by a committee review," resulting in the "transfer and merging of its production function to the [National] Broadcast Division," while the MPD's library holdings are to be "integrated [with]in the newly created Management Information System Division (MISD)."[42]

In reading *Tinig*'s coverage of the closure of the MPD to make way for the MISD, I adapt media industries studies scholar John Caldwell's critical perspective on the "managed self-disclosures" of studio executives and film industry personnel. Caldwell asks: "How does one intelligently unravel the many cultural, conceptual, economic, corporate, social, professional, and interpersonal strands of self-disclosure that are constantly thrown at viewer and scholar alike as part of industrial habit?"[43]

In what follows, I adapt Caldwell's industry studies perspective to think about the *Tinig* article as an instance of managed self-disclosure on the part of a Philippine state institution. Since institutional realities, like industrial ones, are always multiply constructed, an analysis of the PIA's self-representation involves "cross-checking sources" (e.g., juxtaposing the claims of the *Tinig* article with the PIA circulars it references and interviews with archivists from the MISD and the former MPD); taking nothing at face value; and exploring areas of tension, contradiction, and debate.[44]

Read via this critical lens, the primary rhetorical objectives of the *Tinig* article are justification and reassurance with regard to the major changes triggered by the dissolution of the PIA's largest unit. The article seeks to justify the closure of the MPD on the grounds that during its last three-year period (2001–3) the MPD saw "decreasing annual income in

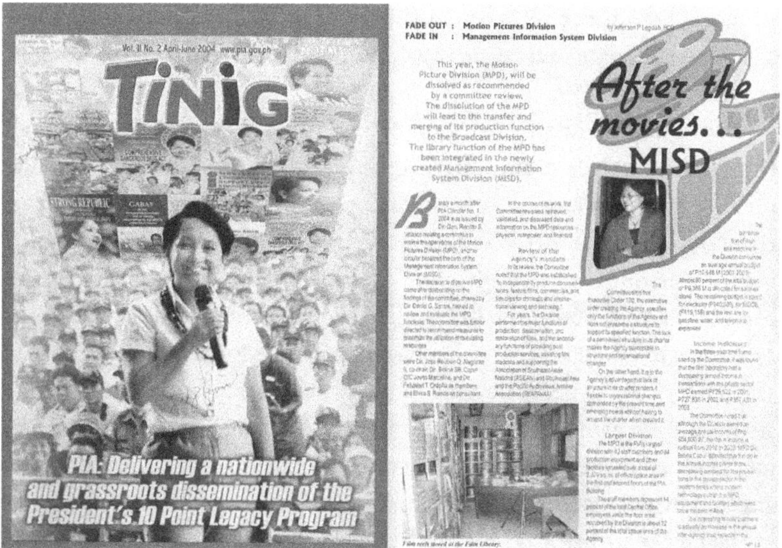

2.6 An article in the 2004 issue of the PIA newsletter *Tinig* (Voice) discussed the rationale for the dissolution of the MPD and the creation of the MISD. The then-president Gloria Macapagal-Arroyo is prominent on the issue's cover.

transactions with the private sector," a steep drop in loans from the film library (although loans of stock footage remained strong), and decreasing film restoration work.[45] "With the above figures, the Committee noted that the outputs/services of the MPD could hardly justify its manpower . . . , its total space area . . . , and its huge financial resources (P10.948 M average annual budget). Thus, the Committee decided, the resources of the MPD are underutilized."[46]

In a 2014 interview, Capul refutes the financial rationale for the dissolution of the MPD: "They claimed a lack of funding . . . but I'll tell you that while we had funds allotted solely for laboratory film processing in the GAA [General Appropriations Act under the Department of Budget and Management], we never touched that because we lived on income from the interagency film productions commissioned by other government agencies."[47] Capul's contention is corroborated by the *Tinig* article, which suggests that the decrease of 372,091 pesos in private sector transactions from 2001 to 2003 was compensated for by a dramatic increase of 8.44 million pesos in interagency income from film services from other state entities in the same period. The article explains: "This means that although the demand for film services from the private sector decreased, the income generated from the inter-agency transactions dramatically increased thereby, suggesting increasing utilization of the film lab facilities for government projects."[48]

Alongside its justificatory objective, the second aim of the article (highlighted by the subheading, "DG Velasco's Reassurance") is to allay possible concerns among MPD staff by pledging that "there would be no reduction or demotion in rank as well as no reduction in compensation for the personnel of the Division."[49] In its unfailingly optimistic tone, the *Tinig* article reads like internal PIA propaganda seeking to forestall resistance to or anxiety over the sweeping institutional overhaul about to take effect. The hyperbolic tone of the article's conclusion, for example, strikes an inspiring note while directly addressing MPD staff members facing redeployment or compulsory retirement:[50] "As for the employees affected by the reorganization, a moment will come when they can regale in the fact that they have sacrificed, have toiled, and have taken part in furtherance of the grand design to achieve a more efficient and effective delivery of public service."[51]

Capul recalls the MPD closure's impact on personnel in less sanguine terms: "Our film production people, those working in the laboratory, were all retooled. Engineers, for example, were sent to computer centers to acquire new skills. Our film restorers were retooled for the digital world. Those who were able to survive are still around. . . . But some of the people in the laboratory, especially those older restorers who were really skilled, say at repairing film sprockets, were rather old to be retooled."[52] Thus, while some former MPD personnel were transferred to the newly created MISD or retrained to acquire new skills, highly skilled motion picture restorers considered too old for such "retooling" were forced to retire, resulting in a loss of valuable competencies for the country's archival film preservation initiatives. It is now widely recognized that the hands-on knowledge of seasoned archivists is indispensable; it is not only legacy media (obsolescent carriers and formats) but also legacy skills (expertise in outdated media) that must be preserved to maintain "contextual integrity."[53] By 2014, the PIA—Southeast Asia's premier film restoration lab in the 1990s—no longer had a single employee comfortable with projecting the 16mm and 35mm films in its collection, though the agency's film projection equipment remained in good working order.

The most striking instance of internal contradiction in the *Tinig* article is its reportage of the decision to shut down the MPD under the section heading "PIA Circular No. 3":

> The [MPD review] committee recommended two options for the management: (1) to fully rehabilitate the division, which would entail capital infusion to upgrade its equipment and facilities to be at par with the present standard; or (2) to dissolve the MPD in its entirety and transfer its production function to the Broadcast Division.
>
> PIA Circular No. 3, Series of 2004, dated April 26 *articulated the management's option*.[54]

The actual text of Velasco's third circular, however, contains no mention of the first recommendation of the MPD review committee reported by the *Tinig* article—that is, to allocate greater funding to the MPD in order to "rehabilitate" its "equipment and facilities to be at par with the present standard." As the article noted, paraphrasing Capul, the downturn in the MPD's private sector income was caused by both the "decreasing demand for film productions" and the fact that MPD's formerly cutting-edge equipment and facilities were outdated and in need of an upgrade.[55] The closure of the MPD, as another subheading of the article emphasized, was "not a reflection of non-performance" on the part of MPD personnel but was due to the fact that, in Capul's words, "its equipment and facilities [had] seen better days."[56] In short, the recognition that the MPD's outdated technology would eventually undermine its income-generating capacity strongly suggests that the PIA needed to allocate more, not fewer, resources to this historically high-performing, high-profile unit.

For the most part, the *Tinig* article attempts to rationalize the closure of the MPD as inevitable, that is, as a mere implementation of an MPD review committee's impartial findings. On the contrary, however, the review committee's first recommendation had not been to shut down a major division with a highly regarded film lab and film archive, but to infuse it with capital. A technologically upgraded MPD might have become more efficient and competitive in a hybrid, transitional moment when established photochemical cinema and digital information technologies were merging. Choosing to overlook the committee's first recommendation to upgrade the MPD through capital infusion, the PIA management instead decided to shut down an internationally recognized unit that employed the largest number of its personnel and was as old as the agency itself. As Edmondson remarks with poignant clarity, "What can take decades of effort to create can also be quickly unmade by the stroke of a bureaucratic pen."[57]

LESSONS FROM THE FALLOUT, OR, WHAT IS TO BE DONE?

The dissolution of the MPD in 2004 destroyed not only its production and postproduction capabilities but also the archival film collection that those competencies actively preserved. When asked about the consequences of the MPD's abolition, Capul noted the loss of financial and staff support for its archival storage facilities as well as a loss of promotion and circulation for its collection.[58] Whereas the PIA had once housed a well-known film archive whose titles circulated through well-publicized exhibitions, such public-facing film initiatives ended with the MPD's closure. The MPD's dissolution squandered the considerable status and authority it had amassed over time, both indispensable attributes for audiovisual archives that must win the public's trust in their institutional permanence.[59] The aftermath of this state film archive's demise is a cautionary tale with several important takeaways.

First, audiovisual archiving must be recognized as distinct from traditional librarianship centered on paper-based collections; failure to do so can unwittingly wipe out a film collection. Circular No. 4, creating the MISD, unceremoniously incorporated the PIA's film and video collection with the rest of its print library, ordering the "integration of all PIA document collections in print, film, video, photo and slides" under the PIA Library.[60] As a UNESCO report emphasizes, "Audiovisual recordings are particularly vulnerable and require special attention for their long-term security."[61] Equating film archives with other "document collections"—for which books and print materials are the primary point of reference—disregards the specific requirements of audiovisual preservation and can instigate the decline of film holdings. The Philippines has a tropical, maritime climate characterized by high temperature and humidity and plentiful rainfall.[62] In contrast, conservation of analog audiovisual media like photochemical film demands storage conditions in which temperature and humidity are carefully regulated. For their part, digital audiovisual media require not only management of individual carriers (such as DVDs) but also monitoring of the stored files' integrity.[63]

The directive to integrate the agency's audiovisual holdings into the rest of the PIA Library inaugurated chronic underfunding and deterioration for the PIA film collection, since a climate-controlled environment is costly to maintain. Following the MPD's closure, the PIA's film holdings were stored in the basement and second floor of the PIA building on Visayas Avenue, Quezon City; the basement holdings were flooded during

Typhoon Ondoy in 2009. By 2013, they had deteriorated to such a point that they were disposed of by the PIA.[64] New inventories of the surviving PIA collection were prepared when the PIA's audiovisual holdings were eventually transferred to the NFAP.[65]

Second, the fate of the PIA film collection underscores the dangers of a purely financial perspective on the nation's cinematic past combined with a shortsighted valorization of digital media to the detriment of analog collections. The twin justifications for the closure of the MPD were both financial and media-technological: the need to reduce costs combined with the rise of digital media, which was thought to render analog film superfluous. That the PIA's film collection should have been devalued due to the growing importance of information technology invites a revisionist reference to an old adage: those unaware of media history might be doomed to repeat it. Recall that the advent of acetate film led to the misguided destruction of early nitrate films. In the Philippines, the state bureaucracy's narrowly monetary interest in the PIA film collection led to a deeply ironic situation in which a government archive (the PIA) devalued state film collections in its care (e.g., the NMPC and MTRCB-FAP films) because they were seen as having little or no commercial value.[66]

Digitization is not synonymous with preservation, since digital media become outdated even more rapidly than analog works do. As Karen Gracy notes, "While 35 mm film was the industry standard for over one hundred years," new digital formats are continually replacing each other. "In the last fifteen years there have been over twenty-five different professional, industrial, educational, and consumer digital moving image formats," which means that content must constantly be transferred and no single digital format or playback system can be considered a permanently durable medium. Although online streaming of movie files from sites like YouTube provides convenient access, the image and sound quality of such highly compressed files fall below preservation standards. Storing high-quality uncompressed digital moving images is expensive, requiring massive amounts of storage and vigilant maintenance. This means that contemporary film preservation is a hybrid affair, combining photochemical processes to preserve the first hundred years of cinema as well as digital asset management.[67]

The closure of the MPD and the devaluation of its film collection in 2004 stemmed from a flawed all-or-nothing logic in which the influx of digital media was perceived to render photochemical film entirely irrelevant. In contrast, Giovanna Fossati emphasizes that audiovisual media are "inherently transitional"; the analog-to-digital transition is only one of several major shifts in film history (e.g., transitions to sound cinema, to color film stock, and to competition and convergence with television and new media). Seen in this light, the advent of digital movies does not spell the death of photochemical cinema but expresses the ontologically transitory character of media in general.[68] It follows that photochemical cinema is not worthless, just as digital media cannot provide an "ultimate format'" for preservation purposes.[69]

Third, the posthumous fate of the MPD collection raises the issue of the government's role in archival film preservation and calls attention to the problem of short-term presidential appointments to top posts at state film agencies. Capul recalls that, as former head of the MPD, she resisted the proposal to abolish the division. She recounts the following conversation in Taglish with Director General Velasco: "He said, and he was very very clear, since I was fighting for [film] preservation [under the MPD], 'Well, if the government itself doesn't care [*hindi inaasikaso*], why do you push for it?' I answered, who is the government? It's people who are on top and who can do something."[70] Whether accurately recollected memory or embellished anecdote, this purported exchange distills questions of state custodianship over culture—specifically the Philippine government's historical failure to pay attention to, look after, and care about the nation's film heritage (all semantic valences of the Tagalog verb *asikaso*)—as well as issues of accountability on the part of officials "who can do something" about film preservation.

Later in the same interview, as I was explaining my view that the state should not be motivated solely by market forces but should also preserve and restore commercially unprofitable films of public interest, Capul responded: "In that sense I agree with you that the government has been remiss in terms of appreciating that [the importance of film preservation]. . . . Market forces are market forces, they are business-minded. But the government needs to see [the public interest in film preservation] and intervene. That seems to be what is lacking or absent. Especially since the leaders at government organizations are always changing [*papalit-palit*], as though they're just passing through."[71] I interpret Capul's last sentence to be a recognition that the changeable (*papalit-palit*), short-lived ("passing") nature of presidential appointees to leadership positions in key state film entities like the PIA and the FDCP has historically had adverse effects on film preservation efforts, since much depends on whether or not the appointed official recognizes the value of audiovisual archiving.

Fourth, a partial solution to the previously mentioned difficulties lies in securing a firm legislative mandate to assure the autonomy of a national institution for audiovisual archiving. The need for "a national policy for the preservation of moving images in the Philippines" was recognized in SOFIA's earliest policy papers.[72] Autonomous governance, a sustainable organizational structure, and legislative security are the thrust of various position papers presented to the House of Representatives in 2017 and 2021.[73] A legislative mandate that assures the autonomy and sustainability of a national audiovisual archive is the holy grail of the archive world, but few institutions actually enjoy this protection, as Edmondson acknowledges: "Unlike other major memory institutions, many of the world's audiovisual archives lack a statutory base, charter or equivalent authority which defines their role, their security and their mandate. They are therefore vulnerable to challenge and change, and their permanence can be illusory. This highlights the need to achieve appropriate decrees, laws, and long-term policies to sustain these institutions."[74] Since complete statutory self-governance for audiovisual archives is often unattainable, Edmondson calls semiautonomy the "desirable minimum." In practical terms, semiautonomy for audiovisual archives requires a legal mandate to guarantee "perpetual succession" and "'arms-length' funding" to ensure that projects, priorities, and decisions are not beholden to "external sponsors, authorities, or a parent organization." If an audiovisual archive cannot be completely self-governing, then it must be meaningfully consulted in governance. Crucially, "The archive [should be] led by a director or executive team with a professional background in the audiovisual archiving field."[75] In the absence of relevant legislation in the Philippines, presidential appointees to head film-related state agencies with an archival function (such as the FDCP and PIA) have not come from a professional audiovisual archival or curatorial background. In contrast, by law (i.e., the Philippine Librarianship Act of 2003), only licensed librarians can be employed in Philippine government libraries.[76] In Australia, the NFSA's path to autonomy confirmed in Edmondson's mind the need for it to be helmed by "experienced audiovisual archivists" rather than "career bureaucrats without curatorial backgrounds."[77]

The institutional histories reconstructed in this chapter attest that these conditions for semiautonomous archival governance have not been met in important Philippine state archives devoted to film. When appointed officials to state audiovisual archives lack a background in moving image preservation, meaningful consultation with experienced professional archivists at these institutions, whether at the middle management or staff level, is a vital safeguard against decisions that state bureaucrats without curatorial experience may implement, without fully realizing the harmful effects such decisions may have on the media heritage in their care. Founding president Agustin Sotto recounts that SOFIA was originally organized as a "professional organization" of "middle management" archivists who hoped to shield their audiovisual collections from "the territorial imperatives of top-level management."[78]

A final takeaway is that cultural stewardship, while vested in state memory institutions and the people who work there, implicates a wider public as well. Broad-based support for audiovisual archives in the Philippines cannot be achieved without giving the public straightforward, reliable access to such archives. Distilling the lessons of Australia's "sustained public campaign by advocacy groups" to achieve statutory autonomy for the NFSA, the general principles adopted by the 2004 Future of the Archive conference at Canberra asserted that cultural stewardship for national audiovisual archives rests not only with the government but also with these archives' stakeholders.[79] Media producers, researchers, curators, archivists, and professional associations constitute every audiovisual archive's broader community of stakeholders.[80] In contrast, the defunding and near decimation of important state film archives in the Philippines have occurred largely out of the public eye. No strident public advocacy arose to take Filipino government officials to task; both the unremarked demise of the PIA film collection after 2004 and the withering of the first FAP in the late 1980s went largely unopposed. Despite SOFIA's decades-long efforts, lack of legislative support and public indifference to the Philippines' imperiled film archives persist.

Core stakeholders for Philippine film archives consist of archivists, researchers, collectors, and film and television workers. My hunch is that a wider community of stakeholders for imperiled Philippine film archives has failed to emerge for several interrelated reasons that include but are not irreducible to the state of the Philippine economy. The long gap between the withering of the FAP and establishment of the NFAP (1986–2011) severely circumscribed access to audiovisual collections. Historically, no broad community has become accustomed to relying on—or appreciated firsthand the value of—archival film institutions in the Philippines. Without being readily and continually accessible to the public, the present-day NFAP/PFA (like its predecessor, the PIA-MPD) lacks a sizable base of users invested enough to advocate vigorously on its behalf in the public sphere. In the absence of convenient, long-running access to state film archives, those with a personal or professional interest in Philippine film history have turned elsewhere: to films available online; to the conglomerate media archive of ABS-CBN; or to informal archival initiatives and private collections, as discussed in chapter 5. The Philippines' tenacious—but insufficiently broad-based—archive advocacy movement is thus caught in a chicken-and-egg situation: lacking established, enduring archives, few stakeholders can be mobilized to press for an archive that endures. Absent a critical mass of users reliant on state media archives, a broad-based advocacy that demands legislated autonomy and sustainability for a national audiovisual institution has historically failed to coalesce.

ARCHIVING THE DICTATORSHIP: A MANIFESTO FOR "POOR ARCHIVING"

The last two sections of this chapter revisit the impact of the PIA-MPD's closure on specific NMPC propaganda films in its collection and focus on the archivists who persevered under inhospitable institutional conditions for audiovisual archiving.

The declaration of martial law was broadcast on television at 7:15 p.m. on September 23, 1972, ushering in the indefinite temporality of martial law. Following the declaration, Marcos clung to the presidency for fourteen more years, well beyond the two terms allowed by the Constitution at that time. As Benedict Anderson notes, Marcos was a "complex hybrid," both exemplifying and departing from the traditional oligarchic political system that preceded his presidency. On the one hand, he dissolved Congress, the seat of oligarchic power. (The balance and solidity of the oligarchic system depended on congressional rule, which allowed for oligarchic families to take turns at the wheel of state.) On the other hand, Marcos took oligarchic excess to extreme limits: beyond private armies and local courts, he wielded the National Constabulary, the army, and the Supreme Court as instruments of his autocratic rule, moving bossism from the countryside into cronyism on the scale of the national economy. Initial support for martial law dissipated by the late 1970s due to the venality and brutality of the regime. As favored military officers grew wealthy and corrupt, Communist guerrilla forces expanded, their leftist nationalist vocabulary taken up by intellectuals, the clergy, and the middle class.[81]

In the course of my research on the NMPC propaganda films at the PIA, I encountered two versions of the declaration. The first version, *From a Season of Strife* (NMPC, 1972, 16mm, color, 10 min.), opens with Marcos intoning the line that ushered in the dictatorship: "As of the twenty-first of this month, I signed Proclamation Number 1081 placing the entire Philippines under martial law." Marcos addresses the camera in medium shot, sitting slightly forward in his presidential chair, several microphones placed on the desk beside his elbow (figure 2.7). The authoritativeness of frontality and direct address is undermined by the dictator's often decentered eyeline, his gaze aimed at off-screen cue cards. Marcos's reading of the proclamation is accompanied by a voice-over and inspirational choral music that portray martial law as the solution to the country's ills. The final images are of headlines touting the regime's anticorruption initiatives, a view of Manila Bay against the backdrop of the Mariveles Mountains, and a low-angle zoom into a close-up of the Philippine flag waving in the wind.[82]

In contrast to the opening excerpt of the declaration in *From a Season of Strife,* a second version of the same speech in my digitized copy of *PFM Message on the Declaration of Martial Law* (NMPC, 1972, 16mm, b/w, 30 min.) is marred by numerous technical flaws. The first of six long takes appears to be a camera test, without synchronized sound, that should have been edited out (figure 2.8). As Marcos reads the proclamation, a brief glimpse of the dictator is followed by nearly half a minute of a blank, black screen (figures 2.9 and 2.10). That we hear sound in the absence of an image at the beginning of *PFM Message* suggests, according to Olgado, that the lens cap might have been left on, covering the lens of either the 16mm projector or the digital camera recording the projected image at the beginning of the digitization process.[83] The dirt on the margins of the frame suggests that dust and debris might have been captured during the process of makeshift digitization, recalling Paolo Cherchi Usai's warning that handling, copying, and migration frequently introduce new flaws.[84]

Michel Chion conceptualizes the *acousmêtre* as an off-screen sound that is heard without its source in the film world being visible.[85] The acousmatic is thus the opposite of visualized sound, that is, sound that is synchronous with its on-screen diegetic source.[86] Chion's discussion focuses primarily on intentional examples of the acousmatic voice involving deliberate decisions about off-screen sound.[87] However, in *PFM Message*, the process of make-do digitization indicates not an intentional refusal to show the dictator whose voice we hear but an accidental acousmatism: Marcos's voice is not exactly off-screen; rather, his deteriorated image is blocked and unmigrated, producing an inadvertent avisuality in which the space and time of Marcos declaring martial law in 1972 is briefly

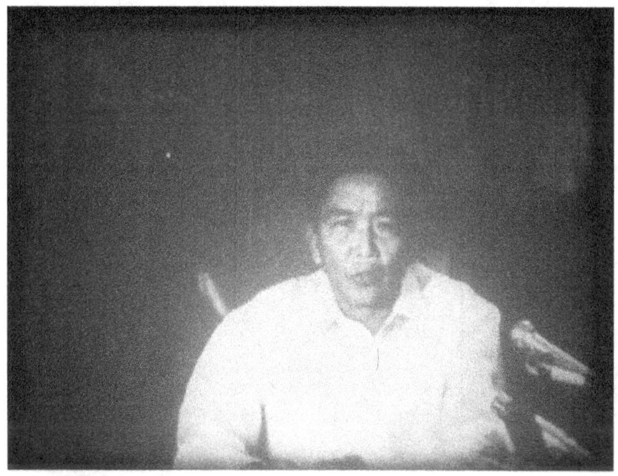

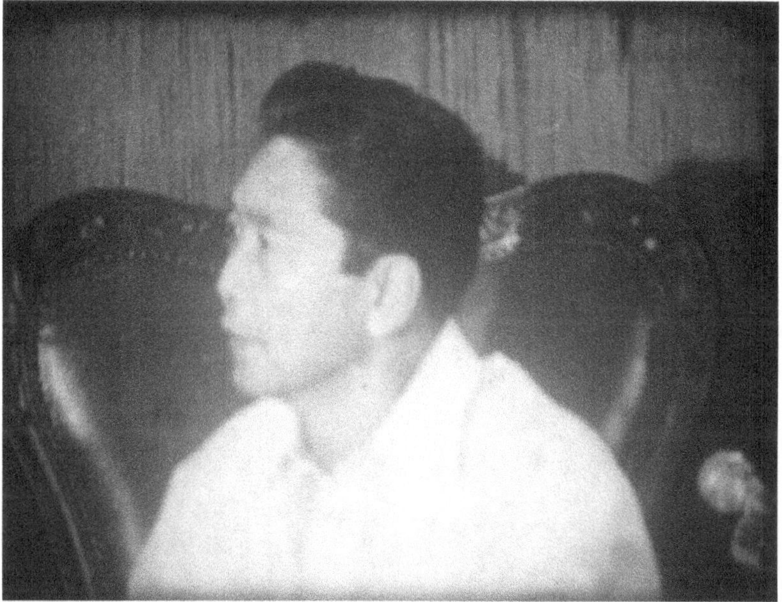

2.7 Digitized copies of the NMPC martial law films yield different versions of Ferdinand E. Marcos announcing its imposition. In *From a Season of Strife*, Marcos directly addresses the camera and the viewer. Film still.

2.8 *PFM Message on the Declaration of Martial Law* (National Media Production Center, 1972) opens with what appears to be a camera test. Film still.

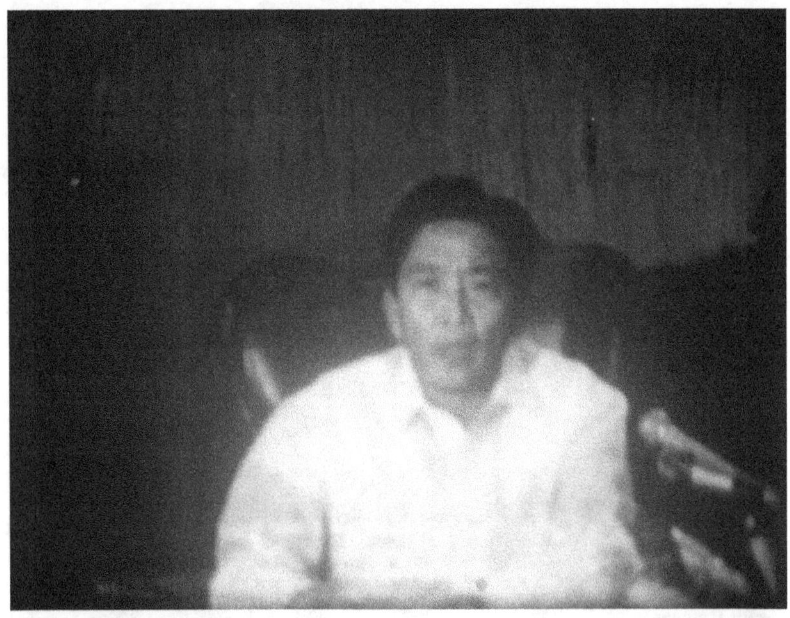

2.9 & 2.10 Following a brief glimpse of the dictator, most of the opening lines of the declaration are heard over a black screen in *PFM Message on the Declaration of Martial Law*. This is possibly due to a failure to remove the lens cap of either the 16mm film projector or the digital camera during digitization. Film stills.

overwritten by a lens cap that stubbornly belongs to the space and time of its analog-to-digital migration in 2015. This accidental error makes the sound and image tracks unexpectedly multitemporal and unintentionally acousmatic. For viewers of this particular copy of the proclamation, Marcos is inadvertently transformed into an *acousmêtre*. Once the lens cap problem is corrected during the transfer, Marcos is progressively de-acousmatized, rendered more and more ordinary. The authoritative quality of his avisual voice erodes once the deterioriated visage of the dictator is revealed.

In the eighteen seconds before we finally *see* Marcos impose martial law, *PFM Message* is simultaneously acousmatic and avisual. In *Atomic Light*, Akira Mizuta Lippit's evocative exploration of the crisis of visuality sparked by World War II, Lippit defines avisuality as "a specific mode of impossible, unimaginable visuality," simultaneously invisible yet within the realm of the visible.[88] More than a mere "antithesis of the visible," avisuality names a kind of paradoxical vision registered not via sight but through other senses. Following Lippit and Chion, then, my low-budget digital copy of *PFM Message* is both avisual and acousmatic: as I watch the black screen where the presidential image ought to have been, the infamous declaration is reduced to off-screen sound. Marcos's failure to appear is not the result of a secretive, deliberately produced invisibility. To justify the imposition of martial law, Marcos was meant to be both seen and heard, unambiguously audio-visioned as an awe-inspiring strongman. In its archival afterlife, however, this decomposing and imperfectly migrated Marcos propaganda film has become a casualty of the regime's own cultural policies. Like its accidental acousmatism, the unintended avisuality of this footage, indicative of rushed digitization and symptomatic of a larger anarchival condition, voids the visual track where the dictator ought to have appeared. Lippit writes of "a category of complex visuality, a system of visuality that shows nothing, shows in the very place of the visible, something else: *avisuality*."[89]

My MPEG file of *PFM Message on the Declaration of Martial Law* is a highly imperfect copy in other ways as well: without having inspected the original film element, Olgado notes that the digital images suggest water damage or a dye issue during coloring; early stages of vinegar syndrome and mold; bad splices; and, throughout, visible scratches on the emulsion (figure 2.11).[90] The literally pinkish tone undermines Marcos's rhetorical red-baiting while visualizing the ephemerality of film as medium, since color is the most "unstable component" of moving images.[91] Marcos

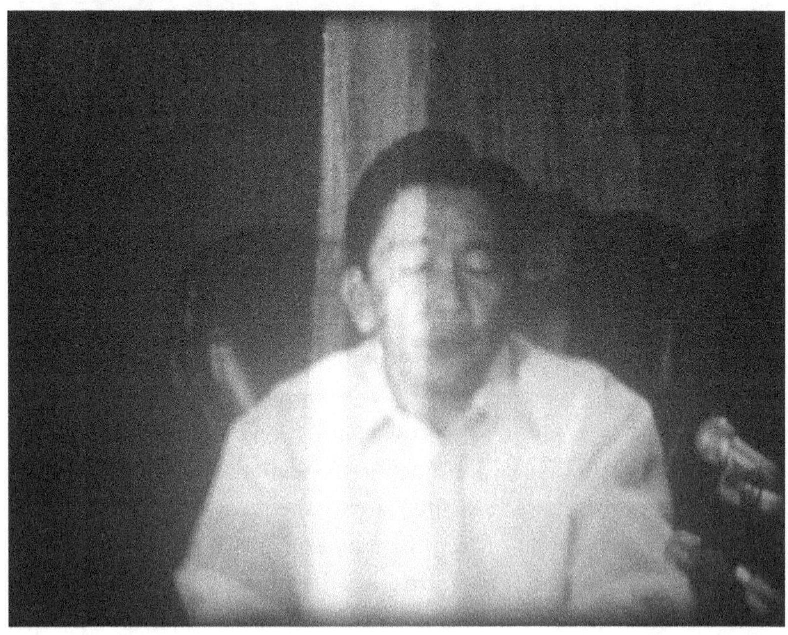

2.11 "Poor images" of the Marcos dictatorship in *PFM Message on the Declaration of Martial Law* are the result of mold, bad splices, visible scratches on the emulsion, early stages of vinegar syndrome, color dye issues, and possible water damage. Film still.

himself delivers a poor performance: forgetting his lines, he fumbles for notes on his desk and squints to read his cue card.

Hito Steyerl's work emboldens me to champion the eloquent poverty of this rushed, collaborative image. Like other poor images, it would qualify as "a lumpen proletarian in the class society of appearances."[92] Access, not technical polish or the pristine fixity of the original, was the priority for everyone involved in the makeshift digitization of these NMPC propaganda films. The resulting poor-resolution image testifies to a history of institutional deprioritization and underfunding, just as the tightly controlled circulation of these films recalls prior acts of bureaucratic obstruction. The converted analog film is now resurrected as a low-quality digital movie, one that undermines the naive notion that digitization is the equivalent of preservation. Digital migration in this access copy of *PFM Message* does nothing to curtail the dilapidated image and sound, nor does it restore the degraded acetate source film. Yet the loss of both the original work's fixity and its contextual integrity need not be bemoaned, since digitization and access create new meanings and horizons of reception. The makeshift digital migration brings to the foreground content-to-carrier relationships that are usually obscured in more polished transfers.

In that sense, an ironic media-historical reversal is at work here: Marcos declaring martial law, so terrifying and life-extinguishing in 1972, is reduced to a less powerful, more distant, diminished, and occasionally foolish-looking figure in this digital transfer. The poverty of the image attests to a history of underfunded state institutions and mismanaged archives where, as Steyerl puts it, "a whole heritage of film prints is left without the support of a national culture."[93] The credits of both 16mm films tell us that these productions were once prioritized by multiple government ministries; several decades later, these propaganda films are forgotten by the very state agencies entrusted with their care. The FAP was established but also undone by the Marcos dictatorship; the anarchival precarity that followed ended up endangering the propaganda of the Marcos state itself. But the gradual death of the dictatorship's filmic legacy is double-edged. On the one hand, it whittles the official culture of a once all-powerful regime down to size. On the other hand, the loss of visible evidence abets a national amnesia about the Marcos period that frustrates demands for historical accountability and enables the Marcos dynasty's resurgence in national politics.

In *Audiovisual Archiving: Philosophy and Principles*, Edmondson writes that the best practices of well-funded, established archives may be ill-suited to embattled archives in the global South. He writes, "The lack of resources in limited situations will be exacerbated if measured by the standards of the affluent, and simply lead to inaction and paralysis brought about by helplessness and fear. A different paradigm is needed," one that involves "buying time and keeping things going, . . . do[ing] the best that one can under the circumstances. If the best equipment is not available, and a lower grade digital copy from an endangered carrier is possible, it is better than doing nothing."[94]

Those words inspire me to try out a kind of manifesto for poor archiving, for which the keywords might be *improvisation*, *bootstrapping*, and *making do*. In the OED, the verb *bootstrap* means to make use of existing resources to improve or uplift one's present conditions, while *to make do* indicates that one is managing with, getting by or getting along, using only what is ready to hand, even if it is, as in the makeshift digitization of the Marcos propaganda films, only an inferior approximation of kinescoping, as discussed in the introduction. Making do as a practice of poor archiving is, then, a distinctly scrappy affair that involves collective efforts to make the best of meager resources. Such practices do not represent a permanent solution; nonetheless, poor archiving must be defended rather than patronized. Auratic qualities like context linkage and fixity must be conceded as lost, since making do as an exercise of archival power is a practice of buying time and creating conditions for access, however limited. The English phrase "making do" approximates for me a Filipino idiom, *gawan ng paraan* (from the verb *gawa*, "make," and the noun *daan*, "path"), an exhortation to the listener to find a way, to forge a path even in the face of known obstacles. If, as Ramesh Kumar suggests, different times and places call forth different archiving cultures, I suggest that committed and creative forms of making do are a defining characteristic of Philippine audiovisual archiving; so is perseverance, which I explore in the final section of this chapter.[95]

ON ADVOCACY, PERSEVERANCE, AND SURVIVAL

Activists and stakeholders engaged in the long-haul struggle to secure the autonomy and sustainability of audiovisual archives risk hopelessness and burn out. Writing of the NFSA campaign, Edmondson reflects: "For the advocacy groups, the risk was always one of exhaustion and despair about ever reaching their goal. *That the campaign persisted for as long as necessary was in itself a major achievement*."[96] In a similar vein, Ann Cvetkovich's collaborative work with queer feminist scholars and activists prompted the following question: "How can we, as intellectuals and activists, acknowledge our own political disappointments and failures in a way that can be enabling? Where might hope be possible?" In her musings on "political depression," Cvetkovich notes that in order to "tackle the work that needs to be done and to create the pleasures that will sustain us," we must find "a vision of hope and possibility that doesn't foreclose despair and exhaustion."[97] In what follows, I link anthropologist Elizabeth Povinelli's discussion of activist perseverance to these reflections on political disappointment. To my mind, persistence is itself an achievement given an inhospitable state context for audiovisual archiving.

In *Economies of Abandonment*, Povinelli asks why some people are able to endure, that is, "to persist beyond the point of exhaustion for other people" under late liberalism. She looks closely at an alternative social project in Australia that harnessed smartphone video cameras and GPS technology to actualize indigenous knowledge about culture and the landscape. Of several boat trips that she and her indigenous colleagues took on the Daly River for the Anson Bay Mobile Phone Project, Povinelli recounts a particularly hazardous trip on a ten-foot dinghy in 2008. State and private corporate financing for the project was scant; the material conditions of this attempt to cross rough waters to reach Banagula, a beach on the southern shore of one of the Daly River's estuaries, were far from ideal. The dinghy's motor, the only one the group could afford, was too weak to overcome the large waves; the boat itself was punctured and missing a paddle. This meant that the boat was, at times, in danger of capsizing, while those on board risked hypothermia and constantly collided with one another. Fuel was limited, and the food supply consisted of roadkill that hunters on board had brought for the trip.[98] Assessing their efforts, Povinelli writes: "We eventually made it to Banagula. On other days we don't make it back or do so barely. But we keep meeting and trying to raise resources to support the project. *We are neither defeated nor are we successful. We persevere* . . . [although] the actual lives supporting this ethical practice hardly seem sufficient to achieve its goals."[99]

Despite federal legislation to recognize indigenous peoples' rights to self-determination in 1976, Povinelli notes that the conditions of indigenous life "in terms of health, education, wealth, life expectancy, and mental outlook" have barely been ameliorated and are still worse off relative to those of most other Australians. The lives of these activists and their families are thus marked by lower life expectancy rates, violence in their communities, and the threat that small infractions incurred during the project might harden into a criminal record leading to incarceration. Over the years, the difficulties that her indigenous friends faced gradually reduced the number of people still involved in the project who were on the dinghy back in 2008. Povinelli's work, then, emphasizes the problem of enduring and the realities of depletion and attrition in real-world struggles.[100]

Povinelli's twin concerns—*how to endure as one strives to persevere*, together with the *effort to change the conditions in which one's persevering occurs*—are extremely resonant for those who have lived through the demise of key film archives in the Philippines.[101] Continuing to care for and care about Filipino audiovisual archives requires "determination and optimism"—two traits Edmondson saw as integral to the NFSA's struggle.[102] Like the story Povinelli relates about the diminishing collective of friends and fellow activists she collaborated with in Australia, the decentralized advocacy for a Philippine audiovisual archive persists, but always risks doing so in depleted form.

As for the Australian state, a government that, after the 2007 intervention, "refused to fund any projects that could not demonstrate a market outcome," and whose agents levied fines on Povinelli's group for their underequipped boat's failure to comply with safety regulations—none of its actions amounted to the state's literal killing of the activists involved, although it made the path to their goals ever rougher and steeper.[103] As Povinelli explains: "In other words, those of us on the boat trying to cross Anson Bay are not being killed by the state in any way that would be recognizable as state killing. . . . *Most opposition to alternative social projects happens in a different way. An authorless wager is made that very few people will be able to continue to persevere in the face of prevailing material obstacles.* They will not be able to sustain their perseverance."[104]

The notion of the state's authorless wager is profoundly relevant to the experience of SOFIA archivists who witnessed the death of the first NFAP as well as the demise of the PIA-MPD and who sheltered the rescued holdings of LVN, only to see their efforts come to naught a decade later. From my ongoing conversations with seasoned Filipino film archivists since 2012, I come away with the impression that they are by turns frustrated, dispirited, and exhausted by the many struggles their advocacy has faced over the years. Yet they persevere in various formal and informal archival initiatives. Arrayed against these archivist-activists is an authorless wager, a bet no one in particular has placed. The authorless wager of the dominant system is that under such conditions of precarity, the alternatives proposed either will not endure or will never become ascendant because those proposing this otherwise to the status quo will eventually become too exhausted to continue.

Povinelli's chapter closes on what I read as a note of political minimalism (as opposed to political utopianism): "This otherwise may lie in shattering the life-world in which a person finds herself situated, but it also might mean maintaining a life-world under constant threat of being saturated by the rhythms and meanings of another. . . . *In these situations, to be the same, to be durative, may be as emancipatory as to be transitive.*"[105] This political minimalism suggests that under such "reduced conditions of life" (in this case, the life span of aging audiovisual collections as well as the lives of cultural workers who struggle to preserve them), *to merely have managed to endure* might be viewed as a substantial accomplishment.[106] This political minimalism—or minimal radicalism—does not demand success. Recalling Edmondson's earlier quote on persistence as itself a "major achievement," political minimalism recognizes endurance and perseverance both as prerequisites for social and cultural movements and as limited, but not meaningless, accomplishments on the part of those advocates who have neither won nor been vanquished across decades of underfunding and undervaluation.

Edmondson's and Povinelli's reflections on exhaustion and persistence open up multiply posed questions of archival survival operating at various scales. From the 1980s to the present, the demise of the Marcos era FAP and the defunct PIA-MPD attests that many significant Philippine film archives fail to survive or are always on the verge of coming undone, their carefully accumulated collections becoming tragically redispersed as state-institutional supports fall away. This means that many seasoned advocates who try to ensure archival survival have in fact already lived through the converse, having witnessed the closure of the FAP, the PIA-MPD, or both. Though some prime movers in the audiovisual archive advocacy have become inactive, those who persevere have had to come up with tactics to survive various film archives' actual or imminent deaths. They have, in one form or another, grappled with the question of how to outlive an archive's collapse or, put differently, how to outlive the authorless wager of state indifference without the films degrading beyond repair and the archivist-activists themselves succumbing to exhaustion.

The Philippine audiovisual archivists I discuss in this book, whether formal memory professionals, scholars, or informal curators and collectors, have been given drafts of the manuscript as it evolved; some replied to my requests for comments, some did not. To the best of my ability, I have incorporated all the feedback and requests for revisions I have received over the years. The present chapter and a shorter journal article version published in *Plaridel* in 2018 incorporate the feedback and revisions specifically requested by Vicky Bejerano and Bel Capul, whom I met with in person while I was in Manila that February and who subsequently emailed me their approval of my revised draft.[107] At the first of these in-person meetings, a two-hour conversation about my chapter draft on the PIA, I spoke candidly with both Bejerano and Capul about the issue of risk-taking in this project and of having been emboldened by Edmondson's essay on audiovisual archivists who made the decision to be "ethical troublemakers," acting on principle rather than in obedience to misguided bureaucratic decisions.[108] I laid out my understanding of both Bejerano and Capul as being ethical troublemakers who were nearly, but not quite, whistleblowers (since the PIA documents I used as sources were officially released with the cabinet secretary's approval). I also told them that I would not publish the book chapter or the *Plaridel* article without their approval. In response, both Bejerano, who is a longtime *plantillado* (permanent) employee of the PIA, and Capul, who had recently retired from the PIA but was staying on in a consultative capacity, confirmed that they were in favor of publication. When I asked both women why they were supportive of my publishing this research, Capul said, "Why? Because we are for archives. We are for learning from what happened." Bejerano concurred. "It's all factual," she began, then asked rhetorically, "*Kung hindi ko matapon* [*ang mga* records], *bakit ko hindi i-she-*share?" (If I couldn't bring myself to throw out these records, then why wouldn't I share them?), adding that documents are memories that shouldn't be discarded.[109] When I asked them whether my discussion of enduring and persevering on the part of archivist-activists was on point, Bejerano teared up and nodded.

Archival survival does not entail only the preservation of celluloid or vigilant continual migration of digitally born films. It is also a question of surviving the casual indifference, wait-it-out complacency, or pointed ill will of the state and being willing to speak out when necessary. Under such circumstances, the Philippines' decentralized audiovisual archival advocacy demands an activist and ethical form of enduring despite exhaustion on the part of behind-the-scenes cultural workers in beleaguered memory institutions. Archival survival is not the equivalent of a revolution in Filipino audiovisual archiving, an ideal, enduring, positive transformation in which Philippine film history is forever safeguarded by a beneficent state. On the ground, archival survival is closer to a politically minimal, nonutopian, nonidealized aspiration for the preservation of the Philippines' fragile audiovisual archives, an aspiration forged by the lessons of various film archives' vexed institutional histories.

In reflecting on the exhaustion and burnout faced by all activists and advocates in a protracted uphill battle, one modest aim of this chapter has been to bring these largely unnoticed stories of archival loss and survival to light, cognizant that, in a worst-case scenario, such published histories might one day outlive the imperiled works in these audiovisual collections. A similar impetus to temper expectations animates my admission, throughout this book, of the necessarily situated, interpretive, and incomplete character of any historiography of the unfolding present. To have reconstructed the complicated institutional history of the posthumous PIA-MPD as it intersects with other state and nongovernmental film entities might seem like too politically minimal an endeavor. Nonetheless, it discerns that the ground-level realities militating against the preservation of Philippine cinema are too thorny to be held to an impossible political-archival ideal.

CHAPTER THREE

Privatization and the ABS-CBN Film Archives

The largest footprint in Philippine film archiving belongs not to chronically underfunded government-run collections but to the audiovisual collection managed by the country's largest media conglomerate, ABS-CBN. While the first two chapters of this book center on state film archives and collections—the FAP, the PIA, and the NFAP/PFA—this chapter and chapter 4 offer an analysis of the ABS-CBN Film Archives. Restorations released on DVD and other distribution windows under the banner "ABS-CBN Film Restoration Presents" totaled 185 digitally restored and remastered titles by July 2020, on the eve of the corporation's broadcast shutdown by the Philippine Congress.[1] As such, ABS-CBN's restoration output far outstrips the approximately 18 film titles restored by the NFAP/PFA as of August 2020.[2]

Over the last decade, the NFAP/PFA (under the FDCP) and ABS-CBN have emerged as the two dominant players whose "archival processes and priorities" and concept of "heritage" have become naturalized in the Philippine audiovisual archive scene. Bernadette Patino has critiqued both "the narrative that high-end digital restoration and exhibition is the ultimate tool to preserve the medium, and the definition of feature-length narrative cinema as the premier expression of national identity." The degree to which it has "normalized the privatization of archival access" notwithstanding, the ABS-CBN Film Archives "cannot be left to compensate for the failures of state or independent archival institutions, despite its state-of-the-art facilities."[3]

The Philippine situation reflects global shifts in audiovisual archiving. As Karen Gracy observes, the last few decades have seen palpable "changes in the balance of power" between not-for-profit archives that regard film as cultural heritage and commercial archives that view film as corporate assets that can be profitably reused.[4] Given limited state funding for film preservation worldwide, the equilibrium of audiovisual archiving has tilted toward commercial entities that rerelease, sell, or license media content and see preservation through the lens of corporate asset protection, profit, and market appeal.

Unlike other commodities, media content is "a product that is not 'used up' in consumption." Whereas goods like food or beverages are expended on ingestion, film content "can be consumed over and over again without additional units having to be produced." Although extra costs are entailed in distribution and exhibition, in general, "media products can be sold and resold indefinitely without incurring significant additional production costs," irrespective of "how many audience members ultimately consume the media product." It follows, as Philip Napoli remarks, that "media industries tend to re-use, repeat, and repurpose existing media content rather than producing new content," provided that the entities in question are the rights holders to the content they repurpose.[5]

One reason that media conglomerates like ABS-CBN have a more prolific film restoration output than government film archives like the NFAP/PFA is that corporations often control the intellectual property rights for much of their collections. As Ray Edmondson explains, old films don't have the "antiquarian value inherent in rare books, paintings, or ancient maps" because of copyright complications. For many state archives, a film collection can be "more of a financial liability than an asset," since the ability to generate revenue resides in copyright ownership rather than physical possession.[6] Moreover, film preservation demands vigilant upkeep via controlled archival storage conditions or costly digital infrastructures.[7]

The commercial value of archival films for their rightsholders partly explains why ABS-CBN, with its origins in broadcast radio and television, has been more committed to film archiving, preservation, and restoration than the Philippine government, since the latter sees little economic value in its custodianship of the nation's cinematic patrimony.[8] Historically, broadcast and cable television networks dependent on recycled cinema have been quicker than film studios to recognize the market value of archival titles. As Edmondson notes, "The beginnings of an economic rationale for audiovisual preservation" surfaced in the mid-twentieth century when the vast movie libraries of film studios—which in earlier decades had destroyed, discarded, or melted old reels for silver—became reusable content for the voracious new medium of television.[9]

Until very recently, the institutional stability of the ABS-CBN Film Archives stood in marked contrast to the histories of short-lived state-run film collections. Unlike the sometimes adversarial relationship between government archivists and state bureaucrats with noncuratorial backgrounds, ABS-CBN's head archivists enjoyed good relations with the parent corporation's top-level management. The conglomerate had a clear financial interest in retaining skilled archivists to watch over the long-term welfare of its audiovisual collection (in my earliest visits in 2005, the basement entrance sign read "Corporate Assets Division" rather than "Film Archives"). For over two decades, the ABS-CBN Film Archives grew its collection and cultivated a skilled archival staff under a stable leadership core. Tragically, this track record of institutional stability was disrupted by the July 2020 congressional decision to deny the renewal of the conglomerate's legislative franchise. From the ABS-CBN Film Archives' founding in the early nineties to its congressional shutdown in 2020, the stability of its staff and collections had offered an encouraging contrast to the historically Sisyphean character of state-run film archives in the Philippines. That the ABS-CBN Film Archives should also be subjected to anarchival peril had been unthinkable in the Philippine audiovisual archive world until 2020.

THE ABS-CBN SHUTDOWN AND ITS ANARCHIVAL WAKE

Prior to its broadcast shutdown on July 10, 2020, by a Duterte-controlled Congress, ABS-CBN was "the Philippines' largest media outfit and the crown jewel of the Lopez business empire" as well as "the largest free-to-air TV broadcast station in the country." In 2016, it owned nineteen radio stations, twenty-six television stations, and eight television affiliates and relay stations across the archipelago; its sheer geographic reach gave the broadcaster 49.5 percent of the daily national audience. It operated two cable channels, one of which (SKYcable) was also a broadband internet service provider, in addition to a global subscription television network, The Filipino Channel (TFC). Headquartered in California, TFC reached audiences in Europe, North America, the Middle East, and the Asia Pacific. An agreement with Globe Telecom allowed ABS-CBN's media content to be distributed to mobile devices; lastly, the conglomerate operated a Philippine franchise for the global amusement park brand Kidzania.[10] Before its broadcast operations ceased in July 2020, ABS-CBN commanded a weekly domestic audience of seventy million over television and radio.[11] But ABS-CBN's influential reach was stymied in 2020 by Duterte's allies in the House Committee on Legislative Franchise. Congress ultimately refused to renew ABS-CBN's application after its initial twenty-five-year legislative franchise (renewed in 1995 via R.A. 7966 under the Ramos presidency) had expired. The Duterte government accused ABS-CBN of unfair reportage, tax evasion, hidden foreign ownership, and unlicensed cable channel operations, all allegations the conglomerate denied.[12]

In hindsight, the nonrenewal of the media giant's broadcast franchise was several years in the making. Duterte may have been swayed by the old enmity between the Lopezes and his occasional political allies, the Marcoses.[13] Once in office, Duterte repeatedly denounced ABS-CBN for airing political advertisements critical of his candidacy in 2016 while failing to broadcast pro-Duterte ads purchased by his campaign. He later faulted the network for biased reportage against his administration. By late 2019, Duterte had made three public declarations of his intent to thwart ABS-CBN's franchise renewal and advised the Lopezes to "just sell" the media outfit.[14]

A broad chorus of voices opposed the Duterte government's nonrenewal of ABS-CBN's broadcast franchise. A general public backlash, an unsuccessful Supreme Court petition, and protests (by celebrities, displaced workers, leftists, journalists, and human rights groups) pushed back against the franchise denial as "a grievous assault on press freedom" through which Duterte silenced media outlets critical of the extrajudicial killings and state-sanctioned violence carried out in the name of his drug war.[15]

The Philippine audiovisual archive community was devastated by news of ABS-CBN's shutdown and the potential impact on its Film Archives. A sizable portion of Philippine cinema's archival afterlives is in the care of an embattled media conglomerate, part of an unfolding history of ephemeral state film entities and media outfits shuttered by feuds between presidents and oligarchs. Established in 1993, the ABS-CBN Film Archives' audiovisual collection held an estimated thirty-six hundred titles and their associated rights in addition to costumes, memorabilia, and film-related print materials.[16] The archives' films are held in two insulated, climate-controlled film vaults for medium- and long-term storage. Since 2003, the archives has been housed in the basement of the Eugenio Lopez Jr. Communications Center in ABS-CBN's Quezon City headquarters, its vaults and acclimatization rooms protected by a fire-suppressive system.[17] The ABS-CBN Film Archives was widely regarded as the Philippines' "de facto national film archive" before (and arguably even after) the NFAP's reestablishment in 2011.[18]

In July 2020, shortly after the nonrenewal of the conglomerate's legislative franchise, unit head Leo Katigbak expressed concern over the fate of the Film Archives' collection: "We're hoping that there will be some people left [in the unit]. I also want to make sure that the air-conditioning and humidity controls [in the storage room] are still running once we're gone." Katigbak worried that history might repeat itself, given that "the master copies of all programs" were destroyed when the military raided ABS-CBN following the declaration of martial law in 1972. "We are trying to avoid something similar from happening. So to the extent that we can protect [the film archives], we will protect it."[19] That same month, a message attributed to Katigbak circulated in Philippine chat groups: "We have a few titles left in the pipeline that were completed, but the shutdown means there will be no further funding. As such, movies that are already deteriorating will probably not be saved by the time we have resources again."[20] Adverting to the commonly held perception that the majority of ABS-CBN's operations would remain closed until the end of Duterte's presidency, the message steeled the local archive world for the anarchival jeopardy that lay ahead.

In the aftermath of the network's broadcast closure on August 31, ABS-CBN's Film Restoration and Archives Unit was forced to go on hiatus as the conglomerate began laying off four thousand workers.[21] By September 2020, two-thirds of the ABS-CBN Film Archives' workers had been let go, with only a third of the archive staff on the technical side remaining, according to an ABS-CBN archivist who participated in a SOFIA virtual seminar in September 2020. By the following February, I learned that even that archivist was no longer with ABS-CBN. At a January 2022 presentation on the ABS-CBN film restoration campaign *Sagip Pelikula* (Save cinema), Leo Katigbak highlighted three effects of the ABS-CBN shutdown: staff reductions from twelve to five people; stoppage of DVD releases; and an end to collaboratively outsourced digital restorations.[22] Katigbak elaborated on these impacts via email:

> We pretty much have no resources to do much of the work we needed to do.... Having 5 people do the work of 14 also limits what we can do and pursue.... Given the long tail nature of the business and ABS-CBN continuing to hemorrhage money, we are not a priority if there are fresh funds, so we are hoping to continue as best we can. I was able to secure some budget for restoration in 2022. It's minimal but it will get some work done.... Scanned and enhanced is a stopgap but we hope to go back to restoration in full.... But most people seem to be happy to just get the sharper images even if scratches and discoloration are still there.[23]

By 2021, ABS-CBN had restored over two hundred titles. Since the conglomerate's franchise denial in 2020, severe staff and budget reductions have resulted in the ABS-CBN Film Archives "digitally scanning and enhancing" titles rather than outputting fully "digitally remastered and restored" works; the latter require costly outsourcing to collaborative partners.[24]

The massive layoffs at ABS-CBN in 2020 unfolded over a pandemic year when the national unemployment rate rose to 10.4 percent, a fifteen-year high.[25] That year, the Philippine economy contracted by 9.5 percent ("the worst on record since World War II"), according to the IBON Foundation; 4.5 million Filipinos lost their jobs while the Philippine government "underspent its 2020 budget" rather than provide an economic stimulus. By January 2021, the Philippines' COVID-19 response ranked "79th out of 98 countries worldwide" and was the "worst performer in Southeast Asia." The IBON Foundation remarks: "Perhaps not coincidentally, what the four worst performing countries in Asia [the Philippines, Bangladesh, Indonesia, and India] have in common is that the pandemic hit as they all struggled with authoritarian leaders and democratic decline."[26]

In what follows, I interweave the story of the FAP's demise and the rise of the ABS-CBN Film Archives against the political tapestry of the tumultuous Marcos-to-Aquino period and the fortunes of the Lopez family, the country's most durable transmedia dynasty. I revisit the cultural policies and economic dilemmas of the post-EDSA period, when key state-produced films were privatized. The end of the chapter zooms in on a consequential moment in the privatization of the state's film holdings: ABS-CBN's 2001 acquisition of the rights and interests of four films produced by a government agency, the defunct ECP.

PRIVATIZATION IN THE POSTDICTATORSHIP PERIOD

Privatization as a historical outgrowth of the Philippine state's economic woes is central to the story of Philippine cinema's anarchival condition, directly enabling the emergence of the ABS-CBN Film Archives. The decline of the Marcos era state film archive upon Cory Aquino's accession to the presidency in 1986 opened the door to the corporatization of a significant portion of the nation's remaining audiovisual archival holdings by ABS-CBN, a media company founded by the Lopezes, one of the country's foremost oligarchic families.[27] Privatization is defined as "the divestment of government-owned or -controlled corporations and acquired assets, and the transfer thereof to the private sector."[28] Given that most of the Philippines' extant films are now held by ABS-CBN—including studio era classics from LVN Pictures and the critically acclaimed government productions of the ECP—privatization must also be understood as a process whereby older films are treated primarily as corporate assets to be repurposed through carefully timed release "windows" in niche and ancillary markets (e.g., cable, DVD, and online platforms).[29] In addition to these first and second senses of privatization (as government divestiture and corporatization), privatization names an archival context in which access and preservation (e.g., appraisal, valuation, curatorship, and restoration) are driven by a market logic. Profitability now looms large in the calculus of Philippine film preservation.

The dominance of commercial audiovisual collections over not-for-profit state archives and the parallel rise of concentrated ownership by media oligopolies from the late 1980s onward are not unique to the Philippines; scholars have tracked the shift to private, commercial film archives in the US context and the rise of conglomerate Hollywood.[30] Aspiring to a generative (rather than denunciatory) critique of ABS-CBN's role in Philippine film archiving, I offset this chapter's focus on oligarchic media consolidation and privatization with a subsequent chapter that focuses on the queer cinephilic pleasures facilitated by ABS-CBN's restoration efforts and archival advocacy campaign.

A final caveat: many years spent visiting archives—whether in the Philippines or elsewhere, film-centered or print-based, state-run or commercial—have convinced me that archives are (primarily) people. By this I mean that archival functions are actualized by cultural workers who exercise archival powers of appraisal, selection, preservation, restoration, and, crucially, access. In this regard, the ABS-CBN Film Archives is not just a division of a sprawling oligarchic media conglomerate. As media scholars note, ownership does not completely foreclose the actual practices and products of media entities.[31] As such, it is not corporate leadership but the archivists with whom I have worked, chiefly Mary del Pilar and Julie Galino, who personify the ABS-CBN Film Archives to me as a researcher.[32] In their roles as archival gatekeepers but also as oral historians of the institutions they helped shape, these women facilitate research access in ways that entail considerably less red tape than in state-run archives.

As Edmondson notes, those who use archives put their trust in other people, not "impersonal" corporations or state agencies.[33] Striking proof of that axiom is LVN Pictures' donation of its memorabilia collection not to ABS-CBN but to Mary del Pilar personally, under her custodianship while the collection is housed in the corporation's climate-controlled vaults. When I last spoke to her in 2018, del Pilar, a founding SOFIA member who retired the following year, planned to bequeath that collection to a successor archivist at ABS-CBN in turn.[34] In that case, the continuity demanded by archival safekeeping would be carried out personally rather than organizationally, a point that bears reflection. Though ABS-CBN is not a public research facility, the helpfulness of its archivists toward researchers explains why ABS-CBN's collection was perceived as a de facto national film archive, since filmmakers and scholars regularly turned to it for access to the Filipino cinematic past. This is precisely why the archive community was so crestfallen by its shutdown in 2020.

MEDIA CONSOLIDATION: THE ABS-CBN STORY

On the surface, the historical evolution of the Philippine media juggernaut ABS-CBN reads as a story of localization: an initially American-owned radio factory and broadcast television license were eventually acquired by Filipino entrepreneurs who successfully ushered in a commercial broadcast era. In truth, however, the "ABS-CBN story" is better apprehended as a cautionary tale about political influence, oligarchic consolidation, and corporate resilience.[35] As historian Alfred McCoy demonstrates, the Lopez media empire flourished under multiple presidential patrons who span the prewar, postwar, and post–martial law eras of Philippine history: Manuel L. Quezon (1935–44), Elpidio Quirino (1948–53), Ramon Magsaysay (1953–57), Corazon Aquino (1986–92), and Fidel Ramos (1992–98).[36] Conversely, oligarchic businesses are also vulnerable to animosity from the executive branch. The Lopez empire—encompassing print and broadcast media, finance, and a key energy utility, the Manila Electric Company (Meralco)—was nearly decimated upon Marcos's imposition of martial law in 1972. Shortly after the fall of the dictatorship in 1986, Cory Aquino acted quickly to reinstate Lopez control over holdings Marcos and his cronies had expropriated, prompting McCoy to describe Aquino's presidency as an era of oligarchic restoration.[37]

The origins of Philippine television can be traced to postwar foreign investment in radio: in 1946, American entrepreneur James Lindenberg opened the Bolinao Electronics Corporation. Named after his wife's hometown in Pangasinan, the plant assembled radios using imported components and parts left over from World War II. Two years later, strict importation laws forced the company to abandon radio assembly and shift to radio broadcast. By the early 1950s, Lindenberg had sold both his company and his television franchise—the first such license in the country—to Judge Antonio Quirino, President Elpidio Quirino's younger sibling. Judge Quirino renamed the company the Alto Broadcasting System (ABS), airing the first commercial television programming in the Philippines in 1953 on Channel 3. Three years later, Eugenio Lopez Sr., who had acquired the *Manila Chronicle* newspaper and a clutch of radio stations in the late 1940s, founded another network, the Chronicle Broadcasting Network (CBN). Lopez's 1958 acquisition of ABS, incorporated under the old name, Bolinao Electronics Corporation (BEC), set the stage for the eventual rechristening of the merged media entities under the corporate name ABS-CBN in 1967.[38] The corporation's official history mythologizes CBN's 1958 acquisition of ABS as a friendly negotiation in which Lopez and Judge Quirino sealed the deal by scribbling their signatures on a table napkin.[39] McCoy, however, references an alternate version in which politics, rather than friendship, enables the historic merger: "According to one account, President Magsaysay repaid a political debt to the Lopezes by foreclosing on government loans to radio stations owned by Antonio Quirino . . . , thus facilitating expansion of the Lopez network."[40]

As Amando Doronila notes, the "concentration of newspapers in the hands of wealthy families" begins in the 1920s under American colonialism. By 1969, a handful of clans had accumulated the majority of media holdings; some owned radio and television stations in addition to newspapers and a diverse array of other businesses. Doronila's critique of conglomerate media's tendency to cluster ownership in the hands of a few bears repeating here:

> The emergence of media giants . . . offered Filipinos a diversity of points of view, but one which was limited to the agenda of public debate set by the conservative political and economic outlook of the newspapers. Lost in this plurality was the reporting of the social grievances of the peasantry. . . . The postwar concentration of the media . . . [is] more diversified [than that of prewar days] and includes an amalgamation of print and broadcasting facilities. The competing interests of the media owners have assured the plurality of views in the media, but only within the context of capitalist liberalism.[41]

The assets of oligarchically controlled Philippine media outfits would be seized and redistributed to Marcos cronies beginning in 1972. Marcos expropriated and reallocated media control to his favored circle but did not put an end to the system of elite-controlled media, which was quickly reinstated upon the overthrow of the dictatorship. The first year of Cory Aquino's presidency would see provincial oligarchs reinstalled in political posts and Manila elites recovering corporate control.[42]

RENT-SEEKING: OLIGARCHIC FAMILIES AND THE STATE

The Lopez family were the dominant media oligarchs both before and after the martial law period. By the late 1960s, the Menzi and Soriano clans had diversified into print media with the *Manila Daily Bulletin* and the *Philippine Herald*, respectively; other prominent families added radio and TV holdings to newspaper ownership: the Elizalde family of industrialists owned DZRH on radio and Metropolitan Broadcasting Corporation's (MBC) Channel 11 on television; the Roces family, which helmed the *Manila Times* and other newspapers, controlled DZTM and Associated Broadcasting Corporation's (ABC) TV 5.[43] Leading the pack in the race for broadcast media consolidation were the Lopezes, beginning with a trilingual provincial newspaper business in the late 1920s (the Iloilo-based Spanish- and English-language *El Tiempo* and a Hiligaynon edition, *Ang Panahon*).[44] The Lopez media empire peaked with ABS-CBN, which, by 1972, had grown to become "the Philippines' largest network, with two TV stations (Channels 2 and 4) and seven radio stations in Manila, three provincial TV and 14 radio stations, and three radio affiliate stations."[45] Throughout his career as a print, radio, and television mogul, Eugenio

Lopez Sr. deployed the news media for political ends, ranging from the *Times-Tiempo*'s support of Quezon's Nacionalista Party in the Visayas in the 1930s, to the *Manila Chronicle*'s initially warm relationship with Quirino in the 1940s, to its reportage on the Marcos regime's corruption in the early 1970s.[46]

In his groundbreaking analysis of Philippine history through the lens of elite political dynasties, "'An Anarchy of Families,'" Alfred McCoy nuances the so-called weak state thesis by arguing that the Philippines combines a debilitated central government with a powerful family-based oligarchy.[47] Elsewhere, McCoy states, "Simply put, rents—restrictive state licenses that allow holders to gain a monopoly or oligopoly over a particular market—have served to strengthen a few fortunate families at the expense of both economic growth and government revenues."[48] Building on McCoy's work, Caroline S. Hau ruefully opines, "If the poor are always with us, so too, it would seem, are the elites." Hau notes that "the idea of 'strong' elites has been one of the most important, if not the dominant, lens for viewing and understanding the history, politics, and current state of affairs in the Philippines," emphasizing that the singular and plural forms of this keyword, "elite" and "elites," "convey the simultaneous homogeneity and heterogeneity of this group."[49]

The relationship between a weak nation-state and formidable dynastic clans is characterized by "rent-seeking," that is, elite families' attempts to obtain economic advantages through government regulation in the form of state licenses (e.g., for broadcast, import, or export), low-cost government loans, favorable taxation, and other concessions that create artificial monopolies or oligopolies.[50] Historically, Philippine presidents have awarded rents to elite families to whom they were politically indebted; oligarchic clans command political office on the national and/or local scale, landed wealth, and sometimes private provincial armies, all of which enable these powerful families to deliver votes to particular political candidates. McCoy writes, "Philippine presidents used the state's licensing powers as bargaining chips in their dealings with national and local elites, thereby creating benefices that favored the dominant political families."[51] McCoy's insight holds, though in the inverse direction, for Duterte's punitive stance toward ABS-CBN in 2020, when he used the state's licensing powers to deny, rather than favor, the franchise renewal of an elite-owned media conglomerate. Attentiveness to entrenched oligarchic rent-seeking practices is particularly germane to an analysis of Philippine media because, as influential families like the Lopezes have long known, "broadcasting constituted an extreme form of rents, one exceptionally vulnerable to state regulation."[52]

The Lopez family's shrewd understanding of the links between media ownership and political power began with Eugenio and Fernando's father, Benito Lopez, whose newspaper, *El Tiempo,* helped him to secure Iloilo's first governorship in 1903. Assassinated by a rival political faction years later, the boys' father left Eugenio and Fernando a modest inheritance (a single hacienda and a small printing press) from which the brothers built a combined fortune valued at US$300 million by 1973, the very wealth that the dictatorship would seize.[53]

THE MARCOS-LOPEZ FEUD

The Marcos-Lopez conflict evolved from an initial alliance. Casting aside his own presidential bid, Fernando Lopez ran alongside Ferdinand Marcos as the latter's vice presidential candidate in the 1965 and 1969 elections; in both polls, their combined ticket emerged victorious. In 1968, Ferdinand and Imelda were guests of honor at the inauguration of ABS-CBN's state-of-the-art broadcast center, helmed by Eugenio Sr.'s eldest son, Eugenio "Geny" Lopez Jr., and located at the triangular lot bordered by Bohol Avenue (now Mother Ignacia Ave.), Scout Albano Street (a portion of which is now Eugenio Lopez Drive), and Sergeant Esguerra Street; this remains the present-day location of the ABS-CBN complex in Quezon City.[54] By 1971, however, a Marcos-Lopez breakup was underway, with the two sides offering different explanations for the rupture: "According to Marcos, the Lopezes were demanding concessions to advance their interests. According to the Lopezes, Marcos was demanding shares in their family corporations."[55]

Marcos's 1972 proclamation of martial law and his first letter of instruction banning the private ownership of media took deadly aim at the Lopezes' considerable holdings in publishing, radio, and television. The *Manila Chronicle*'s printing press was sold for a pittance to Imelda Marcos's brother Benjamin "Kokoy" Romualdez, who used it to issue the *Times Journal.* Crucially, the state's confiscation of privately owned media voided all prior broadcast licenses. By 1973, Roberto S. Benedicto, a key Marcos crony, had taken full control of ABS-CBN facilities to air programming for Benedicto's Kanlaon Broadcasting Corporation (KBS-9) and

Banahaw Broadcasting Corporation (BBC-2) without compensating the Lopezes.[56] Indeed, broadcast and cable television in the martial law era was firmly in the hands of the dictatorship, with various channels run by Benedicto; Malacañang official Gilberto Duavit; and two agencies, the Ministry of Information and the NMPC, both under Gregorio Cendaña; "for all intents and purposes, though, only Ferdinand Marcos had his hand on the switch."[57]

The most spectacular episodes of the Marcos-Lopez conflict are legendary: how the dictator imprisoned Geny Lopez in 1972 and then blackmailed Geny's ailing father, Eugenio Lopez Sr., into ceding control of Meralco the following year; how the old man died in California without seeing his heir; how a daring jailbreak rescue by family members in 1975 flew Geny out of the Philippines in a six-seater Cessna under the military's nose; and how, a decade later, Geny returned in triumph from political asylum in the United States, where he had been a key anti-Marcos figure, to helm a prosperous, resurgent ABS-CBN in the Aquino and post-Aquino periods.[58]

DUTERTE VS. ABS-CBN

Neither Marcos's nor Duterte's deep animosity toward the Lopezes should be mistaken for an anti-oligarchic stance. Marcos betrayed instructive parallels with bitter rivals among the traditional oligarchy, such as Benigno "Ninoy" Aquino Jr. (whose 1983 assassination helped spark Marcos's overthrow) and Eugenio Lopez Sr. (whose massive wealth had been dispossessed by Marcos a decade earlier).[59] In hindsight, Marcos represented not the end of the old oligarchic system of rent-seeking but its apotheosis under new hands.[60] Similarly, Duterte's anti-oligarchic rhetoric was a facade for a regime that cleared the way for its favored circle of elite economic players.

Critics have also discerned parallels between the shuttering of ABS-CBN in both the Marcos and the Duterte era. Maria Ressa writes: "Every time a budding dictator is set to consolidate power in the Philippines, he attacks the Lopez family."[61] Political analyst Millard Lim observes, "In 1972, FM [Ferdinand Marcos] sought the demise of ABS-CBN. In 2020, President Rodrigo R. Duterte (PRRD) is seeking the same." Lim contrasts Marcos's "military solution"—the declaration of martial law and the government seizure of media outlets in the name of a national emergency—with Duterte's "legal solution."[62] Following the ABS-CBN shutdown, Duterte boasted that he had dismantled an (unnamed) oligarchic family without recourse to martial law.[63]

Following the denial of its legislative franchise, ABS-CBN continued to operate its cable channels and retained a limited free-to-air domestic presence equivalent to roughly 34 percent of its former broadcast stations.[64] The loss of its nationwide news broadcasts on radio and television has resulted in a pronounced "cultural vacuum." Media scholar Rolando Tolentino notes, "The government has forced a kind of killing off [of] information flow in . . . vital [rural] areas" not reached by its rival, the Global Media Arts Network (GMA). The shutdown of ABS-CBN exerts a "chilling effect" on media freedom: "If you do not accede to the opinion of the tyrannical government, then you can be shut down. If they could do it to a media conglomerate such as ABS-CBN, then they can do it to a smaller yet critical outfit such as the alternative press or online platforms."[65] Tolentino's prescient warning was confirmed two months later, when catastrophic floods in Isabela and Cagayan Provinces overwhelmed local communities; on-the-ground provincial news reportage was markedly absent. As typhoon survivors had long maintained, ABS-CBN's regional stations, especially in remote areas outside the urban capital, are critical to disaster relief efforts.[66]

FILM AND CULTURAL POLICY POST-EDSA

Unfolding over a few days in late February 1986, the EDSA People Power Revolution that successfully overthrew the Marcos dictatorship and installed an opposition candidate hailing from the traditional oligarchy, Cory Cojuanco-Aquino, was a historic four-day "concatenation of events" that was years in the making.[67] Jaime Cardinal Sin's urgent appeals for public support to shield anti-Marcos rebels, broadcast over the Catholic station Radio Veritas, prompted more than two million Filipinos to surge into Metro Manila's main thoroughfare, EDSA. Caroline S. Hau describes EDSA People Power as a "relatively bloodless" revolution in which Marcos government troops, daunted by the withdrawal of US support and intense national and international media coverage, refused to open fire against an anti-Marcos coalition composed of the middle class, Catholic clergy, leftist activists, and the urban poor. Cory Aquino was sworn in as president on the same day that Marcos and the First Family fled Malacañang to seek exile in Hawaii.[68]

If Marcos demonstrated that a punitive president could devastate elite fortunes, Cory Aquino's counterexample affirmed how quickly successful rent-seeking under a sympathetic president could reinstate the old oligarchy's control over popular media. Within months of Aquino's accession to power, the crony-controlled BBC-2 frequencies were returned to the Lopezes; cable TV was deregulated; and ABS-CBN's franchise was recovered and the network relaunched, after which it "vault[ed] to first place among the five networks in less than a year."[69]

The Aquino administration's enthusiasm for private media conglomerates was inversely proportional to its scant interest in cultural policy. Aquino disappointed nationalist intellectuals who hoped that she would act decisively to "develop a true Filipino people's culture, which shall be non-partisan, multicultural, pluralistic, liberative, and democratic."[70] Cultural critic Doreen Fernandez recalls that shortly after Aquino took the reins of government, her newly appointed minister of public information, Teodoro Locsin Jr., "announced that culture was a low priority. The remark reverberated through the art circles and was met with dismay by all who had suffered through Imelda Marcos's idea of art and culture."[71] Writing two years into Cory's term, Fernandez held out hope that policy planning under the newly organized Presidential Commission for Culture and the Arts would bear fruit. In hindsight, however, Aquino's cultural policy legacy was checkered at best, bearing out "the public perception . . . that there is lack of government interest in art and culture . . . because of President Aquino's concentration on the economy, the military, and politics."[72]

Historically, Philippine politics has invested great power in the executive branch while failing to continue cultural policies across disparate presidential administrations. Cory Aquino's decision to honor the bloated foreign debt accumulated under the Marcos dictatorship, rather than repudiate an estimated US$15 billion in external loans, saddled her term with a crushing economic burden. In such a climate, debt servicing took fiscal priority while allocations for culture were deprioritized.[73] Aquino's cultural policies evinced a deep suspicion of state intervention into culture, which had been personalistic and propagandistic under Marcos.[74]

Leery of state support for film being used for propagandistic and corrupt ends, the Aquino administration investigated fiscal malfeasance at the Film Development Foundation of the Philippines (formerly the ECP) and the Manila Film Center.[75] By and large, however, it took a "hands-off" approach to cinema, ending many Marcos era film initiatives while retaining the problematic policy of excessive taxation. In the first month of Aquino's presidency, her Memorandum Order 2 created a task force to oversee various film-related agencies bequeathed by the Marcos regime. Four years would pass, however, before its membership was formalized via Memorandum Order 274.[76] Narrowly concerned with state film agencies' assets, liabilities, and property rights, Memorandum Order 274 failed to offer cultural policy guidelines to inform the task force's work, nor did it sketch a vision, however inchoate, for the domestic film industry. The memorandum order openly acknowledges that government film entities had not yet "normalized operations" four years into Aquino's term.[77]

In interviews, filmmaker and task force head Cirio H. Santiago articulated the film industry's demand for "tax shelters and reductions, plus rationalization of taxes for both local and imported productions."[78] Echoing this concern, film historian Nicanor Tiongson identifies "onerous taxation" as one of the "principal problems" of the film industry in the post-EDSA period. Analyzing data from 1989, he notes that cumulative government taxes (amusement tax, value-added tax, withholding tax, cultural tax, and other duties) routinely sapped 52 percent of a domestic film's gross returns.[79] The huge tax burden imposed by the state, combined with the devaluation of the Philippine peso, resulted in soaring production costs for a film industry dependent on imported film stock and equipment.[80] Local film producers attempted to stay afloat by resorting to quickie filmmaking—limiting film projects to a truncated forty-five-day schedule in order to cut costs—but the steep drop in quality made domestic movies even less competitive as Hollywood films flooded the Philippines' unprotected film market. These structural problems, exacerbated by the rise of home video and piracy, resulted in a "marked decline in the number of film productions, film hits, and even new movie houses" by 1990.[81]

ARCHIVE IN CRISIS: DE PEDRO'S 1986 FAP REPORT

In the immediate post-EDSA period, relations between the FAP, headed by Director General Ernie de Pedro, and Aquino's task force on film were extremely strained. While doing research at the PIA, I came across an incomplete copy of a May 1986 report, "Overview of the Film Archives," penned by de Pedro and addressed to Executive Secretary Joker Arroyo.[82] De Pedro's report adopts a defensive tone in response to criticism of the Film Archives of the Philippines (FAP) in a task force report dated April 6, which remarked, "Not much has been done in film preservation and film research allegedly because of a lack of equipment and financing."[83]

In response, de Pedro's report itemizes the Film Archives' achievements: through statutory deposits of "over 220 master negatives" as well as donations and temporary deposits, the FAP built up a significant national collection of over 2,140 domestic and foreign titles, including rare early films.[84] Objecting to the task force's mention of the Manila Film Center's "flooded basement," de Pedro maintains that the "film vaults, being elevated by several feet, have never been flooded, although the Archives Level itself was flooded during a freak storm in July 1985."[85] De Pedro further asserts that twenty-four-hour temperature and humidity controls at the Film Archives means that its "storage vault passes the technical standards of the FIAF [International Federation of Film Archives]," a feat that "NO OTHER FILM STORAGE FACILITY in the Philippines—NMPC; Film Library; UP [University of the Philippines] Film Center; Ayala Museum; LVN Archives; Sampaguita Studios or Premiere Studios—matches."[86]

De Pedro asserts that the FAP managed to maintain its important and expansive collection despite profound organizational chaos and institutional neglect. As mentioned in the first two chapters of this book, the FAP was founded in 1981 and initially subsumed under the CCP before being reclassified under the ECP in 1982.[87] When the ECP was dissolved in 1985, the FAP was transferred to the BRMPT.[88] The BRMPT, a censorship agency, was abolished a month later to make way for a review and classification board, the MTRCB.[89] The MTRCB inherited responsibility for the FAP in October 1985, only seven months prior to the submission of de Pedro's report to the newly installed Aquino government.[90] In practice, however, "the MTRCB took the Archives under its fold" only in 1988. The FAP collection remained in the Manila Film Center's basement until 1992, when it was moved to the MTRCB's Quezon City office.[91] The tumultuous institutional history of the FAP contrasts strikingly with the stability of the Philippine state's commitment to film taxation and censorship, regardless of regime change. To take one telling example, the MTRCB, a film censorship agency, survived the Marcos-to-Aquino transition and is still operative today.

The significance of de Pedro's report lies in its detailed account of the organizational confusion, institutional deprioritization, and underfunding that engulfed the FAP upon the ECP's dissolution:

After telexes from film archives around the world impressed upon the office of then president Marcos the incongruity of the situation—(the censors "cut" the film[s], while the archives sought to preserve them)—President Marcos ordered that a corrective E.O. [executive order] be prepared by the Office of the Government Corporate Counsel. The draft was referred to, and endorsed by, the officials of the Film Academy, the BRMPT Chairman, and the Chairman of the Presidential Commission on Reorganization. . . . When the BRMPT was superseded by the Movie and Television Review and Classification Board (MTRCB) as per Presidential Decree No. 1986 promulgated October 5, 1985, its Chairman likewise decided not to include the NFAP in its budget.

The promulgation of the corrective E.O.—proposing to place the NFAP as "an autonomous operating unit" under either the Office of the President (as in the case of the film censors) or the CCP—was, however, overtaken by the revolutionary events of February 1986.

AS THE LAW NOW STANDS, the NFAP is officially under the jurisdiction of the MTRCB. BUT AT NO TIME since October 1, 1985 did the NFAP draw from MTRCB any centavo for its archiving activities or for the salaries of its staff. For October and November 1985 at least, the Film Development Foundation decided to advance staff salaries.[92]

In response to domestic and international criticism of the Film Archives' transfer to a censorship body, the Marcos government apparently drafted, but never released, a "corrective executive order" that would have placed the FAP directly under the Office of the President or within the jurisdiction of the CCP (given the CCP's long-standing commitment to SOFIA-led archiving initiatives in the post-dictatorship era, the latter might have been a good move had it gone through). Unfortunately for the FAP, the Marcos regime was overthrown before the Film Archives found a stable institutional home. In the aftermath of the EDSA revolution, the MTRCB failed to disburse funding for the Film Archives under its wing.

As is painfully clear from de Pedro's report, funding emerges as the most pressing problem for the post-EDSA FAP. As a private foundation, the Film Development Foundation of the Philippines could not be expected to underwrite the FAP's operating costs. De Pedro makes an urgent plea for a 2 million peso annual budget allocation for the FAP; to generate these moneys, he suggests that the Film Archives might "share in" various film-related government taxes.[93]

Though the Aquino government acted quickly to restore oligarchic control of media, it failed to extend support to an ailing FAP. My research has not uncovered any response to de Pedro's report from the Aquino government, whether via the task force or the Office of the President. Absent government allocations to sustain its staff and operations, the FAP could not have remained operational for much longer; it appears to have withered during the early years of Aquino's regime.[94] The collapse of the short-lived FAP, one of Southeast Asia's earliest audiovisual archives, ended the Philippines' aspiration to become a regional film depository for "ASEAN countries which have no film archives yet."[95] The FAP's institutional death coincides with the emergence of ABS-CBN's corporate film archives, a privatized substitute for what de Pedro had once called the "national archive for audiovisual images."[96]

ECP FILMS AND ABS-CBN

In her July 1988 State of the Nation address, Cory Aquino dissimulated her privatization program's neoliberal logic within a rhetoric of public service: "Due care must be exercised in the disposition of assets that belong to the people. We must get the most we can for the people, in as fair and transparent a manner as possible, leaving no room for the smallest doubt about the integrity of the procedure and the people involved." Claiming that "the Privatization Program has generated P11.2 billion in gross revenues," Aquino went on to stress the urgency of privatizing additional government assets.[97] The privatization program aimed to sell off nonessential state assets as quickly as possible while "generating maximum cash recovery" through an open bidding process. In the auctioning of state assets, winning bids consisted of the highest offer accompanied by the largest up-front cash payment. Cory Aquino told attendees at a 1987 investment conference, "We want cash at the barrel-head because that is what we need to fuel our recovery and growth."[98]

Zinnia F. Godinez argues that the Philippines' foreign debt crisis (estimated to have swelled to US$28.6 billion by 1988) and the dismal performance of several public sector enterprises were the rationale for the Aquino administration's espousal of privatization. A portion of the proceeds was promised to government projects like the Comprehensive Agrarian Reform Program.[99] Godinez cautions that criteria for evaluating the success of Aquino's privatization program must include both a decreased budget deficit and successful socioeconomic reforms. She also echoes concerns that privatization might inadvertently further the concentration of wealth in the hands of oligarchic families: "Lessons from recent history have brought to mind the possible substitution of private monopolies for public monopolies. . . . A related concern is the concentration of wealth, particularly since most of the NPAs [nonperforming assets of the government] have been sold through an auction/bidding to facilitate asset disposition. Critics abound with such terms as 'privatization means familization' because most of the NPAs sold have gone mainly to large family-held corporations."[100]

Concerns that privatization might ultimately benefit oligarchic families rather than the public interest have been borne out. In particular, the privatization of the productions of the ECP—the most critically acclaimed of all state-sponsored films—was immensely advantageous to the ABS-CBN Film Archives. As advertised in the classified section of the *Philippine Star*, the "Invitation to Bid" issued by the Department of Finance Privatization and Management Office in February 2001 opens with a hyperbolic banner: "A BUSINESS OPPORTUNITY AWAITS YOU!" (figure 3.1). Promoting the "rights and interests" of four films produced and formerly owned by the ECP—*Oro, Plata, Mata* (Gold, silver, death; dir. Peque Gallaga, 1982); *Himala* (Miracle; dir. Ishmael Bernal, 1982); *Misteryo sa Tuwa* (Mysterious delight; dir. Rosauro de la Cruz, 1984); and *Soltero* (Bachelor; dir. Pio de Castro, 1984)—this classified ad caught the eye of a visionary archivist, Mary del Pilar, at ABS-CBN; the conglomerate went on to offer the winning bid.[101] I vividly remember how, when I was a junior scholar more than a decade ago, government film workers referred in awestruck tones to the *subasta* (auction) of a handful of critically acclaimed feature films produced by the short-lived ECP. Only much later did I fathom the significance of this sale.

The four ECP-produced films are emblematic of what has been called the Philippine New Cinema or the Second Golden Age of Philippine film—a period of artistic accomplishment beginning in 1975 (three years after the declaration of martial law) and ending in the February 1986 People Power Revolution that ousted Ferdinand and Imelda Marcos from power.[102] Tiongson writes, "The New Cinema, which refers to feature films characterized by innovativeness and artistic integrity, was born in the 1970s and grew through the 1980s because of the confluence of social and cultural conditions prevailing during those decades," namely, a generation of filmmakers familiar with international film movements

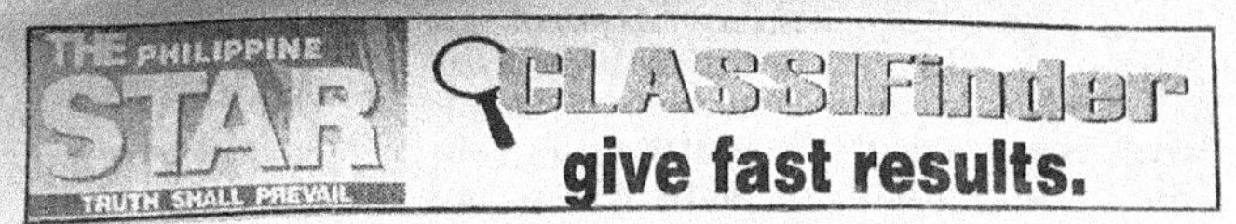

SATURDAY, FEBRUARY 24, 2001

A BUSINESS OPPORTUNITY AWAITS YOU!!!

Republic of the Philippines

Department of Finance

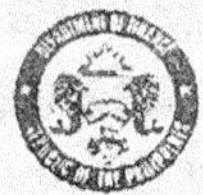

PRIVATIZATION AND MANAGEMENT OFFICE

INVITATION TO BID

Rights and interests of the Privatization and Management Office (PMO) over the films: ORO, PLATA, MATA, HIMALA, MISTERYO SA TUWA and SOLTERO **formerly owned by the Experimental Cinema of the Philippines (ECP).**

The above mentioned films are being offered separately on an open price basis.

Offers will be received, opened and tabulated in the presence of the bidders on 23 March 2001 at 10:00 a.m. at the PMO Conference Room, 6th Flr. North Davao Mining Corp. Bldg., 104 Gamboa St., Legaspi Village Makati City.

Interested parties may request for duly authenticated copies of the **Asset Specific Bidding Rules (ASBR)** and **Asset Specific Bidding Form (ASBF)** for a nominal fee of P500.00. Please contact Mr. John Baldemor or Ms. Maureen B. Valiente of the PMO Marketing Department at 817-0136 loc. 258

North Davao Mining Corporation Building
104 Gamboa Street, Legaspi Village, Makati City
Tel. No. 8170136 connecting all departments
Fax (632) 893-3453/818-0906/818-4591

P.S. February 24, 2001

3.1 The Privatization and Management Office's "Invitation to Bid" on the rights and interests of films produced by the Experimental Cinema of the Philippines. *Philippine Star*, February 24, 2001.

and auteurs, and "a new social consciousness" emerging from anti-Marcos activism.[103]

Himala and *Oro, Plata, Mata* were among ABS-CBN's earliest high-profile "digitally restored and remastered" titles, released on DVD in 2012 and 2013, respectively (figures 3.2 and 3.3). Both films model the accomplishments of two government institutions that fostered the emergence of the New Cinema in the 1970s and 1980s: the MIFF and the ECP, the latter under the executive directorship of the dictator's eldest daughter, Imee Marcos (formerly Imee Marcos-Manotoc). Film historian Joel David suggests that the answer to the New Cinema's central paradox—why did aesthetically accomplished, politically engaged cinema flourish during the repressive Marcos regime?—lies in the conditions of production and exhibition that these two institutions, the MIFF and the ECP, were able to provide.[104] David calls the ECP a state "machinery of total institutional support." The key ingredients for the ECP's ability to generate ambitious, critically acclaimed films were as follows: "the production of scriptwriting contest winners, subsidies for worthy full-length film proposals, tax rebates for deserving productions, [and] exhibition of otherwise shunned or banned releases."[105] Additionally, Tiongson singles out the Film Ratings Board (FRB) (which incentivized quality film productions by giving them tax rebates) and the Alternative Cinema Program (which "produced some of the best scripts and films of the 1980s," including *Himala* and *Oro, Plata, Mata*) as the most commendable initiatives of an otherwise underfunded and artistically compromised ECP.[106]

In his nuanced account of the cultural policy contradictions at work in the ECP, David recalls that Imee Marcos-Manotoc, then embroiled in a quarrel with her mother, Imelda (who helmed the MIFF), tapped leftist intellectuals and opposition filmmakers to help establish the ECP.[107] This raises the question of how the state benefits from its perceived tolerance of dissent, as the Marcoses endeavored to present themselves as enlightened patrons of national culture. Tiongson opines that the ECP was created by Marcos "in an attempt to give his regime a wash of liberality."[108] The calculated choice of Imee Marcos-Manotoc to head the ECP, given her well-publicized rows with her mother and the popular perception of her as a rebel within Malacañang, was instrumental in attracting leftist artists to the ECP. This may explain why the films of the Philippine New Cinema often evinced a political radicalism and a defiance of state censorship in their content (*Himala* thematizes peasant revolt while *Oro, Plata, Mata* links sexual decadence with aristocratic excess) yet relied on a

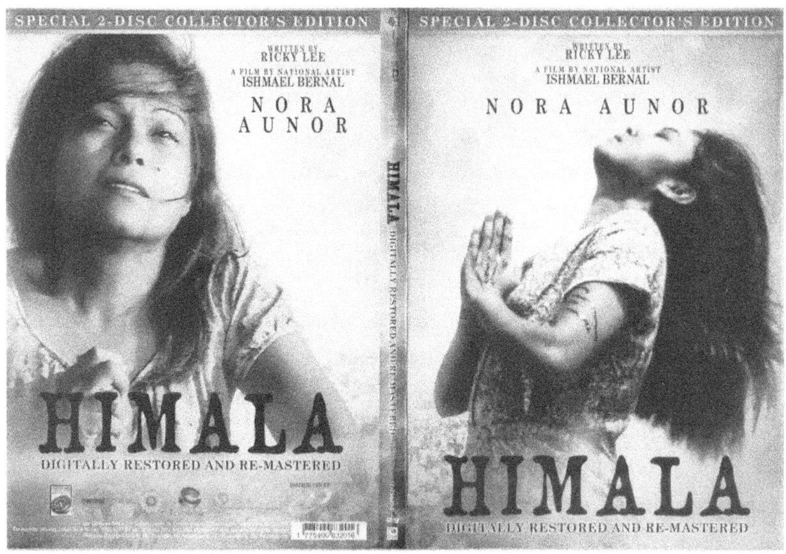

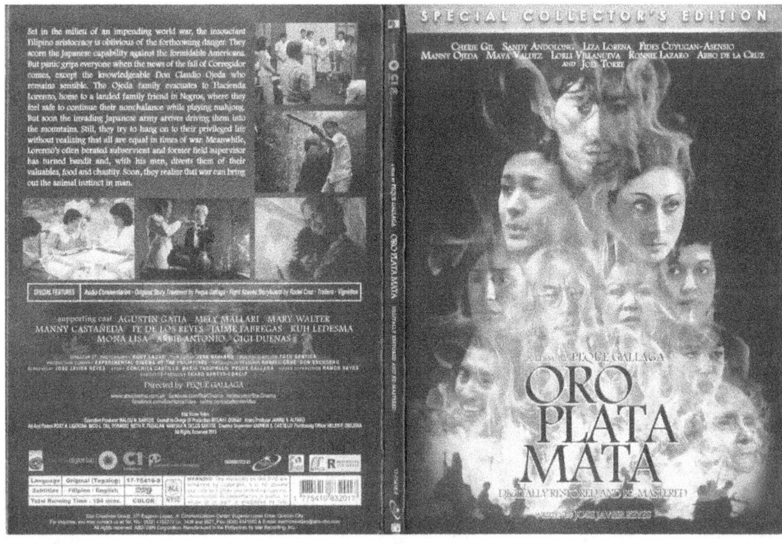

3.2 & 3.3 To launch its high-profile restoration of canonical films by well-known stars and auteurs, ABS-CBN released on DVD "digitally restored and remastered" versions of *Himala* (Miracle; dir. Ishmael Bernal, 1982) and *Oro, Plata, Mata* (Gold, silver, death; dir. Peque Gallaga, 1982) in 2012 and 2013, respectively. The rights to these critically acclaimed productions by a state agency, the Experimental Cinema of the Philippines, were acquired by ABS-CBN in 2001 under the government's privatization program. DVD covers. Author's collection.

degree of complicity with the Marcos administration in their production and exhibition.

By 2001, the year of ABS-CBN's acquisition of the rights to ECP productions, key components of the Aquino era privatization program—the Committee on Privatization and the Asset Privatization Trust (APT)—had expired. Although the success of the Aquino government's privatization program remains in question, subsequent presidential administrations chose to continue on the path to privatization. In 2001, President Joseph Ejercito Estrada's Executive Order 323 reaffirmed the government's privatization policy, creating the Privatization and Management Office (PMO) under the Department of Finance, the very office that issued the invitation to bid on the ECP films.[109]

The deeds of absolute sale for the four ECP films executed between the PMO and ABS-CBN in 2001 recount the complicated fiscal provenance of these films. In 1982, the ECP ceded its rights to *Himala*, *Misteryo sa Tuwa*, *Soltero*, and *Oro, Plata, Mata* as "security for the loan granted by DBP [Development Bank of the Philippines] to the Experimental Cinema of the Philippines." In 1986, the defunct ECP (which had been abolished the year before) defaulted on more than 11 million pesos in financial obligations to the DBP (11,847,000 pesos, to be exact). The following year, the assets and liabilities of the DBP and the Philippine National Bank (which included the rights and interests of ECP film properties) were transferred to the Philippine government.[110] (The latter move was in keeping with the Philippine government's disposal of nonperforming assets held by the PNB and the DBP, two government financial institutions whose "rehabilitation" was stipulated by the World Bank as a condition of their US$300 million economic recovery loan package in 1986.)[111] Estrada's Executive Order 323 having established the PMO as the "successor agency of the APT," the PMO approved the disposal of the Philippine government's rights and interests in the ECP films through public bidding. Offering 1.5 million pesos for the rights to *Himala*, ABS-CBN won the public auction and added one of the best-known works of the New Cinema to their Film Archives' growing collection.[112]

The corporate privatization of films widely regarded as the only cinematic masterpieces produced by the Philippine state may strike some as ironic. I have attempted to situate ABS-CBN's acquisition of the intellectual property rights to the ECP films at the crossroads of several histories: oligarchic media ownership; economic and cultural policies that led to ballooning foreign debt, the collapse of the FAP, and the neoliberal privatization of state assets; and global processes characterized by the "increasing commodification of our moving image heritage," as Karen Gracy puts it.[113] The profit motives of a commercial media network inevitably constrain the nature of ABS-CBN's archival efforts, which focus on mainstream features rather than audiovisual works rich in "cultural and historical value" that "have little or no commercial value." Conglomerate control over intellectual property rights impacts all facets of archival work, "including decisions about selection, preservation, and access to film heritage." Commercial entities leverage their copyright ownership, funding resources, and technological advantages in pushing for their market-driven preservation agenda.[114] As film archives around the world are more and more dominated by such logics, the question of preservation of the past to secure access for the present and the future shifts to a link between temporality and profitability.

None of this is intended as an accusatory critique denouncing the emergence of ABS-CBN as a (now imperiled) powerhouse of archival film preservation and restoration in the Philippines. Indeed, ABS-CBN's DVD releases of digitally restored New Cinema titles point to both a sense of corporate custodianship over the country's dwindling cinematic archive and a canny awareness of the economic realities of film preservation, which favor the restoration of marketable canonical films. (Films like *Himala* and *Oro, Plata, Mata* feature well-known directors and stars and are widely regarded as the gems of the ABS-CBN Film Archives collection.) To its credit, however, ABS-CBN has decided to restore other, less canonical titles. Countering the tendency to prioritize only those films with "the most market value and a high degree of consecration," as Gracy puts it, ABS-CBN also elected to digitally restore and recirculate *T-Bird at Ako* (T-bird and I), a lesbian film classic beloved by queer subcultural audiences and cinephiles, which forms the subject of the next chapter.[115]

Media technologies often generate meanings and consequences in excess of the intentions and ideologies of those who funded and conceived of them, as demonstrated by Brian Larkin's analysis of the "unintended outcomes" of British colonists' introduction of radio networks and mobile cinemas in Nigeria.[116] Emphasizing the "autonomous power" of technologies, Larkin argues that media often generate "technical and social potentials outside their sponsors' control." Sometimes, the intention to produce certain types of social subjects through the cinema results in a "disordering of these ambitions."[117] As the next chapter elaborates, the heteropatriarchal ideologies of the Marcos era are at work in *T-Bird at Ako*, a star vehicle that both spectacularizes and criminalizes a sexually minoritarian subculture. However, its digital restoration and rerelease also enable modes of queerly anachronistic reception in which this intended subjectivation backfires.

CHAPTER FOUR

Queer Anachronisms and Temporalities of Restoration

T-Bird at Ako

> The definition of a classic really evolves over time. It's not just the old critically acclaimed award-winning movies per se, but films that have taken on an iconic status due to [the] director, stars, representation of an era and the like. . . . The [ABS-CBN] restoration campaign focuses on directors primarily. In the case of the 33-year-old [film] *T-Bird at Ako*, it's vintage Danny Zialcita with his snappy dialogue and witty repartee. It's also the last time that Nora [Aunor] and Vilma [Santos] co-starred in a movie and with such a daring theme for its time.
>
> It is uncommon for big stars to act in a film that touches on gay themes. Also, it is one of [director Danny] Zialcita's more memorable films with intact material.
>
> —LEO KATIGBAK, head of ABS-CBN film restoration

When ABS-CBN officially launched its film restoration campaign in 2012, journalistic coverage hyped its high-definition (HD) digital restoration of two prestigious 1982 ECP films, *Himala* (Miracle) and *Oro, Plata, Mata* (Gold, silver, death) (cf. figures 3.2 and 3.3). In the eyes of reporters, the aura of cultural consecration surrounding these multiawarded titles made them unquestionably worthy of a high-profile restoration.[1] Leo Katigbak describes these "true classics" as "marquee titles" vital for promoting ABS-CBN's restoration campaign, rebranded "Sagip Pelikula" (Save cinema), in 2015. *Himala*'s restoration epitomized the Philippine media juggernaut's ambitious plans to create "something like a 'Criterion Collection for local films.'"[2] A virtuoso collaboration between three major talents of Philippine New Cinema (director Ishmael Bernal, screenwriter Ricky Lee, and actress Nora Aunor), *Himala* was the media giant's prize acquisition from the windfall of the ECP's privatization, as discussed in chapter 3.[3]

In contrast, the rationale behind ABS-CBN's decision to rerelease a digitally restored and remastered version of *T-Bird at Ako* (T-bird and I, aka Lesbian love) on DVD and other platforms was less self-evident, although the overt queerness signaled by its title was more titillating.[4] When the restored version premiered at the University of the Philippines Film Institute in 2015, Katigbak was repeatedly "asked about ABS-CBN's selection process of classic titles to restore."[5] I read this as an implicit request to justify ABS-CBN's restoration of a queer commercial movie instead of another prestigious New Cinema title from its vaults. As highlighted in the first epigraph to this chapter, Katigbak's savvy responses expand the notion of a classic film to include not only "old critically acclaimed, award-winning movies" (read, *Himala*) but also movies that command "an iconic status due to [the] director, stars, [and] representation of the era." The archives head proceeds to cite the stylistic signatures of the film's director, Danny Zialcita; its pairing of major stars and its "daring" exploration of "gay themes."[6]

This chapter explores *T-Bird at Ako*'s provocative treatment of queer themes in the context of a star-driven courtroom drama helmed by a prolific commercial director. It delves into the classed, gendered, and racialized aspects of its two rival female superstars' personae and the lesbian cinephilic pleasures generated by the frisson of their much-anticipated onscreen encounter. The chapter's archival takeaways center on the multiple temporalities of ABS-CBN's restoration of a "lesbian classic" of Philippine cinema, as follows.

First, restoration and rerelease do not only aim to return a work to a more pristine, supposedly "original" state; they also initiate present- and future-oriented processes of circulation among new audiences.[7] Second, the retrospective reception of *T-Bird at Ako* enabled by new distribution and exhibition contexts resignifies star images in an overtly queer light and teaches contemporary moviegoers what earlier nonnormative audiences loved about Philippine film history (i.e., a queer archival pedagogy). Third, the temporal twists of the prior statements—pairing "new" with "retrospective," and the oxymoron "older LGBTQ+ audiences" (given that "queer" and "trans" were not prominent in the lexicon of 1980s Manila)—already flag the dissonances confronted by my reflexively anachronistic approach to the film, one that I hope will prove generative. *T-Bird at Ako* deploys an urban queer vernacular rooted in early eighties Manila that I juxtapose with the more intensely transnationalized argot of ensuing decades and elsewheres.

Avoiding a reflectionist understanding of *T-Bird at Ako*—the assumption that a commercial Tagalog movie hit accurately mirrored lesbian life in 1980s Manila—means bearing in mind that what we would now classify as the gender performances and sexual proclivities of the past cannot be recovered in an unmediated sense; as Anjali Arondekar reminds postcolonial scholars of sexuality, the archive is not a transparent "source."[8] My analysis attempts to tease out the sedimented subject effects produced by the movie's exploitation of classed and racialized star-fan dynamics in its spectacularizing depiction of queer urban subcultures, on the one hand, and the disciplinary strictures of Catholic and Marcosian heteronormativity, on the other.

T-Bird at Ako is a window into the subcultural queer lexicon of 1980s Manila. Terms like *T-bird*, *lesbian*, and *tibo* do not coincide with today's LGBTQ+ vocabulary, which is North American and Anglophone in orientation but global in circulation. To navigate this tension, I reflect on the willfully anachronistic terminology that queer, trans, and feminist analyses sometimes bring to bear on older works that resonate with current concerns. The larger stakes of my reading of *T-Bird at Ako* are methodological. On the one hand, I think through the chronological improprieties implicated in our encounters with queer archives; on the other hand, I am mindful of the founding impetus of "queer Asia as critique": to push "queer theory . . . to overcome its Euro-American metropolitanism," as Howard Chiang and Alvin Wong put it.[9] Moreover, thinking trans-ness and Asianness together unsettles the presumed "universality of transgender experiences" grounded in Euro-American frameworks in favor of a "focus on minor traditions of nonnormative embodiment" that have "generally not made their way into the mainstream of scholarship," as Howard Chiang, Todd Henry, and Helen Hok-Sze Leung argue in their essay "Trans-in-Asia, Asia-in-Trans."[10]

LESBIAN CINEPHILIA IN A STAR-STUDDED ROMANCE

T-Bird at Ako is primarily remembered for the formidable star power commanded by its two female leads, Nora Aunor and Vilma Santos. This was not the first time that the two box office queens were brought together in a film whose diegetic romantic conflict alluded to an off-screen cinematic rivalry. The ABS-CBN restoration was packaged as a two-disc box set that put *T-Bird at Ako* at the top of a double bill with *Ikaw ay Akin* (You are mine; dir. Ishmael Bernal, 1978), another of the two stars' four on-screen collaborations.[11] Though on friendly terms with one another throughout their careers, at the height of their popularity as teen idols in the early 1970s, their enormous and devoted fan following—collectively known as Noranians and Vilmanians—fervently disputed the merits of their preferred stars (e.g., which of the two, Nora or Vilma, was the more talented or more beautiful). These fan debates over beauty were overtly racialized, given that Nora was dark-skinned while Vilma was fair-complexioned, an issue to which I will return.

From a commercial standpoint, the genius of *T-Bird at Ako* lay in its decision to intensify its dual-superstar brew by eschewing the formulaic heterosexual love triangle of their prior films (i.e., two women compete for the same man's love) in favor of a same-sex entanglement. In the movie, Nora plays a highly successful defense attorney, Sylvia Salazar, who experiences a sexual-existential crisis as a result of taking on two separate cases in which the defendants each claim to have killed a man in self-defense. In the second of these cases, Sylvia (Nora Aunor) is the pro bono defense lawyer of the beautiful but impoverished Sabel (Vilma Santos), a "low-class beer dancer" and "hospitality girl" (both euphemisms for a female sex worker).[12] In playing a cerebral feminist lawyer who finds herself irresistibly drawn to her client, Nora-as-Sylvia "uses her famous powers of understatement to convey the confusion, discomfort, and amazement of emotional awakening," as one film reviewer puts it. On the threshold of sexual epiphany, Sylvia asks herself: "Could she be a lesbian?"[13]

The queering of the box office formula that exploited Nora and Vilma's legendary archrivalry alluded not just to long-standing rumors about Nora's real-life lesbianism; it also hinted at the homoerotic desire at the heart of the star system in general and Nora's and Vilma's female fan following in particular.[14] In the popular imagination, the terms *Noranian* and *Vilmanian* evoke a fandom composed primarily—though not exclusively—of lower-income rural and urban women employed in domestic work, as well as *bakla* or *bading* (both fluid terms that encompass a spectrum of subjectivities, ranging from gay men to transwomen, that are not entirely equivalent to North American LGBTQ+ categories).[15]

In the famous heterosexual "love teams" of these superstars in their teen years, Nora and Vilma far outshone, both in charisma and in professional longevity, their male partners on and off the screen.[16] Chrishandra Sebastiampillai clarifies the operative distinction in the two women's star rivalry: Nora was an award-winning singer, whereas dancing was the cornerstone of Vilma's star persona.[17] I read *T-Bird at Ako* as a queer subversion of the heteronormative romantic coupling typical of their movies. To that end, the film's lesbian tandem makes knowing use of Nora's early star text as a "boisterous and tomboyish girl" who "walks like a lesbian."[18]

Publicity around *T-Bird at Ako* exploited its superstar lesbian angle to the hilt. One print advertisement during the film's initial theatrical release announces: "The superstars together perhaps for the last time!" (figure 4.1). The tagline from another contemporaneous print ad, subsequently uploaded to a fan website, reads: "Rivals in real life, lovers on the screen. The greatest superstars in their most dramatic and perhaps last encounter on film. This is the movie experience of a lifetime."[19] A promotional photograph of the two stars in one another's arms conveys the pleasures of same-sex intimacy as the diegesis does not, given that the fictional character Sabel consistently rebuffs Sylvia's romantic overtures in the plot (figure 4.2). This publicity snapshot of the two movie queens hugging on set—Nora's intense gaze directed off-screen while Vilma smiles directly at the camera, apparently reveling in their suggestive physical intimacy as the weight of her right hand draws Nora's embrace closer—fulfills the promise of lesbian cinephilia more explicitly than the tepid, unsatisfying scenes that finally made it onto the screen.

The spectacular lure of a star-driven, lesbian-themed box office hit recalls Patricia White's analysis of lesbian cinephilia in classical Hollywood cinema and 1990s lesbian independent video. (Philippine cinema's star system—in both the studio period and the poststudio era that Nora and Vilma dominated—was modeled on Hollywood's.)[20] As White notes, "Female homoerotic desire is in a sense foundational to the star system, which as common (and marketing) sense would have it, appeals primarily to women." Its dependence on female audiences and their "same-sex star crushes" notwithstanding, commercial cinema has often "seemed to disavow the fact that lesbians were part of the 'general public' who bought tickets."[21] White offers this incisive analysis of

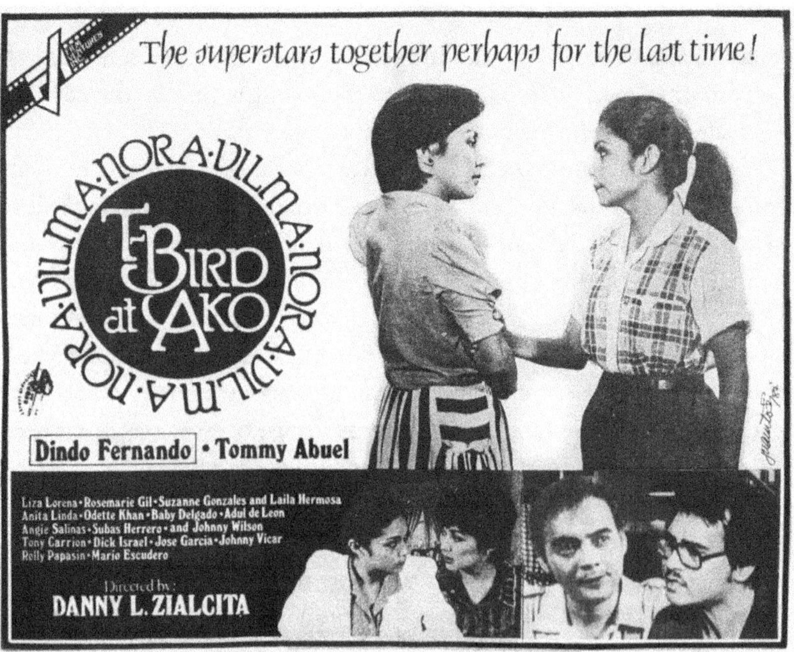

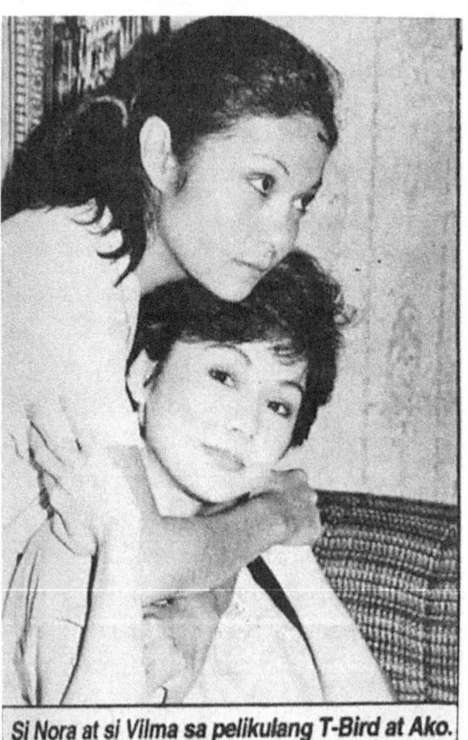

4.1 Print advertisement for *T-Bird at Ako* (T-bird and I/Lesbian love; dir. Danny Zialcita, 1982) during its initial theatrical release. Courtesy of Simon Santos.

4.2 A publicity image posted online said to have accompanied a film review in the entertainment magazine *Parade* dated September 22, 1982. The caption reads: "Nora and Vilma in the Film *T-Bird at Ako*." Source: Cruz, "T-Bird at Ako."

cinematic pleasure via lesbian cinephilia: "Lesbianism is both a social identity and a psychosexual investment in loving women. One goes to the movies and can evaluate what one sees there 'as a lesbian,' at the same time that something in the cinema experience calls forth, confirms, and specifies lesbian identities. I think it makes a kind of intuitive sense to link 'gynophilia'—love of women—with cinephilia—love of movies, to recognize that cinema's stock-in-trade, the eroticized image of Woman, is also addressed to us."[22]

White underscores that, for the most part, the lesbian spectator's "desire is solicited by the cinema, but not represented therein."[23] Departing from mainstream cinema's usual practice of "ghosting the lesbian," in Terry Castle's apt phrase, *T-Bird at Ako* frankly solicits and represents lesbian desire both diegetically and in the movie's promotional paratexts.[24] Cannily addressing women-who-love-women in the audience while simultaneously calling out and calling forth the girl-girl star crushes integral to Noranian and Vilmanian fandom, publicity for *T-Bird at Ako* included a game segment in one television variety show in which female contestants acted out scenes from the film.

In a snapshot of one such TV segment, likely taken from the long-running noontime show *Eat Bulaga!*, two female contestants reenact a dramatic scene in the film in which Sabel and Sylvia give one another a hard slap after the former flatly refuses the latter's advances (figure 4.3).[25] A gigantic movie billboard for *T-Bird at Ako* forms the backdrop of the scene. The top of the billboard reads, "The clash of the superstars in the most explosive story to hit the screen!" while the center of the billboard features the movie title radially framed by the two stars' names, mimicking the credit sequences at the beginning and end of the film. (A reviewer explains that filmmakers "came up with a circular 'billing' so you couldn't tell whose name appeared first," thus symbolically according equal importance to the screen queens.)[26] In the foreground of the photograph, two fan-contestants are costumed according to character. The competitor playing the femme Sabel/Vilma (*center left*) is attired in a dress, while the other competitor playing Sylvia/Nora (*center right*) wears an outfit a good deal more masculine than any of Nora's costumes in the film. This small but significant modification in what appears to be an otherwise faithful fan reenactment articulates, I think, her queer fans' desire to see Nora sport a more explicitly butch sartorial style than *T-Bird at Ako*'s costume design allowed.

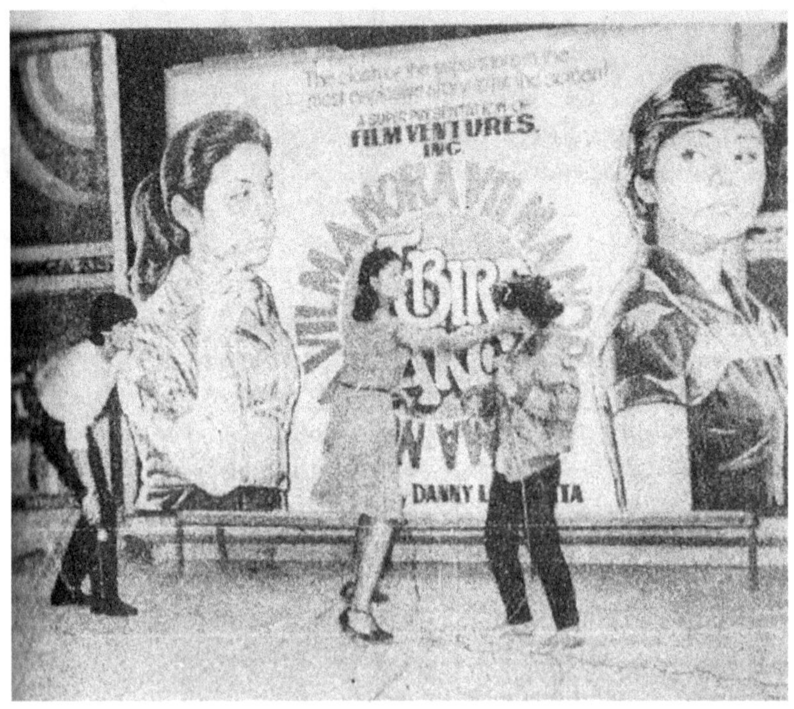

4.3 Fan contestants on a television variety show reenact a climactic scene from *T-Bird at Ako*. *Parade*, August 26, 1983.

CLASS DISPARITIES AND THE RACIAL POLITICS OF MESTIZA STARDOM

Identifying as one of the many "men who dream of becoming Nora Aunor," Jorge Demafeliz, a lifelong Noranian and overseas Filipino worker in Riyadh, recalls a kindergarten memory. As a child, he overheard two housemaids quarreling about the relative merits of Vilma versus Nora. One of the women asserted, "Vilma is mestiza. Nora is *negra*! Vilma is beautiful. Nora is ugly" (*Mestisa si* Vilma. *Negra si* Nora! *Maganda si* Vilma. *Pangit si* Nora). In response, the author's aunt chastens the Vilmanian, replacing the racist epithet *negra* with the connotatively positive term *morena* (a dark-complexioned girl). "Don't ever say Nora is ugly," the aunt warned. "She is beautiful and a wonderful singer. And she is not *negra* but *morena*" (*Hindi siya negra—morena*).[27] In addition to exposing the racialized dimensions of the two performers' star texts, Demafeliz's recollection condenses the classed and gendered dimensions of the stars' loyal following, among whom lower-income provincial and urban women and *bakla* were prominent.

The dialogue of *T-Bird at Ako* forthrightly references racialized casting practices and ideologies of beauty in the Filipino movie industry. Sabel/ Vilma is repeatedly referred to as *maputi* (white) by other characters. When she first learns that Sylvia/Nora posted her bail, Sabel is wary and derisive: "Are we relatives? That seems unlikely. Our skin color is different" (*Magkaiba tayo ng kulay*). Such dialogue reflexively alludes to skin color as a point of contention between Vilmanians and Noranians while also acknowledging the profound degree to which Nora's star image upended the racial logic of mestizo/a stardom. As demonstrated by Nicanor Tiongson in an influential 1979 essay, the colonial aesthetic common to both theater and popular cinema boils down to a simple maxim undergirding a racialized politics of casting: "White is beautiful" (*Maganda ang maputi*). In Tiongson's classic essay, Nora is mentioned as the sole exception to the rule of mestiza stardom in contemporary Philippine cinema.[28]

In the poststudio era, Nora, the first "brown beauty" (*kayumangging kaligatan*) of Philippine cinema, forced an unprecedented break with the film industry's reliance on mestizo/a stardom, the practice of casting fair-skinned actors with foreign features in leading roles. Nora's defiance of the film industry's axiom "White is beautiful," so prominently foregrounded in *T-Bird at Ako*, has never again been replicated on such a scale by another Filipino film star. As I have elaborated elsewhere, Nora's superstardom broke away from a racialized politics of casting that enshrined fair-skinned mestizo/a performers as the apex of physical beauty and cinematic glamour. In the studio era, matinee idols were invariably mixed-race actors whose light skin and European or American features allowed them to be packaged as local approximations of Hollywood stars. More than a figure of race mixture, the mestizo/a star in Filipino cinema is also imagined as situated between the "whiteness" of the Hollywood star or of the post/colonial elite and the "brownness" of lower-income urban audiences who constitute the bulk of the nation's filmgoers. Nora became the first nonmestiza star of Philippine cinema and, at the peak of her popularity in the late 1960s and early 1970s, the most powerful star in its history.[29]

In its depiction of an ultimately one-sided lesbian courtship, *T-Bird at Ako* emphasizes racial logics and class disparities between strong queer earners (coded as either butch or androgynous, like Sylvia) and the economic vulnerability of the beautiful straight women they ardently desire (like the feminine Sabel). This casts butch-femme relationships in a purely transactional light, suggesting that Rubia (Leila Hermosa), the girlfriend of one of Sylvia's legal clients, Maxie (Odette Khan), is not a queer femme but, rather, a cynical gold digger. Similarly, the narrative suggests that Sabel was slow to choose her cash-strapped ex-boyfriend Dante (Dindo Fernando) over Sylvia due to a sense of financial indebtedness to Sylvia, not genuine homoerotic attraction. The assumption that butch lesbians and T-birds are obliged to compensate femme women for their romantic or sexual companionship brings to mind a similarly insidious logic remarked by contemporary ethnographers. Ryan Richard Thoreson's research on LGBTQ+ activism in the Philippines reveals that in exchange for social acceptance, many tomboys and *bakla* are expected to be economically productive workers. Queer "breadwinners" are obliged to support their relatives while remaining single and are discouraged from starting new families of their own.[30]

IN DEFENSE OF QUEER ANACHRONISM

To my mind, the scholarly challenges posed by *T-Bird at Ako*'s politics of gender and sexuality involve issues of anachronism, translation, and language that implicate not only English and Tagalog-based Filipino but also the Western-derived LGBTQ+ vocabulary that gained global currency decades after the film's initial release in 1982. The movie uses the terms *lesbian*, *tomboy*, *T-bird*, and *tibo*. While this nomenclature is rooted in early eighties Manila, only the first two terms dovetail with contemporary LGBTQ+ and Filipinx usage. The title word *T-bird*, for example, is a strongly generational term no longer current in local jargon, though it was still in use among diasporic Filipina communities in Hong Kong in the 1990s and perhaps elsewhere beyond that decade.[31]

Linguistic, political, and historical forces have come to bear on the term *Filipino* itself. The *x* in *Filipinx* attempts to replace the *a* in *Filipina* and the *o* in *Filipino*, unsettling the binary genders presumed by nouns of national-cultural belonging in favor of gender inclusivity, expansiveness, and the move toward nonbinary identification espoused by some (though not all) feminist, queer, and trans communities.[32] In response to Dictionary.com's addition of "Filipinx" and "Pinxy" entries to its online lexicon in September 2020, several commentators denounced what they saw as a neocolonial imposition of a term that gained currency in Philippine American contexts onto a domestic setting in which the word *Filipinx* does not enjoy popular usage.[33] This rhetoric tends to valorize the "homeland" as the definitive locus of cultural authenticity while invalidating migrant experiences of multilingualism and cultural contact. At a Cinema Sala roundtable that posed the polemical question, "Are we Filipinx?," panelist Marrian Pio Roda Ching recalled an illuminating historical precedent discussed in Dawn Bohulano Mabalon's historiographical study, *Little Manila Is in the Heart*.[34] Mabalon recounts that the words *pinoy* and *pinay*, widely embraced in the Philippines as popular synonyms for Filipino and Filipina, respectively, are neologisms of diasporic (i.e., not national) origin that initially referred to Philippine American subjectivities.[35] Historically evolving modes of self-naming are messier than assumed dichotomies between the "authentically" domestic-as-national and the "inauthentically" diasporic-as-colonial would suggest.

While doing research for my own remarks at the roundtable, I came to realize that the *x* in *Filipinx* marks the intersection between the gender-transgressive aspects valued by trans and queer communities and the translocal realities of the Philippine diaspora. The contemporary push to replace the masculine *o* and the feminine *a* in Spanish-derived nouns and adjectives points to a shared history of colonization between Latinx and Filipinx experiences, alluding to earlier debates around *Latinx* that emerged in the Latino/a/x community from 2004 onward.[36] Thus, while *Filipinx* bears the imprint of colonialism and neocolonialism (what Vicente Rafael calls "white love"), it also registers what we might consider (following José Esteban Muñoz) a "brown" horizon of affect, contact, and solidarity between Philippine migrants and overseas Filipino/a/x workers (OFW) and Latinx communities.[37]

The eponymous, self-described "T-bird" character in the narrative, Maxie, played with bravado by actress Odette Khan, is considered a woman by the film's protagonists (though bilingual characters refer to Maxie in English as "she," Maxie never uses a gendered pronoun reflexively; Filipino pronouns are gender-neutral). In contrast, a contemporary LGBTQ+ perspective is likely to refer to Maxie as Filipinx and to hear an echo of trans masculine subjectivity in Maxie's declaration "*Lalaki naman ako* [After all, I'm a man], from top to bottom." Such contemporary viewers might opt to use *he* or the nonbinary pronoun *they* to refer to Maxie. Having wrestled with these temporal, political, sexual, and linguistic incommensurabilities, I have resolved to refer to Maxie as *he* in my analysis. That is, I have decided to reflexively espouse a queer use of anachronism rather than risk reinscribing the hetero- and cis-normativity that, to twenty-first-century eyes, already pervades the film.

I am hardly the first viewer to confront such quandaries in queer Asian cinemas.[38] An anonymous contribution to the lifestyle website Spot.ph titled "Revisiting the Lesbian-Themed Film Classic T-Bird at Ako," posted a year before the ABS-CBN restoration, notes: "This movie's significance is probably *better appreciated today* than when it was released in 1982 . . . but 'T-Bird' is also *a product of the sexism of its time*, all the more *compounded by the spicy dialogue* that is a trademark of a Zialcita movie."[39] The dichotomy between "the sexism of its time" and a "significance . . . better appreciated today," one that is exacerbated by the acerbic wit typical of a Zialcita film, raises the question of anachronism, that is, the imposition of an LGBTQ+ and/or Filipinx interpretive lens onto a place and period—1980s Manila—to which it does not chronologically belong. Scholarship on Philippine gender and sexuality also problematizes the term *queer* as such. In his ethnographic study of LGBTQ+ activism in the Philippines circa 2008 through 2011, Thoreson argues that *queer* is useful as an "expansive," "etic" term referring to "all those who diverge from a predominant sex and gender system" while acknowledging that the term is "rarely used" in LGBTQ+ advocacy in the Philippines.[40]

One entry point into the debate on anachronism and language in queer historiography involves David Halperin's important reminder that past sexual cultures were not organized along the homo/hetero binary familiar to us today. For example, ancient Greek pederasty is not synonymous with modern homosexuality.[41] Halperin's warning—against projecting modern sexual rubrics as universal or transhistorical—articulates what has been called the "alteritist" position in queer historiography. In this view, the first ethical principle of a history of sexuality is to "understand our own inability to understand" the "erotic particularities" of the past, resisting the tendency to tell stories about past others that cast our profoundly different predecessors as versions of our present selves.[42]

The alteritist warning is well taken; without obviating it, I also see the value of queer feminist theorists' resistance to this position. Edgar Allan Poe's short story "Ligeia" (1838), for example, closes with a scene of apparent lesbian spectral possession involving the narrator's dead wife, Ligeia, and her recently deceased substitute, Rowena. Valerie Rohy acknowledges that such a presentist reading can only be "historically illegitimate," since Poe's story predates the medicalized constitution of *lesbian* and *homosexual* as deviants. The lesbian resonance of "Ligeia" is historically implausible, "but just the same," Rohy writes, "it hangs before our eyes." Such queer optical illusions in older works are anamorphic images, visible only when seen at an angle, considered from the perspective of "the wrong time."[43] Carolyn Dinshaw might call this an "intentional collapse of conventional historical time" that registers the queer need for "affective connection—a touch across time."[44] Felt correspondences with intractably different pasts—the glint of lesbianism in Poe, the flash of trans masc or gender nonconforming subjectivity in *T-Bird at Ako*—pose hard questions about historical anachronisms and the legitimacy of transtemporal, cross-cultural interpretations.

The transgressive genders and sexual desires depicted in *T-Bird at Ako* often strain against the confines of a commercial, star-driven blockbuster and the language of the film's own time. As such, my consideration of *T-Bird at Ako* aspires to hold two interpretive polarities in generative tension with one another. On the one hand, I probe the historically grounded queer vernacular pedagogy the movie offers. The film defines the terms *T-bird*, *lesbian*, and *tibo* in historically specific ways for the benefit of diegetic characters and off-screen audiences alike. On the other hand, my analysis unfolds within a willfully anachronistic, retrospective reception framework that sees *T-Bird at Ako* as part of a pleasurable and usable queer past.

A QUEER VERNACULAR PEDAGOGY

Early in the film, Babette (Suzanne Gonzales), another lawyer at Sylvia's firm, reads a dictionary definition of *lesbian* aloud while conducting research for Maxie's legal defense:

> BABETTE: According to Daniel Webster, a lesbian is a female homosexual. . . . According to the Keynes report, *Reader's Digest*, November issue 1959, 90 percent of all women are born lesbians. It just depends on the circumstances. . . . Good thing I wasn't included. I belong to the 10 percent. I'm all woman.

Having just cited a 1959 report stating that 90 percent of women are born lesbian but that their ultimate sexual orientation will depend on their environment, Babette blithely maintains she is one of the 10 percent who are not lesbian, but "all woman." Babette's conflation of gender (being "all woman") with sexual orientation (being straight) is not unusual in casual Filipino/a/x conversation. In contrast to transnational LGBTQ+ vocabularies that distinguish between sexuality and gender, the Philippine context is characterized by "the flexibility of sexuality [*sekswalidad*] and gender [*kasarian*] as polysemantic terms."[45] In *T-Bird at Ako*, this conflation gives rise to heteronormative logics that align gender identification with presumptive heterosexuality. Maxie's girlfriend, who is cheating on him with a cis man, explains with a shrug: "I'm a woman, so I need a man."

Yet alongside *T-Bird at Ako*'s gender essentialism, the film also evinces a keen interest in the fluid queer lexicon (in English and Tagalog) circulating in Manila at the time of its production. Several scenes offer a subcultural vernacular pedagogy for both characters and audiences. In the first of these, Sabel learns from her friend Perla (Baby Delgado) that *tibo* means lesbian and that a person's sexual orientation can't be gleaned from appearances. When Sabel objects that Sylvia doesn't look like a lesbian, Perla says she was once stalked by a beautiful *tibo* who looked like Elizabeth Taylor. This offhand remark suggests that a woman who desires other women may look conventionally feminine, though elsewhere the film reverts to its penchant for collapsing gender presentation with sexual orientation. Yet this blurring can be read multivalently.

In an essay on transnational and transcultural "Filipino/a tomboy masculinities and manhoods," Kale Bantigue Fajardo analyzes the work of Nice Rodriguez, a writer who has lived in both Canada and the Philippines. Both Fajardo's incisive discussion of Rodriguez's short stories and the latter's interview responses to Fajardo are remarkable for capturing the rich messiness and barely translatable complexity of what Fajardo describes as Rodriguez's "transculturated use of the term butch" both as an "approximation of tomboy" and as a lived, fluid naming situated in "a kind of gender-nonconforming, transgender Filipino masculinity/maleness/manhood, in addition to female masculinity or lesbianism."[46] Particularly striking are Rodriguez's remarks about the incommensurability between North American and Tagalog understandings of "tomboy": "Tomboy is such a lame word in North America. It doesn't have the same meaning in Tagalog. Butch, lesbian and dyke were approximations of what I meant. I learned about transgender and transsexual much later. . . . It took me a while to know the difference between the two. I am more comfortable with Tibo and Pars [Filipino variations or equivalents of 'tomboy'] but like I said the terms I used were approximations."[47]

Rodriguez's remarks to Fajardo help me make sense of *T-Bird at Ako*, a film in which the dialogue moves restlessly between overlapping approximations that are seen as both equivalent and yet not quite synonymous: *tibo* is and is not "lesbian," which is and is not coextensive with "T-bird," which is and is not translatable to *babae* (woman) or *lalaki* (man). Fajardo remarks of Rodriguez's writing, "There appears to be slippage or overlap between 'lesbian' desire and sex and tomboy transgenderism or transsexualism." Rather than fault this "lack of absolute clarity or transparency," Fajardo emphasizes the way in which Rodriguez, writing in and between queer worlds in Manila and Toronto, "highlights Filipino queer or transgender transnational sex-gender fluidities."[48] While different words for nonheterosexual or nonheteronormative sex/gender identifications and practices have different effects, it's worth bearing the title of Julia Serano's online *Transgender Glossary* in mind: "There is no perfect word."[49]

In another scene in *T-Bird at Ako*, Maxie defines being a T-bird in terms of emphatic maleness (being a *lalaki*) and aggressive masculinity (*machong-macho*). While the movie does not elaborate on the significance of the *T* in *T-bird*, fieldwork on Filipinx communities overseas in subsequent decades may help fill in the gaps. Nicole Constable's 1997 study of Filipina domestic workers in Hong Kong explains, "The terms *T-bird* (short for 'thunderbird') or *tomboy* in Filipino slang refer to a lesbian; particularly one who adopts a masculine style of dress. A T-bird, I was told, is 'a gay,' but the term can also allude to a lesbian style of dress, common among Filipina workers."[50]

Ambiguously referring to both sexual orientation (lesbianism) and gender presentation (a butch sartorial style), *T-bird* alludes to classic muscle cars and the associated term *tomboy*, whose transnationalized twenty-first-century meanings encompass a spectrum of practices and identities related to sexuality and gender. In a 2008 study, Fajardo writes: "In Manila and other locations in the Philippines, *tomboy* is a term used to describe a range of gender and sexual practices and identities, including (1) woman-identified lesbianism often transculturated via white U.S.- or European-based notions of gender and sexuality, (2) working-class female-to-male transgender or transsexual embodiments and formations of masculinities where tomboys identify and/or live as lalaki (males/men), and (3) neither 'women,' 'lesbians,' or 'men' but an entirely different third or fourth gender formation."[51]

Awareness of linguistic nuance, cultural hybridity, and transnational flows in queer vocabularies demands an attentiveness to processes of vernacularization, that is, the translation (not straightforward reproduction) of transnational concerns into locally legible politics, which queer, trans, and feminist scholars of Asian media have variously conceptualized as "transculturated,"[52] "translingual" engagements that might foment "transversal queer alliances."[53] As Thoreson notes, the long shadow of US cultural, military, and economic imperialism and the widespread use of English in the Philippines have enabled the diffusion of transnational LGBTQ+ frameworks and vocabularies, even as those same conditions "foster suspicion and hostility toward Western and transnational projects."[54] Local understandings of *tomboy*, *lesbian*, *tibo*, and *T-bird* push back against homogeneous notions of global queering. This sensitivity to vernacularization is where *T-Bird at Ako*, with its keen ear for the pleasures of repartee, double entendres, and sharp turns of phrase, excels.

Though the translated English title, "Lesbian Love," seems relatively straightforward, the original Taglish (hybrid Tagalog and English) title deserves some reflection. In the bilingual phrase "T-Bird at Ako," the opening English word conveys a Filipinx queer subjectivity in a foreign tongue, while the ensuing Tagalog words, *at ako*, meaning "and I," invite viewer identification with a referentially ambiguous diegetic character. The T-bird in question could be Maxie and/or Sylvia, while "I" could be Sylvia, Sabel, Babette, or the social audience member whose experience of the film creates a relationship with queer subjectivity. The ambiguity of the title centers on the interpretive undecidability of Sylvia, who at the beginning of the film wonders aloud at her possible lesbianism: "What if I meet a woman I'm physically attracted to?" At the plot's dramatic climax, however, Sylvia's declaration of love for Sabel is explicitly male-identified: "Sabel, I'm crazy about you alone. I'm all man" (*Sabel, sa'yo lang ako sira. Lalaking lalaki*). The semantic ambiguity of the title and the interpretive ambivalence surrounding Nora-as-Sylvia (is s/he a man, a woman, a *tibo*, a T-bird, or a lesbian?) highlight the protean meanings of terms like *tomboy* and *T-bird*, which might refer to "male or masculine-identified females" or to a "(transgender) tomboy."[55]

The chronological impropriety of my analysis, which anachronistically fast-forwards, freezes, and rewinds between moments of gender normativity and a spectrum of queer potentialities opened by my retrospective encounter with *T-Bird at Ako*, aspires to a temporal unruliness. Rather than deriding *T-Bird at Ako* as embarrassingly old-fashioned, "not-quite-queer-enough," and politically behind the times, I am, like Elizabeth Freeman, "emotionally compelled by the not-quite-queer-enough longing for form that turns us backward to prior moments, forward to embarrassing utopias, sideways to forms of being and belonging that seem, on the face of it, completely banal. . . . *We can't know in advance, but only retrospectively, if even then, what is queer and what is not.*"[56]

QUEER DESIRABILITY ON TRIAL

T-Bird at Ako opens with a dramatic courtroom scene in which Maxie is being cross-examined by a bullying prosecutor (Johnny Wilson). Charged with homicide, Maxie claims that he stabbed his girlfriend's ex-boyfriend in self-defense. Maxie testifies that the ex-boyfriend stormed into the couple's home, enraged at having been jilted in favor of Maxie; Maxie subsequently stabbed him with a kitchen knife. The prosecutor's ensuing attempt to cast doubt on Maxie's testimony unfolds as a misogynist, homophobic, and transphobic diatribe. The prosecutor expresses incredulity that Maxie, whom he persists in misgendering as "Maximina" and regarding as a woman, would have "sufficient strength to overpower an angry man." Above all, the prosecutor refuses to believe that Maxie's girlfriend Rubia would have preferred Maxie to her former boyfriend. Addressing Maxie in Taglish while gesturing toward Rubia, the histrionic prosecutor asks:

> PROSECUTOR: Do you expect this court to believe that you possess sufficient strength—as cousin to Hercules and equal to Samson—that you have sufficient strength to overpower an angry man, who is superior to you physically?
>
> MAXIE: He was a small guy and he was drunk. There was nothing I could do about that.
>
> PROSECUTOR: And now you want the court to believe that this woman [gesturing at Rubia], the epitome of beauty, this mysterious woman involved in an abnormal love triangle, is in love with a creature from *The Planet of the Apes* like you?
>
> SYLVIA: Objection, your honor. The defendant has a name.
>
> JUDGE: Objection sustained. The private prosecutor is reminded to refrain from using such language. The defendant is still a human being with all the rights attached to that existence. You may proceed.

PROSECUTOR: What I'm trying to point out to this court, Your Honor, is the fact that this beautiful woman cannot conceivably be in love with this . . . this . . . [sputters] human being![57]

This over-the-top exchange is punctuated by various characters' reaction shots: Sylvia, trying to control her impatience; Rubia, proud of Maxie for standing up to the pompous prosecutor, but also uncomfortable with their queer relationship being thrown into the public eye; and the judge, increasingly annoyed by the prosecutor's grandstanding. Reproaching the prosecutor for his dehumanizing characterization of Maxie, the judge reminds the prosecutor of the defendant's human rights. (The film's brief invocation of human rights likely had a different significance in the Marcos period—during which it had a pronounced antidictatorship resonance—than in the era of gay rights and LGBTQ+ activism.)[58]

Most strikingly, this hyperbolic courtroom scene construes the question of the credibility of Maxie's testimony as a question of whether an "attractive" (read, conventionally feminine) woman would ever choose a T-bird over a man. The use of the courtroom drama as a framing device for a film that advocates a measure of tolerance and respect for lesbians, T-birds, and *tibo* motivates the repeated demand, articulated both by the prosecutor and, later, by Sylvia herself, that Maxie mount an explicit defense of not only a queer person's desire but also a queer person's desirability.

Sylvia puts the question directly to Maxie in a subsequent scene:

SYLVIA: Explain to me why you should be loved more than a man.

. . .

MAXIE: Whatever a man lacks, I can make up for. [*Kung anong kakulangan ng lalaki, pinupuno ko.*] I know, if I were a car, I would be missing a part. That's why I'm considerate, thoughtful, and faithful. In short, I am mother, father, brother, sister, friend, and lover.

When Maxie asks whether Sylvia has come to doubt his account of events, Sylvia replies in the negative but points out that the prosecutor has managed to shift the terms under which the trial is conducted:

SYLVIA: The direction of the trial has changed. It's become a question of whether a woman could possibly love a lesbian over a man.

> MAXIE: Objection, attorney. I'm not a lesbian, I'm a T-bird. . . . There's a difference. . . . A lesbian is like a star-fruit [*balimbing*], a turncoat, two-sided. A woman's body, a man's heart, but sexually restless [*malikot*]. A T-bird is hypermacho. Like a Texas fighting cock that fights past death. A purebred [*purong-puro*].

At such moments, the movie is less concerned with Sylvia's existential question ("Am I a lesbian?") than it is simultaneously fascinated and repulsed by the question of a T-bird's desirability. Any answer to the repeatedly posed question of whether a femme cis woman could possibly love a lesbian or a T-bird more than she could love a man is foreclosed by the film's normative, gender-essentialist logic, repeated throughout, that a "woman needs a man," and by its persistent conflation of sexual orientation and gender presentation (the prosecutor is incredulous at the thought that Rubia, a feminine-presenting cis female, could be a lesbian). *T-Bird at Ako*'s central question is urgently posed and articulated before transgender sociopolitical movements, particularly their mainstreaming of the prefixes *cis-* and *trans-*, had denaturalized the link between gender identity, expression, embodiment, and assigned sex at birth; and before the distinctions and convergences between various subjectivities—butch lesbian, female-to-male (FTM), and a spectrum of trans and nonbinary identifications—had been explored and debated. This is not to assert that the film is dated, only to acknowledge that the terms of my anachronistic analysis are not those of the film's own milieu.

According to Sabel, a *babae* ("woman," a category of gender) cannot be a lesbian (a category of sexuality). Similarly, in Maxie's monologue, the masculine "purity" of a T-bird is conflated with a sexual preference for cis women. Maxie contrasts the T-bird's "faithful" sexual orientation and "pure" gender identity with a lesbian's "turncoat" quality, figuratively conveyed by the word *balimbing* (a multifaceted starfruit). Combined with the adjective *malikot* (naughty, playful, or restless), *balimbing* in Maxie's disparaging usage connotes lesbian androgyny and/or a "traitorous" bisexuality.

Though never critically recognized as an "auteur" of Filipino cinema, Danny Zialcita was a prolific mainstream filmmaker active from the 1960s to the 1980s. Highly improvisational on set, Zialcita habitually disregarded the script, which reportedly led to clashes with screenwriter and LGBTQ+ activist Portia Ilagan over the film's heteronormative ending.[59] Exploring sexually risqué themes such as marital infidelity and homosexuality in an upper-class milieu, Zialcita films were best known for campy rapid-fire dialogue and verbal zingers that gave his movies a knowing, worldly quality.[60]

Given the improvisational character of Zialcita's filmmaking style, authorship of Maxie's interpretively rich, impossible to translate dialogue is hard to pin down: Are these the words of queer-identified screenwriter Portia Ilagan, or were these generated by the actress, the director, or both in the course of filming the scene?

Visually, much of the conversation unfolds as a shot-reverse-shot sequence between Maxie and Sylvia, their reflections prominent in medium close-ups and medium shots as they lean against a glass door (figures 4.4 and 4.5). The visual doubling of the characters and the combative tone of their conversation tend to cast them as diametric opposites rather than potential allies. Sylvia, the feminist and possibly lesbian or T-bird lawyer, is reserved, serious, and cerebral; Maxie, the boastful, homicidal T-bird, is a loose cannon. From this scene onward, Maxie's role in the plot dwindles; when we next see him, Maxie will have caught his girlfriend in bed with another man and killed them both.

Maxie confesses to the dual homicide in the presence of police officers but expects Sylvia to get him acquitted based on the doctrine of *destierro*, a controversial Philippine law that protects the so-called honor killing of a woman who has besmirched the family honor (figure 4.6), Citing a husband's right to kill his wife and her lover upon catching them in flagrante delicto, Maxie, who identifies as Rubia's husband on the basis of his provision of financial support, expects Sylvia to mount a vigorous defense on his behalf. Visibly shocked and exasperated, Sylvia refuses to take on Maxie's defense, stating flatly: "She was not your spouse." The T-bird's character arc ends abruptly with this brief scene, filmed decades before the emergence of feminist arguments for the repeal of *destierro* and queer legislative advocacies for the legalization of same-sex marriage.[61]

In contrast to what *T-Bird at Ako* imagines as a zero-sum rivalry between T-birds, *tibo*, lesbians, and cis males, Fajardo's fieldwork on Filipino seamen, conducted nearly two decades after the initial release of the film, suggests that what were once considered "watertight" heterosexual masculinities have begun "to leak, revealing instead the connections and fluidities between conventional and transgender masculinities."[62] While *T-Bird at Ako* explores friendships and romances between straight and

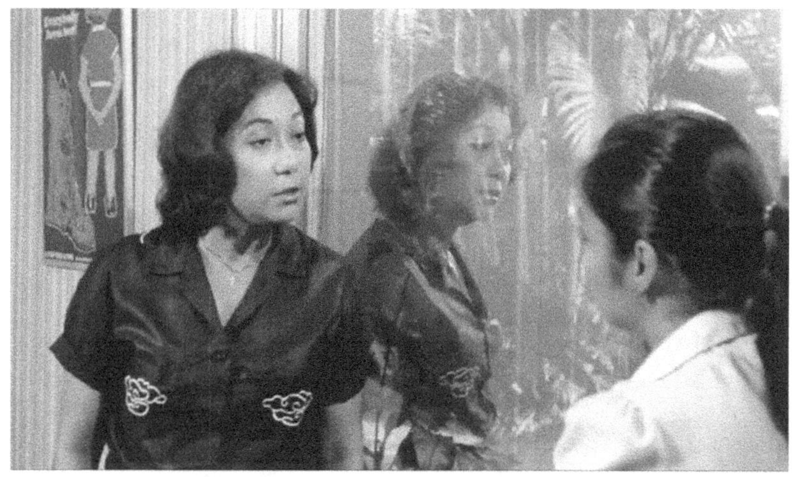

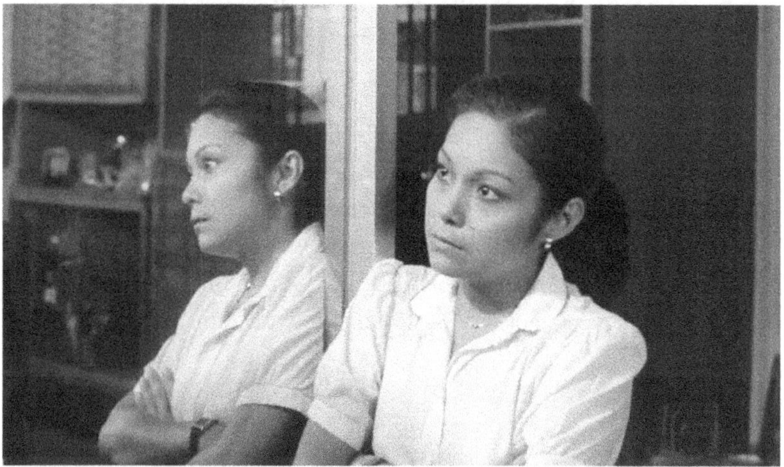

4.4 & 4.5 Motifs of doubling and reflection are prominent in the conversation between Maxie (Odette Khan, left) and Sylvia (Nora Aunor, right) in *T-Bird at Ako*. Film stills.

queer femininities among its fictional characters (Sylvia, Babette, and Sabel), the film is palpably more anxious about female and trans masculinities, depicted as the perverse opposite of heterosexual cis male masculinity. The demonized Maxie kills two cis men who are romantically involved with Rubia in the film: the first in self-defense and the second in a jealous rage. The implication is clear: straight women and lesbians can be friends while cis men and T-birds are bitter enemies; cis women will "naturally"

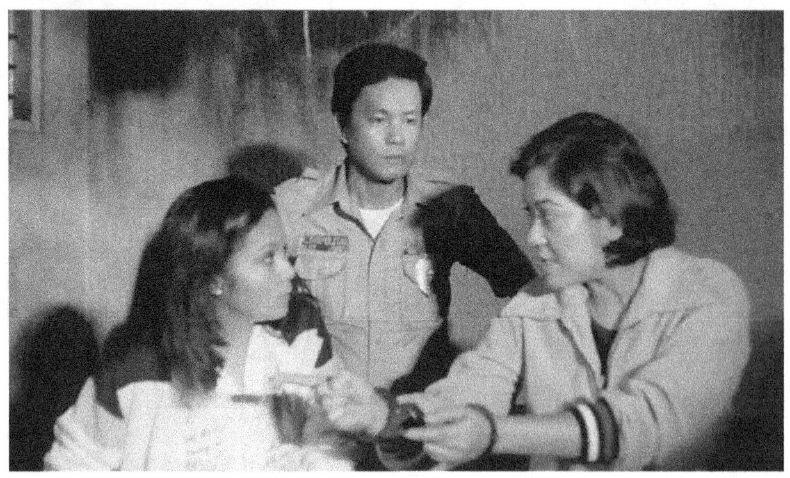

4.6 In *T-Bird at Ako*, a handcuffed Maxie confesses to dual homicide in the presence of a police officer but expects Sylvia to get him acquitted based on the legal doctrine of *destierro*. Film still.

prefer the former. In precluding, then, what Fajardo would call "a more expansive and inclusive understanding of Filipino masculinities," *T-Bird at Ako* articulates a particular vision of same-sex sociality and desire among characters who identify unproblematically as women while foreclosing a more relational view of cis, trans, straight, and queer masculinities.

COMPULSORY HETEROSEXUALITY AND THE MARCOS FAMILY ROMANCE

What Libay Linsangan Cantor calls the "heterocentric happy ending" is a mainstay of depictions of lesbians in Philippine cinema, from the "gender-bending comedies" of the studio era to the explicitly lesbian-themed narratives of the eighties. In such narrative resolutions, "the female-bodied persona of such characters—who are often presented as mannish tomboys, or even butch lesbians who do not self-identify as such—get 'rescued' or 'turned' back to being heterosexual when a cisgendered-identifying male body expresses his love for her, tries to woo her back to heterosexuality, and succeeds." Cantor notes that the triumph of compulsory heterosexuality in these endings is mirrored by a corresponding return to conventional gender presentation: "The mannish tomboy is no more, replaced by a feminine-dressed leading lady to partner with her dashing prince charming."[63]

When Sabel rebuffs Sylvia in *T-Bird at Ako,* the spurned lawyer implores Jake (Tommy Abuel), a male attorney whose courtship she has repeatedly ignored, to sweep her off her feet and "make [her] feel like a woman." Aghast to learn that Sylvia is in love with another woman, Jake admonishes her: "If you're a woman, be a woman!" Jake gives Sylvia an ultimatum: "If you're coming back to me, you'd better be dressed like a woman, with the body and heart of a woman inside it" (*Kung babalik ka, naka damit babae, katawang babae, pusong babae ang nasa loob*). By the end of the movie, a chastened and smiling Sylvia goes on a date with Jake wearing a colorful striped dress; apparently, sexual preference, gender presentation, and embodiment are now appropriately aligned.

The film ends with a split-screen freeze-frame that parallels the final heterosexual couplings of both Sylvia and Sabel (the latter has decided to marry her ex, Dante). This unsatisfying straight ending recalls the Hollywood characters played by lesbian icon Marlene Dietrich. While Dietrich's androgynous heroines might initially cruise women, they would invariably end up with men. Writing of the Dietrich film *Morocco* (1930), Andrea Weiss wryly observes, "This flirtation with a woman, only to give the flower to the man, is a flirtation with the lesbian spectator as well, by offering a potentially lesbian ending only for the film to conclude heterosexually."[64] In the case of *T-Bird at Ako*, however, our immersion in the fictional narrative is punctured almost immediately, as the extradiegetic star names "Nora" and "Vilma" are rapidly superimposed over the screen in different fonts (figure 4.7). The "happy" heterocentric ending is overshadowed by screen credits that pointedly remind us of the thrill of casting two superstars in a lesbian romance.

The heteronormative ending of *T-Bird at Ako* is prefigured throughout the movie by mise-en-scène: the wall art and foreground/background dynamics of various settings moralize against same-sex relationships by implying Roman Catholic and Marcosian arguments for compulsory heterosexuality. On the first night that Sabel sleeps over at Sylvia's house, Sylvia creeps into the former's bedroom and ogles Sabel's sleeping form. Sylvia's voyeuristic sexual objectification of Sabel is implicitly reproached by a large crucifix over Sabel's bed (figure 4.8). In their first romantic quarrel, Sabel refuses to choose Sylvia over her ex-boyfriend; their altercation unfolds in front of a religious painting of Jesus surrounded by worshippers

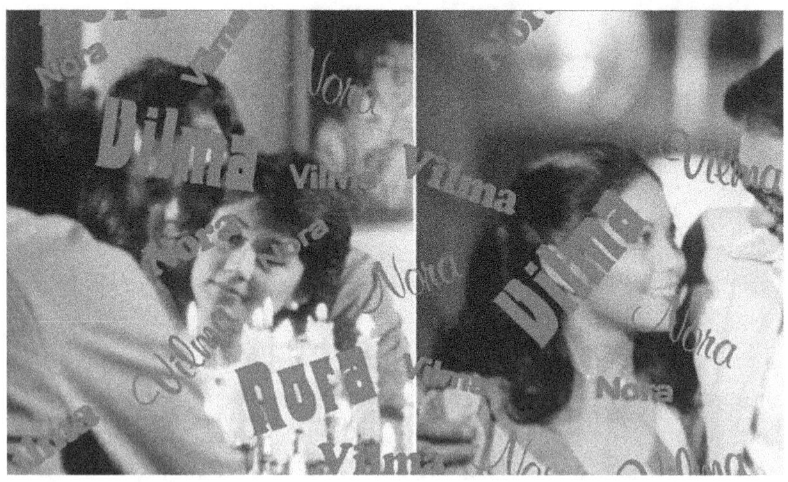

4.7 *T-Bird at Ako*'s final split-screen shot of Sabel (Vilma Santos) and Sylvia's heterosexual "happy ending" is disrupted by screen credits of the two superstars, their names exploding onto the screen. Film still.

in a composition reminiscent of the Last Supper (figure 4.9). Most strikingly, the climactic breakup scene takes place in a public setting where Sylvia arrives to find Sabel staring up at a portrait of the conjugal dictators Imelda and Ferdinand Marcos, in the company of other dignitaries (figure 4.10). While narrative absorption usually works to occlude the profilmic, this is an instance in which, as Laura Mulvey puts it, "The time of the film's original moment of registration . . . suddenly burst[s] through its narrative time. . . . The now-ness of story time gives way to the then-ness of the time when the movie was made."[65] The Marcos portrait is strangely out of place in a melodramatic narrative that makes no overt references to the turbulent twilight years of the regime in which these performances were first filmed.

Robert Diaz describes queerness in Marcos era Manila-based cinema not only as "mark[ing] intimacies between economically and politically marginalized individuals in the city that challenge hetero-patriarchal notions of sexual behavior, affiliation, and consanguinity" but also as "embody[ing] the urban dweller's willful attachment to the wrong objects of affection."[66] Diaz's analysis is germane to Sylvia's queer desire for Sabel, which would be reprehensible in a predominantly Catholic Manila under martial law. In his reading of *Manila by Night* (dir. Ishmael Bernal, 1980), the Marcos era film whose affectionate depiction of a lesbian drug pusher

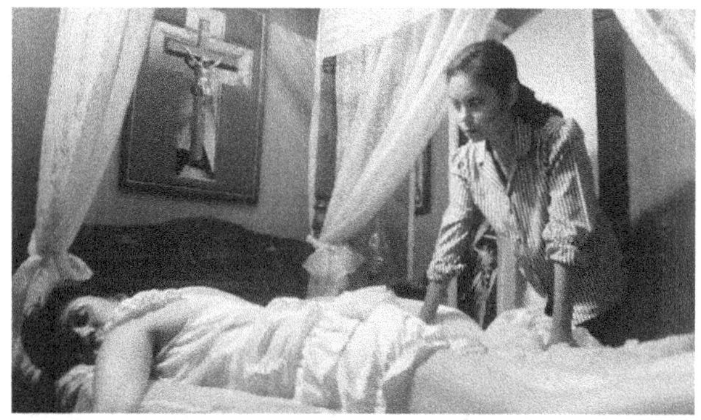

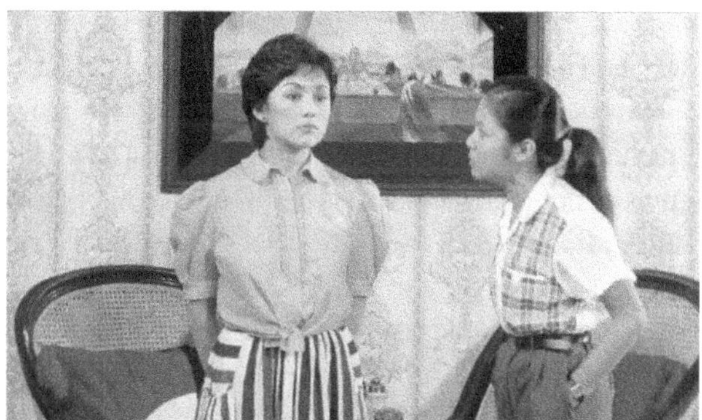

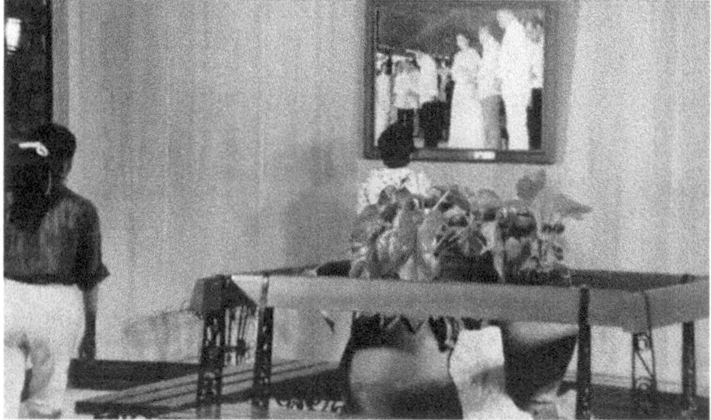

4.8 The religious wall decor in several scenes appears to comment on the narrative action. A crucifix above Sabel's bed implicitly reproaches Sylvia's voyeurism. Film still.

4.9 Sylvia and Sabel's first romantic quarrel unfolds against the backdrop of a painting reminiscent of the Last Supper. Film still.

4.10 The climactic breakup scene begins with a shot of Sabel staring fixedly up at a portrait of Imelda and Ferdinand Marcos in the company of other dignitaries. Film still.

makes it the primary New Cinema intertext for *T-Bird at Ako*, Diaz argues that "the characters' way of orienting their love . . . presents a powerful counter-discourse to the often-rehearsed narratives around love proliferated by the conjugal dictators to maintain a foothold on their rule."[67] In *Manila by Night*, released two years prior to *T-Bird at Ako*, queer love is an affront to the heteropatriarchal family romance that, as Talitha Espiritu and others have shown, formed the ideological bedrock of the Marcos dictatorship.[68]

Such scholarship helps me make sense of *T-Bird at Ako*'s conspicuous use of the Marcoses' portrait in a scene that culminates in queer heartbreak. The scene in which Sabel rejects Sylvia begins with a long shot of the women, their backs turned. The static camera holds for the duration of Sylvia's movement as she enters from the foreground, walks around a planter, and joins Sabel in the background; the latter gazes fixedly at a portrait of the Marcoses throughout (see figure 4.10). In a garrulous movie filled with chatter, this brief moment of silence, the stars' faces turned away (denying spectators mainstream cinema's usual visual frontality), invites us to notice the only face partially turned toward both camera and viewer in the frame: that of Imelda Marcos in the farthest background plane.[69]

An impatient Sylvia utters the first line in the scene: "Is there a problem? Why did we have to meet here?" Though Sylvia's annoyance might be due to the inconvenience of meeting outside when they are already living together (Sabel has been Sylvia's houseguest since the beginning of her court case), the question might also express Sylvia's aversion to meeting in a public place that openly professed its adherence to the Marcos regime and was, by implication, inhospitable to queers. As the scene unfolds, the push and pull of the two women's biting exchange, Sylvia articulating her desire for Sabel, Sabel rejecting it as a sin in the eyes of God, ends with each woman giving the other a hard slap on the cheek only a few feet away from the Marcoses' portrait, now off-screen. As *Manila by Night* and *T-Bird at Ako* suggest, modalities of queer life flourished even in the most strictly policed quarters of the Marcosian City of Man. Whether intentionally or not, the staging of queer discipline and defiance reveals a cinematic political unconscious: in *T-Bird at Ako*, the restoration of heteronormativity occurs in a space that reads as a figurative altar for the dictatorship.

OF RUMORS AND SUBCULTURAL QUEER PLEASURES

> Rumor and gossip constitute the unrecorded history of gay subculture.
>
> Something that, through gossip, is commonplace knowledge within gay subculture is often completely unknown on the outside, and if not unknown, at least unspeakable. It is this insistence by the dominant culture on making homosexuality invisible and unspeakable that both requires and enables us to locate gay history in rumor, innuendo, fleeting gestures and coded language—signs that should be recognized as historical sources.
>
> What the public knew, or what the gay subculture knew, about these stars' "real lives" cannot be separated from their star images. Whether these actresses were actually lesbian or bisexual is less relevant than how their star personae were perceived by lesbian audiences.
>
> —ANDREA WEISS, *Vampires and Violets*

Arguing for the historiographical value of gossip about movie stars in the formation of 1930s gay subcultures, Weiss makes several interconnected claims: first, that the so-called truth value of rumor with reference to specific stars is not what matters most. To infer a history of audience responses that have been rendered invisible and unspeakable, we must focus instead on how subcultural perceptions of certain gay and lesbian media icons—encoded as rumor, gossip, and innuendo—may be understood as a process of transcoding dominant cultural elements into "shared private values."[70]

Across a five-decade transmedia career spanning radio, television, film, and theater, Nora Aunor has generated a significant amount of gossip. In January 2011, *Showbiz Portal* ran an item headlined with the juicy question, "Nora Had an Affair with a Lesbian Named Portia Ilagan?" A Noranian reportedly "wrote to denounce Portia Ilagan, former student activist" and "admitted lesbian," for "all of a sudden declaring in public and on radio that she had an affair with Nora Aunor." The fan denied this as a vicious rumor and maintains that Ilagan "should have just kept silent about it and not stain[ed] the reputation of the one and only Superstar."[71] Though the fan letter did not identify Portia Ilagan as *T-Bird at Ako*'s screenwriter, Ilagan's public disclosure of her alleged affair with Nora casts the movie in a different light. Later that year, in October 2011, *Yes!* magazine offered readers an exhaustive profile of Nora's celebrity career, noting, "The biggest question mark hanging over Nora's personal life has to do with the persistent rumors linking her to women."[72]

The magazine's glamorous profile of Philippine cinema's first superstar is introduced on the cover with the tagline "And yes, she had a big crush on archrival Vilma" (figure 4.11). In the interview, Nora relates that, years before making *T-Bird at Ako*, she waited for hours in Vilma's hotel lobby to give her a bouquet of roses. Vilma politely invited her up to her suite, but when she got there, Nora was tongue-tied. She gave the rival star the bouquet and left after ten minutes. Laughing off the entire episode in retrospect, Nora notes that she and Vilma are now old friends and that Vilma serves as the godparent of Nora's fourth child.[73] This titillating anecdote was reprised in a 2015 video of a celebrity interview in which Nora retold the story on the eve of the premiere of ABS-CBN's restoration of *T-Bird at Ako*.[74] Patricia White notes that girl-girl star crushes are "the data of lesbian spectatorship theory."[75] Nora's thrilling admission of her teenage infatuation with Vilma echoes the positionality of lesbian spectators who have had crushes on these very stars.

Today, the *Yes!* interview is best remembered for Nora's measured confirmation of long-standing rumors regarding her sexual orientation. Remarking that her "rugged demeanor" (code for Nora's increasingly butch sartorial style as she aged) is rooted in a childhood tomboyism, Nora opines, "We shouldn't be ashamed of what we are. . . . Why not be whatever we are?" (*Hindi natin dapat ikahiya kung ano tayo. . . . Kung ano tayo*, why not, *di ba*?)[76] In third person, the interviewer recalls pouncing on the opportunity to ask Nora a long-simmering question:

> So is she [Nora] a lesbian?
>
> I'm still thinking about it. I sometimes think that's kind of what I am. [*Iniisip ko pa. Pakiramdam ko paminsan-minsan, parang gano'n na rin ako.*] Then she lets out a hearty guffaw.
>
> Is she bisexual?
>
> And then she lets out another hearty laugh. 'Maybe that's what I am. If that's what I am, it's still fun, right? At least, anything goes, that kind of thing. [*Baka nga gano'n ako. Kung gano'n ako, masaya pa rin, di ba? At least, pwede ka kahit ano, 'yong gano'n.*][77]

Nora's disclosure, which sent ripples throughout the Philippine entertainment world, is marked by a certain evasiveness. In Nora's syntax, the oft-repeated word *ganoon* ("like that," or "in that way") is an ambiguous predicate that enables a set of ellipses. Instead of saying "I might be a lesbian"

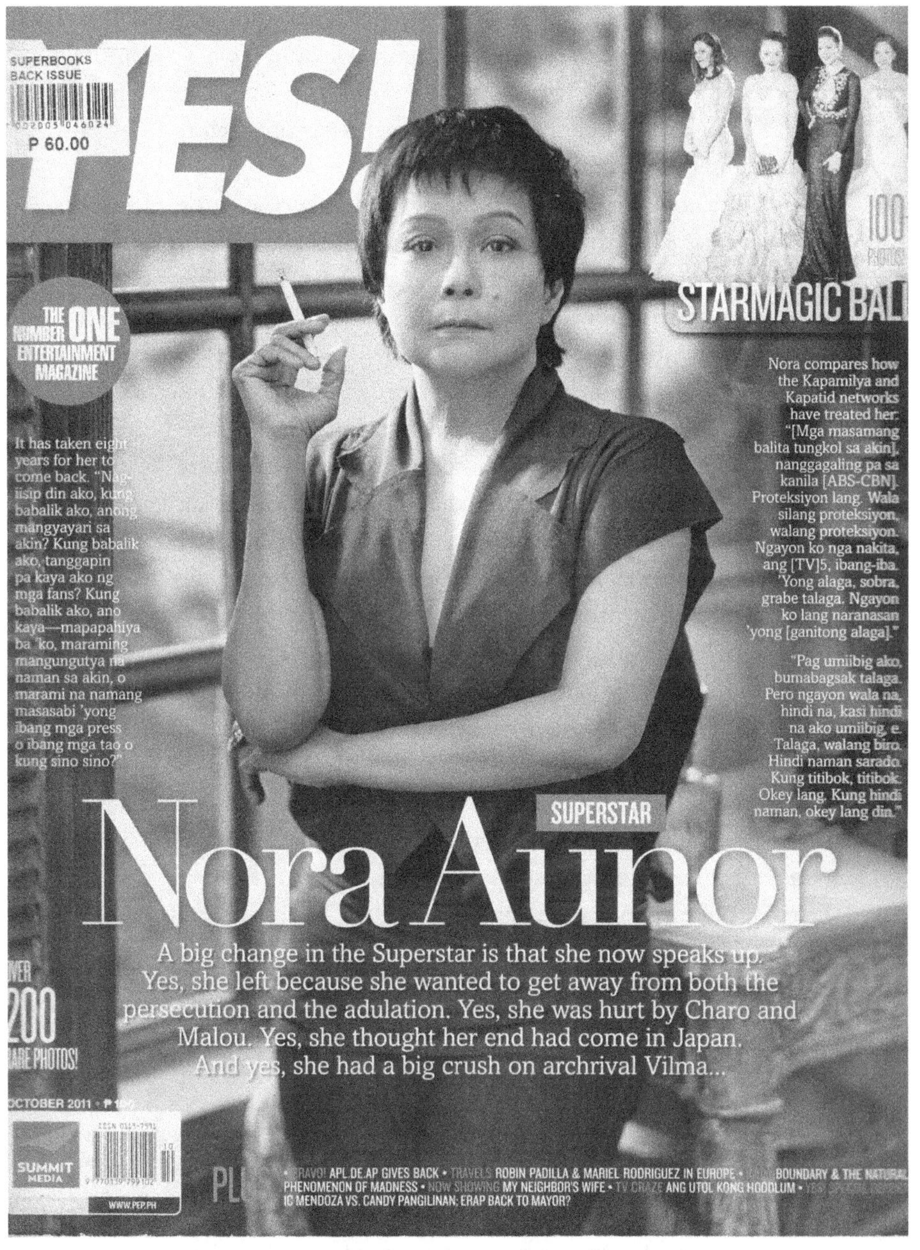

4.11 Nora Aunor's tell-all interview is the cover story of the October 2011 issue of *Yes!* magazine. The last sentence of the main cover line reads, "And yes, she had a big crush on archrival Vilma." Author's collection.

or "Maybe I am a bisexual," she tells her interviewer that she might be "that way." As several scholars have clarified, coming out and explicit disclosure, while crucial to post-Stonewall LGBTQ+ visibility politics in the United States, are not central in Philippine and other Asian queer cultures, where reticence and tacit acknowledgment prevail.[78]

As White notes, the farther-reaching significance of a female celebrity's coming out is the fact that it also "mak[es] their lesbian *audiences* visible."[79] More important than Nora's affirmation that she may be "kind of" queer is the fact that she has always had a queer audience that wanted her to be not-straight and gender nonconforming. My hunch is that in the years prior to Nora's 2011 revelation, queer viewers of a certain age were fascinated by *T-Bird at Ako*, relishing scenes in which Nora momentarily disrupted her expected roles to "act out that rumored sexuality on the screen."[80]

For queer feminist film scholars, the tactics by which lesbian audiences wrest pleasures from heteronormative mainstream cinema center on stardom and oppositional interpretive strategies that isolate moments of narrative, gesture, and performance, infusing them with forms of subcultural knowledge (like gossip). For White, the central question is how "marginalized groups . . . negotiate a pleasurable response to dominant cultural productions that would seem to exclude them," in effect "resolving the contradiction between desire and denial, delectable image and depressing story."[81] Three decades before Nora admitted to her fans that she "might be that way," *T-Bird at Ako*'s allusion to the superstar's rumored lesbianism invited subcultural audiences to seize moments of queer pleasure from an otherwise phobic, normative film.

THE SHOWGIRL AND THE KISS

> Traditionally, the woman displayed has functioned on two levels: as erotic object for the characters within the screen story, and as erotic object for the spectator within the auditorium, with a shifting tension between the looks on either side of the screen. For instance, the device of the show-girl allows the two looks to be unified technically without any apparent break in the diegesis. A woman performs within the narrative; the gaze of the spectator and that of the male characters in the film are neatly combined without breaking narrative verisimilitude.
>
> —LAURA MULVEY, "Visual Pleasure and Narrative Cinema"

Recalling on the work of Christian Metz, Laura Mulvey discerns three looks particular to classical Hollywood cinema: first, that of the camera recording the profilmic situation; second, that of the viewer facing the screen; and third, that of characters addressing each other within the world of the story. The first two looks, that of the camera and of the audience, are elided and conflated with the third, the gaze of the character, to reduce awareness of the constructed nature of the film and maximize spectatorial involvement. The spectacle of the showgirl's performance fuses the scopophilic, sexually objectifying male gaze of the diegetic characters with that of the spectator without calling attention to this melding of looks on- and off-screen.[82] However, in a striking departure from the gendered Hollywood conventions Mulvey identifies, the showgirl scene in *T-Bird at Ako* depicts Vilma-as-Sabel performing not primarily for cis male characters but for Nora-as-Sylvia alongside *tibo* and T-birds in the diegetic audience who are prominent in the staging and editing of the scene.

Sylvia had first heard Sabel described as a dancer whom other T-birds were crazy about in a bar called "Scene 1, Take 1." (The bar's reflexive name emphasizes the constructed nature of the movies.) Alluding to an earlier Vilma Santos film, *Burlesk Queen* (Burlesque queen; dir. Celso Ad. Castillo, 1977), Sabel's showgirl scene occurs right after Sylvia asks herself what would happen if she ever fell for a woman. This showgirl performance, replete with sultry looks, fuchsia-leotard-clad hip gyrations, and lingering crotch shots, provokes Sylvia's agonizing experience of same-sex desire. Sylvia falls for Sabel, and falls hard.

Sabel performs at the center of a dance floor surrounded by diegetic audience members (figures 4.12–4.21). In the first half of the scene, the space of the bar is conspicuously divided along gendered lines: toward the front of the bar where Sabel's dance begins (i.e., the first end of the axis of action revealed by the camera; figure 4.12), Sabel is surrounded by what appear to be cis male, presumptively straight audience members (figure 4.16). Reverse shots reveal the back end of the bar where Sylvia and her colleague Babette are seated near several T-birds and butch lesbians (figure 4.13). Diegetically, the prominence of queers in the mise-en-scène recalls Maxie's prior statement that Sabel has a T-bird following at the club (figure 4.17). Two particularly rakish androgynes—whom viewers might regard variously as T-birds, tomboys, butch lesbians, or transmasculine persons—are seated on barstools in the right foreground of the frame, clearly enjoying the show. Extradiegetically, they also elicit what White calls a subcultural "whoop of recognition" in other T-birds, *tibo*, and

4.12–4.21 Sabel dances for the gazes of Sylvia, Babette (Suzanne Gonzales), and various T-birds in *T-Bird at Ako*. Film stills.

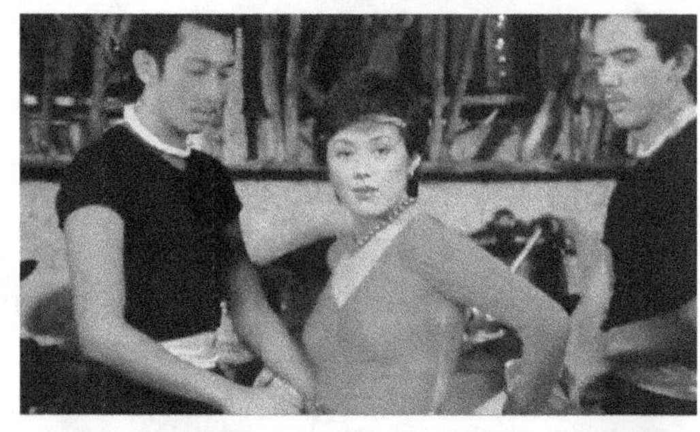

4.12

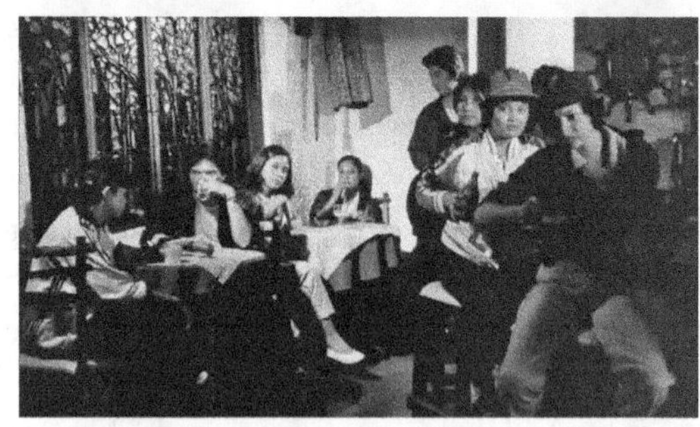

4.13

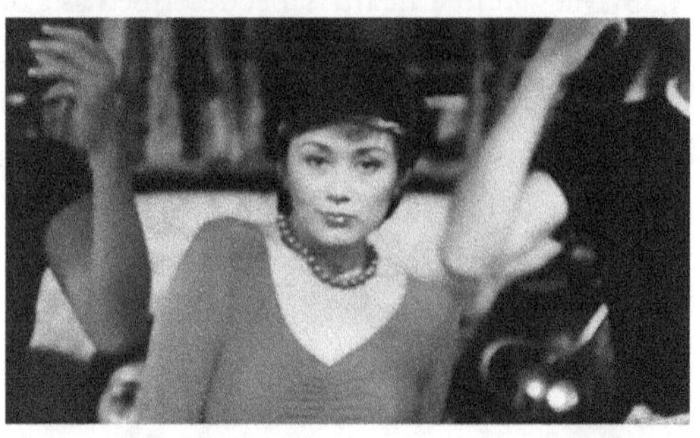

4.14

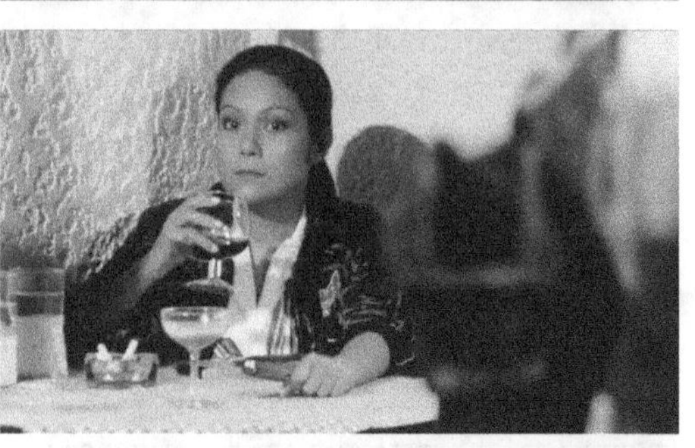

4.15

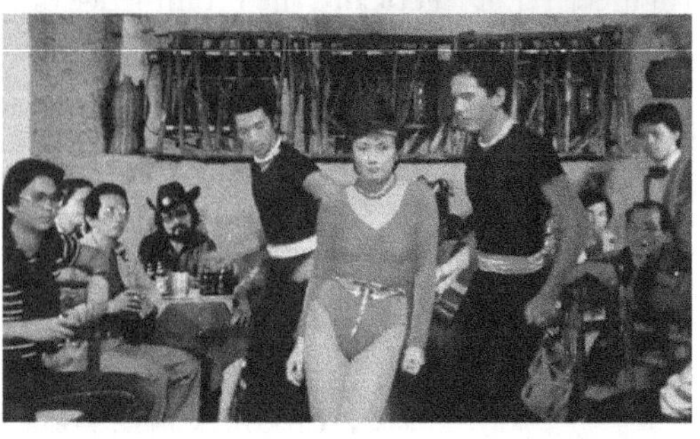

4.16

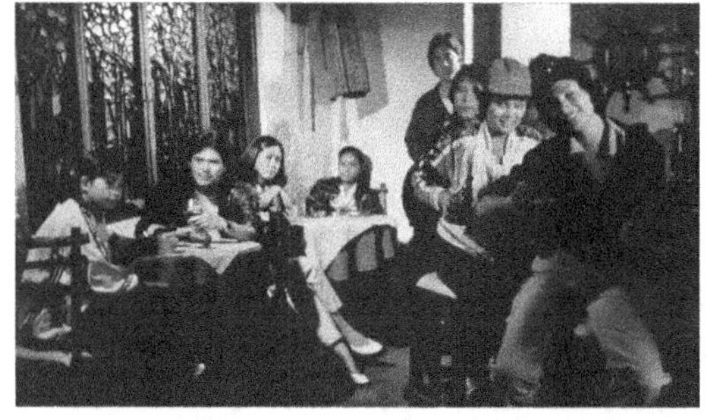
4.17

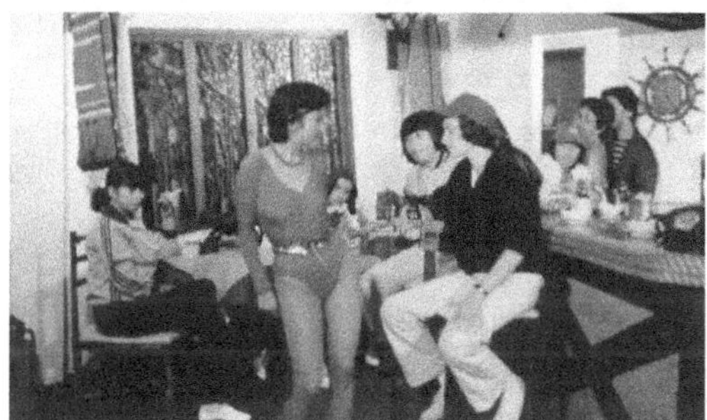
4.18

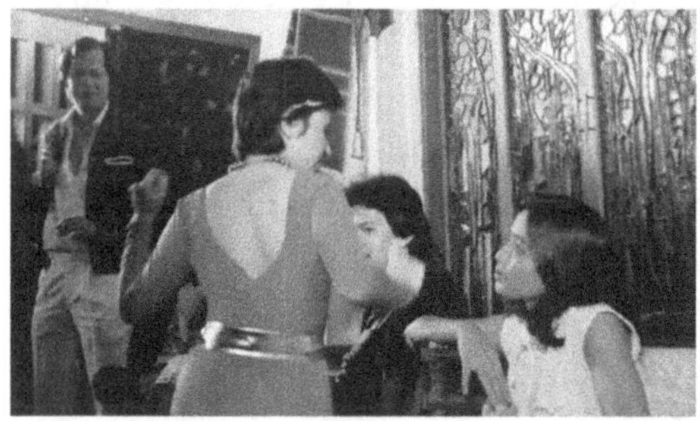
4.19

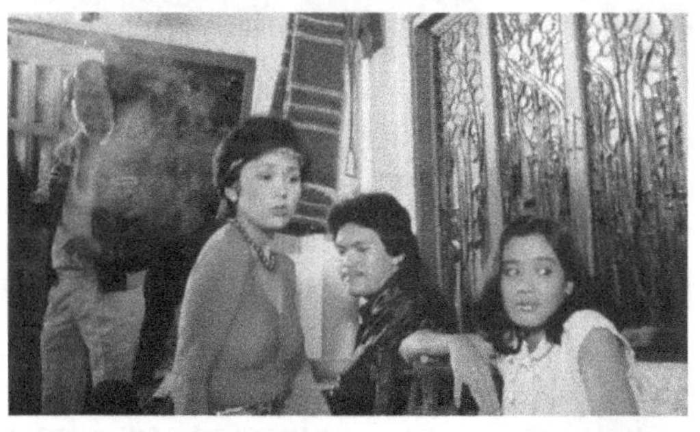
4.20

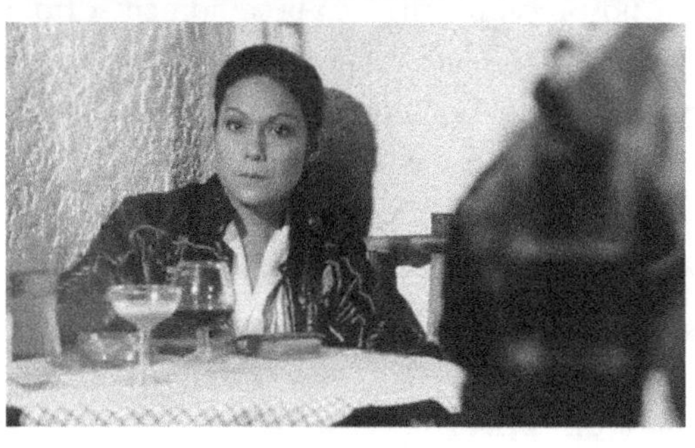
4.21

queer spectators who recognize the sartorial codes and bodily demeanor referenced by such overdetermined moments.[83]

To the campy, crooning lyrics of a disco song that describes Sabel as a "sexy lady," Sabel makes her voluptuous way from the front to the back end of the club, flanked by two flamboyant male dancers, her eyes on Sylvia for much of that time. In a mixed space where various sexualities and genders are on display, Sabel's eyeline is never directed toward the cis men in the audience, who are denied closely framed reaction shots. Rather, for the most part her gaze is directed frontally toward the camera (figures 4.12, 4.14, and 4.16), which the shot-reverse-shot pattern suggests might correspond to the eyelines of the T-birds sitting in the right foreground of the reverse shots, or to the gaze of Sylvia, who is centered in the background plane. Sylvia puts down her brandy glass at one point, disconcerted by the directness of Sabel's intense look (figure 4.15). Point-of-view editing and framing emphasize moments when Sabel swivels her hips while looking directly at unnamed T-birds (figure 4.18), Babette (figure 4.19), and Sylvia in turn (figures 4.20 and 4.21). For queer audiences, identification as a "tenacious insinuation of ourselves into the picture," as White puts it, becomes that much easier when Vilma-as-Sabel is diegetically performing for Nora-as-Sylvia and for a straight female, lesbian, T-bird and/or trans masc gaze, thus allegorically making public the private protohistories of subcultural Filipinx reception.[84]

In another scene cut to the measure of lesbian cinephilia, Sylvia and Sabel have just quarreled over Sabel's planned return to her job at the bar.[85] They make up when Sabel plants a quick, entirely unexpected kiss on Sylvia's cheek, one that lands just to the side of the latter's lips. Whether Sabel's intention is platonic or romantic is unclear. The ensuing medium close-up dwells on Nora's pitch-perfect, characteristically understated performance as Sylvia. The camera holds on an astonished Sylvia's priceless reaction shot, her bemusement giving way to muted delight and a veiled ardency as the flicker of a hope that Sabel might return her affections flashes across Sylvia's face. This moment was relished in 2014 by an anonymous fan in an online post recalling the "ten best moments" from the "lesbian-themed classic *T-Bird at Ako*": "One evening, Isabel leaves Attorney Sylvia's home to go to work—something that Attorney Sylvia makes a fuss over because she understands what Isabel means precisely. Isabel assures her host that it would just be for tonight. She gives her a buss on the cheek, and Nora performs what could be the classiest blushing captured on film."[86]

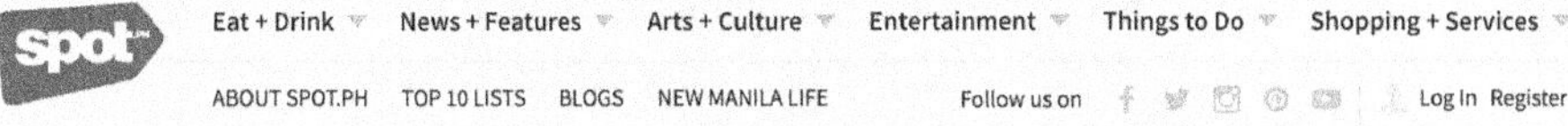

Entertainment

Revisiting the Lesbian-Themed Film Classic *T-Bird at Ako*

Here are 10 best moments from this landmark 1982 film by Danny Zialcita, starring Nora Aunor and Vilma Santos.

Apr 20, 2014

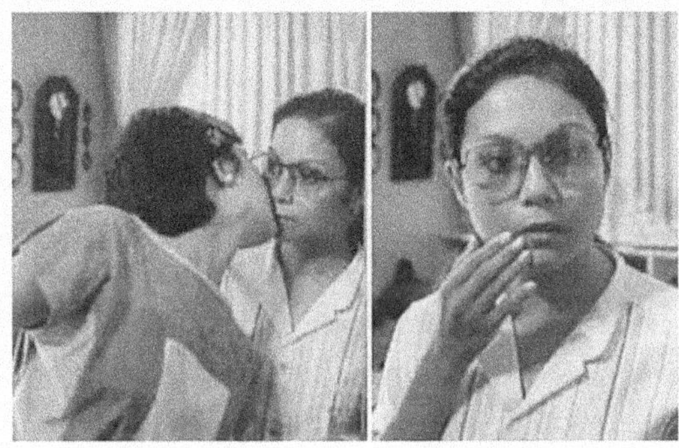

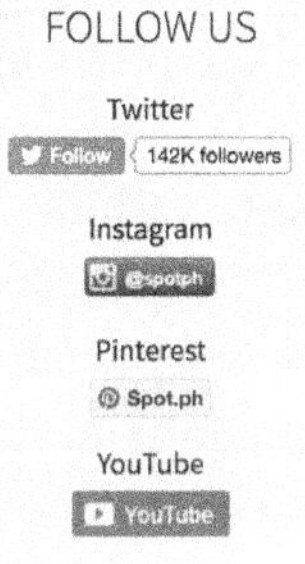

Nora gets an all-too-brief whiff of Vilma in this scene.

9. Vilma's buss on Nora's cheek

One evening, Isabel leaves Attorney Sylvia's home to go to work-something that Attorney Sylvia makes a fuss over because she understands what Isabel means precisely. Isabel assures her host that it would just be for tonight. She gives her a buss on the cheek, and Nora Aunor performs what could be the classiest blushing captured in film.

4.22 Vilma-as-Sabel's queer "buss" on Nora-as-Sylvia's cheek and the latter's priceless reaction shot are relished by an anonymous fan post on spot.ph.

Two screenshots, one of Vilma-as-Sabel's queer "buss" on Nora-as-Sylvia's cheek, and the latter's stunned reaction as her fingers lightly graze the spot where Sabel's lips had nearly touched her own, is captioned: "Nora gets an all-too-brief whiff of Vilma in this scene" (figure 4.22).[87] The fan post confirms that this scene—one in which Nora is stunned, titillated, and aroused by Vilma (note that the diegetic characters' names have fallen away)—is a singular moment cherished by queer audiences.

As the faded color of the images and the date of the post indicate, the screenshots were likely captured from an unrestored commercial DVD copy of *T-Bird at Ako* released by Paragon Home Video in 2008. As Mulvey points out, DVD spectatorship is emblematic of what she terms "delayed cinema," particularly the tendency of retrospective spectatorship through newer digital platforms to disrupt the linear causality of narrative time (which, in *T-Bird at Ako*, marches toward a heteronormative closure) in favor of a cherished "detail or previously unnoticed moment."[88] Whether restored or not, older films recirculated on DVD offer "the possibility of returning to and repeating a specific film fragment . . . interrupting the flow of film, delaying its progress."[89] In the screenshot relished by the anonymous film buff, cinephilic viewers exert power over the image: "The star succumbs to stillness and repetition." Digital viewing delivers the pleasures of the stars' iterable kisses, close-ups, lines, and performances to the "possessive spectator" who selectively screens and manipulates movie fragments. Yet in contrast to Mulvey's claim that "the possessive spectator commits an act of violence against the cohesion of the story," in this case, the desire to replace the heterocentric ending of *T-Bird at Ako* with an act of cinephilic stasis (in a screenshot) or by re-viewing cherished moments on DVD, is an attempt to repossess a previously elusive "lesbian classic" of Philippine cinema that had not been readily available, delivering it to queer pleasures.[90]

RESTORATION IN A COMPARATIVE LIGHT

The consecrating, conservative tendencies of film archives take many forms. First, archives create recognized canons by including or excluding works deemed worthy or unworthy of archival preservation. Second, archives tend to address narrow demographics, strongly correlated with socioeconomic privilege and education, who feel welcome at museums, libraries, and other memory institutions. Finally, film archives tend to reproduce rather than challenge existing expectations about films and their audiences.

As noted in chapters 1 and 3, the state's archival restoration priorities are rooted in an auteurist canon that privileges mainstream genres. Constrained by limited state allocations, the NFAP/PFA's restored titles are predominantly canonical and homogenizing, centering nearly exclusively on critically acclaimed male filmmakers based in Manila as representative of a so-called Philippine national cinema. Chapter 3's approximate listing of eighteen film titles collaboratively restored by the NFAP from 2012 to 2020 is largely auteur-driven.[91] The majority of the directors are male luminaries of the studio and poststudio eras and the New Cinema (the only director to command three NFAP/ PFA-restored titles, i.e., 25 percent of their restoration output, is Brocka, Philippine cinema's most recognizable auteur). Auteurs of alternative cinema are also represented. Jo Atienza is one of only three female directors included in the NFAP/PFA list for her codirection of the experimental short *Sa Maynila* (In Manila). (The other two women filmmakers are Marilou Diaz-Abaya and Olive La Torre.) Finally, the NFAP/PFA's restored titles are dominated by Manila-based productions, with only one title made outside the Tagalog film industry, the Hiligaynon film *Ginauhaw Ako, Ginagutom Ako* (I am thirsty, I am hungry). In contrast, ABS-CBN has restored no works of regional cinema. These numbers reflect the extremely low survival rates of vernacular cinemas on photochemical film, as discussed in chapter 6.

In contrast, ABS-CBN Film Archives, whose restoration work its archivists perceive as lying somewhere between market pragmatism and corporate social responsibility, is both better funded and more commercially oriented.[92] New Cinema masterpieces are emphasized in promotional trailers and videos that seek to brand ABS-CBN Film Archives' restorations as a prestige catalog of modern classics.[93] The promotional emphasis on ABS-CBN's restoration of critically acclaimed auteurist cinema is understandable, given that the economic realities of film preservation favor the restoration of well-known art films with a potentially high market value.[94] Contravening that promotional emphasis, only eleven New Cinema titles are listed in ABS-CBN's 2018 restoration inventory, representing a mere 7.3 percent of its total restoration output to that point.[95] In actuality, restorations of titles by Star Cinema, an ABS-CBN subsidiary, accounted for 82 percent of their restorations by March 2018.[96] This too is understandable since, for ABS-CBN, archiving is a means of preserving Star Cinema's enormous content library for future repurposing across various distribution platforms.

A crucial although possibly unintended benefit generated by ABS-CBN's film restoration campaign—one that it has not trumpeted in its prestige-oriented, star-driven publicity—is that its focus on restoring commercial movies has resulted in greater inclusivity of women filmmakers.[97] While only three films by women filmmakers are represented in the list of the NFAP/PFA's restorations as of 2020, ABS-CBN had by 2018 restored forty-eight titles helmed by eight female directors; women-directed films represented 32 percent of its restoration output.[98]

I am not suggesting that a corporatist gender diversity agenda underwrites ABS-CBN's restoration campaign; nor am I arguing that queer-positive politics were the primary motivation for the restoration of *T-Bird at Ako*. Instead I offer the modest observation that the prolific volume of ABS-CBN's restoration effort opens a modicum of space for minoritarian voices and themes within mainstream Tagalog cinema to be re/encountered by contemporary audiences.[99] As the seventy-seventh restoration undertaken by ABS-CBN Film Archives, *T-Bird at Ako* is not among the conglomerate's highest-profile projects, though its marketing did exploit the potential of the superstars' collaboration in one of the earliest commercial films to focus on lesbian desire.[100] Given the NFAP/PFA's limited slate of government-funded restorations, a film with *T-Bird at Ako*'s particular mix of ingredients—a commercial star vehicle that explores Manila's lesbian and tomboy subcultures—would have been an unlikely candidate for restoration by the national film archive.

Gina Marchetti describes mainstream cinema as a "meeting ground" for subcultures in two senses. First, commercial films about subcultures exploit the curiosity of general audiences who are possibly "titillated" by the prospect of exploring subordinate groups' styles and ways of life. Second, such movies are consumed by subcultural audiences who read these films against the grain of the dominant culture that produced them.[101] This rings true for *T-Bird at Ako*, whose depiction of the T-bird social and sexual scene in early 1980s Manila is an admixture of the "dread and fascination" that for Dick Hebdige characterizes mainstream media's ambivalent response to "spectacular subcultures."[102] (Anecdotally, a relative my age recounts that in her 1990s varsity college basketball team at the University of the Philippines, Diliman, lesbians campily referred to themselves and to one another with the acronym EKT, for *eee, kadiri, tomboy*! [Yikes, disgusting, a tomboy!]. This expression perfectly distills mainstream culture's mixture of dread and fascination toward queer subjects, here being ventriloquized by a sporty *tibo* herself.) In light of subcultural studies' contributions to the study of film spectatorship, we can begin to understand ABS-CBN's restoration and recirculation of *T-Bird at Ako* as addressing both the heteronormative worldview of a general audience (particularly in 1982) and subcultural audiences then and now (regarded as a niche market by ABS-CBN) whose retrospective reception is facilitated by the movie's rerelease.

In media economics, the nondepletability of a movie as a commodity that can be repeatedly consumed has one crucial implication for conglomerates like ABS-CBN: revenue from movies, even older ones, can be stretched across a much longer span of time.[103] This insight is central to the media industrial concept of the "long tail," first introduced by Chris Anderson in the early years of the twenty-first century.[104] The concept has become a buzzword in media economics, summarized by Kevin McDonald as follows: "Long Tail signifies the growing importance of niche markets and the subsequent shift from relying exclusively on massively successful commodities to more modestly successful commodities that generate value over longer periods of time."[105] Historically, the emergence of home video "creates a vast array of ancillary markets 'downstream,' and taken together these return more money than theatrical release windows and the Web."[106]

In the case of the restored and rereleased *T-Bird at Ako*, ABS-CBN could expect most of its revenues to be generated over time in ancillary markets via carefully scheduled releases, known as a "windowing" distribution strategy.[107] The distribution windows of ABS-CBN's restored films involve international film festivals and/or local red-carpet premieres, broadcast television, pay-per-view cable television, DVD distribution, and online platforms.[108] To create demand across these distribution windows, the marketing around *T-Bird at Ako* relies on interviews in which Nora and Vilma lend their star power to ABS-CBN's restoration campaign. In separate interviews included as bonus features on ABS-CBN's restored DVD release, Nora emphasizes the importance of rescuing film history (*sagip pelikula*) and recalls director Zialcita's predilection for changing lines on set. For her part, Vilma highlights the importance of restoring the works of important Filipino auteurs, reflects on her own body of film work as having held up a mirror to the lives of women (*salamin ng totoong buhay ng kababaihan*), and gleefully recalls the slaps (*sampalan*) and "crispy lines" in the script that were evenly distributed (*hating-hati*) between Nora and herself in *T-Bird at Ako*.

Harnessing Nora's and Vilma's star power to constitute a public for restored archival films appears to have worked: according to the *Philippine Star*'s coverage of the red-carpet premiere, "Nora graced the event and showed her support for ABS-CBN's film restoration project. Noranians and Vilmanians also flocked to the venue."[109] The exhibition and commercial release of restored films are always attempts to bring an archival public into being—the subject of the epilogue to this book. For *T-Bird at Ako*, that archival public appears to have dovetailed, at least in part, with two sets of audiences usually excluded from the viewers targeted by film retrospectives and exhibitions of newly restored films. First, the highly gendered, classed, and generational segment of Philippine moviegoers known as Noranians and Vilmanians; and second, a subcultural queer counterpublic, some of whom may already have identified as one or both of these stars' fans. Called into being by the retrospective pleasures of *T-Bird at Ako*, this serendipitous convergence of film fans, queer cinephiles, and an archival public-in-the-making for the preservation of Philippine cinema might be the most unexpected virtue of ABS-CBN's restoration campaign.

CHAPTER FIVE

Informal Archiving in a Riverine System

Video 48 and the Kalampag Tracking Agency

Turning from formal collections to informal archives—from video stores to curatorial undertakings—this chapter argues for an expanded sense of both archiving and archivists, one that registers the crucial work of the curators, video store clerks, collectors, and cinephiles whose labor enables both mainstream and alternative Philippine cinema to flow to a wider public, in effect functioning as figurative headwaters for the riverine circulation of archival Philippine cinema.[1] This chapter's focus on informal archives seeks to rectify the unwitting "tunnel vision" that characterized my early research for this book, which was focused solely on formal state and corporate archives and the organized advocacy of SOFIA. Only gradually did I realize that these formal collections and initiatives—accessible to me as a career academic with long-standing ties to archivists—are not the avenue of first resort for most interested film buffs looking for hard-to-find Philippine titles.

For many, streaming platforms like YouTube and Netflix are go-to resources for Philippine cinema, but online holdings, while vast and eclectic, are neither representative nor exhaustive, not least because much of the country's audiovisual media has never been digitized or commercially released. Cost is another barrier to entry: subscription-based video-on-demand (SVOD) services entail monthly paywalls that few Filipinos can afford. User penetration relative to population in the Philippine SVOD market segment was approximately 5.73 percent in 2022, in contrast to well over 40 percent in the United States, which had the highest user penetration of SVOD globally.[2] The 6.6 million Filipino SVOD users estimated for 2022 are a fraction of the overall Philippine population, which exceeded 115 million that year.[3] Between formal archives like those maintained by the NFAP/PFA and ABS-CBN (whose gatekeeping functions can be forbidding since neither offers ready access to the general public) and the at-your-fingertips convenience of streaming services for those with high bandwidth connectivity (a convenience that masks the workings of proprietary algorithms, data harvesting, and hidden advertising), other important informal archival nodes exist.[4]

By *informal archives*, I am referring to collections that do not call themselves archives or conform to the official policies of organizations like the International Federation of Film Archives (FIAF) yet nonetheless collect, maintain, and make available swaths of Philippine cinema that would otherwise be neglected and inaccessible. Those who run these informal collections—individual collectors, volunteer curators, store owners, or shop workers—are not professionally trained archivists, but they epitomize an unmistakable archival consciousness. I argue that informal archives like Video 48 and the Kalampag Tracking Agency function as headwaters for the Filipino film scene without which the waterways of Philippine cinema would long ago have run dry.

Video 48 names both an online blog and a legendary brick-and-mortar video store devoted to the Tagalog-language, feature-length fiction films produced by the Manila-based film industry.[5] Dubbed "the last video rental shop in Manila," the physical store was founded by Simon Santos in 1988, two years after the collapse of the first FAP and twenty-three years before the founding of the NFAP, in an era when Betamax was the prevailing home video format.[6] For over thirty years, Video 48 was an indispensable fixture of Metro Manila's mediascape, beloved by cinephiles and extolled by glowing journalistic coverage.[7] A fan-collector of print materials (movie ads, film magazines, photographs, lobby cards, posters, *komiks*) and all manner of movie memorabilia since the 1960s, Santos later expanded his holdings to include Betamax and VHS videotapes, laser discs, VCDs, DVDs, and digital movie files as well as toys and action figures.[8] The shop's striking display of Santos's eclectic collection gave Video 48 a pronounced museological quality.

In addition to the storefront located at 48 West Avenue in Quezon City (the address for which it is named), the Video 48 blog begun in 2007 offers a sprawling online version of Video 48, "a virtual online library and archive on Philippine cinema." Sharing Santos's contagious love of Philippine cinema without recourse to a paywall, the site offers the passionate cultural work of a lifetime (images, filmographies, articles, and trivia) to online visitors for free.[9] An archival consciousness animates both the (partially closed) physical and (ongoing) virtual iterations of Video 48. Santos maintains that "movies by our great filmmakers like Gerardo de Leon, Lamberto Avellana, Manuel Conde, Lino Brocka, Ishmael Bernal, Celso Ad Castillo, [and] Mike de Leon, among others, should be made available. They must be seen and appreciated." Only then can Filipinos be "made to realize the importance of past and present cinema in our culture and in our lives."[10]

For its part, the Kalampag Tracking Agency is a two-person microcuratorial project helmed by Merv Espina and Shireen Seno that retrieves and recirculates experimental and avant-garde shorts from Manila's alternative film and video scene. Circulating across a variety of venues—from paradomestic events in the organizers' own residences to community-based screenings to international museums and film festivals—Kalampag's screening programs recover and recirculate often badly deteriorated, experimental titles.[11] Prior to Kalampag's efforts, experimental and avant-garde short films and videos were largely overlooked by both the SOFIA-led archive movement and the NFAP/PFA, even though the latter had such titles in its own collection. Historically, the restoration and preservation efforts of SOFIA, the NFAP, and ABS-CBN have focused on auteurist, feature-length "classics" of Philippine cinema, precisely those masterworks of the domestic film industry that Video 48 made available on the home video market. In contrast, the Kalampag Tracking Agency retrieves and disseminates alternative cinema crafted in a minor, noncommercial mode—short films and videos made outside the confines of the domestic film industry. From 2016 to 2017, as a direct result of Kalampag's efforts to raise the profile of Filipino experimental film and video, the NFAP transferred eighteen experimental 16mm and 35mm films made between 1992 to 2003 to digital formats.[12]

A collaborative curatorial undertaking, the Kalampag Tracking Agency first coalesced when Espina and Seno put together a screening program at the invitation of the 2014 Experimental Film and Video Festival in Seoul. As indicated by the Tagalog onomatopoeic word *kalampag*—a "rattling sound or a bang" that "implies that . . . machinery is somehow damaged"—the program sounds an alarm, calling attention to systemic problems that beset Philippine experimental cinema.[13] Chief among these are problems with access, distribution, and archiving as well as a dearth of scholarship and documentation, since short experimental works have been largely overlooked in Philippine film studies and art history.[14] Seno and Espina highlight the archival impetus of their work, especially in terms of the promotion, preservation, and migration of analog films and videos to digital formats:

> We wanted a body of works that rattled the system at least for a brief moment in time. . . . The Kalampag Tracking Agency . . . treats the screening program as a method, an ongoing process of investigation and a means to not just promote these works, but more importantly, to preserve them as well.
>
> We use the opportunities provided by festivals, archives, museums, art spaces and other platforms that have invited the screening program to access equipment that we don't have in the Philippines. In this way, we have been able to make newer and better transfers of several works. Each screening is slightly different, as there are always slight improvements here and there.[15]

Seno and Espina's notion of archival preservation has little in common with professional audiovisual archivists' protocols and practices. For an ultra-low-budget initiative like Kalampag, storage in temperature- and humidity-controlled vaults and regular migration using costly digital infrastructure are fiscal impossibilities. Instead, Kalampag's archival modus operandi is to facilitate better-quality digital scans of analog-born titles via donations in kind.[16] This is a crucial, ingenious form of making do, archival preservation-as-access conducted in an inventive, collaborative, minor mode.

This chapter begins by elaborating two bases for a comparative analysis of Video 48, a retail shop, and Kalampag, a screening program. In juxtaposing two seemingly disparate case studies, the chapter foregrounds, first, private-to-public archival circulation. Both Video 48 and the Kalampag Tracking Agency are informal archives that facilitate essential flows between private collections originating in exclusive insider film circles and a broader public audience who would otherwise be unable to access most of these films. Santos is a collector with strong ties to established filmmakers and the mainstream film industry, while Espina and Seno move in the close-knit world of alternative filmmaking.[17] Second, both Kalampag and Video 48 recover and revalue residual media, offering historical snapshots of various eras whose formats and carriers span the transition from tangible to virtual media. The chapter offers a spatial analysis of Video 48, both as an urban hub for local movie cultures and in terms of its cinephilic store layout. This is followed by a discussion of Kalampag's efforts to generate new digital transfers and conduits for the distribution and exhibition of historically peripheralized experimental films. I analyze four short films featured in Kalampag's screening program for the March 2018 Glasgow Short Film Festival: *ABCD* (1985) and *Juan Gapang* (Johnny crawl, 1986) by Roxlee (Roque Federizon Lee); R. J. Leyran's compilation short *Bugtong: Sigaw ni Lalaki* (Riddle: Shout of man, 1989); and Tito & Tito's *Class Picture* (2011).

This chapter argues for an understanding of the archival circulation of Philippine cinema as a riverine system for which informal archives such as Video 48 and the Kalampag Tracking Agency function as crucial headwaters. Straddling both formal and informal media spheres, such collections are more concerned with improvising pathways to access than with deferring to the interests of rights holders (who, in the case of older or marginal works, might not be readily identifiable or reachable).[18] As elaborated in previous chapters, the formidable archival vacuum that surrounds Philippine cinema dwarfs the comparatively small number of extant titles. Amid such anarchival conditions, the older mainstream, theatrically released Tagalog-language films that comprised the core of Video 48's holdings are, in effect, "alternative" cultural fare even within the borders of its own nation-state; domestically produced nonfiction genres, such as the experimental shorts foregrounded in Kalampag's screening programs, are even more marginalized.

A RIVERINE SYSTEM OF ARCHIVAL FLOWS

Although I had originally hoped to explore Video 48 and the Kalampag Tracking Agency as beacons of hope in the crisis-ridden history of Philippine film archiving, both of these informal archives have been endangered by anarchival ephemerality. As I drafted this chapter in the first COVID-19 pandemic summer of 2020, a neighborhood electrical fire spread to the office and archival storage spaces of Green Papaya, the Quezon City residential-cum-arts space for which Kalampag's Merv Espina served as curator. The June 3 fire that engulfed "Manila's oldest artist-run space" damaged VHS tapes as well as laptops and hard drives containing digital transfers and research. Extinguishing the flames reduced paper materials donated by filmmaker Roxlee and others in the experimental community to "soggy bricks." Espina notes that some of the surviving materials were themselves "veterans of disaster, already surviving the 2009 Ondoy flooding," but many other holdings, including some works featured in Kalampag screenings, were burned and/or soaked.[19]

Less than a month later, Simon Santos announced the partial closure of Video 48 on Facebook: "Video 48 will cease operation as a video sales and rental shop, but it will remain open as a hobby, collectible and memorabilia shop. . . . Being an ardent movie enthusiast, I will still maintain and continue running my Video 48 blog and FB page."[20] Among the many expressions of gratitude and support prompted by this announcement, several registered the crucial contributions of Video 48 as an informal archive while others requested continued access to its movie library.[21] Santos explained that the store's closure was prompted by several reasons that were exacerbated by the pandemic. As Video 48's proprietor, he was unable to get the Optical Media Board's approval to operate, "since one of their requirements is to get accreditations from any video suppliers, [and] all video suppliers had closed shop." The worsening financial situation of the Video 48 store was compounded by temporary shutdowns at the onset of the pandemic. Eventually, Santos recalls, "I, with my family's blessing, decided to close it permanently."[22] The palpable consternation that echoed across local film circles in the wake of these events confirmed that Video 48 and the Kalampag Tracking Agency were indispensable watersheds in Philippine cinema's already attenuated riverine system of archival circulation.

In suggesting that archival circulation might be generatively construed as a riverine system, I do not mean to undervalue the crucial differences between river ecologies and media systems, nor am I advancing an environmental media argument. Rather, the modest aim of my proposed analogy is to highlight salient parallels between archival film circulation and running-water ecosystems.[23] River ecologies exemplify biodiversity; similarly, the cinemas of the Philippines are far more variegated than a default focus on Manila's feature-length fiction films apprehends. Like river systems, media circulation is fed by multiple streams. The brackish freshwater-and-saltwater estuaries often formed by rivers recall the hybrid character of archival circuits in which formal and informal practices and collections commingle. In the course of their movement through time and space, rivers, like media, leave things behind, and their sediments accrete on riverbanks (as the film *Bugtong* bears out, serendipitously deposited traces can be fertile). The flow of rivers may be perennial or seasonal, rapid or sluggish, unhindered or dammed up. Drought, pollution, and political toxicity result in alarmingly unhealthy river ecosystems or kill them off entirely. Likewise, the circulation of audiovisual media, especially as works age, fluctuates between ready access, bottlenecks, and total unavailability. With rivers, as with media, streams might be free-flowing, diverted, or barred. The circulation of movies as "a question of provision and denial" calls our attention to the political, highly asymmetrical distribution of resources.[24] Similarly, river dams produce enormous gains for some at the cost of immense harm for others (to wit, indigenous communities' fifty-year resistance to hydroelectric dams along the Chico River system in Kalinga and Mountain Province, located in the Philippine Cordilleras).[25] Given that rivers are extraordinarily valuable to the Earth's ecosystems, restoring and managing rivers involve balancing the conflicting needs and claims of diverse stakeholders in contexts where "the distinction between pristine and degraded systems is disappearing rapidly."[26] Dissenting perspectives on access, restoration, and stakeholder consultation likewise underpin audiovisual archiving.

PRIVATE-TO-PUBLIC COLLECTIONS

To a certain extent, every serious film scholar is a kind of film collector. The researcher's propensity to collect is amplified for those who do research on Philippine cinema, given the shortage of available materials for study in physical archives or on online platforms. In my experience, teaching or studying Philippine cinema means drawing on a personal archive of "ripped" digital movie files, DVDs, or videocassettes as well as collecting paratextual materials (books, journals, clippings, and ephemera from film-related events, such as brochures and catalogs released to coincide with film festivals, retrospectives, exhibits, or restorations.)[27] Earlier generations of collectors and scholars I've met owned 35mm, 16mm, or Super 8 film prints.[28] They also recorded televised broadcasts of movies on Betamax and VHS, just as, for contemporary researchers, sharing digital movie files on discs, portable drives, or via streaming links is a common practice. The media provenance of such files varies from ripped commercial VCDs or DVDs to from a filmmaker's or producer's copy on Vimeo or an external USB drive, a DVD, or a DCP.

The fantasy of perpetual availability—normalized for those who study film in contexts where a variety of physical and online archives, libraries, and retailers can be expected to hold much of the back catalog for the oeuvre in question—is not part of the assumptive horizon for those with a historical interest in Philippine film. Circumscribed access to Philippine cinema, structured by anarchival conditions, serves as a deflating corrective to what Lucas Hilderbrand dubs "access entitlement," that is, fantasies of "infinite and instant access to specific movies or shows" that are more likely to characterize the expectations of media consumers in the global North than in the global South.[29] Those who study Philippine cinema are well aware that commercially available videos are difficult to track down beyond their shelf life at video stores and that an even wider array of domestically produced films have never been released on videocassette or DVD. This explains why films from Video 48's extensive collection from the late 1940s onward are so sought after, since many of these titles are out of print or were never commercially released for home video, though selected titles could be obtained directly from major studios like LVN and Sampaguita on a special-order basis.[30]

For experimental works, the majority of which have never enjoyed formal distribution, circulation is even more restricted. Unless one is fortunate enough to score a Vimeo link shared by the filmmakers themselves (whether gratis or for a fee), most of these works are not available online, whether via YouTube, subscription streaming services, or illicit movie downloads. Nick Deocampo, the only major scholar to offer a sustained historiography of Philippine experimental cinema, has called attention to the limited, often ephemeral distribution and exhibition of alternative short films. In his groundbreaking book *Short Film: Emergence of a New Philippine Cinema* (1985), Deocampo notes that the exhibition of experimental and avant-garde works is sporadic, occurring largely through television stations and screenings at community centers and schools; "after the screenings, the films are soon unheard of." Undergirding these exhibition issues is a deeper problem with circulation (whether via a formal distributor or self-distribution on the part of the filmmaker): "Distribution has a long way to go before it can vitalize alternative film production and make it a viable business or artistic enterprise."[31] Given that the problems Deocampo identified nearly four decades ago have not been surmounted, the Kalampag Tracking Agency's screening programs confront the question of alternative circulation for experimental cinema anew.

For these reasons, collections that bridge the divide between the exclusive world of filmmakers and cinephiles, on the one hand, and a broader audience of local and international media consumers, on the other, are extraordinarily valuable. Hilderbrand's remarks on cinephilia as bound to "unavailability and the joy of seeing something against the odds" is germane here. If, as Hilderbrand suggests, "films that play hard to get are the ones we want the most," then that yearning is particularly acute for film buffs who must contend with the rarity of older Filipino films in a market awash with Hollywood product.[32] As Teddy Co puts it, "In our country, . . . we've not had a proper archive for years. . . . By default the collector becomes the archives, shall we say, he takes on the role of the archives."[33] The informal archives explored in this chapter lie at the crossroads of the private cinephilic collection and the public circulation of Philippine movie titles that would be nearly unobtainable for interested viewers without insider connections to mainstream or alternative film scenes.

Barbara Klinger's observation that collecting removes mass-produced media commodities from the public sphere, transposing them into a private archival sanctum, probably holds true for the collections of most audiophiles and cinephiles.[34] Crucially, however, Santos, Espina, and Seno reverse the usual public-to-private flow of individual collecting. Rather than accumulate publicly available films at home, Video 48 and Kalampag operate in the opposite direction, offering selections of their personal insider collections to wider audiences: in the case of Video 48, to the general paying public for purchase or rental at its retail store or for free at its online blog; in the case of Kalampag, to audiences in various Philippine venues (in microcinemas, community contexts, and public outdoor screenings within and outside Manila), international film festivals, and workshops.[35]

The community-oriented collecting of Video 48 and Kalampag, which spans both formal and informal media economies, departs markedly from the "hardware aesthetic" of wealthy collectors in the global North, epitomized by the figure of the "male technophile or gadgeteer." What Klinger calls a "white male technocentric ethos" involves "exacting standards that demand pristine visuals in original aspect ratios and crystalline soundtracks."[36] In contrast to this technocentric ethos, Kalampag and

Video 48 prize not so much technical polish (though both strive to obtain the best available transfers) as the very act of (often imperfect) retrieval and renewed access itself.

Straddling the personal realm of the private collection and the public character of video stores and film exhibitions, Video 48 and Kalampag are crucial informal nodes in a riverine archival system because they reroute rarefied insider collections to public circulation, making them available to a wider range of audiences. Simon Santos, the collector-proprietor of Video 48, is an insider to industry cliques whose store attracted A-list patrons in its heyday (New Cinema auteur Lino Brocka's borrower's card is now one of the gems of his collection). One interviewer notes that Video 48's prominent clientele, which included National Artists, directors, writers, and actors, constitutes "a who's-who of Philippine cinema, a list that will send any film student into spasms of ecstasy."[37] If the noncorporate, specialty video store is not just a space of capitalist consumption but also a convivial site at which video store owners, clerks, and customers could "talk film" in a spirit of camaraderie, then Video 48 at its height must have been a veritable salon of cinephilic "sociability."[38]

In contrast to corporate marketing rhetoric that interpellates the media consumer as a knowing "insider," for both Video 48 and the Kalampag Tracking Agency the insider status of the collection is real, not imagined.[39] While some of Kalampag's screening programs originate in the institutional collections of MOWELFUND and the UP Film Center, more than half of its audiovisual holdings are sourced from copies shared by filmmakers or friends in the experimental film community. Shireen Seno recalls that the seeds of her personal "hoard" were digital movie files gifted by film critic Alexis Tioseco, while Merv Espina concurs that his stash derives from movie files shared by "immediate peers."[40] As noted earlier, most of these short films were never formally distributed.

RESIDUAL MEDIA AND HISTORICAL RETRIEVAL

As Charles Acland observes, "It is striking how infrequently work has addressed the aging of media and cultural forms directly." The term *residual media* names the persistence of "reconfigured, renewed, recycled, neglected, abandoned, and trashed media technologies and practices" as "these accumulate in landfills, . . . archives, or attics." Residual media remain understudied in Philippine film scholarship, which has rarely focused on "the processes by which technological forms and related cultural practices age and are selectively revitalized."[41] The rediscovery and revitalization of forgotten works of Philippine cinema are central to the work of both Video 48 and the Kalampag Tracking Agency as informal archives. Acland refers to scholarship on residual media as "studies of 'living dead' culture."[42] The phrase "living dead" calls to mind the reanimation of eclipsed media artifacts and technologies, while "the half-life of media forms and practices" tells us that aging audiovisual culture is characterized by a considerable reduction in their potency due to the passage of time.

Breathing new life into outmoded media artifacts is core to the practice of collecting. In a 1931 essay, Walter Benjamin describes collecting as "the renewal of existence," a practice that reinvigorates the historical life of the collected object: "To a true collector the acquisition of an old book is its rebirth. . . . To renew the old world—that is the collector's deepest desire when he is driven to acquire new things."[43] That collectors of residual media are motivated by a profound sense of history is evident in their propensity to organize artifacts in historically meaningful ways—to wit, the Video 48 blog's historical periodization of web pages, from prewar and postwar Tagalog stars and movies, to the 1950s to the 1980s. Similar to Barthes's *amator*, collectors are lovers with a particularly historical inclination. Michelle Henning writes that they "attempt to mend the rift that modernity violently produces between the present and the past," sometimes taking on the role of a "surrogate mourner" for forgotten lives and events.[44]

In a sense, nation-states are (or ought to be) the foremost collectors of their country's collective past, charged with amassing those artifacts of material culture that have been sacralized as "national heritage."[45] In repeatedly failing to value its own national audiovisual past, then, the Philippine state can be described as a deficient or failed collector of its national cinema. Faced with a government that has never been a passionate collector of its own moving image history, archive advocates and private collectors have stepped in as surrogate mourners for Philippine cinema.

In this light, SOFIA's search and rescue of the numerous film reels that LVN studios dumped onto an open-air basketball court in 1994, devalued both by LVN and by the producers who declined to reclaim them, can be recognized as a kind of Ur-story for the archival collection and resacralization of Philippine cinema at the turn of the millennium. As poignantly recounted by Clodualdo del Mundo, "a total of 1,471 reels in rusty tin cans," exposed for months to "intense summer heat and later to torrential rains," had become a de facto trash heap of "abandoned and orphaned films" at the point when SOFIA intervened.[46] Collecting and salvaging are acts of sacralization that uproot films from contexts in which their worth is unrecognized (i.e., the profane sphere where outmoded commodities are seen as garbage) so as to reinvest them with significance in the context of a carefully amassed collection (i.e., the sacred, ritual context that converts dross into collectibles).[47] In salvaging these titles, SOFIA acted as surrogate mourners for a devalued trove of Philippine cinema, a role that collectors like Simon Santos and self-described "hoarders or accumulators" like Merv Espina and Shireen Seno have since come to occupy.[48]

VIDEO 48: A SPATIAL ANALYSIS OF A VIDEO MECCA

In contrast to major corporate video store franchises like Video City, which had several branches in the 1990s and early 2000s, Video 48 was an independently owned "video mecca" specializing in the feature-length output of the Manila-based, Tagalog-language film industry.[49] Daniel Herbert defines a *video mecca* as a prestigious specialty video store regarded as a "destination" by cinephiles; such establishments often invite the devoted reverence of its loyal customer base and the video store clerks that work there.[50] Joshua Greenberg analyzes the video store as a historically specific "consumption junction" between the media content industry, "video hardware and software manufacturers," and the social audience.[51] The near-total collapse of the brick-and-mortar video rental business worldwide by the 2010s, experienced by legitimate stores and bootleg shops alike, is widely attributed to the decline of DVDs and the advent of streaming media and internet piracy.[52] Despite the shift from physical stores to online platforms, it is important to bear in mind that the tangible media culture of the video store was a precursor to the current era of online digital entertainment, since video stores exemplified the media industry's decisive shift to decentralized film distribution and a flexible, customizable, and highly personalized movie culture.[53]

In a 2019 interview, Emely Serreng, a video store clerk who had worked at Video 48 for a decade, recalled that while students, academics, writers, directors, and collectors remained the bedrock of the store's customer base, the number of visitors had plummeted in the preceding five years, from ten customers a day when she was hired in 2009 to a handful of visitors a week. Video 48 adapted to the downturn by decreasing new acquisitions, reducing staff, and focusing on the most durable aspect of its long tail business: Filipino Cinema.[54] While Hollywood productions and world cinema made up half of the store's holdings in early years, international fare accounted for only 20 to 30 percent of the collection by the time I interviewed Serreng, with Tagalog titles constituting the rest of the inventory; new acquisitions consisted solely of the latter.[55] I speculate that Tagalog films—vintage classics, star vehicles, and auteurist masterworks—were the most durable aspect of Video 48's niche market, remaining in steady demand despite competition from online video platforms and media piracy precisely because these Filipino titles remain largely unavailable online. While a bounty of images and information can be accessed for free on the Video 48 blog, watching the actual movies in Santos's collection required a physical visit to the West Avenue store.

If, as Herbert argues, video meccas enjoy the status of "informal film schools," reciprocally "supporting and supported by a community of cinephiles and intellectuals," then Video 48's historical importance to researchers, movie buffs, and the entertainment industry in Manila was enabled by its location at the bustling commercial end of West Avenue, Quezon City.[56] (This aspect of Video 48 anticipates the "geocinematic hermeneutic" theorized by David James in relation to minor cinemas, elaborated later in this chapter with reference to Kalampag.) Within a three-mile radius of Video 48 are the corporate headquarters of two Philippine media giants, ABS-CBN and the broadcasting company GMA Network, as well as the intellectual and artist communities fostered by nearby campuses: the University of the Philippines, Diliman; Ateneo de Manila University; and Miriam College. In this sense, Video 48 has for decades been a vibrant part of a local movie culture that it energized with archivally conscious cinephilia.

Located on the ground floor of a building owned by Santos's family, Video 48 at the time of my August 2019 research visit was flanked by a skin care clinic and a pastry shop. Given the building's sleepy exterior, a first-time visitor might be surprised to find a gurgling fountain in the courtyard lobby and an art gallery, also family-owned, upstairs.[57] Video 48's retro logo, rendered in a bold yellow 1970s-style font and outlined in red, was emblazoned on two glass doors that opened into the shop; underneath it, a laminated photo of Alfred Hitchcock welcomed customers inside (figure 5.1). Just beyond the threshold beckoned an eclectic feast for the eyes. Through the open door on the right, one glimpsed autographed headshots of Filipino movie stars whose decades-long careers began in

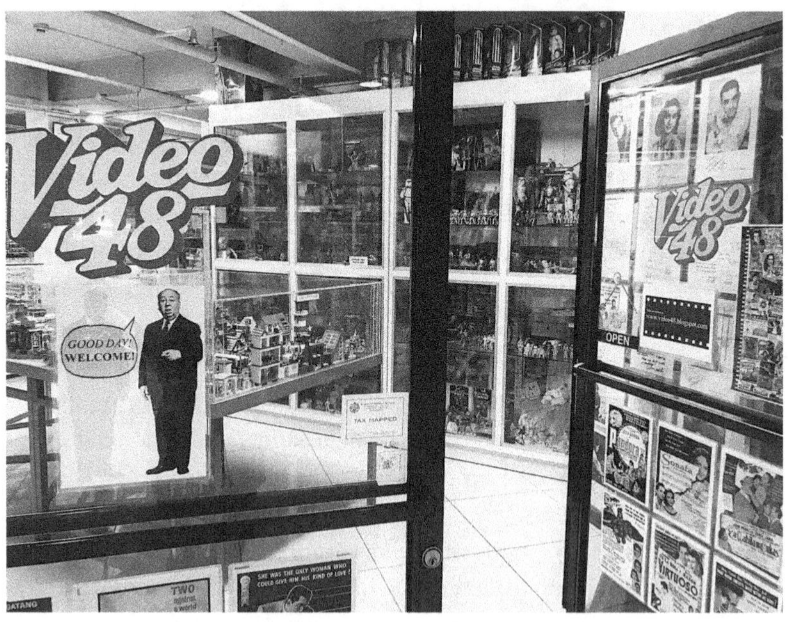

5.1 The striking entryway and store layout of Video 48 reflect the archival, cinephilic, and pop cultural sensibilities of owner-collector Simon Santos. Photo by author, August 2019.

the fifties and sixties: action king Fernando Poe Jr., popularly known as FPJ; glamour queen Susan Roces, FPJ's widow; and legendary comedian Dolphy. Glass cases at the center and borders of the store displayed LEGO building models as well as action figures and collectibles from Hollywood franchises and the US professional basketball team the Chicago Bulls. The left wall next to the entryway featured a miniature compendium of publicity material—magazine covers, movie posters, and cover art—spanning FPJ's career from 1955 to 2003.[58]

The striking store layout of Video 48 invited the fantasy of unlimited access to sedimented movie knowledge, all available, as it were, in a wide panoramic panning shot as one entered the shop. The shop's contents represented a fraction of Santos's vast audiovisual collection, which far exceeded the available display space (his extensive world cinema holdings were piled from floor to ceiling in a separate storage room). The overall effect was sensory overload: there was almost too much to appreciate and discover through the cosmopolitan sensibility of the shop's owner-collector, Simon Santos. Clearly, this was the collection of someone who loved FPJ, Philippine cinema, Hollywood, international art cinema, sports, and global popular culture in the same breath.

Scholars underscore the importance of a spatial analysis of video stores that unpacks their cultural geography as interactional spaces.[59] An individual video store's distinct "architecture of classification"—that is, a particular shop's way of arranging its media collection on shelves and in aisles—is a "material spatial manifestation of ideas about how movies should be organized and thus conceptualized and understood." Along with "conceptual divisions," a shop's ordering and allocation of space for various titles express perceived interconnections and degrees of importance ascribed to various items in the collection.[60] My spatial analysis of Video 48 confirms the tangible privileging of mainstream Tagalog movies in a collection that includes both domestic and international film titles. The centrality of local productions in the store's cultural geography mounted a powerful argument for the archival value and cultural significance of Philippine cinema.

As with bookstores, the floor plans of video stores were conventionally dominated by central modular aisles organized by genre to facilitate customer browsing; as such, most video stores resembled "open stack" libraries where patrons perused items at will.[61] In contrast, Video 48's store layout departed from the conventional browsing-oriented spatiality of video rental stores. The store's entryway was reminiscent of a pop cultural museum: glass cases with not-for-purchase collectibles were centered in the shop's foyer. On the back wall behind the shop counter, DVD and VHS cases flanked a flat-screen TV and a DVD/VCD deck (figure 5.2). Visually scanning from left to right, the eye first met Hollywood movies on DVDs, arrayed in an L-shape immediately to the left and underneath the screen; however, such titles took up only about 15 percent of the store's most prominent display case. The majority of the most conspicuously displayed titles, approximately 85 percent of the remaining wall space, consisted of Philippine cinema on VCD (on the lowest shelves below the screen), DVD (immediately to the right of the screen), and VHS (behind the counter); the spines of these video cases were arranged alphabetically, without classificatory labels (figure 5.3).[62] Tagalog movies on DVD and VHS were thus spatially privileged as the heart of the media collection.[63] This is especially the case in comparison to the Hollywood laser discs and VHS tapes housed in the far right corner of the store, or the piles of assorted VCDs on the floor near the pillars of the shop (figure 5.4).

In keeping with the sensibilities of the store's fan-collector-proprietor, American and Filipino popular cultures were intermingled in eclectic

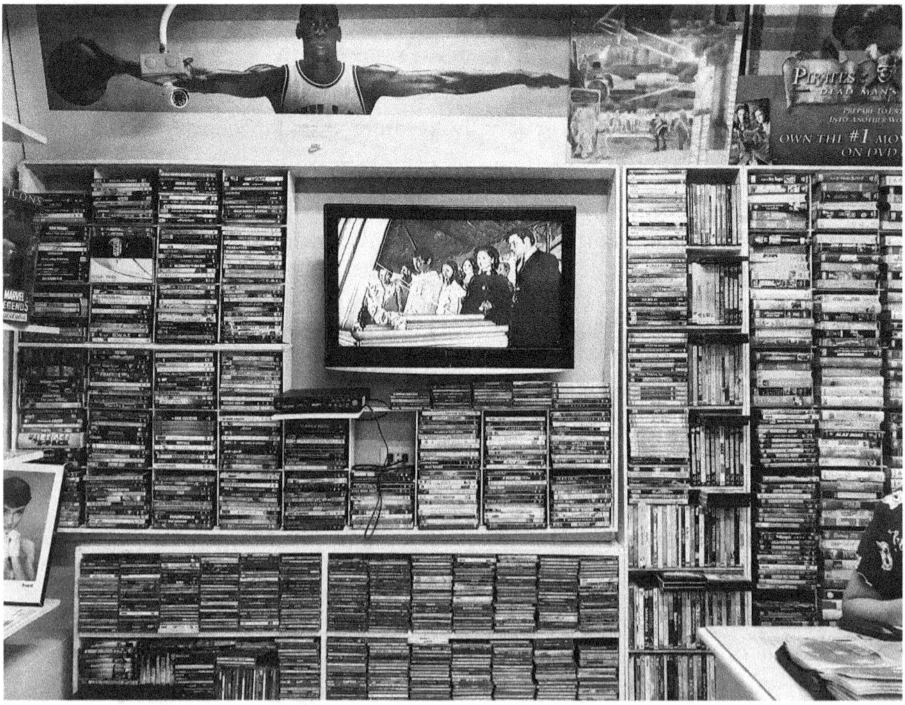

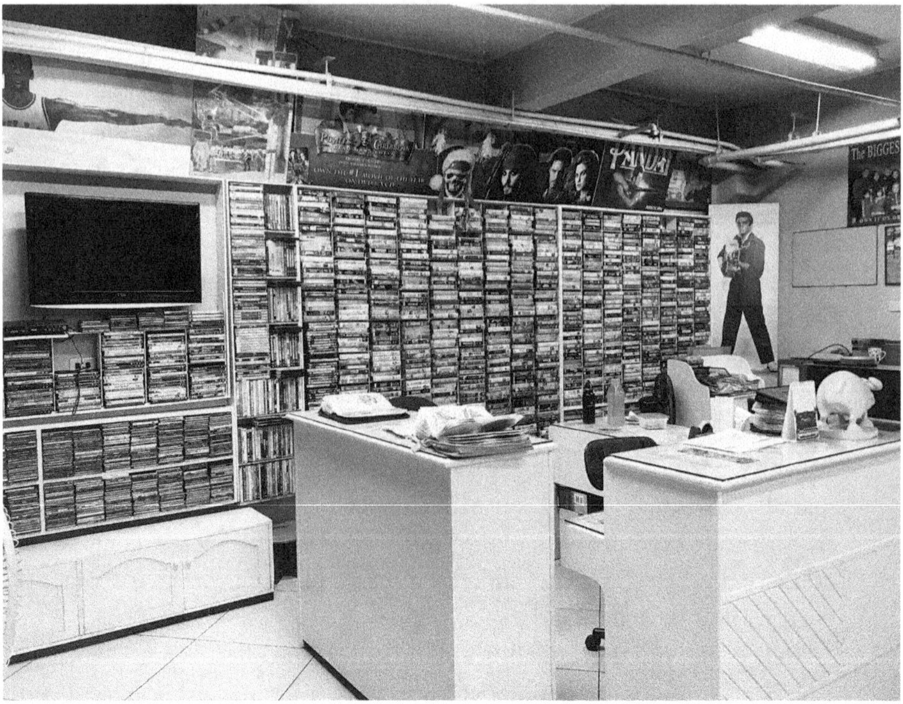

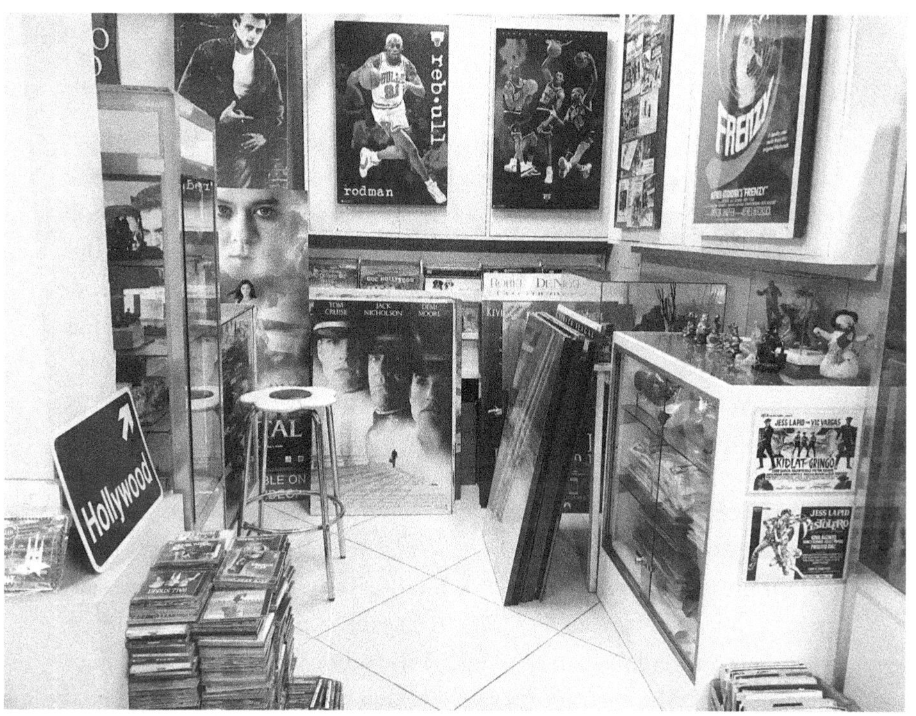

5.2 (*opposite top*) On the left side of the back wall of Video 48, Hollywood movies on DVD and Tagalog cinema on DVD, VHS, and VCD are arranged in loose alphabetical order around a TV screen and a DVD/VCD deck playing a scene from *Patayin sa Sindak si Barbara* (Terrify Barbara to death; dir. Celso Ad. Castillo, 1974). Photo by author, August 2019.

5.3 (*opposite bottom*) Displayed behind the store counter, Tagalog movies on DVD and VHS are spatially privileged as the heart of Video 48's collection. In this interactional space, browsing patrons are drawn to the counter where the video clerk is stationed. Posters and other memorabilia intermingle American and Filipino popular culture in eclectic ways. Photo by author, August 2019.

5.4 (*above*) The store layout of Video 48 condenses the historical rise and fall of media formats. Older media carriers like laser discs and VCDs are de-emphasized, shelved in a corner of the store. Photo by author, August 2019.

ways: the Filipiniana movie collection's top margin was demarcated by a line of posters from Hollywood tentpole franchises (e.g., *Star Wars* and *Pirates of the Caribbean*) and a poster for the ABS-CBN television series *Panday*, while its right flank was adorned with a larger-than-life poster of Elvis Presley (see figure 5.3). Only the leftmost third of the titles on the back wall were fully available for customer browsing; located behind the shop counter, the majority of the DVDs and videotapes were highly visible but physically out of reach for customers. The cultural geography of the store thus drew the browsing patron immediately inward, closest to the counter where the video store clerk was stationed.

Today, the few brick-and-mortar video stores that remain standing are nostalgic spaces of residual media that point to the multiple, media-archaeological temporalities of cinephilia and videophilia. Laura Mulvey writes of cinephilia, "The object of [cinephilic] love is at a crossroad in its history, between technologies, eras, and so on that bring its multiple temporalities into sharp relief."[64] Similarly, Kathleen Williams conceptualizes the video store as an interstitial space of persistence: "There are in-between spaces in which an older media technology, object, or practice is forced to persist with the present through the desires and interests of media consumers. In this process, new values are attached to objects and practices, demonstrating that the meaning attached to media is circulatory and negotiated."[65]

As a media-archaeological space of persistence, Video 48 offered a snapshot of the historical rise and fall of media formats. The advent of the VHS and DVD era "dramatically democratized" film collecting as video collecting. While the higher price point and low market penetration of laser discs in the United States and elsewhere lent that format a "boutique identity," VHS and DVD enjoyed a much higher market share, with DVDs eventually supplanting VHS as the dominant home video format from the late 1990s to the first few years of the twenty-first century.[66] Accordingly, Video 48's store placement emphasized titles on VHS and DVD and de-emphasized laser discs and VCDs. File duplication went on discreetly in the desktop computers located behind the counter (figure 5.3). Laser discs, an older but more elite boutique format in comparison to VCDs, were displayed in a corner, partially obscured by framed movie posters but still close to eye level (figure 5.4). The store's VCDs, a newer format than VHS and laser disc but less likely to be prized as collector's items, were piled nearby on the floor and were below eye level. A cheap, highly compressed format on a low-density CD carrier, VCDs were devalued for their poor audiovisual quality. They dominated East Asian and Southeast Asian home video markets from the late 1990s to around 2005, their prevalence eventually eroded by the ascendancy of DVDs, which offered better audiovisual quality at increasingly more affordable prices.[67] With both legal movie releases and pirated knockoffs of television and film titles circulating widely on VCD throughout East, South, and Southeast Asia at the turn of the millennium, media scholars argue that "mixed Asian legal and illegal VCD capitalism" shaped "a specific pan-Asian transnational and transcultural space of consumption and exchange."[68]

As an interactional space, Video 48's layout positioned the store clerk as the primary resource for finding movies. In the absence of browsable aisles, the store's spatiality invited one to scan displayed titles on the walls, consult posted lists, and interact directly with the clerk, who consulted the shop's computerized database and hard copies of selected subcollections to recommend titles. Spatially, then, the customer's reliance on the clerk-as-curator, already in place in conventional video stores where categorized aisles occupy the bulk of the space, was intensified in Video 48. During my visit, its uncategorized wall displays prompted my frequent interactions with staff member Emely Serreng as I foraged through this informal archive. The titles of the laminated lists on the counter conveyed their canonical and auteurist organizing logics: Urian Best Pictures from 1976 to 2014; the Golden Globes' Best Foreign Films from 1949 to 2015; the films of Ishmael Bernal, Mike de Leon, and Lino Brocka. After a few minutes' conversation about my film tastes, Serreng produced well-worn paper copies of more lists, some typed and faded, others handwritten: "Tagalog Classics," "Independent Films," "Nora Aunor." While most of the holdings were commercially released on home video formats (Betamax, VHS, VCD, or DVD), a substantial number have never been available for purchase. My guess is that these were recorded from off-air cable or television broadcast or shared by a filmmaker, collector, or cinephile. Beyond the comprehensive database on the store's computer, the clerk deferred to store owner Santos as the final and most accurate source on a particular title's availability. The customer's inability to access a master list of the store's holdings, as well as the astuteness with which Serreng divined my interests (producing lists, looking up a particular actor's name, and confirming relevant titles from memory), convinced me that, as with all formal libraries and archives, the true finding aid to Video 48 as media mecca is not a catalog but a person—whether Santos as cinephilic owner-collector or Serreng as knowledgeable clerk-archivist.

KALAMPAG TRACKING AGENCY: FROM ARCHIVE TO AUDIENCE

In the Philippines, the marginalization of short experimental cinema is more than a century old, dating to the 1910s. The growing dominance of feature-length filmmaking and Hollywood values positioned shorts as a minor cinema. To the short film as countercinema, Deocampo ascribes both nationalist authenticity and the "fecundity" of early cinema.[69] *Short Film*, Deocampo's desideratum for alternative Philippine cinema, sketches three sets of challenges faced by experimental cinema, which he calls an "other cinema" to the commercial film industry: "The following remain absent: an audience, a distribution network, [and] an archive mainly for short works like super-8 films."[70]

Kalampag attempts to address these three issues. With regard to the first two challenges, experimental cinema's audience problem is inextricable from the shortage of distribution pipelines and exhibition venues for alternative cinema. Clodualdo del Mundo Jr. maps experimental cinema as existing on the outermost margins of a Philippine film scene composed of three concentric circles, with mainstream cinema at the center, niche indie cinema just outside it, and experimental and documentary films at the farthest periphery.[71] Given the marginal, anticommercial status of experimental cinema, Anna Marie de Guzman wryly observes, "Experimental films are not meant to be easy." If audiences find them "daunting and confusing," this is because such works provoke a reorientation of "entrenched cinematic habits."[72] The striking features of experimental shorts—anti-illusionistic manipulation of cinematic plasticity, refusal of narrative, and political radicalism—are prominent in Kalampag's curatorial choices. Such works shocked government censors in the twilight of the Marcos regime and remain profoundly unsettling for domestic audiences weaned on "the commercial values of Hollywood and the melodramatic conventions of Filipino cinema."[73]

To survive, experimental works went underground, searching for "an audience that is yet to be tapped."[74] Deocampo's belief in experimental short cinema's untapped but extant audience prefigures what Jasmine Trice has called the speculative public ardently imagined and cultivated by contemporary Philippine independent filmmakers.[75] In one of his twelve commandments for independent filmmakers, iconic independent animator Roxlee enjoins: "Thou shalt not lose hope, even if you have a small audience for now; the bigger audience may be meant for the next generation."[76] Espina and Seno speak of "giving access back to the artists themselves," who are thrilled that a forgotten work has been found; Kalampag also brings these works to a younger generation of artists and audiences unfamiliar with older media.[77]

Historically, the distribution of experimental and avant-garde film and video has "been undertaken by small specialist organizations . . . operating in a subsidized economy via low wages, volunteer labor, and state funding. Sustaining such organizations—and hence the visibility of experimental work—has frequently proved extremely challenging."[78] As a two-person microcuratorial collaboration between Espina and Seno, the Kalampag Tracking Agency's informal archiving, distribution, and exhibition of experimental cinema are grounded in the lived realities of unsalaried, volunteer labor, in contrast to projects funded by the government or by established cultural institutions.[79] As such, the long-term viability of Kalampag is overdetermined by the prime movers' ability to find the time and the resources to keep the project going. At the time of our 2018 interview, for example, Kalampag's plans were put on hiatus since Seno had just given birth to her first child.[80] Soon after the June 3, 2020, fire that damaged their holdings, Green Papaya began collecting donations to fumigate surviving materials.

The third issue, which concerns the archival lacunae surrounding Filipino experimental cinema, is ruefully glossed by Kalampag's curatorial notes: "No one knows where films showcased in Manila's first National Festival of Short Films in 1964 can be found, yet we still have feature films from this period."[81] The acute archival marginalization of experimental film and video is not unique to the Philippines. In addition to lost titles and budgetary constraints, the difficulties of archiving experimental film worldwide include keeping them "alive not only physically but also culturally—in cinemas, museum galleries, or in new media formats" in the face of the general archival disregard that besets experimental works.[82] In a 2012 article written at the cusp of the worldwide shift to digital theatrical projection, archivists at the Deutsche Kinemathek Film Museum in Berlin anticipated that the near extinction of 8mm and 16mm production would cause digital carriers to default on distribution options, making small-gauge films rarely projected specialist artifacts "kept under strict protection and only available for serious study by scholars, or for the creation of new masters."[83] Their prediction is confirmed by the Philippine experience, where the decline of experimental film on film was underway in the early 2000s.[84]

The archival challenges and frustrations faced by Kalampag are even more acute. Seno and Espina typically do not work with preprint elements, instead making do with multiply migrated, later-generation access copies. Because Kalampag lacks original filmic elements and works primarily from analog video transfers of Super 8mm or 16mm films, its efforts are markedly survivalist: Espina and Seno describe their attempts to output the highest resolution transfers possible, using the personal and institutional networks that materialize with specific screenings to facilitate film and video digitization as donations in kind.

Audiovisual media are context-dependent, that is, reliant on the technology through which a work in a historically specific medium, format, or carrier can be experienced. Accordingly, the archival principle of context linkage aspires to reconstruct the technological context of past works. Film archives strive to maintain not only reels of celluloid but also the skills and technologies pertinent to their original exhibition context. The on-the-ground realities of Philippine audiovisual archiving, however, make context linkage and fixity (restoring the work to its "original, unaltered form") impossible archival ideals.[85] Kalampag focuses on more modest, pragmatic, and achievable aims, providing access for contemporary audiences and generating better-quality versions of previously lost works.[86]

Experimental filmmakers' aesthetic manipulation of footage in postproduction has rarely been documented, making the technological and institutional history of the avant-garde notoriously difficult to reconstruct.[87] This makes the input of filmmakers themselves—when obtainable—key to archivists seeking to work with the original audiovisual materials.[88] Screenings attended by "several generations of artists and filmmakers" who "exchanged ideas, talking history, aesthetics, and process" yield an important oral history component to Kalampag's work in the context of meager or inaccurate documentation.[89]

THE FILMS OF ROXLEE: *ABCD* AND *JUAN GAPANG*

Crucially, Kalampag has recovered and recirculated the work of Roxlee, described by Tilman Baumgärtel as "the foremost art animation filmmaker of the Philippines and a frequent habitué of the [Goethe-Institut] film workshops" in the 1980s and 1990s.[90] Roxlee's twelve commandments for independent filmmakers urge originality, resourcefulness, and thrift ("shoot with a limited budget but with unlimited ideas") while renouncing the commercial star system. Telling young filmmakers not to be discouraged by harsh critics or the lack of local audiences, Roxlee advises: "aim for international release" and "work up to your last breath."[91]

Despite Roxlee's stature as a pioneering experimental animator operating outside the industry, there is little published writing on his rarely screened works.[92] Thanks to Kalampag's efforts, digital scans of Roxlee's Super 8mm films have been deposited at the Asian Film Archive in Singapore. Espina recalls that Kalampag's evolving digital transfers from Super 8mm film for Roxlee's *ABCD* (1985) and *Juan Gapang* (1986) involved multiple collaborators and institutions:

> We transferred these from the original Super-8 a few times. At first at Toronto's LIFT, then at Boston's Balagan Films, then finally through the Asian Film Archive (AFA) in Singapore. The AFA transfer might be the highest resolution ones that we have. AFA digitized all the Super-8 that Rox[lee] has at the NFAP. . . . Shireen [Seno] and I mixed and matched the sound files from other versions for the [Kalampag] program. For *ABCD*, that file is actually a more recent collaboration with Pow Martinez . . . [for] a screening that Yason Banal programmed as part of Green Papaya's participation in *No Soul for Sale* at the Tate Modern [in 2010]. When we worked with the Super-8 of *ABCD*, we discovered some extra frames in the beginning that were not in the video reference files we had access to earlier.[93]

The confluence of new lightweight Super 8mm film cameras (introduced by Kodak in 1964) and sociopolitical upheaval enabled the flowering of alternative cinema in the seventies and eighties. By 1971, when youth-led rallies and demonstrations against the Marcos government were at their height, student filmmakers documented the protest movement on Super 8mm.[94] The renaissance of Filipino experimental filmmaking in the seventies and eighties was subtended by the political ferment of the First Quarter Storm, the martial law era, and the economic crises that wracked the country in the final years of the Marcos dictatorship.

Roxlee's five-minute experimental animation Super 8mm film, *ABCD*, telegraphs the political, economic, and social tumult of the late Marcos period. As Anna Marie de Guzman notes, Roxlee's "singularity as a filmmaker rests on a multiplicity of artistic strategies that he utilizes with the ease of a master juggler: animation, dark humor, political commentary, [and] unmitigated nihilism, among others." Often "urgent and feral" in tone, Roxlee's use of montage creates an "intensely frictional visual space that is both messy and beautiful."[95]

Masquerading as a children's alphabet, *ABCD* offers a searing political critique of the Marcos regime. The animation short opens with hand-drawn cartoons illustrating its intertitles—"A AS IN ANIMATION," "B AS IN BEARD," and "C AS IN CIRCLE"—accompanied by a subtly discordant track combining harmonica chords, whistling, humming, and percussion. This deceptively innocuous beginning hints at disturbing undercurrents: a man turns into a pig; an inkblot becomes a scream. With "D AS IN DICTATOR," a silhouetted hand turns into a gun that blows a person's head off; "E AS IN EVIL" comments explicitly on unconscionable state violence (figures 5.5 and 5.6). Interspersing a variety of animation techniques—black-and-white drawings, paint on glass, inkblots, found images, and photo collages—the short's initially playful mood turns increasingly darker. "M FOR MILITARIZATION" is punctuated by a rapid-fire montage: news photos of protests against the Bataan Nuclear Power Plant, indigenous minorities' calls for self-determination, soldiers in tanks, and police brutality against student activists are intercut with text from the Philippines' Military Bases Agreement with the United States (figure 5.7). Throughout *ABCD*, political critique is peppered with toilet humor and sexually explicit visual jokes.

In the last two minutes of the film, the soundtrack switches to a man's voice reading a Catholic prayer, *Ama Niamo*, a Bikol-language version of the Our Father. The piety connoted by the vocal track is at odds with the indignation depicted on the image track. In the section "Q FOR QUESTION," an outraged cartoon figure asks, "WHY IS THE PHIL. IN DEBT WHEN WE ARE RICH IN NATURAL RESOURCES?" One fist raised in the air, another figure replies, "BECAUSE OF INTERNATIONAL MONETARY FUND? BECAUSE OF AMERICAN IMPERIALISM." The film closes with a call for solidarity ("U FOR UNITY") in the face of political apathy (in "Z FOR ZZZZ" a man falls asleep with an erection, alluding to the numbing proliferation of escapist *bomba* or sexploitation films). Roxlee's deft visual and audial rhythm, combined with the witty, free-associative, and nonlinear structure of *ABCD*, balance didacticism with levity.

The film *ABCD* was completed in 1985, a year before the popular ouster of the Marcos government; this was the same year that saw the publication of Deocampo's germinal book *Short Film*. Deocampo's account is particularly valuable because he was simultaneously a historian and a prime mover in the experimental film scene. His claim that shorts in the seventies and eighties combined aesthetic innovation with political boldness is particularly relevant to *ABCD*. The period's "restless" alternative cinema, forged in

5.5–5.7 Roxlee's *ABCD* (1985) uses a range of animation techniques—black-and-white drawings, paint on glass, ink-blots, found images, and photo collages—to denounce the militarized suppression of dissent under the Marcos regime. Film stills.

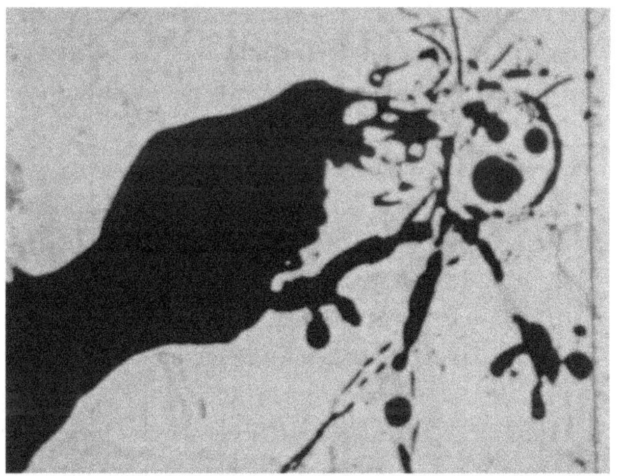

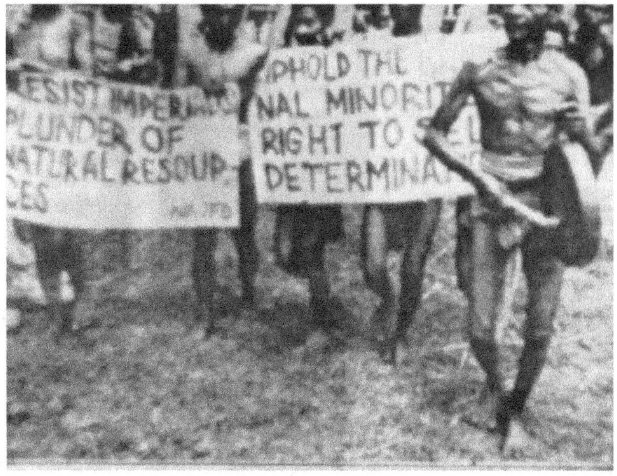

the charged milieu of social, political, and economic chaos, foregrounds film's "role in social change" and contends with the "threatening presence of a Board of Censors that can quash any attempt to reveal political and social realities."[96]

Juan Gapang (Johnny crawl), one of Roxlee's best-known, multi-awarded works, is a six-minute live-action film made in 1986, the year of the Marcos regime's ouster. The eponymous protagonist crawls on all fours in a variety of directions and settings. Clad only in white body paint, white tights, and a long black wig, the silent, ghostly male figure creeps through foliage, logs, tunnels, railroad tracks, stairways, overpasses, and roads crowded with curious pedestrians or clogged with cars and jeepneys. The film is a social allegory that recasts the Filipino everyman figure, Juan de la Cruz, into Juan Gapang, a suffering, vulnerable character who must go through life literally on his knees. *Juan Gapang* offers a surreal critique of the degree to which poverty and political repression under the Marcos government had reduced Filipinos to a groveling existence.

The short film's memorable settings allude to the turmoil of the times. Juan crawls past a building facade littered with strike and protest signs (figure 5.8); the Manila Film Center, site of the regime's deadly excesses and home of the first FAP (figure 5.9); and Manila's central artery, EDSA, where a multitude toppled the dictatorship in 1986, the very year that *Juan Gapang* was released. Musician Joey Ayala and visual artist Javy Villacin collaborated on a soundtrack in which ethnic pop instrumentation is overlaid with a garbled voice recording. Throughout, the clatter of a film projector adds another percussive stratum. In the absence of live sound for the Super 8mm footage, Ayala and Villacin "recorded [the soundtrack] like a live performance, playing as they projected the film, so you can still hear the projector."[97]

What Espina calls the characteristically "dirty sound" of experimental cinema's make-do filmmaking tactics parallels the imperfect yet ingenious forms of make-do kinescoping employed by MOWELFUND and memorialized by Kalampag. For *ABCD*'s soundtrack, the filmmakers jammed along with the footage and the noise of the projection equipment, producing a remarkable extradiegetic admixture of the musical and the machinic. These postproduction tactics are echoed in the make-do migrations pioneered by filmmakers at the MOWELFUND Film Institute, whose archival holdings form the basis of some of Kalampag's screening programs.[98] MOWELFUND's analog-to-digital film and video transfers recall CCP technicians' approximation of kinescoping by using a digital camera to record projected

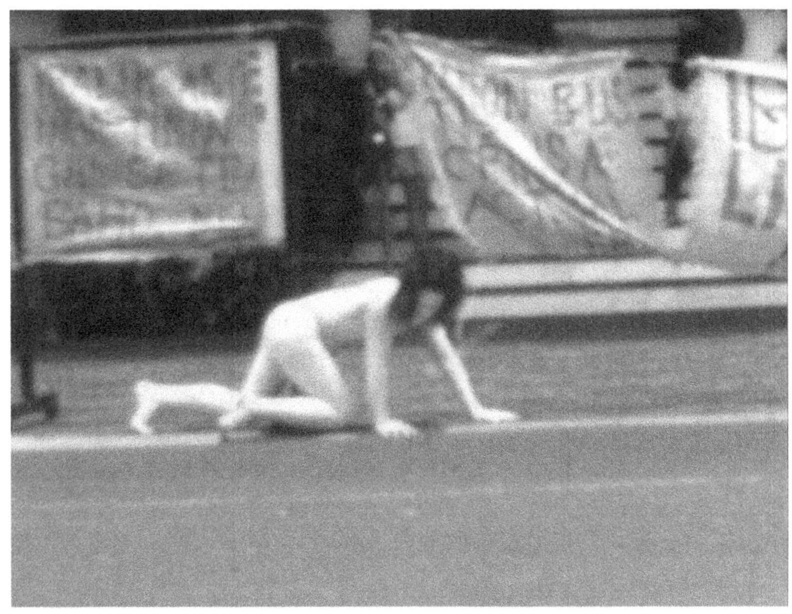

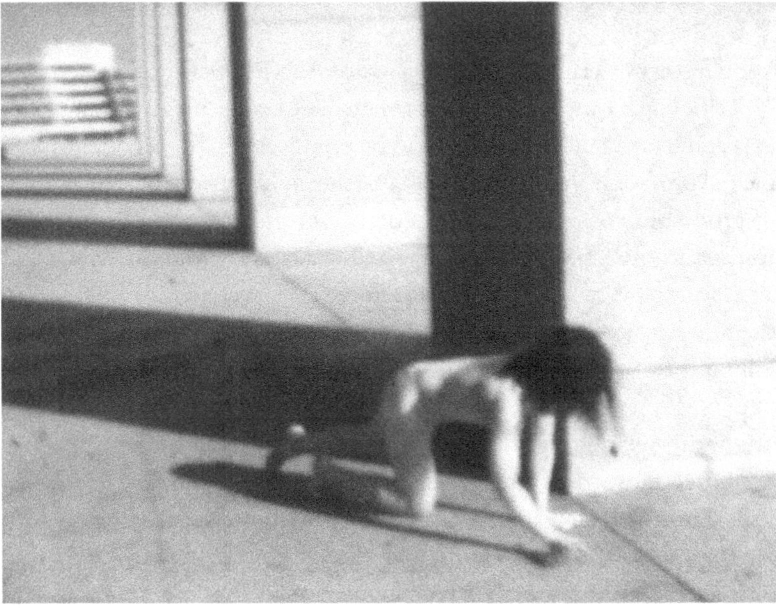

5.8 & 5.9 The protagonist in Roxlee's *Juan Gapang* (Johnny crawl; 1986) crawls past street protests and the pillars of the Manila Film Center, metonymic of the Marcos dictatorship's fatal excesses. Film stills.

images on a blank wall.[99] Espina recalls filmmaker-archivist Ricky Orellana's description of these makeshift transfers: "Ricky said, 'We don't have the luxury of kinescoping. For us, this is kino' [*Walang kino-kino e. Ito na 'yung kino sa amin'*]. That's how they did it, they just project it on a wall . . . and aim a camera at it [*tutukan nalang*]. Sometimes, you can hear them drinking in the background."[100] Like the postproduction recording of a live music soundtrack along with the sound of the film projector in *ABCD*, the MOWELFUND access copies remediated by Kalampag recorded the ambient sound of the work's screening and transfer contexts. Recovering the ideal fixity of an original work is beside the point. Rather, Kalampag's curators, MOWELFUND's archivists, and the experimental filmmakers themselves value renewed access and the "evolving" character of the work. Espina recalls, "Sometimes, Roxlee himself doesn't really remember the original or what the other versions were. . . . So it's also an evolving work because it's always different."[101]

BUGTONG, OR, LEFTOVER CINEMA 1

In his history of avant-garde cinema in Los Angeles, David James observes: "Specific apparatuses and institutions mediate between a given minor cinema and its spatiality and allow it to be produced."[102] For Manila's experimental film scene in the 1970s to 1990s, the crucial mediating apparatuses of production were the MOWELFUND Film Institute and the Goethe-Institut, whose collaboratively organized workshops made film equipment and mentorship by international directors available to aspiring filmmakers; the PIA-MPD, whose film laboratory processed their works; and the UP Film Center as co-organizer.[103] These institutions are credited at the beginning of many films in Kalampag's screening program; by distributing, promoting, exhibiting, and archiving such overlooked works, Kalampag itself functions as a vital mediating apparatus of dissemination.

What Baumgärtel calls the "Sine-Kino connection" (a neologism combining Tagalog and German words for cinema) refers to a period of intense collaboration between German and Filipino filmmakers and institutions from the mid-1970s to the early 1990s.[104] The peak of the Sine-Kino (or, alternately, "Kinosine") exchanges occurred under Uwe Schmelter's directorship of Goethe-Institut Manila, when MOWELFUND and the Goethe-Institut sponsored two major production workshops for alternative cinema annually.[105] In particular, the legendary optical printing workshops led by German experimental filmmaker Christoph Janetzko in the late eighties and early nineties had a lasting influence on the local film scene.[106] By the 2010s, however, this extraordinary clutch of Sine-Kino works was largely inaccessible and in danger of becoming a lost cinema in its own right, if not for the work of Kalampag.

One product of the Janetzko workshops recirculated by Kalampag is R. J. Leyran's *Bugtong: Ang Sigaw ni Lalaki* (Riddle: Shout of man; 1989), made in response to the workshop theme of "collage."[107] Leyran's compendium of decayed footage from mainstream Tagalog films offered an ironic take on the masculinist culture of violence that underpins the 1980s *bakbakan*, or action movie, genre. The first three shots of the compilation film frame the action film footage to come: images of Anita Linda leading a Catholic family prayer, likely drawn from a melodrama, are followed by comedian Dencio Padilla whistling the national anthem, "*Bayang Magiliw*." This ironic opening and a repeated motif—extreme close-ups of a male bystander's blank gaze at the unfolding violence—retool the genre conventions of the *bakbakan* as a send-up of a nation-state in the late Marcos and early Aquino period that feigned religious piety and patriotism while brutally silencing dissent. Over the course of the three-minute short, we revisit the iconic action heroes of the eighties, Lito Lapid and Bong Revilla, along with heavies like Paquito Diaz, Ruel Vernal, and Charlie Davao (figures 5.10–5.12). Female victims slain by gunfire (such as Beverly Vergel) or action heroines brandishing machine guns themselves (Carmi Martin and Marissa Delgado) are prominent in the second half of *Bugtong*.

In *Bugtong*, conspicuous decay undermines star power, instead inviting us to contemplate the twists and turns of these movie fragments' archival afterlives. The extreme deterioration of the image track is comparable to the degradation of early nitrate celluloid, even though the footage dates only from the 1980s. *Bugtong* looks old before its time because its footage was "salvaged from a commercial studio dumpster" that Leyran and fellow workshop participants found half submerged in a nearby creek.[108]

The rescue of *Bugtong*'s decomposing footage from a New Manila dumpster can be understood through what James calls a "geocinematic hermeneutic." A geocinematic analysis attends to "the relationship between the way a city figures in a film and the way it figured in the filmmaking," since avant-garde films tend to inscribe their own spatial origins.[109] Instantiating such geocinematic dynamics, *Bugtong* attests to the place-specific emergence of an alternative film scene in Quezon City, a district of Metro Manila where two of the oldest major movie studios, LVN and

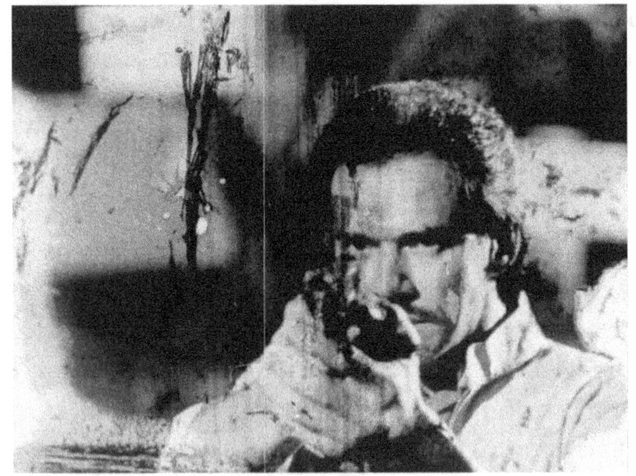

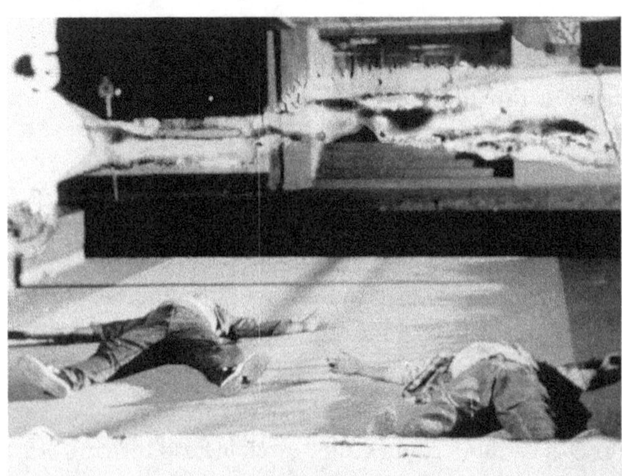

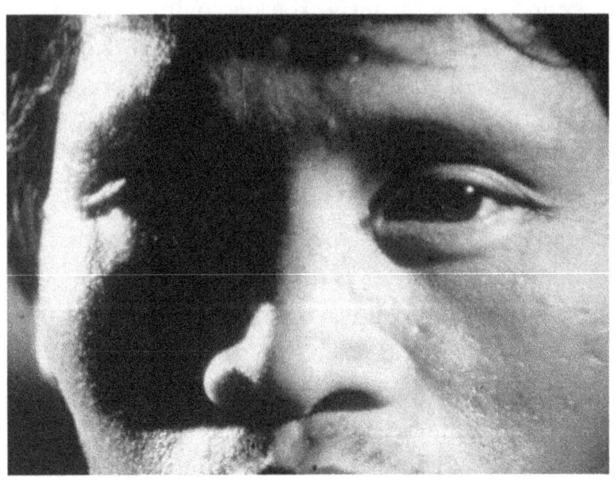

5.10–5.12 In *Bugtong: Ang Sigaw ni Lalaki* (Riddle: Shout of man; dir. R. J. Leyran, 1989), decomposing footage of stars from 1980s Tagalog action movies (*bakbakan*) is intercut with the visual motif of a male bystander's blank gaze. Film stills.

Sampaguita, were located. Teddy Co, himself a participant at the Janetzko workshops, recounts that the "film footage [used in *Bugtong*] was found in a creek near Mowelfund." MOWELFUND, which Janetzko writes was the "main venue" for the three workshops he led between 1988 and 1992, and the film laboratory of the PIA where their work was processed, are also located in Quezon City.[110] The national capital region of Metro Manila itself is the geographic center of the Philippine film industry.[111]

Orellana speculates that LVN Pictures—a former major studio turned postproduction facility and film lab for the commercial film industry—was the likely source of footage used by Leyran and other workshop participants, such as Cesar Hernando. A filmmaker, collector, and production designer acclaimed for his work on the social realist New Cinema of the early eighties, Hernando was a trusted collaborator and friend of auteur Mike de Leon, grandson of the LVN studio founder. According to Orellana, Hernando was the participant-conduit between the alternative cinema workshops at MOWELFUND and the mainstream films "developed, processed, and printed" within the LVN compound:

> Cesar Hernando was partly responsible for connecting some of the workshoppers to LVN. MOWELFUND, [located] on Rosario Drive corner Ylang-Ylang Street, is walking distance from LVN along P. Tuazon Avenue. One would just cross Aurora Boulevard, walk a few meters, and you would arrive at LVN. The LVN compound had postproduction facilities, which were used by mainstream movies. So that's the reason why outcuts from 35mm movies were dumped . . . in the garbage where the films were found. . . . I don't know if some of the workshoppers might have gone to Sampaguita as well, which was a bit further away, but also nearby, within New Manila. . . .
>
> The decaying films were a shared workshop resource within the workshop group. . . . They were drawn to the decaying process [of the outcuts] of commercial films, which gave this colorful image that originally wasn't there, due to the mold or fungus growing on the emulsion layer of the film.[112]

Confirming the geocinematic quality of *Bugtong*, the proximity of MOWELFUND to centers of film production allowed the participants of the Janetzko workshops, some of whom had ties to the mainstream film industry, to serendipitously retrieve the footage. *Bugtong* both tells the story of how it was made—in keeping with avant-garde cinema's "tendency to allegorize the mode of their production"—and attests to "the story of

[its] own spatiality."[113] A bravura example of making do as an exercise of archival power, *Bugtong* makes a virtue of anarchival precarity, turning cinematic dregs into a resource for avant-garde experimentation and making witty, creative use of mainstream cinema's decomposing remains.

CLASS PICTURE, OR, LEFTOVER CINEMA 2

The story of *Bugtong* and of other archival films lost and found reminds us that movies themselves have life histories, entering unexpected streams of consumption, circulation, and duration.[114] In carefully recording their transfer processes for evolving works (e.g., optically printed Super 8mm films digitally scanned to H.264 codec), Espina and Seno engage in a form of media-archaeological "tracking," tracing the twists and turns of what Giovanna Fossati calls the "archival life of film in transition."[115]

In particular, Kalampag foregrounds the afterlives of nearly dead media in experimental shorts that rework cinematic leftovers. According to Seno's and Espina's curatorial notes, Tito & Tito's 2011 film *Class Picture* was "shot on expired [film] rolls and short ends that would otherwise have been destined for the trash bin."[116] Espina reflects, "Using the debris of the commercial industry and turning it into art is a recurring process in the program."[117] Kalampag is drawn to works by directors who "take advantage of what's there, the surplus and garbage of the industry," whether those be "films they found in a creek by a major studio," as in *Bugtong*, or filmmakers who "take advantage of someone else's trash," such as the "tail ends of films in *Class Picture*."[118] Seno, a member of the art and film collective Tito & Tita, elaborates on the salvaging of filmic detritus in *Class Picture* as follows:

> A lot of the younger film artists here have been shooting recently on expired film, because that's all we can get now. *Class Picture* is by this collective that I'm a part of, Tito & Tita, but at the time it was two guys who made that work, Gym Lumbera and Timmy Harn, that's why it was Tito & Tito in the credits. They were able to get the short ends as a donation from [independent filmmaker] Sari [Raissa Lluch] Dalena. The short ends are the leftover film at the ends of works. So they chopped them up and made a new roll, basically.[119]

Given that few companies still manufacture commercial photochemical film globally, Tito & Tita learned from other "DIY artist-run film labs around the world" who "coat stripped film with their own mixture of emulsion" to produce "homemade film."[120] Asked why experimental filmmakers would do this in an era when anyone with a smartphone can quickly shoot a video, Seno responded:

> It's like recycling. If you've shot a roll and you don't like what you've shot, you can strip it and recoat it; you don't have to buy [new film]. . . . People who work with [photochemical film], myself included, feel it has a soul. It has a tangibility; it has so much more of the unexpected. It's the organic quality of it that you treasure. You want the accidents to happen. You don't want to just press a button and see it right away [*agad*]. You want this unexpectedness.[121]

Class Picture defamiliarizes a durable genre of school photography through a ghostly repurposing of leftover media. The four-minute 16mm film diverges from several conventions of class photographs. First, the subjects—coed students and a teacher from an elementary school in Balete, Batangas—repeatedly pose not for a static snapshot but for several long takes.[122] The first of three long takes shows all the girls in the class; this is followed by a shot of all the boys in the class, then a third shot of all the students together with their teacher. The fourth long take, however, deviates from the conventions of class photographs by showing the female schoolteacher by herself (figures 5.13 and 5.14). Lumbera asks, "Why is it that, for class pictures . . . there's never a solo shot of the teacher alone?"[123] Shot duration increases across the first three long takes, from twenty-two seconds to nearly a minute, dragging out the kids' fidgeting as they struggle to hold the pose.

Second, the setting of Tito & Tito's *Class Picture* is a lakeshore rather than a school. Silhouetted against the sky over Taal Lake, the subjects in the foreground are static, while the waves in the background ripple continuously behind them. *Class Picture* makes its subjects appear and disappear instantly against the background by juxtaposing long takes of the school kids and their teacher with empty shots of the coastal horizon via rough jump cuts. These abrupt appearances and disappearances—which recall early cinema's "stop-trick" or substitution splice—gives the film a pronounced ghostliness.

Third, and most crucially, the faces of the students and their teacher are completely unrecognizable due to what would conventionally be considered exposure problems in the film, resulting in an extremely murky, low-contrast image where the water, the sky, and the human figures all look equally gloomy, faded, and indistinct. As with *Bugtong*, which reveled in the aesthetic power of cinematic decay, *Class Picture* makes a virtue of what would normally be considered poor cinematographic exposure by making do with recycled short ends of outdated film stock.

Expired film is characterized by reduced photosensitivity, requiring more light than the manufacturer's stated film speed. Mindful of this, the filmmakers shot *Class Picture* at high noon with an aperture setting five f-stops over that of the original ISO to overcompensate.[124] Despite these precautions, the faces are still spookily illegible, thus undercutting the most basic function of the class picture as a clear visual record of one's school days. The work is silent except for brief portions immediately preceding the title and the end credits when the sound of wind and waves are audible. Using a vintage 16mm Bolex that captures only silent images—the same camera used on many MOWELFUND experimental shorts in the past—the filmmakers recorded location sound on their cell phones. Their decision to use sound sparingly in *Class Picture* further deepens the film's ghostly quality.

Class Picture's overall effect is thus profoundly eerie; rather than regard expired tail ends as flawed materials for filmmaking, Lumbera and Harn clearly revel in the moody, enigmatic quality of the bluish sepia footage. Reversing the naturalized voyeurism of film spectatorship, the subjects look at an audience who can't quite see their faces.[125] The ghostly quality of *Class Picture*, which was shot in 2011 but feels a century older, derives primarily from its recycling of residual media. As Seno notes, the short ends of expired 16mm film were "perfect for the haunting idea of *Class Picture*. [Because] we can't see anything, it becomes a sort of painting, almost; [it has] that painterly quality."[126]

Balete, the Batangas municipality acknowledged in the end credits, is Lumbera's hometown. As Lumbera notes, the Balete setting is likely to strike Filipino audiences as another otherworldly detail: "We felt it was such a magical place, a place named for the enchanted trees where, it is said, so many spirits [*ispirito*] live."[127] The similarly named Balete Drive in New Manila is synonymous with urban legends about a ghostly "white lady," an intertext for the final long take of the isolated teacher, the spookiest figure in the film. Lumbera elaborates on the ghostly figure of the teacher in *Class Picture*: "Why is the teacher scary? Because we aren't used to seeing the teacher alone. . . . But we know that she is alone, as the last person to stay after school. She is the one who stays there constantly,

5.13 & 5.14 The shadowy faces of elementary school students and their teacher are illegible in *Class Picture* (Tito & Tito, 2011), shot in Balete, Batangas, using the short ends of expired 16mm film rolls. Film stills.

while the students continuously change. We don't acknowledge it, but this is what is actually scary."[128]

Teachers are gendered female and imagined as isolated in the film and in the preceding remark. Lumbera's comment induced self-ironic laughter on my part; listening to Lumbera, I realized that I had been spooked by a figural variant of myself. Cognizant of its unnerving quality, the filmmakers never screened *Class Picture* for its subjects. "We never showed them the film. Because we felt . . . they might find it really scary. But sometimes we think about those kids, we wonder where they are and how they're doing, and we want to go back and check on them." Pushed to elaborate on the grounds for this decision, Lumbera added: "We felt it wasn't important that we show it to them. The film process produced another entity that included them. . . . The experience of shooting the film by the lake, that was cinema. It was more important that the event happened, and that the camera recorded the event."[129]

Maintaining that the profilmic event was the core cinematic experience, Lumbera regarded the final output as another "entity" that was not reducible to the subjects themselves. Ultimately, Lumbera claims, neither the names of the filmmakers (already obscured by their professional appellation, Tito & Tito/a) nor the identities of the schoolteacher and her students were essential to the film, which is why the final 35mm film version of *Class Picture* omits final credits in their entirety, further heightening the film's enigmatic quality: "In the last [35mm] cut, there are no credits. We wanted it to be so mysterious that you didn't even know who made it. . . . What matters is that the idea exists and was given form."[130]

As John Powers remarks, "Undoubtedly, some of the pleasure of avant-garde cinema is the ingenious use and misuse of technology" by "exploiting the technology's built-in limitations."[131] Working with expired film to produce imperfect exposures was only the beginning of *Class Picture*'s ingenious misuse of cinematic technology. After the expired film was developed, it was digitized through Tito & Tito's version of make-do kinescoping. Lacking the funds for a telecine transfer, Lumbera and Harn projected the film negative onto white cartolina paper using a 16mm projector; this projected image, in turn, was captured on an HD camera.[132] Lumbera speculates that this "DIY telecine process" resulted in the bluish-tinted frames in *Class Picture*. The digitized negative was then converted into a positive image using the "invert" effect on editing software.[133] Lumbera characterizes Tito & Tito's creative process as unintentional (*hindi sinasadya*), intuitive, and organic: "We just went with the flow of the process and the situation [*dinadala lang kami ng proseso at sitwasyon*]." Epitomizing leftover cinema's innovative misuse of cinematic affordances, both *Bugtong* and *Class Picture* make a virtue of film's ephemerality, making do with deteriorated footage or expired film to use imperfection as the vehicle for aesthetic imagination.

CONCLUSION: TWO PROPOSITIONS FOR INFORMAL CIRCULATION

INFORMAL-TO-FORMAL CIRCULATION: IMPROVISING ACCESS IN A RIVERINE SYSTEM

My first proposition is that the dovetailing of formal and informal audiovisual circulation provides indispensable modes of access for Philippine movies beyond those provided by formal archives. In *Shadow Economies of Cinema*, Ramon Lobato demonstrates that "informal distribution is a central rather than marginal feature of film culture"; the informal side of the worldwide movie economy is "a global norm rather than an exception or deviation."[134] Lobato expounds: "Formality refers to the degree to which industries are regulated, measured, and governed by state and corporate institutions." In contrast, "Informal distributors are those which operate outside this sphere, or in partial articulation with it. . . . Informal distribution is mostly nontheatrical and is characterized by handshake deals, flat-fee sales, and piracy."[135]

If, as Lobato states, "formal theatrical exhibition is no longer the epicenter of cinema culture," then I would argue that formal archives are not the epicenter of access to film history.[136] The two informal collections I have discussed—Video 48 and the Kalampag Tracking Agency—provide ample support for this claim. Formal and informal archival flows interpermeate, as in a river system. For example, one can buy a legal DVD or Blu-ray copy (thus participating in the formal system of film distribution) but then make copies for others without securing permissions from the rights holders, thereby crossing into informal modes of circulation that are harder to track. Instantiating informal-to-formal archival flows, ABS-CBN staffers regularly purchased copies of hard-to-find titles at Video 48 for research and training. The ABS-CBN Film Archives requires permissions from producers and rights holders before making copies of media for researchers like myself; its sister subsidiary, Star Cinema (aka ABS-CBN Film Productions), is one of the Philippines' most prolific film production and distribution companies. Yet while I was at Video 48, where digital files ripped from commercially released DVDs were copied to blank discs or USB flash drives as a matter of course, I learned that ABS-CBN was one of Video 48's long-standing clients.[137] This bears out Lobato's important insight that "there is a great deal of traffic between the formal and the informal" media economies.[138] Formal and informal circulation of archival films dovetail rather than being mutually exclusive.

The best-known informal film practice, media piracy (especially in the global South), has many persuasive scholarly champions. Lobato reminds us not to discount "the efficiency of piracy as a distribution model," offering an alternative understanding of piracy as a "redistributive" form of access.[139] Scholars question the idea that illegal access stymies the formal sale of movies, instead highlighting the economically productive aspects of piracy, which are implicitly institutionalized in Hollywood's own piracy-dependent practices of promotion and distribution.[140] Piracy discourse has been criticized as the paranoid protectionism of the global North, one that reinforces geopolitical inequities.[141]

Informal media practices—which include piracy but are not reducible to it—flow continually into the formal film economy; the informal copy cultures of the global South feed formal archives and prominent media companies. Examples abound: buyers from university libraries, state collections, and corporate media archives were regular consumers of pirated media sold in the illegal DVD stalls of Mexico City and Hanoi.[142] Baumgärtel recalls that the University of the Philippines Film Institute's media collection in the aughts was stocked with "classic and cult films" on pirated DVDs, an indispensable resource for faculty and students alike.[143] Rolando Tolentino caps his stinging rhetorical question "Who in the Philippines is not a pirate?" with the observation that "media piracy has been crucial to the ongoing renaissance of Philippine cinema through independent digital films" from 2005 onward.[144] Tolentino's assertion is echoed by Keith Deligero, a prime mover of the Binisaya film movement, who notes that Filipino indie filmmakers learned from pirated DVDs of international art cinema and that local indie film production and postproduction remain dependent on pirated software.[145]

To be clear, the practices of the Kalampag Tracking Agency and Video 48 do not fall under conventional understandings of media piracy. Joshua Neves and Bhaskar Sarkar convincingly assert that demonizing low-cost, informal duplication obstructs a deeper understanding of Asian media cultures' "improvised infrastructures."[146] I am persuaded by Lawrence

Liang's influential analysis of "porous legalities" in India as "often the only modes through which people can access and create avenues of participation in the new economy." Learning from Liang's provocations about Asian media copy cultures and the need to critically interrogate the naturalized fetish for legality, I approach the informal circulation enabled by both Video 48 and Kalampag as examples of an "elastic legality" that extends across both formal and informal spheres.[147]

The first decade of the new millennium saw the decline and eventual "decimation of the brick-and-mortar video rental business."[148] In the aftermath of the steep downturn in video rentals worldwide, Video 48's shift from a rental to a sales-based model meant that it operated beyond the "'first-sale' principle" of video sell-throughs.[149] It nonetheless remained a highly respected media business targeted by pirate DVD entrepreneurs based in Quiapo.[150] At the time of my visit a year before the store's closure, Video 48's prices were modest. Historically, a borrower's membership required a deposit of 500 pesos (approximately US$10) plus a rental charge of 60 pesos ($1.20) per title; with the decline of its rental business, most customers purchased a digital copy on DVD or a portable drive, with costs ranging from 150 to 500 pesos ($3 if sourced from a DVD, $10 if transferred from a VHS or laser disc). I speculate that Video 48's practices elicited no objections from the Manila media industry because its contribution as a readily accessible archive of Tagalog cinema far outweighed any real or imagined revenue leakage. Video 48 was itself the victim of Quiapo pirate DVD vendors posing as customers; their knockoffs still bore Video 48's logo on their photocopied covers.[151] (Several film scholars have urged a revaluation of Quiapo, a historic but now run-down district whose once-infamous pirate DVD market—much diminished since 2011 due to anti-piracy raids—laid "the foundations for a nascent alternative film scene," as Jasmine Trice puts it.)[152]

For its part, Kalampag's archival retrieval and recirculation of experimental cinema depend on a culture of sharing and generosity within an alternative film community that is largely indifferent to copyright issues, though that older ethos is gradually being eroded by a gallery model that emphasizes rarefied "editioning." Seno recalls that the seeds of her own collection of experimental titles began with the cinephilic sharing exemplified by film critic and archive advocate Alexis Tioseco and filmmaker Roxlee in the early 2000s.[153] The alternative film community's historical emphasis on sharing rather than copyright, however, is giving way to a more profit-centered gallery model:

LIM: Is that the ethos? Mostly sharing, not very worried about rights?

ESPINA: I think so. And it's not just this generation but the generation before. . . . "Oh, you haven't seen it? Oh, here's a copy." There was that kind of generosity. Not so concerned about proper protocols. Nowadays, it's more like here's a copy, but don't tell my distributor or my producer, or my gallery, that type of thing. . . .

SENO: Well, the whole art value system works on the idea of editioning. You don't want it to be seen, you want it to be this prized, very little-shown work that collectors can have the luxury of having. . . .

ESPINA: I really think that by having more access to this material, by uploading this stuff, you create more value. People would want to see it more because maybe they're exposed to it. [In contrast, say you] made that video that no one has seen and at some point, people just forget about it. [SENO. Yeah.] How is that valuable? And then, a lot of the time, it's just burned on a DVD, and that DVD is probably going to rot in four years. So, yeah, it's a bit silly. (chuckles)

Seno and Espina's incisive critique of rarefied editioning against the backdrop of the extreme archival marginalization of experimental works strikes me as spot-on. In contrast, Kalampag locates value not in the curtailment of circulation but in its unimpeded flow.

Mapping archival circulation as a riverine system demands that Kalampag and Video 48's formal-to-informal movie exchanges, often without the rights holder's imprimatur, be recognized as headwaters for the Filipino film scene, as crucial archival sources without which the waterways of Philippine cinema would long ago have run dry. Coincidentally, Espina used a riverine metaphor when describing Kalamapag as an embankment: "We just happened to save/keep/accumulate and remember a lot of materials that passed our way. This informal circulation of digital files and various media is not uncommon to us. There are several people who do this across generations. Things just flow and sometimes accumulate at certain points of embankment. We just happened to be one of those banks."[154]

Kalampag as a riverbank on which alternative films have accumulated, as one of many stops along a coursing archival waterway, affirms that audiovisual circulation is characterized by "multiple vectors of pathfinding across the cinematic field."[155] Compared with the high barriers to entry at formal archives, informal collections like Video 48 and the Kalampag Tracking Agency allow older titles and marginalized works to circulate more broadly.

ARCHIVAL POTENTIATIONS (OR INFORMALITY AS MAKING DO)

In closing this chapter, I offer a second (briefer) proposition to encapsulate the preceding discussion. Improvisational archival initiatives—exemplified by Video 48 and the Kalampag Tracking Agency—rely on practices of making do that foreground the capacity of such informal yet indispensable archives to "potentiate." I draw this verb from Bhaskar Sarkar's exuberant theorization of piracy as potentiating rather than parasitical. To potentiate is to "build on current productivities, proliferate spontaneous energies, and open up unanticipated vistas of ingenuity. . . . This potentiation is actualized as ground-level economic activities, cultural circuits, and leveling socialities—which then expand and multiply via fecund linkages and feedback loops."[156] Informal archives' potentiation drove new forms of improvisational circulation in a film buff's video store and in the microcuratorial efforts of self-described "hoarders" who track down overlooked experimental works. Their resourceful exercise of archival power as making do broadened access in the face of a pronounced archival vacuum that major corporate and state archives have not been able to fill. Video 48 and the Kalampag Tracking Agency can be understood as generative improvisations that respond to restrictive infrastructures by innovating new ones; without their efforts, even fewer works would have survived to flow through the riverine system of Philippine film archiving.

CHAPTER SIX

Binisaya

Archival Power and Vernacular Audiences in Iskalawags

Archival silence refers not just to lost films or knowledge gaps concerning the collapse of prior film collections. Archival lacunae shape the very conception of Philippine national cinema and the narrativization of its history. Michel-Rolph Trouillot writes, "Historical narratives are premised . . . on the distribution of archival power."[1] As such, attempts to rewrite Philippine film history—with an eye toward nonindustrial filmmaking in a plurality of languages from various regions of the archipelago—wrest archival power away from "imperial Manila."[2] Exerted by and for vernacular cinemas, this is a form of archival power whose time has finally come. From the middle of the aughts onward, digital independent and alternative films made outside Manila's commercial industry in a variety of Philippine languages—"Ilocano, Kapampangan, Pangasinan, Bicol, Cebuano, Bisaya, Hiligaynon, Chavacano, and a host of indigenous languages"—have issued what Katrina Ross Tan calls a "direct challenge" to the "legitimacy of Tagalog as the language of Philippine cinema."[3] As Paul Grant emphasizes, at this point "one would be hard-pressed to make a case for a national cinema that is not polyglot and poly-regional."[4]

The ascendancy of Tagalog in an ethnolinguistically diverse archipelago composed of over 180 languages and more than seven thousand islands is deep-rooted. Constitutional provisions dating from the Commonwealth period declared Tagalog the bedrock for the fledgling republic's national language, thus implicitly demoting other regional and indigenous languages to the status of "dialects." Emphasizing the nation-binding role of language as bridging ethnic, regional, and linguistic differences in the postcolony-to-be, President Manuel L. Quezon's 1936 address to the National Assembly noted, "The Constitution recognizes the fact that there is no common native language spoken by the Filipino people. . . . A language spoken and understood by all . . . constitutes one of the strongest ties that bind the people and foster a unity of national ideas, aspirations, and sentiments." That same year, the Institute of National Language—created by Commonwealth Act 184 and composed of seven scholars representing several major Philippine tongues—was tasked with choosing a single vernacular as the foundation for a national language (*wikang pambansa*). The institute's selection of Tagalog led to Quezon's Executive Order 134, which declared Tagalog the basis of the national language in 1937. Officially called Pilipino in 1959 and rechristened Filipino in 1973, the Tagalog-based national language faced vociferous regionalist resentment among non-Tagalogs who instead championed English and other vernaculars in ensuing decades.[5] As Vicente Rafael remarks, Filipino as national language—"projected as the potential language of cultural authenticity with which to articulate a precolonial past with a decolonized future"—has never entirely fulfilled such aims. English, the legatee of American imperialism and an official language since 1935, is still accorded the greatest social distinction in the hierarchy of Philippine languages.[6]

Cinema accomplished the nation-binding work that constitutional mandates alone could not, disseminating Tagalog to audiences all over the ethnolinguistically diverse archipelago. In the 1930s, the advent of sound led to an unexpected rise in the popularity of domestically produced movies vis-à-vis imported fare. Clodualdo del Mundo Jr. writes, "Although foreign distributors were convinced that sound would not discourage Filipinos from watching films in English and that there was a sufficient number of English-speaking people in Manila 'to warrant the installation of talking equipment,' they did not foresee the boost in local productions that the new technology would provide." Filipino audiences in the thirties patronized local movies in growing numbers, drawn by the sound of Philippine languages. With the decline of Visayan regional filmmaking in the 1970s, Filipino cinema was conflated with one vernacular whose ascendancy was linked to the urban center of the local film industry: "Filipino filmmaking is based in Manila and Philippine films are basically Tagalog.

The dominance of Manila-based movies could also be credited for the spread of Filipino, the Philippine language, which is based on Tagalog."[7]

Tagalog cinema eroded the hold of English but also relegated other vernaculars and regional film movements to off-screen space. "Philippine films are basically Tagalog": historically, the conflation of national cinema with a privileged regional language, echoed in the colloquial use of "Tagalog movies" to refer to Philippine cinema, has produced archival silences that are difficult to redress. Most historiographies of Philippine cinema elide vernacular cinemas other than Tagalog, with a few notable exceptions.

In a pioneering essay, "In Search of Philippine Regional Cinema" (1987), Teddy Co bemoaned a specific casualty of this archival vacuum: "The once-promising Visayan movie industry has never been written about at length by our Manila-based film critics and historians," despite the fact that Cebuano (also known as Bisaya and Visayan, all synonymous terms for the language, the people who speak it, and the Visayas islands as one of the three main regions of the archipelago) "is spoken in Cebu, Bohol, Western Visayas, Negros, in the northern and eastern coasts of Mindanao, and parts of Bukidnon, Agusan, Surigao, Davao, Cotabato, and Zamboanga."[8] Nick Deocampo's monograph *Films from a "Lost" Cinema: A Brief History of Cebuano Films* (2005) likewise laments the archival void surrounding Visayan cinema, which "lost out to more aggressive Tagalog and Hollywood film histories."[9] Grant concurs: "While many regions are today producing some of the most innovative work in the Philippines, historically there is one challenger to Tagalog film hegemony that has its own history, its own 'auteurs,' its own stars and a long tradition . . . of local film writing: Cebu (Sugbo)."[10] Grant's characterization of Tagalog-language, Manila-centric cinema as "hegemonic" implicitly situates Visayan cinema and other vernacular films made outside the national capital as counterhegemonic practices that offer "a powerful retort" to normative conceptions of Philippine national cinema.

Following the peak of Cebuano moviemaking in the late forties and fifties, Visayan cinema declined in the late sixties. Deocampo enumerates the structural reasons for its demise: prohibitively high production costs; the national government's promulgation of Tagalog-based Filipino; the lack of postproduction facilities in Cebu; the eventual "exodus" of Cebuano film talents to Manila; and, above all, the absence of a Visayan-controlled distribution and exhibition system nimble enough to thwart the Manila industry's control over the nation's theatrical market.[11]

Vernacular cinemas' structural disadvantages might be understood in Trouillot's terms as "lived inequalities" that "yield unequal historical power," that is, the tendency to narrate Philippine cinema as synonymous with the Tagalog movies disseminated by the Manila film industry. Grant gives quantitative shape to this archival asymmetry: whereas the earliest surviving Tagalog feature films date from the 1930s, there are only four extant Visayan films from the photochemical era, the earliest from 1969.[12] Sadly, Grant observes, "The Cebuano cinema of the pre-digital age is all but lost."[13] The upshot of the archival vacuum surrounding Visayan cinema is that "the question of a reliable historiography is posed rather dramatically."[14]

This chapter explores the Binisaya movement's wresting of archival power away from the Manila film industry as the country's geocinematic center to reckon with the ongoing history of Visayan vernacular cinema.[15] Learning from Patrick Campos's interview with prime movers of the Binisaya movement, I understand Binisaya in a capacious sense as encompassing, first, a generation of filmmakers in Cebu who began making short films in 2005 prior to launching the Binisaya film festival in 2009 (Remton Zuasola, Keith Deligero, Victor Villanueva, Christian Linaban, Ara Chawdhury, and others). Second, it includes the "film-watching community" their works reach.[16] Third, it includes a new generation of film scholars, Paul Grant and Misha Boris Anissimov chief among them, engaged in excavating the lost history of Cebuano cinema.[17] Binisaya as a community composed of filmmakers, historians, artists, and audiences coalesced via regional film festivals and key institutional hubs in Cebu, such as the International Academy of Film and Television and the Cinema Program at the University of San Carlos (USC), the latter being the academic home of Grant and Anissimov.[18] Some of the prime movers of Binisaya are alumni of USC Talamban: Keith Deligero, Remton Zuasola, and Victor Villanueva were college classmates.[19]

The ensuing analysis of the Binisaya movement illuminates how film scholars and filmmakers have responded to the archival silence surrounding Visayan movies by undoing entrenched absences in the dominant understanding of Philippine national cinema. I begin by recounting how Binisaya scholars work to reconstitute the lost history of Cebuano cinema before turning to Binisaya filmmaker Keith Deligero's 2013 film *Iskalawags* (Scalawags), which is the principal focus of this chapter. Binisaya scholarship and filmmaking leave behind concrete archival artifacts: publications, films, and paratextual materials. Beyond these more expected examples of what constitutes an archival record, however, this chapter locates, in *Iskalawags*, less obvious traces of contemporary struggles in Visayan media culture.

Iskalawags is a nostalgic media archive that registers the formative influence of Manila's popular culture on young Visayan audiences. The collective protagonists of the film—the titular *iskalawags* or "rascals"—are a group of Cebuano boys who eagerly consume action films and pop ballads from Manila. Intranational cultural imperialism and asymmetries between the urban capital and a remote island in Cebu are signaled by the boys' consumption of pirated Betamax and audiocassette tapes, carriers that were long obsolete in Manila by the late 1990s and early 2000s, when the film is set. Sardonic and sentimental by turns, *Iskalawags* champions Visayan language and humor in its multilingual send-up of the hierarchy of Philippine languages as enshrined in school curricula. In its extraordinary climax, the film turns into a self-reflexive ouroboros, simulating a Binisaya informal beach screening in Cebu.[20] The production history subtending the film's finale confirms its value as an affective archive of the early Binisaya movement's audience-building attempts to overcome rarefied film festival circulation through informal outdoor screenings. The chapter closes with a discussion of the Philippines' three most influential film festivals—the Cinemalaya Philippine Independent Film Festival, Cinema One Originals Film Festival, and Cinema Rehiyon (Cinema of the regions)—to highlight the structural challenges posed by film festival distribution and the limits of "poverty porn." I contextualize Binisaya's dream of self-distribution alongside other historical models for the alternative circulation of independent and vernacular films.

Throughout, I draw on interviews with Keith Deligero and other filmmakers as well as video documentation of Binisaya screenings, festivals, and behind-the-scenes accounts of the production and circulation of contemporary Visayan movies in Cebu. I approach these sources not as definitive pronouncements that certify a supposed "truth" or authoritative "intention" behind *Iskalawags* and the Binisaya movement. Rather, in focusing on what John Caldwell might call the movement's own "self-theorizing"—its "self-representation, self-critique, and self-reflection"—I hope to shed light on how Binisaya prime movers understand their work, goals, and tactics vis-à-vis the sobering challenges the movement confronts.[21]

BINISAYA SCHOLARSHIP: "UNEARTHING SILENCES"

In their groundbreaking book *Lilas: An Illustrated History of the Golden Ages of Cebuano Cinema* (2016), Grant and Anissimov describe their response to archival silence as a methodological turn to paracinematic ephemera:

> One of the primary issues faced by the student of Cebuano cinema is the rather rude fact that the majority of the films are now unavailable to screen, thus the moniker of "lost cinema." How could those who undertake writing the history find anything to say about the films if they cannot be seen? . . . We pick up the pieces in the archives, amongst the debris and ephemera, the *para-cinematic* elements . . . that remain, and from there we begin to construct (and here the purposeful nature is explicit) a narrative based on the most concrete evidence we can find.[22]

What Anissimov and Grant describe as a purposeful reconstruction of lost cinematic history through paratextual sources recalls Trouillot's evocative metaphor for the historian's archival labor: "The unearthing of silences, and the historian's subsequent emphasis on the retrospective significance of hitherto neglected events, requires not only extra labor at the archives—whether or not one uses primary sources—but also a project linked to an interpretation."[23] The attempt to unearth neglected histories demands the creative work of interpretation because accreted silences tend to congeal.

In another important intervention, Binisaya scholarship problematizes the category *regional cinema*, a term that enjoys wide usage in many institutional contexts, from film festival circles to academia. Persuaded by such critiques of the regional cinema rubric, I adopt the term *vernacular cinemas* to refer to filmmaking in non-Tagalog languages originating in local communities and ethnolinguistic and/or geographic regions outside Metro Manila. Both Grant (a Binisaya film historian) and Campos (a Manila-based scholar) note the various scales at which the term *regional* can be used in relation to Philippine cinema, from the transnational (e.g., the films of Southeast Asia as a region) to the intra- or subnational level (e.g., the cinemas of the Mindanao, Bicol, and Bisaya regions).[24] Beyond the potentially confusing geographic scales at which the term "regional" might be used, Grant incisively notes that despite its progressive potential, the regional may unwittingly reinscribe the homogenizing tendency undergirding the concept of national cinema. Grant writes:

> The idea of a regional cinema has its obvious appeal; it invokes hopes of a local, sometimes minor, conception of cinema that challenges the aesthetics, fetishized production values and corporatism of dominant national cinemas. . . . Given that a region . . . is a form of local community or territory within a nation, it is in some sense *required to pass first through the difficult terrain of the national*. This is primarily because even while the regional approach offers a more heterogeneous and hybrid expression of what makes up a nation—expressions that give more credence to indigenous, local and perhaps above all linguistic distinctions—it still maintains . . . constitutive parameters that tend towards a *potential homogenization*.[25]

The implicit homogeneity, internal consistency, and ethnolinguistic self-sameness posited by the regional are the focus of Grant and Anissimov's critique: "Are we not, ultimately, faced with an imagined region with a fixed, unified, and coherent narrative?"[26] Their misgivings recall Andrew Higson's germinal critique of national cinema as a "hegemonising, mythologizing process" that amounts to a "form of internal cultural colonialism."[27] Cultural homogenization for Higson is that process by which the culture of a social fragment is projected as the culture of an entire nation. The "national" in national cinema, therefore, does not denote a shared culture that unequivocally unifies a nation; rather, it articulates that which vies for cultural legitimacy on national terms. While the national framework was crucial to the assumptive horizon of cinema studies in its formative years, scholars have come to recognize that the rubric of nation, like that of region, is a boundary effect dependent on "the perimeter of the state."[28] The imagined coherence of such bounded entities has unraveled in the face of multiply scalar worlds, from the subnational to the global.

To posit, for example, a culturally distinct "Cebuano-ness" as the defining feature of Visayan/Cebuano/Binisaya cinema is to fall back on a notion of "cultural expressivity" that ultimately replicates, on the regional level, the very "suppressed internal boundaries and differences" that the national projected and that the regional had hoped to circumvent. Grant and Anissimov ask: "Is there such a thing as *Cebuanoness*? . . . Or is such an essentializing undertaking ultimately futile?"[29] Problematizing the homogenizing premise of cultural expressivity in regional cinema, they prefer to embrace the term *vernacular cinema* to foreground not a unified ethnolinguistic identity (an alleged "Cebuano-ness") but the primacy of language, reception, and circulation. On the one hand, "it is language in the final instance that will determine a Cebuano film," especially given that Visayan as a translocal, interisland language was crucial to Cebuano cinema's historical success.[30] (Pan-Visayan audiences across the archipelago constituted 40 percent of the national film market in the sixties.[31]) On the other hand, the reception and circulation of these films allow us to glimpse "what is of value in the Cebuano cinematic experience" from the perspective of its audiences.[32]

The critique of cultural expressivity by Binisaya scholars is echoed by Vicente Groyon, who analyzes regional film festivals as the motive force behind vernacular filmmaking since 2009, given that festivals are these films' primary funding source, distribution platform, and exhibition venue. Groyon notes that the "regional identities" (i.e., cultural expressivity) exhibited by various non-Tagalog films at the inaugural Cinema Rehiyon film festival in Manila were not articulations of identity; rather, they were generated by "conscious and unconscious" curatorial choices externally "imposed by sponsor organizations." To the degree that Cinema Rehiyon catalyzed an upswing in regional filmmaking while remaining tethered to state agencies in the national capital (i.e., the NCCA), Groyon cautions that received definitions and expectations of regional cinemas at influential festivals—as operationalized by curatorial frameworks—inadvertently replicate the controlling "gaze of Manila."[33]

My central objection to the regional cinema category is its tendency to equate "the regional" with non-Tagalog productions, thus ceding "the national" to the Tagalog-language Manila film industry and reaffirming the latter as the norm against which "the regional" signifies ethnolinguistic diversity. It bears remembering that despite its historical status as the Philippines' geocinematic center, the National Capital Region (NCR) of Metro Manila—the urban center of the Tagalog region in the island of Luzon—is itself (merely) regional and is not coextensive with the Philippines. Unthinkingly applied, the term *regional cinema* threatens to devolve into a polite euphemism for "films from the provinces." By contrast, the insurgent force of vernacular cinemas lies in their capacity to expose the provincialism of Manila culture and the unacknowledged linguistic ethnocentrism that its long-unchallenged dominance fosters.

Reflecting on his years as a co-organizer for Cinema Rehiyon during the Duterte regime's declaration of martial law in Mindanao (2016–19), Patrick Campos recalls a "moment of clarity": "Being in Mindanao for Cinema Rehiyon while remaining acutely aware of being not *from* there,

I had a keen sense of observing Philippine national cinema at a remove, recognizing how it is neither homogeneous nor singular. . . . I grasped quite viscerally what I had known intellectually: that Manila, my own location, was exceedingly 'provincial,' where the norm had been to capture Philippine cinema as an object beheld from an aerial view, obscuring the details of its coordinates." Campos distills the point beautifully: "Manila, my own location, was exceedingly 'provincial.'"[34] The questioning of national cinema provincializes and contests the notion that Manila's "captive culture," as Resil Mojares puts it, is metonymic of the archipelago.[35] The central intervention of the rubric *vernacular cinema* is to oppose a compensatory multiculturalism that merely supplements Manila moviemaking with regional output while leaving Manila's dominance and national cinema's fictive homogeneity intact.

BINISAYA FILMMAKING: *ISKALAWAGS*

The vital themes that undergird Binisaya scholarship—Visayan cinema's archival vacuum, the primacy of language to Visayan audiences, and the domestic variant of cultural imperialism exerted by the Manila entertainment industry—are all explored in Binisaya filmmaker Keith Deligero's *Iskalawags*, a 2013 film that confronts the cultural aporia surrounding Visayan filmmaking and archives the Binisaya movement's audience-building efforts beyond the film festival circuit.

The Binisaya film movement emerged against the backdrop of a pronounced archival vacuum, since Binisaya filmmakers were not reared on Cebuano films. Deligero recalls his creative cohort's belated introduction to Visayan film history through the work of Binisaya scholars: "I don't think any of us grew up watching Cebuano films. We became aware that there was a 'golden age' of Cebuano cinema just recently, when we were already making films ourselves. It's a good thing that we have people like Paul [Grant] and Misha [Anissimov], who are studying Cebuano film history. Because of them, we got to see the films from back then."[36] Of growing up in Cebu, Deligero recalls, "When we were kids, all the pop culture that we were exposed to came from Manila."[37] In keeping with the filmmaker's observations, *Iskalawags* ambivalently memorializes the pleasures of Manila-centric media while proffering a playful and potent alternative to its soft power.

Grant calls Deligero the enfant terrible of Binisaya cinema, "creating work that is independent and uncompromising in the strict sense of both of those terms" and espousing an aesthetic approach markedly different from his contemporaries. "Whereas his colleagues in Cebu approach cinema via genre or art-house conventions, Deligero creates feature-length works that are composed of illicit images and a harsh pastiche of metal, punk and other sonic disturbances." In contrast to the slow cinema approach of other Filipino indie auteurs, "hard-cutting and black comedy take precedence over contemplative cinematography or static narrative" in Deligero's films.[38] While *Iskalawags* offers witty metacommentary on popular genres (particularly the Tagalog action film, or *bakbakan*, and American porn), its unique visual, sonic, and improvisational style makes it a movie without a genre.[39]

In Neil Briones's eleven-minute documentary, *Shooting Iskalawags in Camotes* (2013), Deligero is interviewed on location in Cebu's Camotes Islands.[40] *Shooting Iskalawags in Camotes* (referred to hereafter in shortened form) is directed by one of Deligero's Binisaya collaborators (Briones shares *Iskalawags*' cinematography credits with Deligero) and was completed as a "special class project" for a course taught at USC Talamban's Cinema Program by Misha Anissimov, a Binisaya scholar. As a communal, collective documentary short, *Shooting Iskalawags* is of significant interest because the history and study of subcultures—including cinematic ones—often require recourse to alternative archives, self-generated traces of dynamic but often short-lived creative scenes and aesthetic movements. In hindsight, both Deligero's feature film *Iskalawags* and Briones's behind-the-scenes documentary *Shooting Iskalawags* can be recognized as important archival records of the Binisaya community's filmmaking ethos and commitment to audience building. These cinematic archival documents originate from within the Binisaya scene itself.

Both *Iskalawags* and Briones's documentary are multilingual, unfolding primarily in Cebuano or Visayan, with English and Tagalog words sprinkled liberally throughout. *Shooting Iskalawags* is an extended interview with Deligero, who describes *Iskalawags* as "a story about seven friends who lived in a fishing village in Barangay Malinawon, Camotes Islands." These pubescent boys are the eponymous scalawags, mischievous young rascals who plan to poach the enormous papayas growing just outside the home of their pretty schoolteacher, Ma'am Lina (Dionne Monsanto). Adapted from a Visayan-language short story, "Kapayas"

(Papayas) by Erik Tuban, *Iskalawags* hews closely to Tuban's coming-of-age narrative.[41] At the same time, it infuses the narrative with the shared memories and observations of the collaborative filmmaking team. "It's a compilation of fragments, a mixture of nostalgic memories," Deligero reflects. "It's made up of observations and past experiences. Summers when we were fifth graders. It's a mixture. It's possible to call it autobiographical on the part of Erik Tuban, Gale Osorio, Remton Zuasola, myself . . . Neil Briones, and others.[42] It's the autobiographical childhood of everyone involved in the movie."[43]

In what follows, I explore *Iskalawags* as a nostalgic media archive of a Cebuano boyhood lived under the shadow of Manila's and Hollywood's popular cultural dominance; as a satirical critique that overturns the Philippine hierarchy of languages in favor of the Visayan vernacular; and as a valuable record of the early Binisaya movement's attempts to build a local audience through alternative distribution and exhibition initiatives.

A MEDIA ARCHIVE OF CEBUANO ADOLESCENCE

A nostalgic, nonsynchronous, and materialist media archive of a Visayan adolescence, *Iskalawags* takes a deep dive into its collective protagonists' pop cultural diet: Tagalog action movies, American porn, and punk music from Cavite and Cebu alongside local religious programming. Our delinquent heroes are avid consumers of residual media: bootlegged Betamax tapes watched on a CRT TV, metal audiocassette tapes, and radio shows heard on a transistorized boom box (figures 6.1–6.3).

As Deligero puts it, "The entire point of the movie is that it's a throwback film." Although both Deligero's film and Tuban's short story are retrospectively narrated, the story's temporal setting is never spelled out in either work. Temporal cues are offered primarily in relation to media: the boys' cherished action movie idols (Jeric Raval and Raymart Santago) and a maudlin love song by April Boys suggest that the film is set sometime in the late 1990s or early 2000s. By this time, both Betamax and audiocassettes were long obsolete in Manila. Of outdated media, Deligero muses, "I consider pop culture as chapter markers of history," adding, "The farther you get, the more obsolete are the current things people are listening to. When you say that Betamax at the time was obsolete in the center of the Philippines, it was still being used in farther areas."[44] The profusion of residual

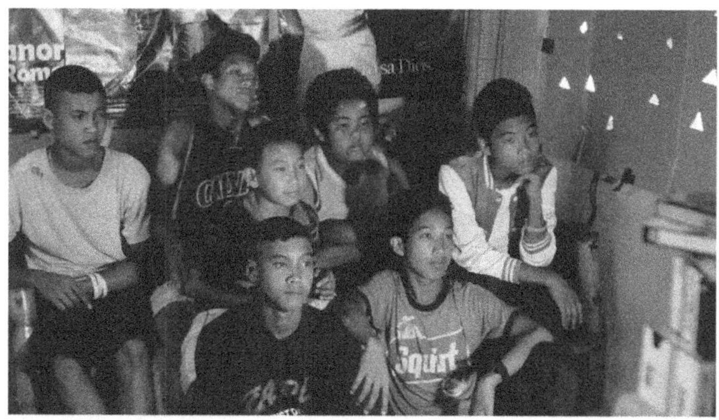

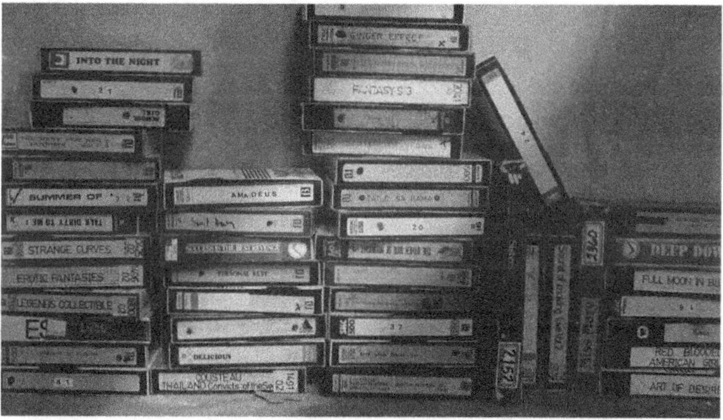

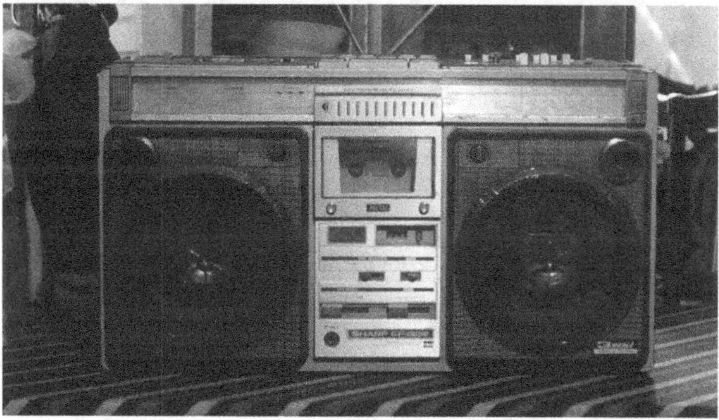

6.1–6.3 The protagonists of *Iskalawags* (Rascals; dir. Keith Deligero, 2013) consume all manner of residual media, from bootlegged Betamax tapes watched on a CRT TV to metal audiocassette tapes and radio shows played on a transistorized boom box. Film stills.

media in *Iskalawags* foregrounds class issues, center-periphery dynamics, and the reciprocal flows of rural-to-urban migration.

As noted previously, the film's title refers to a group of seven teenage boys from the fictional Barrio Malinawon, somewhere on a remote island in Cebu at the turn of the millennium.[45] The boys rakishly refer to themselves as the "*iskalawags*," inspired by a 1997 Tagalog action film of the same title, *Iskalawags: Ang Batas Ay Batas* (Scalawags: The law is the law; dir. Francis Posadas). We are introduced to the young miscreants fifteen minutes into the film: Poldo (Joriel Lunzaga), grandson of the village fishmonger, is constantly mistaken for Elyok (Jonhreil Lunzaga). This recurring joke is conveyed by a brief flurry of two-shots in which the boys, played by real-life twins, appear virtually indistinguishable. Jared Bulldog (Micko Maurillo), the son of Nestor, a *sari-sari* convenience store owner, routinely ignores his friends' wisecracks about his weight (they call him "Tambukikoy" or "Fatty"). The littlest member is the school-smart Liklik (Mark Lourence Montalban), often framed against a classroom blackboard. Romart (Windel Otida), whose mother owns the Betamakan (Betamax shop) where the *iskalawags* voraciously consume videotapes of their favorite movies, is the pretty boy of the group. Palot (Kerwin Otida), the son of a drowned fisherman, is the oldest of the *iskalawags* and their leader. Our narrator Intoy recounts their misadventures in a series of seamlessly interwoven flashbacks.[46] Intoy is brought to life by a composite performance: on the visual track, he appears for most of the film as a teenager played by Reynaldo Formentera, except for the final scene, when the adult Intoy is played by author Erik Tuban himself. On the soundtrack, the adult voice of Intoy's retrospective narration is that of director Deligero. The composite performance behind Intoy highlights the collective authorship of the film's loosely autobiographical vignettes.

Iskalawags' consummate nonlinear editing moves backward and forward in time, emulating the confident achronological style of Tuban's short story (as evident in the author's own English translation of his Cebuano tale). Similarly, Deligero, who got his start as a film and video editor, thinks of his films as "editor pieces."[47] In the short story "Kapayas," narrative past and present are often grammatically conflated by using the present tense and adverbs such as *now*, just as Intoy's narration in *Iskalawags* relates various memories in a manner that is temporally unmoored yet never confusing. (Shots of an English grammar lesson on the past perfect continuous tense might be construed as an inside joke on the editing.) The film retrospectively revisits the boys' teenage misadventures while emphasizing the immediacy of the recollected past for the narrator in the present. The plot to purloin Ma'am Lina's papayas is the *iskalawags'* most daring scheme; scenes where the boys hatch and execute this plan constitute an approximate narrative present and drive home the story's titular erotic motif (as the feminized "forbidden fruit" they yearn to pluck, the papayas are metonymic of the boys' sexual curiosity and raunchy humor). Yet this is only one of the film's many motifs and allusions.

Immediately preceding the title card, the memorable opening scene begins with Palot aiming a toy pistol at Elyok while accosting him with the words "Hoy, Valderama."[48] The line alludes to a classic Tagalog *bakbakan* movie, *Hindi Ka Na Sisikatan ng Araw: Kapag Puno na ang Salop, Part III* (dir. Pablo Santiago, 1990) starring legendary action film icon Fernando Poe Jr., known to fans as FPJ.[49] The first part of the title quotes the movie's most memorable line, in which FPJ's Guerrero, a righteous populist hero, tells the corrupt Judge Valderama that he will not live to see another sunrise. The second half of the title refers elliptically to an idiomatic Tagalog phrase ("*kapag puno na ang salop, kailangan kalusin*"). The idiom makes an analogy between leveling off (*kalusin*) an overflowing measure of rice (*salop*) and cutting an adversary down to size.[50] The Visayan boys' pretend play takes considerable license with the Tagalog source film. Their Tagalog dialogue is a pastiche of the film's title and other snappy comebacks typical of the Tagalog *bakbakan* genre, delivered with a pronounced Cebuano accent by Palot (as the heroic Guerrero), who faces off against Elyok (as the evil Judge Valderama) at the beginning of the scene. With the boys' toy pistols pointed menacingly at each other while the camera zooms in on their faces, their over-the-top parody reimagines Manila's action movies with a dark Visayan twist (figures 6.4–6.6). The scene ends with all the Tagalog-speaking tough guys bested by a Visayan dude played by Bulldog, who shouts, "You're all crazy!" (*Buang kamong tanan!*) in Cebuano before mowing everyone down with a faux machine gun. This note of Bisaya victory is followed immediately by the film's title shot of the *iskalawags'* hand-painted banner. The highly intertextual "Hoy Valderama" scene is itself a motif; the scene is reenacted a second time later in the film, with the boys using their fingers and broken-off twigs to simulate weapons.

As an affective archive of a rural Cebuano boyhood in the 1990s, *Iskalawags* is dense with allusions to the action movie idols of the Tagalog *bakbakan* genre. Various cinephilic, multilingual allusions emphasize that Tagalog action stars offer a thrilling template for Visayan adolescent masculinity. Beyond the film's many nods to FPJ, there are recurring

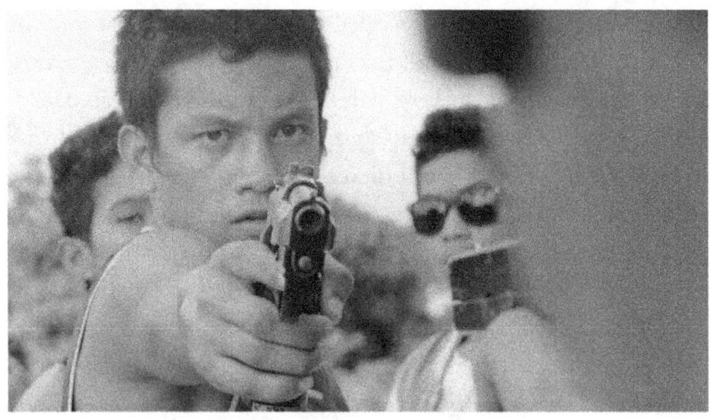

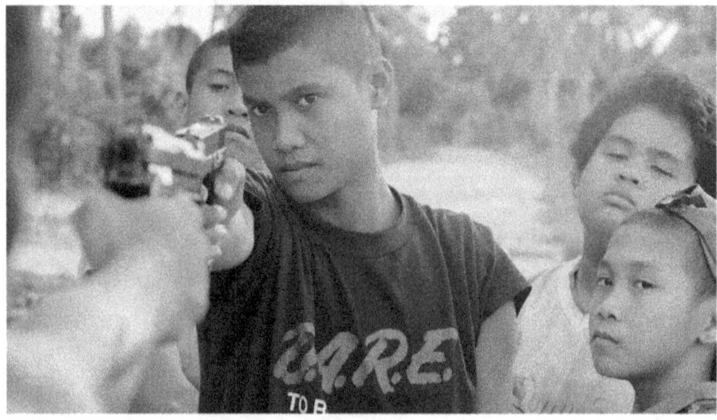

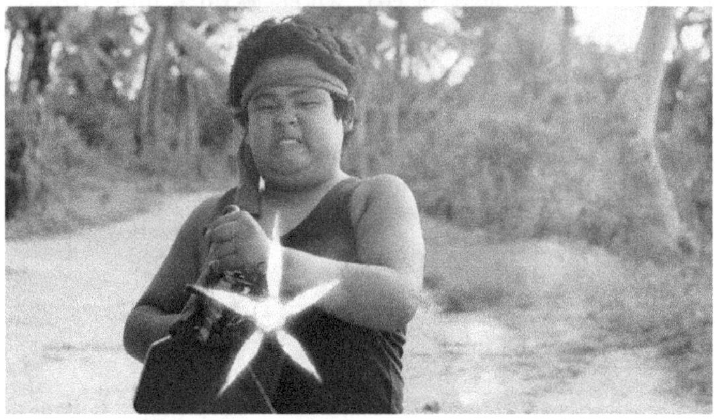

6.4–6.6 The memorable opening scene of *Iskalawags*, in which Palot (Kerwin Otida, *top*) aims a toy pistol at Elyok (Jonhreil Lunzaga, *middle*), alludes to classic Tagalog action movies (*bakbakan*). The Tagalog-speaking tough guys are gunned down by Bulldog (Micko Maurillo, *bottom*), who yells, "You're all crazy!" in Cebuano. Film stills.

references to several other male action stars. "Ramon! Ramon," a music track by the Cavite-based band The Dropouts, plays on the soundtrack as the boys horse around. The Tagalog song pays homage to *bakbakan* star Ramon Revilla. Its lyrics refer to a 1986 film starring both FPJ and Revilla, *Iyo ang Tondo, Kanya ang Cavite* (Tondo is yours, Cavite is his; dir. Pablo Santiago). Stardom and a send-up of dynastic national politics underpin the song's place-bound allusions: FPJ, a presidential contender during his lifetime, was from Tondo in Manila; Revilla, a former senator, hailed from Cavite in Southern Luzon; both Tagalog stars had children who went on to become senators, highlighting how a movie pedigree in the Philippines can launch a political clan.

Both the film and the source story reference action film star Jeric Raval. Raval himself appears in a cameo as the military husband of Ma'am Lina; a faulty motorcycle forces him to return home unannounced in the film's finale. Poldo and Elyok come across Raval's character twice, on his way home to their schoolteacher. Throughout, the *iskalawags* perceive him as Ma'am Lina's husband, not as an extrafilmic action star. That the real-life actor Raval both is and is not playing himself in *Iskalawags* is of a piece with Deligero's idea that "things are and are not themselves," which applies also to the scenes from Binisaya films excerpted in the climax.[51]

A short, shrill musical cue with trumpet and drums marks the tense, wordless confrontation between the *iskalawags* and the soldier-husband played in cameo by Raval. It is a momentary clash of Visayan versus Tagalog cinematic masculinities that goes nowhere, rendering these scenes simultaneously dramatic and absurd. Alluding to American film noir music as a cinematic shorthand for suspense, the brief trumpet and drums leitmotif associated with Raval—which punctuates the "Hoy Valderama" scenes as well—recalls the opening of Henri Mancini's main title music for *Touch of Evil* (Orson Welles, 1958). Deligero notes that "Manila's action films were very Western-influenced, even in their music cues."[52] These references to Tagalog action stars and Hollywood genres, like the recurring motif of group shots in which the *iskalawags* pose directly for the camera, tell us that the Cebuano boys see themselves in the influential scripts offered by Tagalog and American movie genres as the larger-than-life action heroes of their own small-town exploits.

Several scenes show the *iskalawags* clustered around a bulky old TV, watching pirated videocassettes of their two favorite genres, action and porn, at the Betamakan owned by the one of the boys' parents. These frontal direct shots of the group form a recurring motif. The *iskalawags* are a

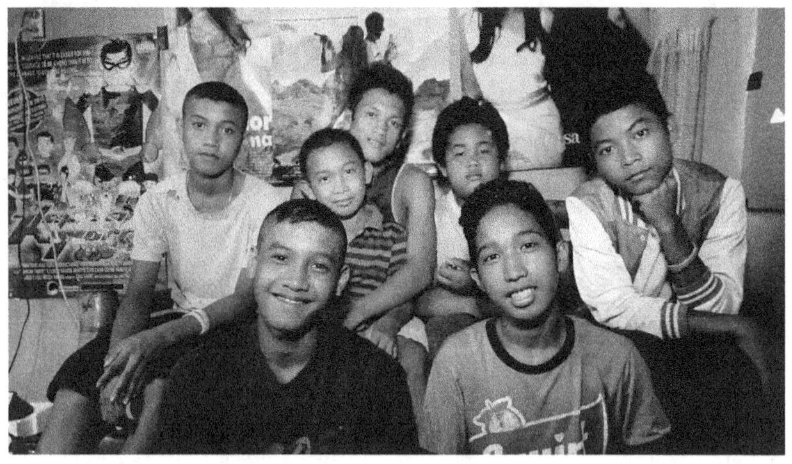

6.7 Recurring frontal group shots frame the *iskalawags* as a diegetic cinephilic audience that often seems to break the fourth wall by looking directly at the extrafilmic audience. Film still.

diegetic audience of dedicated movie buffs who, in one of the film's many self-reflexive touches, often seem to break the fourth wall by looking directly at us, the extrafilmic audience. *Iskalawags* is a movie for and about audiences like them, and like ourselves (figure 6.7).

Perforated sheets of cardboard line the windows of the tiny videotape rental shop, converting it into a makeshift movie theater, as envious townsfolk outside try to get a glimpse. Hanging out at the Betamakan, the boys become avid movie buffs who repeatedly rewatch action flicks or their favorite English-language porn tape, a pirated copy of *Tarzan X: The Shame of Jane*. Bootlegged videotapes consumed in informal small-town screening venues like the Betamakan were childhood staples that the director states he explicitly set out to archive in fictional form: "In every town there's always this house that opens itself to the neighborhood. All the neighbors would watch something at that house, and you'd pay one or two pesos. They would probably be the only house in that town with a Betamax [player]. Outside the door of the house, you'd see a lot of slippers, a lot of kids inside, so it's that kind of thing I wanted to preserve in the film."[53]

Deligero adds that the tapes screened in such houses were invariably bootlegged: "The distributors of those films wouldn't care to sell them in those small islands."[54] In *Iskalawags*, the provenance of obsolete, pirated media not only signifies Camotes Islands' geographic remoteness from

Manila as center but also indexes social mobility and migratory flows. The filmmaker speculates that the folks who ran informal screening houses in rural areas had the means to travel back and forth between province and city: "The rich people who grew up there went away, got those titles, came back, and then rerecorded and rented out that content, all of which are bootlegged."[55]

The film's boldly anachronistic soundtrack combines residual media with contemporary punk music. It juxtaposes a period-appropriate Tagalog love song from 1995, the April Boys' "*Ikaw Pa Rin Ang Mamahalin*" (You'll still be the one I love) alongside underground punk music from the 2010s by the Tagalog band The Dropouts and by Cebuano bands Psychomonkey, Tiger Pussy, and Bombo Pluto Ova (the filmmaker describes the latter as a hybrid of punk, noise, and avant-garde music).[56] Heard over close-ups of an old boom box, these punk tracks were released several years after the movie's ostensible temporal setting at the turn of the millennium, giving the film a quality of nonsynchronous temporal multiplicity. Deligero explains the significance of the anachronistic music and sound design of *Iskalawags*:

> Music functions almost like a narrator; the radio that you see, more than the voice-over telling the story, is like a narrator. Music is a very important ingredient in the films I make. When I think about a film I want to make, I think, "How would it sound if it were music?" So music drives the flow of ideas. When I was imagining the story that my friend Erik Tuban wrote, it sounded so punk. The inspiration came from there. . . .
>
> For me, the [punk] music on the radio is the music that the adult Intoy is listening to. When the *iskalawags* were kids, they were listening to April Boy Regino. Intoy is like the country mouse who went to the city. So maybe he grew up on the island and moved to the city for college, and maybe he became a hipster, sort of. It's how I tried to evoke that nostalgia, mixing the contemporary with the things that were real when the *iskalawags* were young. What they were listening to as kids is not actually punk. It's April Boys, those cheesy ballads, and the angelic radio program, because that's the kind of stuff you hear in the far-flung areas of the country. The farther you get, the more obsolete the current things they're listening to.
>
> . . . We call these really low pop things *baduy*. The settings that are very evident in my films are the things I used to think are *baduy*. And I'm just looking back now, like Intoy, and appreciating what I should have liked a long time ago. It's a big part of the film *Iskalawags*.[57]

Iskalawags performs a nostalgic redemption of lowbrow, trashy popular media, referred to in Tagalog as *baduy* (tacky), revalued through the retrospective perspective of the adult narrator, Intoy. An urban hipster with rural roots and a taste for punk, Intoy has a newfound appreciation for the cheesy pop tracks of his youth. The final scene in which the present-day narrator regretfully recalls the *iskalawags*' past is ambiguous about whether Intoy is leaving or returning to his provincial home. The director remarks, "In the ending, we're not sure whether he's coming back home or getting away from home. That sort of nostalgia came from there."[58]

LANGUAGE HIERARCHIES AND THE MOTIF OF ORATION

Deligero ruefully recalls that he did not listen to Cebuano pop songs growing up because to do so would have been "so not cool." In a Philippine mediascape where all commercially distributed fare is in either Tagalog or English, Cebuano culture can only be disparaged as *baduy*. (That this situation is gradually changing can be attributed to grassroots cultural initiatives such as the Binisaya movement.) The filmmaker explains:

> The official language of the Philippines is Tagalog. There are a lot of other languages all over the Philippines, but the commercial distribution of literature, music, and films is usually in Tagalog. So your options are either that, the Tagalog content, or anything from Hollywood. . . . So, either from the West or from the center of the Philippines.
>
> When we think of local, for example, Cebuano or Ilocano or Bacolod, it's usually considered really *baduy*. . . . I never remember hearing a Cebuano pop song on the radio when I was young. All that's available is Cebuano radio drama or the news, and it would be so not cool if you were a kid who was listening to this, so you're forced to listen to Tagalog songs or punk rock from the West. So that's the question that the film is trying to ask. We are Cebuanos, so why are we listening to other stuff?
>
> . . . For wider distribution, for wider reach, you need to make it in English or in Tagalog. . . . . The film is in Bisaya, which is not the distributed language of films in the Philippines. And that's one of the issues in the politics of the film. People from Manila and everyone else are changing their minds. . . . In recent years, there's been a boom in provincial content. So even pop songs now in Cebu are being sung in Cebuano. It's amazing.[59]

The Binisaya movement attempts to turn the tables on the linguistic pecking order of commercial media by producing and distributing Visayan-language cinema. Accordingly, *Iskalawags* centers Bisaya language and humor against the backdrop of the Philippines' two official languages, English and Filipino. In recurring scenes of oration, kids recite canonical poems and famous movie monologues, whether rehearsed or impromptu, in two of the film's three spoken languages. First, Bisaya—the most prominent language in the film—dominates Intoy's voice-over narration and the majority of *Iskalawags*' spoken dialogue; it is markedly absent, however, from the kids' formal education. Second, Tagalog is the language of the *bakbakan* movies the *iskalawags* watch and reenact, the pop ballad they sing to lift their spirits, and the poems and speeches they rehearse for school contests. Several oratorical scenes explicitly reference August as *Buwan ng Wika* (National Language Month), established via presidential proclamation in 1997.[60] Finally, English is the language of the school system; of pornography; and of Ma'am Lina's lectures on the female reproductive system (in one hilarious, pruriently improbable scene, she tells the class to repeatedly intone "vulva," in unison). Shots of the school's "English garden" are juxtaposed with the Tagalog *Makabayan* Garden (Patriotic Garden), with plants labeled in their respective languages. Notably, the school does not cultivate a Visayan Garden, despite being located in Cebu. Thus, while the film upholds Bisaya, the educational curriculum in its story world does not.

Throughout, *Iskalawags* decenters Tagalog as the language of Philippine movies in favor of Bisaya. In the prologue, Liklik recites a Cebuano version of the Tagalog-language Panatang Makapalay (Rice Pledge) in adherence to a government campaign to "attain rice self-sufficiency" by 2013 by "boost[ing] farmers' morale" and admonishing the national public to be "responsible rice consumers."[61] (The Tagalog name for the Rice Pledge puns on the Panatang Makabayan, or Patriotic Oath, commonly recited by schoolchildren.) The prologue is one of *Iskalawags*' many anachronisms since the Rice Pledge was promulgated more than a decade after the story's period setting.

In *Iskalawags*' unscripted opening scene, Liklik solemnly delivers the Rice Pledge in Cebuano while standing in front of a blackboard that displays the words of an English lesson.[62] A long take of the boy directly addressing the camera while promising to value agricultural crops gives way to a vérité montage of daily life in the fictional Sitio Malinawon.[63] Fishermen bring in their haul while farmers handle corn, *kamote* (sweet potato), and *malunggay* (moringa). Establishing the tonal complexity of the film to come, the prologue is disarmingly equivocal: textured in its sketch of everyday life in a coastal fishing town but ambivalent with regard to state discourses of official nationalism. The prologue ends by cutting unceremoniously to a sign that warns, in Visayan, "Do Not Shit Here" ("*Guinadili ang pag-kalibang dinhi*"), subtly ironizing the government's claim to value the labor of Filipino farmers.

After the title card, another scene of oration ensues at the *iskalawags'* treehouse, this time in halting Tagalog. In contrast to Liklik's perfect Visayan delivery, Bulldog is practicing, with great difficulty, Assunta Cuyegkeng's Filipino-language poem "*Salamin, Salamin*" (Mirror, mirror). The poem's first-person exploration of the painful process of coming to know oneself is consistent with the self-referentiality of Tuban's short story and Deligero's film adaptation, both of which employ first-person narration. Bulldog's many flawed attempts to recite the Tagalog poem punctuate the film, from this early scene of failed memorization to later scenes in which he rehearses the poem alone for the upcoming National Language Month dressed in a *barong Tagalog*. A regional Tagalog garment elevated to official Philippine national attire, Bulldog's costume is a visual analog for the promotion of Tagalog to the status of national language.[64] Instead of shoes, however, Bulldog is wearing slippers, thus undermining his formal outfit, just as he is "talking to nobody," eroding the communicative aspect of his oration.[65]

The compulsory embrace of Tagalog by Visayan students in the Buwan ng Wika scenes conveys *Iskalawags'* tongue-in-cheek critique of Philippine language policy. Like Bulldog's strained recital of the poem, his classmates' oratorical performances are also subpar. One student haltingly recites the Tagalog poem "*Sa Aking Mga Kabata*" (To my fellow youth), mistakenly attributed to national hero Jose Rizal, while Intoy's voice-over explains that Palot was the first among them to grow pubic hair. The coarseness of Intoy's narration drowns out the poem's most famous line ("*ang hindi magmahal sa kanyang salita . . .*"), which reproaches those who fail to love the national language. The next scene is an absurdist one in which students required to don formal national garb have been instructed to kneel in the soil, harvesting eggplants in the Patriotic Garden. Deligero articulates the preposterousness of official attempts to inculcate a love for Tagalog as registered by disaffected Cebuano youth: "Why are we wearing the national costume when we're gardening? Why are things this way?"[66] The Buwan ng Wika segment ends with a student responding in

Tagalog to the question "How can we grow our national language?" Her trite, faltering answer, "By using it in schools, because everything starts in the classroom," is cut off when her microphone fails.

In contrast to these scenes of flawed oration and obligatory nationalism, the *iskalawags* deliver lines lifted from Tagalog action films with aplomb, suggesting that Manila's culture industries do more than formal schooling and legislation to enshrine Tagalog as the national language. The film's final act begins with Palot delivering FPJ's monologue from the Tagalog movie *Asedillo* (dir. Celso Ad. Castillo, 1971), a biopic about a teacher who became a populist rebel hero under American colonial rule. Returning to his hometown, Teodoro Asedillo—played by FPJ in the original film and emulated by Palot in *Iskalawags*—addresses his townmates, who listen warily from behind closed windows. Attempting to clear his name, he describes himself as a thief who steals only from the rich to safeguard the rights of the poor. In *Asedillo*, the townsfolk open their windows and hearts to the earnest protagonist; in *Iskalawags*, the boys gird themselves for that evening's theft of the papayas.

The two memorable cinephilic allusions to FPJ action films that bookend *Iskalawags*—the "Hoy Valderama" exchange from *Hindi Ka Na Sisikatan ng Araw* and the populist monologue from *Asedillo*—provide a spirited counterpoint to the stilted scenes of school oration. Bulldog can never get the assigned poem right but sings a song by April Boy Regino perfectly; Palot and Elyok reenact memorable scenes from *bakbakan* flicks by heart. Clearly, movies and pop songs are more potent transmitters of Tagalog's cultural dominance than high literature. Yet rising above the quotation of Tagalog media is an eloquent Visayan oration nearly co-extensive with the entirety of the film: Intoy's voice-over narration, performed by Deligero himself. The director explains: "He's delivering a speech, he's telling us a story, so Intoy is doing an oration for us, on-screen. In order to reinforce that, because we could not see him until the ending, it was necessary to put in [other] scenes that reflect this idea of oration."[67]

ARCHIVING BINISAYA AUDIENCE-BUILDING

Group shots of the *iskalawags* looking directly at the camera as they consume their favorite movie genres or pose as action heroes pervade the film (see figure 6.7). This motif—frontal shots of the boys as collective media spectators—conveys a central theme: *Iskalawags* is a film for and about movie audiences. A cinematic bildungsroman about young Cebuano film buffs, the film also archives the Binisaya movement's efforts to reach underserved Visayan viewers. In this crucial sense, *Iskalawags* chronicles Binisaya filmmakers' attempts to address an enduring audience problem that impacts vernacular productions even more acutely than Manila-based projects.

As elaborated in the epilogue, what I refer to as Philippine cinema's enduring "audience problem" is this: while ordinary moviegoers in the nation-space may have heard about the country's internationally acclaimed social realist art cinema or indie movies, such films are largely inaccessible to popular domestic audiences given their rarefied distribution and exhibition. Contemporary Philippine indie films—whether Tagalog-language or vernacular productions—are consumed primarily by the film festival circuit's middle-class niche market.[68] For their part, popular Visayan audiences gravitate toward Hollywood films rather than local Cebuano productions.[69] Recognizing that the Binisaya film festival's narrow audience is composed of "fellow filmmakers or people who are trying to get into filmmaking," the Binisaya movement endeavors to reach a broader working-class audience in Cebu and elsewhere in the country. "We just keep strategizing, shooting, and organizing," Deligero says, in order to foster "a revitalized movie-going public interested in Visayan-language films. . . . We're going to keep at it until this thing takes hold."[70]

Binisaya audience-building efforts deserve to be recognized as profoundly local and imaginative forms of making do that circumvent both rarefied festival distribution and theatrical exhibition by organizing local pop-up screenings in urban areas and rural barrios. Conceptualized in 2009, the Binisaya movement actively endeavors to bring Cebuano films to local communities in the "nooks and crannies of the Philippines," as Deligero put it in the fifteen-minute documentary, *A Short History of BINISAYA* (2020).[71] Binisaya has held informal screenings in Manila, Davao, Laguna, and several places in the Visayas: Mactan, Camotes Islands, and Biliran.[72]

Deligero insists that he is an audience member first, a filmmaker second: "In organizing Binisaya, we thought of ourselves as the audience . . . we just happened to be filmmakers ourselves."[73] In a 2019 virtual Q and A conducted in English with my students at the University of California, Irvine, Deligero reiterates this point: "I think you need to make a film to build an audience. You can't build an audience without giving them anything to watch. . . . I always consider myself a member of the audience who happened to have made films. As an audience member, the things I wanted to watch are not being made, so I make it myself."[74]

The motive force behind the Binisaya movement, then, is an audience-building dream, evident in Deligero's definition of Binisaya as both a "filmmaking and film-watching community."[75] "Unless we have an audience," Binisaya filmmaker Ara Chawdhury explains, "any and every attempt to #ReviveCebuanoCinema will fall flat."[76] As Grant points out, the absence of a Cebuano film archive and the historical lack of exhibition venues for Visayan films mean that "screenings of even new Cebuano films in Cebu require an immense amount of footwork to even have a respectable attendance."[77] In contrast to the commercial industry's reliance on focus groups and market testing, Binisaya's audience-building process is, for Deligero, gradual, organic, and interpersonal.[78]

In interviews, Deligero evocatively defines cinema as "a space, a screen, a projector, and people in between."[79] This conception of cinema as a collective audience's public encounter with a projected image is prominent in *Iskalawags*' climactic montage depicting an informal barrio-level Binisaya screening, as a beach audience watches Cebuano films projected on a makeshift bedsheet-as-screen. Thus, *Iskalawags* reflexively stages and affectively archives the Binisaya movement's search for a Visayan variant of what Jasmine Trice has called, in the context of the Manila film scene, a "speculative public": sites and practices of distribution and exhibition that aspire to broaden the domestic audience for alternative film.[80]

In a 2017 interview, Deligero explicates the Binisaya community's animating vision: "Actually '*binisaya*' is a term we borrowed from the faith healers in Cebu. If there is something that the doctor cannot cure, you go to the 'quack' doctor. Basically, what we're trying to do here is to bring back the Cebuano faith in Cebuano cinema by celebrating Cebuano-made films in a space between a screen and a projector: a space, a screen, a projector, and people in between."[81]

Binisaya, then, is the cinematic analog of a Visayan folk cure, a local remedy for the dearth of Cebuano films and the need to cultivate an audience for them. This sense of Binisaya as a mystical animist practice is present in both Tuban's short story and Deligero's film. When Palot runs away, his distraught mother makes offerings to a magical balete tree, entreating the spirits to return her son. This brief, self-reflexive scene—a Binisaya folk practice depicted in a Binisaya film—tells us that when nothing else avails, one takes a chance on faith of a marginalized kind. To cure an ailment as entrenched as Visayan cinema's audience problem,

Binisaya filmmakers affirm a "Cebuano faith in Cebuano cinema" by "taking cinema to the streets."[82]

What Deligero dubs the Binisaya movement's informal "guerrilla screenings" are free outdoor screenings that operate outside the Binisaya film festival (in the latter, paying audiences view movies in indoor urban theaters). In contrast, Binisaya guerrilla screenings are impromptu social gatherings that occupy a zone of porous legality. Deligero reflects: "It's like a guerrilla shoot. You go somewhere and you don't ask for permission, so if the authorities make you leave, you relocate to somewhere else where you won't be chased away. I shoot movies in the same way."[83] Armed with a portable projector and a makeshift fabric screen, Binisaya filmmakers screen films in urban community venues like "basketball courts, basements, and rooftops" and "barrio-level screenings" in remote rural areas.[84] Deligero explains, "We are there to hang out, and we share our films for free with whoever happens to come. That's how it started, and we've had many of these kinds of events."[85] Cheap and laid-back by design, this informal mode of exhibition is more invested in connecting with local audiences than profiting from them.

At their informal outdoor screenings, the organizers usually project a mix of Binisaya shorts: "slow, artsy films"; "documentaries and installation pieces"; and "funny, relatable pieces by Victor Villanueva" whenever audiences grow bored or restless. In a virtual conversation with Deligero in 2021, I asked him how passersby respond to Binisaya's mix of accessible and difficult screenings. He replied: "If you're from a small town and suddenly there's this burst of activity, it's like there's this social event. The tendency is for you to get curious about what's going on [*makikiusyoso ka*]. And since you're already there, you stay to watch." Deligero describes the first-time local viewer of Binisaya's nonmainstream program as an *usisero*—a spectator unaccustomed to but curious about alternative cinema. "Even if they don't like everything or find it boring, they stay to watch because it's a social activity."[86]

The origin story of *Iskalawags* crystallizes around audience responses to an informal 2012 beach screening organized by Binisaya in the Camotes Islands municipality of San Francisco.[87] In an email, Deligero recalls: "A bunch of friends drove to an island to welcome our Tagalog guests, Kei [Katrina Tan] and Kitch [Ana Katrina Marcial]. We went to the beach, rented a cottage and instead of playing party music, we played films from Binisaya, and then random people gathered around to watch with us."[88] Tan concurs: "My impression was that people stopped by, curious to see the films speaking their language. It was a kind of guerrilla screening. The power source we used was the minivan's engine!"[89] Deligero calls this the "memorable" Binisaya screening that "inspired" *Iskalawags*.[90]

Deligero was particularly taken by the reaction of two young boys at that first Camotes Islands screening, briefly glimpsed in a 2012 YouTube video, *Binisaya sa San Francisco* (figure 6.8).[91] The coastal screening unfolded over three to four hours, during which time locals came and went; an average of approximately twenty to thirty viewers gathered at any one time (if such events get too big, Deligero notes, local authorities might step in). The two kids, who look to be eight or nine years old in the YouTube video, stuck around for the long evening of screenings and afterward had a sleepover with the Binisaya organizers on the beach. As Deligero describes it:

> There were two boys, the ones in that YouTube video, who stayed with us until the next day. Come morning, they complained, "What's with the stuff you're showing? They're so awful. We didn't understand a thing" [*"Ano ba 'yong pinapalabas ninyo? Ang pangit, wala kaming naintindihan."*] But they watched everything; they finished it all. They said they expected the kind of films they watched on DVD or TV. But because it was a social activity, they stayed all throughout, and they ended up watching all of it. They complained afterwards, but they watched and experienced it. So, we just explained, "Not all movies need to be like the ones on DVD; films can be like this too." That was probably my most memorable experience interacting with a local audience. . . . This is the reason why I was inspired to make *Iskalawags*. None of the various screenings we did ever gave birth to another film. [*Sa lahat ng mga* screenings *na ginawa namin, hindi naman nanganak ng other* film.][92]

As Deligero tells it, the excitement generated by that informal screening piqued the boys' curiosity about Binisaya. Their reaction was an admixture of alienated impatience and fascination with a Cebuano cinematic experience completely unlike the Tagalog movies commercially available on television or DVD.[93] Reading Tuban's short story "Kapayas" upon his return to Metro Cebu, Deligero recalled the kids' reaction and the beauty of Camotes Islands and decided to shoot *Iskalawags* there.[94]

Iskalawags commemorates its genesis in that first Binisaya screening on Camotes Islands in 2012. As Deligero later explained, "The screening scene in *Iskalawags* was a scene made up for the film to reference what we do in Binisaya."[95] Vérité-style footage of a fictional Binisaya screening was

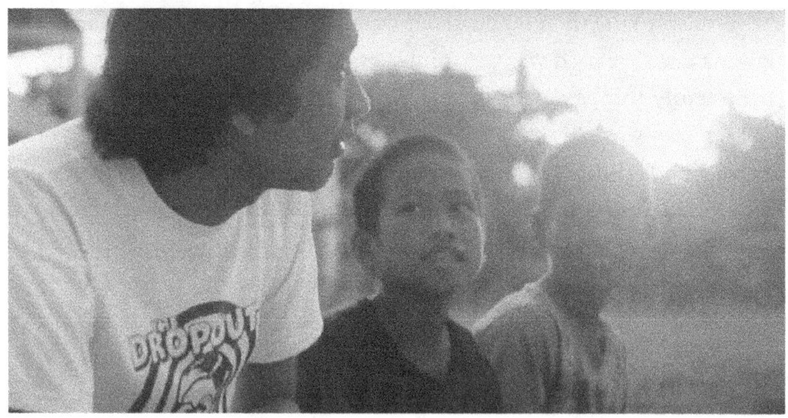

6.8 Director Keith Deligero chatting with the two boys who inspired *Iskalawags* in the 2012 YouTube video *Binisaya sa San Francisco.*

shot on location in Tulang Diot, a remote islet at the back of Camotes' main island, Tulang Dako, where most of the action was filmed. Nearly an hour into *Iskalawags*, we see four figures alight from a boat—a Binisaya cohort that includes the director himself. Diegetically, the footage shows preparations for an evening movie screening in Malinawon that Elyok will attend; extrafilmically, the footage documents the filmmakers setting up that night's shoot in Tulang Diot.[96] As Deligero and other Binisaya members fasten a white bedsheet onto a stage—in Cebuano, the *telon* or large cloth on which the *pasalida*, or movie, will be projected—Intoy walks by and stops to watch. The final act begins, and fictional and nonfictional worlds overlap as *Iskalawags* alludes to its own production in Camotes Islands (figures 6.9 and 6.10).

Preparing for the *iskalawags*' planned papaya caper that evening, Intoy heads home to pilfer a *sanggot* (a long rod tipped with a curved blade, perfect for reaching overhanging fruit). He rejoins the others just as Palot is motivating everyone with the speech from *Asedillo*. All the *iskalawags* are present except for Elyok, who does not take part in the planned theft of the papayas. According to Deligero, Intoy and Elyok are surrogates for the extrafilmic audience in the final act. From Intoy's perspective, we watch the boys head for the papayas, while Elyok's point of view allows us to see the beach screening.[97]

The *iskalawags*' most daring exploit—their attempt to nab Ma'am Lina's papayas under cover of darkness—is crosscut with a fictional Binisaya

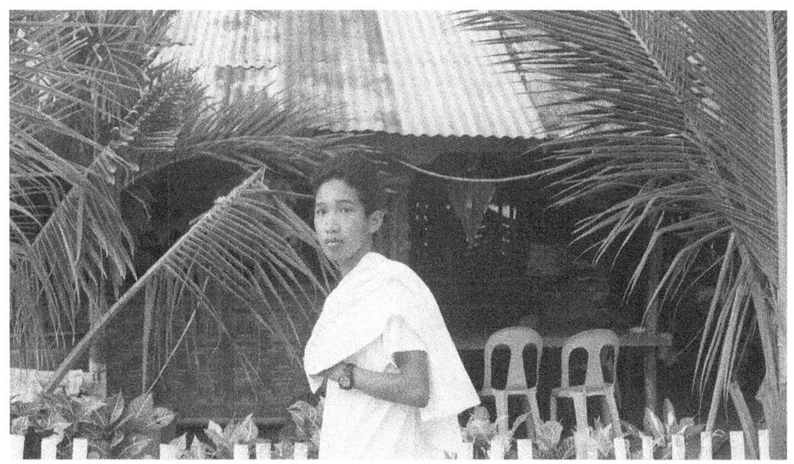

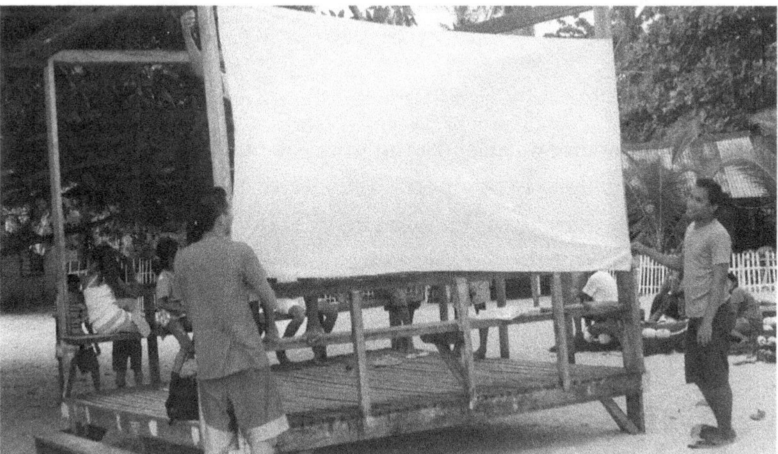

6.9 In a self-reflexive scene in *Binisaya sa San Francisco*, the narrator, Intoy (Reynaldo Formentera, *top*), watches preparations for a Binisaya screening in the Camotes Islands.

6.10 Director Keith Deligero (*above on left*) helps set up the makeshift screen.

screening in Barrio Malinawon. A crowd of over a hundred people watches with rapt attention while seated on the sand. This movie screening, which has no counterpart in the film's literary source "Kapayas," is the most significant departure from the short story. A man wearing a Binisaya shirt next to the projector is identified in the credits as *Iskalawags'* own editor: "Lawrence Ang as the Binisaya Projectionist." Elyok is seated amid the absorbed audience, wearing the same shirt he wore in the "Hoy Valderama" scene (figure 6.11). The faux Binisaya film screening is *Iskalawags'* most

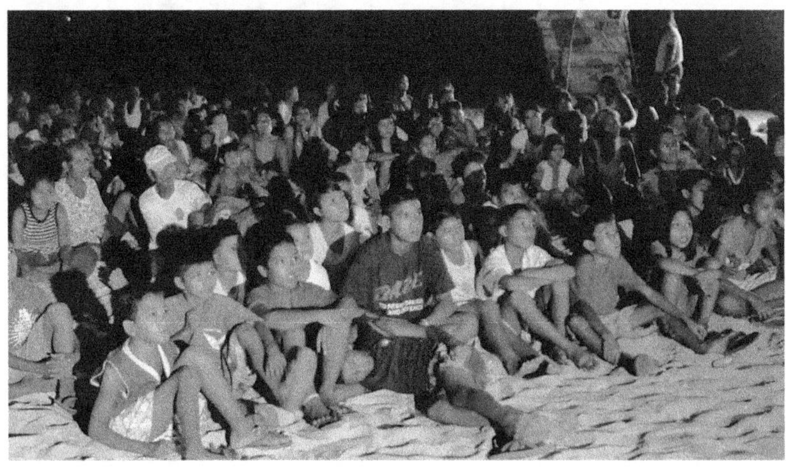

6.11 In *Iskalawags'* climactic montage, Elyok (*front row, center*) is seated amid the audience of a Binisaya beach screening. Film still.

conspicuous instance of anachronism since the film is set a decade ahead of Binisaya's founding. In ouroboric fashion Elyok, a diegetic character in a Binisaya movie, attends a Binisaya guerrilla screening. The implication is clear: the dream of the Binisaya movement is for Visayan audiences—including low-income barrio folk in far-flung islands—to watch films about themselves.

The *iskalawags'* trek through the nipa forest en route to Ma'am Lina's house is intercut with shots of soldiers making their way through jungle foliage in search of communist rebels; this footage is lifted from another Binisaya film, *Ritmo* (Rhythm; dir. Remton Zuasola, 2012). Accompanied by a marching drum on the soundtrack, the soldiers' movements from *Ritmo* are rhymed by the *iskalawags'* nocturnal march. Intoy's voice-over narration reflects that, in contrast to movie ghosts or zombies, the "real monsters" are people "with weapons that terrorize others, including the monster who lashes out at his own weakness with a belt." Lifted from Tuban's short story, this line refers to Intoy's abusive father and foreshadows the violence unleashed by Ma'am Lina's soldier husband, played by Tagalog action star Jeric Raval.

At last, the *iskalawags* arrive outside Ma'am Lina's house. Hidden in the darkness, they see their teacher's illuminated window, where two shadows entwine (figure 6.12). To Intoy, their voices sound "like cats in heat." One voice belongs to their teacher; the other belongs to an unseen man who is not her husband. Most of the boys hide in the foliage outside Ma'am Lina's house, but Palot is bolder, climbing the papaya tree to watch more closely through the window. Forgetting their original goal of stealing the papayas, the boys are transfixed by the sexually illicit acts they inadvertently witness. The *iskalawags* came as thieves but remain as voyeurs.

The deftly crafted montage that follows interweaves what the boys actually see and hear (exterior shots of an illuminated window that resembles a movie screen) (figure 6.12); the movie in their mind (fantasy shots of their teacher enticing her lover, scenes they could not possibly have seen from their vantage point) (figure 6.13); and slightly faded images of the seductive teacher, projected on a movie screen (figure 6.14). Three sets of audiences watch outside Ma'am Lina's window. Multitemporal montage crosscuts between the *iskalawags* in the cornfield, sometime in the late nineties or early aughts, and the audience on the beach in the fictionalized Binisaya screening, implicitly from the 2010s (see figure 6.11). The sequence also implicates us, the extrafilmic audience of *Iskalawags*. In doing so, it violates the temporal norms of parallel editing, which conventionally crosscuts between different diegetic events taking place at the same time.

Deligero maintains that shots of Ma'am Lina enticing her lover or confronted by her husband are not from the movie *Iskalawags*: "Inside the film, they're not watching *Iskalawags*." Though never explicitly mentioned in the film or the source story, these images of seduction and confrontation are from a film-within-the-film that Deligero refers to as *Secrets of Ma'am Lina*, a projection of "gossip in the barrio." Deligero clarifies, "This is the movie in the minds of not just the kids, but everyone in the town, about the open secrets and intimate details the whole town knows."[98] The boys' adolescent titillation at the rumored off-screen coitus between Ma'am Lina and her lover is conveyed by a witty cutaway to a classroom where students repeat the word *vulva* at their teacher's behest, followed by a second shot of Liklik attentively moving an eraser over the clitoral portion of a chalkboard diagram.

The film's climax plays on the metaphor of forbidden fruit symbolized by the papayas. As an unknown lover "devours" their teacher, the narration observes that he was "sucking on the wrong fruit." Ma'am Lina's husband, the soldier played by Jeric Raval, arrives unexpectedly. The husband's voice is distorted, ventriloquized by Deligero-as-Intoy's voice-over. In clumsily delivered Tagalog, the husband tells Ma'am Lina that he came back home because his motorcycle broke down. The montage that follows intercuts the expectant gazes of the Binisaya audience on the sand, the *iskalawags*

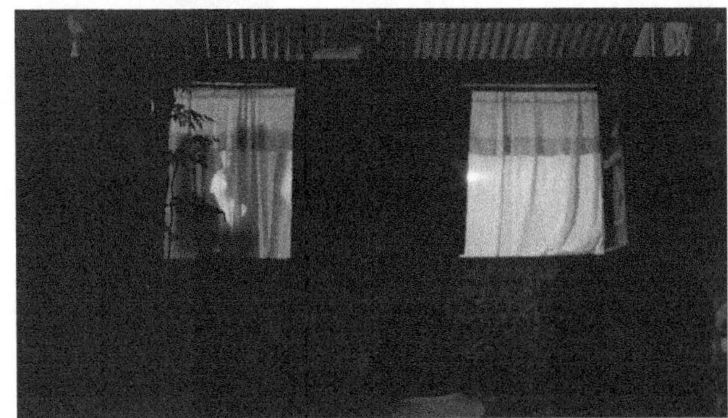

6.12 The schoolteacher's window resembles a movie screen. Film still, *Iskalawags.*

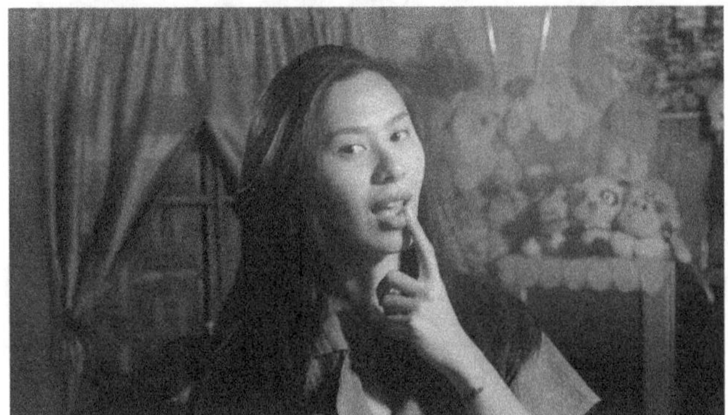

6.13 The boys fantasize about their teacher, Ma'am Lina (Dionne Monsanto), enticing her lover. Film still, *Iskalawags.*

6.14 The imagined seduction scene projected on a movie screen. Film still, *Iskalawags.*

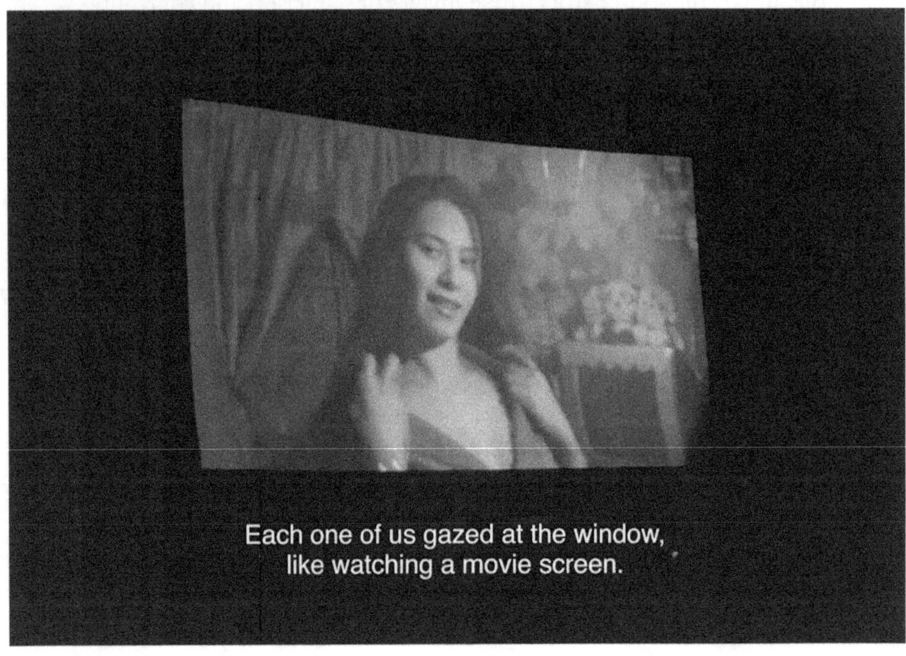

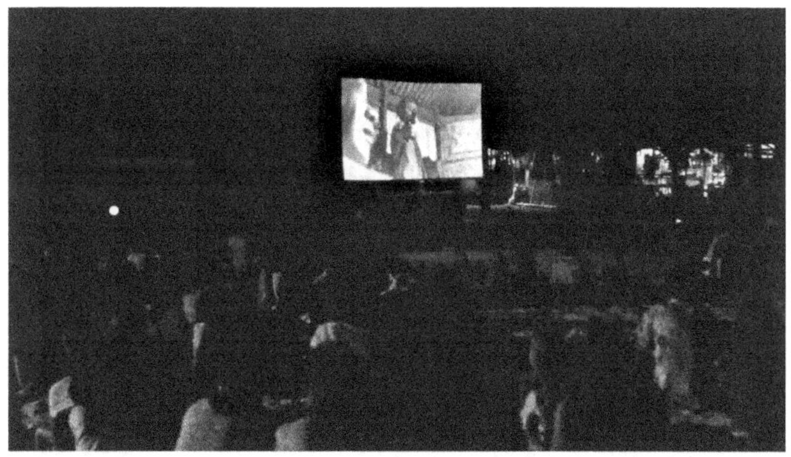

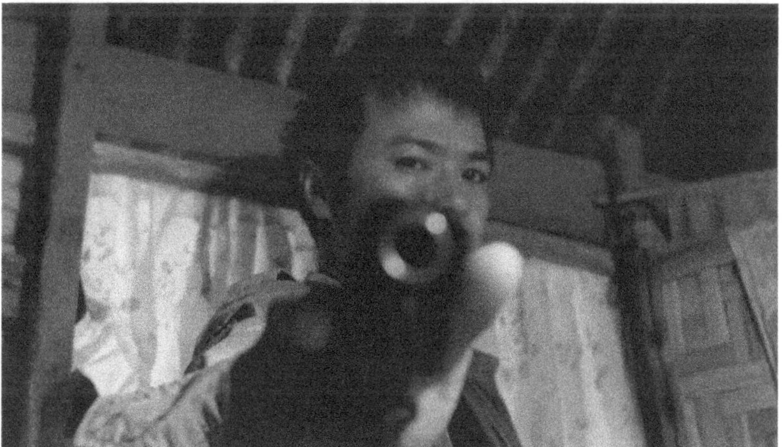

6.15 & 6.16 In *Iskalawags*' film-within-the film (*top*), the soldier-husband (Jeric Raval) aims his gun at Ma'am Lina, watched by several rows of Visayan spectators. In the subsequent medium close-up, he fires directly at the camera (and at the audience). Film still.

in the bushes, and the terrified face of their teacher looking at her enraged husband. In the movie-within-the movie, we see the furious soldier aiming his gun at Ma'am Lina on-screen, behind several rows of seaside spectators riveted by the projected movie (figure 6.15). In a medium close-up, he fires directly at the camera (and at the audience) (figure 6.16).

This brutal act, witnessed by the *iskalawags* hidden outside the teacher's window, is the pivotal traumatic event of their adolescence. Deligero notes, "Violence on-screen is thrilling and exciting, but if it becomes real, it's painful and traumatic. That was the *iskalawags*' experience."[99] The encounter between Ma'am Lina and her mystery lover initially unfolds like a sexploitation film because the *iskalawags* imagine a formulaic depiction of sex and violence, in keeping with the porn and action films they consume. Yet what they actually witness leaves them horrified rather than titillated, scarred for life.

The soldier-husband portrayed by a Tagalog action star emerges as the central deadly figure of this Visayan film's open-ended climax. Raval (tellingly deprived of his own voice throughout *Iskalawags*, his character's single line of dialogue ventriloquized by Deligero) is cast as the film's ultimate villain. Thus, though pruriently masculinist throughout, *Iskalawags* is arguably not misogynist. For all the *iskalawags*' devotion to male action stars, in the final confrontation the sympathies of the young protagonists and of the film itself lie decisively with the woman, Ma'am Lina, not with her soldier-husband as played by Raval. Positioned in intuitive identification with their vulnerable female teacher, Intoy's voice-over narration describes Ma'am Lina's vengeful spouse as a "ghost with a gun" and soldiers in general as "monsters with weapons that terrorize others." Ma'am Lina's murderous military husband, then, is a figure critiqued by "Kapayas" and *Iskalawags* for both state violence against guerrilla insurgents and domestic violence against women, neither of which is condoned by the film or the short story.

Intoy escapes and recounts the story in hindsight, but neither narrator nor audience knows for sure what happened that night. We hear only one gunshot fired at point-blank range, but it's unclear who might have been killed: Ma'am Lina? Her lover? Nor do we know whether the other *iskalawags* made it to safety. In the film's final scene, an older Intoy silhouetted on a boat admits that he fled the scene in terror, abandoning Palot and the other *iskalawags* to their fate. *Iskalawags*' story of intense boyhood friendship concludes abruptly on an open-ended note of confusion, betrayal, and self-reproach: "I don't know where my friends are. . . . I'm sorry."

ARCHIVING PRODUCTION HISTORIES

In shooting the beach screening scene for *Iskalawags* in Tulang Diot, the filmmakers knew that Binisaya films alone would not attract a large local crowd. Cannily adopting a bait-and-switch approach, they began their twilight screening with a Tagalog "maindie" film: a Manila-produced independent film whose well-known star guaranteed crossover appeal. However, the crew faced an additional difficulty: Tulang Diot, Deligero recalls, "has no electrical power at night. The whole island goes dark at 7:00 p.m., after which they have to rely on generators." For this reason, most of the beach screening scene was filmed before the blackout; scenes from three films, a portion of a Tagalog movie followed by excerpts from *Iskalawags* and *Ritmo*, were projected on the large screen. Deligero recalls, "After sunset, to bring in a larger crowd, we started with a maindie film to attract an audience." Reaction shots showing a crowd of over a hundred spectators sitting on the sand were filmed at this time. The director ruefully remarks, "This is how many people showed up [for the maindie Tagalog film]; far more than those who attended the actual screening that this shot refers to" (see figure 6.11). Once a large enough audience had gathered, the projectionist switched to footage from *Ritmo* and scenes from the imaginary film, *Secrets of Ma'am Lina*, shooting necessary scenes before electrical power was cut. This is when the crew "filmed shots of the screen, with the silhouettes of the audience in the foreground" (see figure 6.15). Finally, after 7:00 p.m., when the production shifted to battery power, they filmed "reverse shots of the audience with just light shining on their faces. They're not really looking at a screen, because the electricity had gone out by that time." According to Deligero, "They're just looking at lights. We didn't have a projector because we were just battery-operated at that point, due to the limitations on power."[100]

Deligero cannot recall which shots of the audience were filmed in response to the Tagalog maindie film, to the Binisaya footage, or to the battery-powered lights. Nevertheless, I like to imagine that the editors grafted the audience's reaction shots to the Tagalog movie to scenes from Binisaya films, in effect appropriating Cebuano responses to Manila's commercial cinema on behalf of Visayan vernacular films through shot–reverse shot continuity editing. The climactic montage of *Iskalawags* intercuts the boys' attempt to snatch papayas with the Binisaya movement's desire to poach audience engagement with Tagalog mainstream films in favor of Visayan minor cinema.

As recounted by Deligero and recorded on screen, the production history of *Iskalawags* is a bravura example of making do in the face of a yawning gap between the Cebuano filmmakers' aspirations (to cultivate a sizable, engaged Visayan audience for Binisaya films) and the sobering reality (such an audience could only be lured by a Tagalog movie). Although the movie is fictional and the island screening is staged, *Iskalawags* is an archival record of the difficult conditions faced by Binisaya organizers in their "guerrilla-style" screenings and the resourcefulness with which they overcame challenges to their audience-building initiatives. Deligero remarks, "I see it as a tribute to the inspiration of that first Camotes Islands screening; the act of doing a tribute is basically archiving. Making a film is actually archiving, a nostalgic perspective on the near past."[101]

TO FESTIVAL OR NOT TO FESTIVAL?

> For me as an audience member, watching cinema is like watching somebody else's dream.
>
> —KEITH DELIGERO, in conversation with the author and students

Deligero's remark distills the oneiric quality of *Iskalawags*, particularly its recursive nonlinear editing and strong doses of adolescent fantasy.[102] Above all, the collective consumption of movies in the film's climax tells us that the Binisaya movement is, at heart, a dream about audiences. If, as Rolando Tolentino puts it, "indie films are films in search of an audience," then the scene of Binisaya audience building in *Iskalawags*, which adverts to free-of-charge informal screenings in small provincial towns, breaks the mold of the festival-bound Manila indie film.[103] Nominated for several awards at the Cinema One Originals Film Festival in 2013 and fictionally evoking a Binisaya "guerrilla screening," *Iskalawags* straddles the threshold of formal film festival circulation and informal pop-up exhibitions. The mode of alternative film exhibition archived in *Iskalawags* answers Tolentino's call to "show these films in places that lack full access . . . but do demand alternative narratives about the life of society."[104]

The Binisaya movement is acutely cognizant of the pitfalls of film festivals not only as the principal source of production funding but also as the primary distribution and exhibition channel for indie films. Chawdhury reflects, "Our problem with financing is that none of it is local. For the past years, Cinema One Originals has sponsored our productions," with the result that "they end up owning the films." Given the competitive structure of the festival, "there is no guarantee that we'll get a project from them every year."[105] Such limitations inhere to the Philippines' three top-tier film festivals, widely seen as catalyzing the upsurge in independent and vernacular filmmaking over the last fifteen years.

The first of these annual festivals is the Manila-based Cinemalaya Philippine Independent Film Festival, established in 2005 with funding from both private and state sources. Until 2014, most of the festival's financial support stemmed from corporate tycoon Antonio "Tonyboy" Cojuanco, cofounder of the nonprofit Cinemalaya Foundation, in tandem with government funds from the FDCP, the NCCA, the CCP, and, from 2015 onward, the Department of Budget and Management.[106] The government disburses about 20 million pesos annually to the CCP, 10 million of which is allocated for Cinemalaya's seed grants. Cojuanco, via the Cinemalaya Foundation, covers financial shortfalls. Vicky Belarmino, festival coordinator for Cinemalaya, reflects that the festival was initially conceptualized in 2004 "to revive a dying industry." By February 2021, in the throes of the economic downturn caused by the pandemic, she remarked that "we are again in that state."[107]

The second major domestic festival, also held in Metro Manila, is the corporate-run Cinema One Originals Film Festival, a subsidiary of media giant ABS-CBN. In addition to competing in the festival, Cinema One productions are "automatically programmed in the cable channel of ABS-CBN, with minor rights given to filmmakers to explore further theatrical distribution."[108] *Iskalawags*, Deligero's third film, was a Cinema One production whose higher budget allowed for better production value and enhanced distribution. The director reflects that working under Cinema One resulted in technical polish but also came with a different set of corporatist demands that undermined the supposed autonomy of "independent" filmmaking.[109]

Deligero reflects that his three Cinema One productions—*Iskalawags*, *Lily* (2016), and *A Short History of a Few Bad Things* (2018), "an incidental trilogy on the politics of languages"—are films that only Cinema One would have produced, since other investors would have doubted their marketability. "Even Cinema One has difficulty selling these films. But since they have the money, they have a [film festival] competition, and they need diversity, then we exploited the Cinema One opportunity, exploiting the exploiter. And we benefited too. . . . It amplified our small voice as Binisaya." Cinema One's inclusion of Visayan films led to Binisaya's inclusion "in the list of what counts as Philippine cinema" in the eyes of "critics at the center of the Philippines."[110] Indeed, scholars note that in financing several films that jump-started the Binisaya movement, Cinema One has done more to support Cebuano filmmaking than the central government film entity, the FDCP.[111]

Especially pivotal for the rise of vernacular filmmaking, the third major domestic film festival is the state-funded, noncompetitive Cinema Rehiyon, launched in 2009 as the focal project of the NCCA's Cinema Committee. Initially held at the CCP in Manila, from 2011 onward Cinema Rehiyon has traveled to various regions outside the national capital.[112] Given its archipelagic reach, documentary filmmaker Baby Ruth Villarama hails Cinema Rehiyon as "the true national film festival, a relatively rare but precious occasion to see filmmakers from Luzon, Visayas, and Mindanao come together to create regional networks." However, its limited funding results in lower public visibility than the other two festivals. Moreover, the absence of guaranteed state funding means that the sustainability of the Philippines' foremost vernacular film festival is far from assured.[113] Beyond Cinema Rehiyon, smaller vernacular festivals, such as Binisaya and Lilas Binisaya in Cebu City, have been funded by the NCCA's Cinema in the Regions program. Tan notes, however, that the NCCA's funding is limited and must be augmented by funding from other local state, private, and institutional patrons.[114]

While having the salutary effect of slowing filmmakers' out-migration to Manila by incentivizing them to "remain in their home regions to . . . benefit from local production grants," the drawbacks of film festivals are considerable. Tan cautions that depending solely on film festivals for the production and distribution of vernacular cinemas unwittingly "reinforce[s] the centrality of Manila," since "while filmmaking may have been decentralized, the source of production funds remains relatively concentrated in the capital."[115] Villarama points out that film festival productions typically operate on compressed six-month production and postproduction timelines that weaken quality and leave little time for promotional marketing to "match" films to a potentially receptive audience.[116] In the postfestival context, archival access to these movies is highly constricted and informal, since the vast majority of indie films are never picked up by formal distributors.[117] For all their archival value, *Iskalawags* and contemporary indie and vernacular films more generally are not films that can be accessed primarily via formal archives.

Film festivals draw attention to the structural challenges involving film distribution, taxation, and exhibition that threaten the sustainability of vernacular cinemas' pre-pandemic dynamism. As distribution channels, festivals are regrettably short-lived, with brief theatrical runs and limited exhibition venues. Tan cautions that the viability of vernacular filmmaking remains uncertain: in addition to onerous taxation (a 30 percent amusement tax on film revenues), "funding for productions is volatile and uncertain, no distribution system for regional films exists, and no laws or policies exist to safeguard regional film productions."[118] A particularly pernicious exhibition practice is the "pull-out policy of commercial theaters," defined as "the practice of pulling films from theaters even during the first day of showing if they do not achieve the targeted sales quota," thus foreclosing the possibility of slowly building audiences via word of mouth.[119] The pull-out policy is one of many "deeply entrenched" practices through which Manila-based theater cartels keep a chokehold on Philippine exhibition, stymieing the circulation of nonmainstream domestic films.[120]

Where the Binisaya movement's audience-oriented dreams are concerned, the most serious structural limitation of film festival distribution and exhibition is a gaping "demographic disconnection between the audience and important films," as Villarama puts it.[121] Deploring what he calls the "ironic audience situation of indie films," Nicanor Tiongson pinpoints indie film festivals' demographic disjointedness: "The middle and upper classes become the main audience of indie films, whose main subject matter is the poor."[122] Tiongson's insight deepens the representational critique of so-called poverty porn by grounding it in the structural limitations of festival distribution and exhibition. An oft-cited quote from Cannes Film Festival awardee Brilliante Mendoza articulates the problematic ethos of poverty porn: "These films might be about the lower classes, and it is their stories we are telling, but these films are not *for* them. Our films are for the middle class and the educated people."[123]

One of my students asked Deligero how a filmmaker might avoid the pitfalls of poverty porn when telling stories about impoverished protagonists. Deligero's answer is illuminating:

> The characters in [my] films are not necessarily rich; they are considered, maybe, poor. But personally, my films are a reaction to this trend of making poverty porn. For me, a film only becomes poverty porn when the filmmaker who made a story about poverty is not actually poor [chuckles]. By default, filmmaking is an expensive art form. So, it's usually the privileged who get to make films. When you talk about poor people as an outsider and you tell a story about "them" from your outsider's perspective, and you export all those films into foreign festivals, it's like you're appropriating their lives. The difference from that

> with me is that I'm one of the *iskalawags*. I lived in a place like where they lived. The way I grew up was similar to how they grew up. It's like I'm telling my story, I'm not commenting on whatever social reality exists, it's asking questions more than a commentary on social status. When you think of it as commentary, this borders on what we call poverty porn because you're detached from it.[124]

The crux of Deligero's position on poverty porn hinges on this line: "For me, a film only becomes poverty porn when the filmmaker who made a story about poverty is not actually poor." In contrast to the detached perspective of an outsider for whom the *iskalawags* might be a cipher for the impoverished masses, a (collective) autobiographical experience underwrites the film: "I'm one of the *iskalawags*." More than a mere authenticating gesture, Deligero's answer adverts to the collaborative authors' lived knowledge of lower-income families in rural Cebu. This is evident in his muted caveat—the *iskalawags* are "not necessarily rich" and so might be considered "maybe, poor" by middle-class viewers. Yet at other points in the same Q and A and in Tuban's short story "Kapayas," it's clear that the filmmakers do not regard the *iskalawags* as the undifferentiated "poor." In the final act, Intoy's voice-over reflection about the scarcity of TV sets in his childhood is adapted from a line in Tuban's short story: "In our tiny town, . . . not too many owned the luxury of TV sets. In fact, if you owned one, then you were already considered among the 'rich' and elite members of our little society."[125] As the owner of a Betamakan, Romart's mother, Nang Rosa, would have been one of the barrio's comparatively better-off members (a point Deligero echoes when he refers to purveyors of bootlegged tapes as "rich" returned migrants).[126] In Tuban's story, Bulldog is described as the "son and heir" of his father's *sari-sari* store. Two of the *iskalawags*, then, are children of small business owners, while several other characters are employed in working-class occupations (Palot works as a gardener; Palot's mom, Nang Bising, is a laundrywoman; and Poldo's grandmother, old Susing, is the town fishmonger).[127] In *Iskalawags*, as in "Kapayas," class issues are handled with nuance and complexity, and none of the characters personify abject poverty. In contrast, Deligero's remarks understand "poverty porn" as films made by privileged filmmakers for export to foreign film festivals. Though couched in the rhetoric of social commentary, "poverty porn" films enact a homogenizing appropriation of a classed other, often spectacularizing the poverty they thematize.

OF AUDIENCES AND SELF-DISTRIBUTION

Binisaya was conceived in the aftermath of a hectic final push to complete a film in time for a festival deadline. Emerging exasperated from festival-induced "panic mode," Deligero recalls thinking in Cebuano, "Why do we have to send our films to some other place?" ("*Nganong kinahanglan ta mag-*send *sa atong mga salida padolong sa laing lugar*?")[128] The local, place-bound quality of many Binisaya screenings originates in this founding impulse to show Cebuano films in the Visayas rather than exhibit them elsewhere.

During the COVID-19 pandemic, the closing ceremonies to the online Binisaya 2020 festival excerpted an interview of Deligero originally recorded for the FDCP's celebration of the centennial of Philippine cinema that year. Deligero tells the camera: "The future of Philippine cinema is self-distribution."[129] When I asked Deligero what he meant by this, he emphasized that in order to make films for Cinema One, Binisaya directors were forced to sell off the rights to their own works, stating, "We dreamed of owning our films but we couldn't have made the films without them." For Binisaya filmmakers and their wider community, the holy grail of sustainable self-distribution encapsulates two interrelated dreams: first, aesthetic autonomy; and second, a circumvention of the film industry's "gated, guarded" approach to distribution, where only "films that are sure to make a profit" are picked up by formal distributors. Although Deligero has often envisioned a distribution cooperative, Binisaya filmmakers have yet to discover a viable business model for self-distribution.[130]

Such drawbacks notwithstanding, the history of vernacular cinemas offers illuminating precursors to the Binisaya movement's "guerrilla" modes of film circulation. Innovative exhibition and distribution strategies underwrote the success of an unconventional Cebuano hit from 1975, *Ang Manok ni San Pedro* (Saint Peter's gamecock; dir. Narciso and Domingo Arong). Deocampo relates that the directorial siblings elected to shoot the film in Super 8mm format, then enlarge it to 35mm, to avoid the prohibitive costs of renting 35mm film equipment from Manila. The Arong brothers also sidestepped Manila's monopoly over distribution and exhibition by showing their film outdoors during local fiestas. Barrio-level fiesta distribution proved both lucrative and ingenious. Deocampo calls this a "remarkable feat" that "provided a clear working alternative to the problems plaguing the Cebuano movie industry."[131] More recently, the 2007 film *Hunghong sa Yuta* (Earth's whisper; dir. Arnel Mardoquio,

2007), coproduced by the Brothers of the Sacred Heart as part of a "peace education campaign," doubled its modest production cost of US$20,000 through school screenings in Davao and Manila. Tan writes that the "synergy between the efforts of filmmakers and educational institutions" in the case of *Hunghong* demonstrates the "commercial viability" of vernacular cinema through alternative forms of distribution.[132]

The kinship of these examples to Binisaya tactics is striking, especially their recourse to highly localized distribution and exhibition in noncommercial and outdoor venues. Yet just as the Philippines' long-simmering archival dream is shadowed by anarchival conditions, the sustainability of Binisaya efforts to foster audiences and forge alternative avenues of film circulation remains an open question. Tan notes that several Binisaya filmmakers "have (temporarily?) migrated to Manila to pursue a career in the industry."[133] This recalls Cebuano film talents' "exodus to Manila" in the 1960s, which accelerated Visayan cinema's decline in that decade.[134] In answer to the question "How do you see Cebuano cinema in the future?," Deligero replied darkly: "I am afraid of history repeating itself."[135] During the pandemic in 2021, I asked Deligero whether or not the out-migration of Cebuano filmmakers threatened the vitality of the Binisaya movement. At the time of our conversation, Deligero described himself as living both in Cebu and in Taytay, Rizal, just outside the national capital region, where "rent is cheaper." His response was instructive:

> Everyone's perspective is that when people migrate, that's the end. The general narrative is that filmmakers like Ara Chawdhury and Christian Linaban left, first for Manila, then for the US, because there aren't enough opportunities in Cebu, which is partly true. But my perspective is that migrating will not stop anybody from making films about their home. I was the first to leave Cebu [for Manila], but all the movies I've made from that point onward have been Cebuano films. . . . Every year I do two projects in Cebu, Binisaya and another film at the same time. . . . Remton Zuasola is living in Cebu during the [COVID] lockdown, but also goes back and forth to Manila like me. . . . So I'm worried about the idea that [filmmakers leaving Cebu] will be the end. If that becomes the generally accepted narrative, then history will repeat itself, because people will think there's nothing going on in Cebu cinema. . . . But I firmly believe that even if I or others leave, as long as people are making local films, even if they're no longer living there, Cebuano film is alive and will continue.[136]

The politics of place is far more complicated than where one currently resides: this is the thrust of Deligero's claim. Several Binisaya filmmakers no longer based solely in Cebu have continued to make local films, challenging the assumption that filmmakers' relocation away from Cebu spells the inevitable end of Visayan cinema's resurgence.

Given all that imperils Binisaya and other like-minded vernacular film movements, *Iskalawags* offers one possible answer to the question of how to archive the evanescent but vital accomplishments of minoritarian cinematic subcultures. In *City of Screens*, Jasmine Trice argues that the film audiences so coveted by counterdominant Philippine filmmakers are never given but are, rather, brought into being by circulation. Manila's dynamic but "short-lived" alternative film scenes should not be considered failures but rather as "asymptotic" attempts to realize what she calls a "speculative public." Like an asymptote, a line that nears yet never touches the curve it comes toward, various transient film communities and initiatives have approached, without permanently achieving, the cinephilic audience they long to constitute.[137] Trice's insight is borne out by the continuities between Binisaya's informal screenings and the Mogwai Cinematheque (2007–11), an alternative film exhibition venue in Cubao Expo (CubaoX), described by Trice as "a regular haunt among Manila's early-aughts bohemia."[138] CubaoX's short-lived alternative film scene is cited by Deligero as one inspiration for Binisaya's informal outdoor screenings; the other is his childhood memory of FPJ movies projected in the town plaza of Poblacion Badian in Cebu during summer visits to his grandparents. Deligero recalls, "These are the two models that I merged in Binisaya: the traveling screenings in Cebu from my childhood and the CubaoX hipster scene in Manila in the mid-2000s, like Eric Matti's Mogwai."[139] A through line connects the audience-building dreams of various historical junctures: itinerant provincial screenings in the eighties and nineties; a Manila microcinema from the aughts; and the contemporary Cebuano film scene.

This chapter and the epilogue that follows foreground two aspirations: Binisaya filmmakers' longing to call forth local audiences for vernacular cinema and advocates' dreams of rousing an engaged public supportive of audiovisual archiving. Whether or not such aspirations fizzle out or bear fruit, the history of Philippine cinema offers memorable works that archive, if not the lasting realization, then the impassioned pursuit of those dreams.

EPILOGUE

Of Audiences and Archival Publics

Pepot Artista

What I have been referring to as Philippine cinema's "audience problem" is a decades-long quandary. Put simply, it is the failure of locally produced "serious cinema," broadly defined, to attract a substantial domestic audience, despite these works having gained international recognition via awards or film festivals. This enduring difficulty besets a wide spectrum of films, whether these be 1950s masterworks of the First Golden Age; the social realist New Cinema or Second Golden Age of the 1970s and 1980s; documentary, experimental, and avant-garde works produced on the margins of the industry; or the twenty-first-century digital indie films that now outnumber local mainstream productions. In this epilogue, I suggest that the imagined audiences ardently pursued by various film movements and circulation initiatives are closely linked to the archival publics that media preservation advocates invoke *in potentia*. There is an unrecognized connection between filmmakers' yearning to overcome Philippine cinema's audience problem and audiovisual archiving advocates' hopes of hailing an archival public-in-the-making.

The through line between two of Philippine cinema's foremost challenges—a limited domestic audience and a history of archival precarity—is, as I see it, fairly straightforward. If Philippine cinema (beyond a small number of recently released Tagalog-language blockbusters) commanded an engaged local audience (and, by extension, a robust long tail market for domestic movies), then there would be broader interest in preserving and accessing these films and their history. This is the hinge between Philippine cinema's long-standing audience problem and the absence of a thriving archival public.

PHILIPPINE CINEMA'S "AUDIENCE PROBLEM"

Jose F. Lacaba's classic 1970 essay on *bakya* articulates a late twentieth-century version of today's audience problem. The now dated term *bakya* was an earlier era's derisive name for lowbrow popular culture and its consumers, the so-called mass audience composed of the urban and the rural poor. Revaluing and championing such lowbrow moviegoers, Lacaba explains that *bakya* was originally named after "the wooden slippers worn in lieu of shoes by the poor in the barrios." As such, it refers to "anything that is cheap, gauche, naïve, provincial, and terribly popular." Lacaba compellingly argues that the "*bakya* crowd" does not designate an actual spectator. Rather, the charge of *bakya* articulates the elitist frustrations of filmmakers and critics who castigate supposedly unsophisticated viewers for failing to embrace quality films that have won international acclaim. Lamberto Avellana, National Artist and renowned studio era auteur, "is said to have coined the phrase [*bakya* crowd] in his rage against an audience that failed, or refused, to appreciate his award-winning movies."[1]

The "bakya audience" is shorthand for dynamics of audience stratification along the axes of socioeconomic class, cultural taste, and ethnolinguistic difference. The charge of *bakya*-ness is symptomatic of neocolonial film policies that disadvantaged local films vis-à-vis imported fare. Philippine cinema, whose technological origins coincide with the United States' annexation of the country at the end of the Philippine-American War, has been perennially hamstrung by unrestricted film importation of Hollywood product. As Talitha Espiritu observes, the film importation problem—a holdover of historical "special relations" between the Philippines and the United States—undergirds the class stratification of domestic audiences along linguistic and geographic lines. With the advent of sound, the local film industry began to market Tagalog films to rural *bakya* audiences, eventually prevailing over vernacular movies, while the Hollywood imports that flooded local screens in the absence of protectionist policies became the preferred movie diet of Manila's urban audiences.[2]

According to Petronilo Bn. Daroy, the domestic film industry's reliance on low-income audiences shifted in the 1960s and 1970s, when a surge in nationalist consciousness on university campuses prompted educated middle-class youths to embrace mass culture and, by extension, popular film. Nonetheless, class divisions among Filipino movie audiences persisted, as did the divide between popular audiences and "serious" film critics whose ideas "could not reach the masses."[3]

In the mid-1970s, Lino Brocka, Philippine New Cinema's foremost auteur, defended the *bakya* "mass audience" as follows:

> Too often has the *bakya* crowd been blamed for the sad state of Filipino movies. But what can one expect of an audience that has been fed nothing but secret-agent, karate, fantasy, and slapstick movies since time immemorial? . . . The only way one can elevate local cinema from its present *bakya* status to an artistically acceptable level is to introduce gradual changes until one succeeds in creating one's desired audience. The "upliftment of the motion picture industry" . . . [is] a protracted struggle. . . . The sincere Filipino filmmaker should get over his hang-up about making the Great Filipino Film; he should instead, think seriously about developing the Great Filipino Audience.[4]

In his (regrettably masculinist) polemic against elitist condescension toward popular audiences, Brocka points to the structural underpinnings of lowbrow taste, indicting the commercial movie industry for churning out exploitative, formulaic fare. (Over three decades later, Alexis Tioseco would echo this sentiment in his oft-quoted wish list for Philippine cinema.)[5] Brocka enjoins fellow filmmakers to move beyond audience vilification to audience creation, which Brocka characterizes as a "protracted struggle," borrowing the language of the Left. Brocka's recipe for "developing the Great Filipino Audience" involves selectively appropriating popular elements and infusing these with social relevance without sacrificing spectatorial pleasure.[6] His advice notwithstanding, Philippine cinema's audience problem endures. Today, a presumptively homogeneous "mass audience" is even more untenable, given the emergence of niche markets, increased content production, and new distribution pipelines in the digital era.

A contemporary iteration of the audience problem, one that no longer goes by the outmoded name of *bakya*, unfolds against the upsurge of digital media production. As Patrick Campos notes, indie productions now outstrip the annual output of the commercial film industry, further complicating the already "conflated" term *indie cinema* and giving rise to crossover "maindie" films.[7] Campos offers this sobering assessment: "Like indie's predecessors (i.e., the realist films of the 1970s and 1980s, and the alternative art cinema of the 1980s and 1990s), contemporary indie films have not been easily accessible to the majority of Filipino audiences locally."[8] As one commentator puts it, "Some indies are lucky enough to get picked up by distributors; most of them never reach the audiences they are intended for."[9]

Hollywood fare dominates Philippine movie theaters for most of the year. In contrast, domestically produced commercial cinema makes most of its revenue during the annual Metro Manila Film Festival (MMFF), a one-week period in December when local films' box office performance is bolstered since Hollywood and other foreign film imports are barred from theatrical exhibition. While Hollywood and domestic commercial films enjoy extended screenings in shopping mall multiplexes, Philippine indie cinema's circumscribed distribution results in very brief runs in local film festivals and art house theaters, where they are consumed by a highly specialized audience.[10] Consisting of "primarily middle-class cineastes, students, academics, and the intelligentsia," the audience for indie films, whether made in Manila or by vernacular film movements, is "quite distinct from the bakya or lowbrow movie fans that troop in droves to watch genre films and the MMFF."[11]

Jasmine Trice offers a sustained exploration of indie cinema's audience problem. In her analysis of Manila film culture from 2006 to 2012, the period of digital indie cinema's emergence, Trice explores the "speculative public" addressed by filmmakers, producers, distributors, exhibitors, and community activists striving to develop local audiences for nonmainstream fare. Her phrase "speculative public" refers to a supportive domestic audience for locally produced alternative cinema that has never quite materialized, despite being ardently yearned for by filmmakers and critics alike. Regardless of their ephemerality, Trice argues, various "asymptotic" attempts to cultivate a devoted local film audience are historically significant. For instance, although the alternative microcinemas of CubaoX in the first decade of the twenty-first century were short-lived, Trice argues that these bohemian subcultural venues utopically envisioned a different kind of film culture for the city: one not dominated by middle-class commercialism but instead open to alternatives for social change.[12]

Audience-building projects live on, dovetailing with both the formal and informal archival practices explored in this book. Classic Tagalog movies reach viewers through vintage video stores like Video 48 and restorations by the NFAP/PFA and ABS-CBN; short experimental and avant-garde works find their way to audiences through the Kalampag Tracking Agency's screenings. Binisaya films straddle the boundaries between film festival circulation and "guerrilla screenings," attempting to reach the vernacular moviegoers for which they were made; and commercially restored films like *T-Bird at Ako* strive to hail an archivally conscious public that includes both lower-income movie fans and queer cinephiles.

I became belatedly aware of continuities between various audience-expanding initiatives and the Philippines' riverine archival ecology through conversations with filmmakers and archivists; these moments of oral history have for me a quality of epiphany. At a 2021 SOFIA Q and A following a talk I gave on informal archives, Ricky Orellana reflected that he and Teddy Co "supported Kalampag because it reminded us of the informal practices we were doing so long ago." He went on to recall that MOWELFUND held alternative film screenings at "schools, Luneta Park, and punk venues like Red Rocks Café" in the early 1990s.[13] Similarly, Keith Deligero recalls that the Binisaya movement's informal pop-up screenings were dually inspired by Mogwai Cinematheque (2007–11) at CubaoX and the itinerant Visayan projectionists of his childhood.[14] These casual disclosures alerted me to the unrecognized undercurrents that bind historically disparate initiatives to archival practices and flows.

Movies need audiences to watch them just as audiovisual archives need a public to support them: that avid film audiences, if called forth, might also become an archival public, once roused, is the hinge between two long-standing dreams. The first dream is to cultivate a devoted domestic film audience for alternatives to formulaic fare; the second aspiration is to kindle in that audience an investment in the continued accessibility of the local movies they love.

DREAMING OF AN ARCHIVAL PUBLIC

Every advocate of moving image preservation is likely to have their own story of initiation into the "archival world," as Paolo Cherchi Usai calls it.[15] Clodualdo del Mundo Jr.'s *Dreaming of a National Audio-Visual Archive*, a clarion call for the urgency of film preservation, was my introduction to the archival world of Philippine film. Del Mundo was writing in 2004, seven years prior to the revival of the NFAP, at a moment when "classics" of Philippine cinema circulated primarily on videotape and archival masters of restored films were "written back on film negative . . . from which new projection prints can be made."[16] In that SOFIA-published monograph, del Mundo describes the frustration encountered by Filipino film scholars working under conditions of profound archival loss:

> Imagine this scenario: you are a film scholar doing a study on Philippine cinema. You want to do research on the classics of this Southeast Asian cinema, specifically on the works of renowned Filipino filmmakers like Gerardo de Leon, Lamberto Avellana, Manuel Conde, Lino Brocka, and Mike de Leon. . . . Where do you go to watch and study these films?
>
> . . . You connect with colleagues in the Philippines, and you get the same answer: no copy of the film exists; if there is one, nobody knows where it is kept or who may be holding on to it. You have to settle for stills of the film and secondary materials published in newspapers and magazines. Consider your primary material lost.[17]

The opening of del Mundo's *Dreaming of a National Audio-Visual Archive* uses an attention-grabbing second-person address in the imperative mood ("Imagine this scenario: you are a film scholar") to solicit the reader's empathy, urging his audience to understand what it is like to love Philippine cinema under anarchival conditions. Above all, del Mundo's monograph not only dreams of a national audiovisual archive but also yearns to constitute an archivally invested public, to turn his readers into an active social audience concerned with Philippine cinema's archival predicament and supportive of film preservation efforts.

Over a decade after del Mundo's pioneering monograph, there has been a marked uptick in the country's film restoration output. Reestablished in 2011, the NFAP/PFA has restored works by all but one of the auteurs del Mundo listed. Two of the country's best-publicized film restorations are titles previously bemoaned by del Mundo as locally unavailable: Manuel Conde's *Genghis Khan* (1950) was the NFAP's first film restoration in 2012; Lino Brocka's *Maynila sa Mga Kuko ng Liwanag* (Manila in the claws of light; 1975) was restored the following year.[18] In addition, ABS-CBN has restored several films by Mike de Leon and other auteurs.[19] Recently, ABS-CBN's "digitally restored and remastered films" on DVD have included special features on restoration, vignettes in which Star Cinema celebrities extol the importance of film preservation.

On the one hand, then, the current situation might be considered less bleak than in the early aughts, thanks to the efforts of various individual, corporate, and institutional actors to raise the level of archival consciousness about Philippine cinema and to bring an archival public into being. On the other hand, as Bernadette Patino points out, there are downsides to a restoration agenda focused on commercial feature films. Foremost among these is the privileging of industry-produced narrative films as national heritage, a perspective that elides a gamut of domestically produced works (e.g., educational films, "short films, experimental and alternative works, documentaries, student and amateur films, wartime and martial law propaganda"). Taken together, such overlooked works outnumber those of Manila's commercial film industry. As Patino incisively argues, the focus on narrative feature films reflects hegemonic archival norms that have been "naturalized" by the institutional priorities of government entities (the NFAP/PFA under the FDCP) and corporate archives (ABS-CBN). Likewise, SOFIA embraced the restoration and exhibition of a "canon of primarily industry-made, feature-length narrative cinema" as a pragmatic strategy for appealing to "a wider audience for their advocacies, especially from the film industry itself." While this prevailing archival agenda has rescued and recirculated important films, the focus on restoring and screening feature-length Tagalog films has done "little to address deep-seated archival infrastructure and funding problems."[20]

Hegemonic restoration agendas are one way of eliciting public support; writing about Philippine cinema's anarchival predicament is another. Del Mundo's second-person address and the keywords prominent in the opening of his monograph—*dreaming* and *imagining*—call to mind Michael Warner's influential conceptualization of the public as a collective social fiction: "Publics exist only by virtue of their imagining."[21] Warner argues that a public is constituted by a "circulation of texts among strangers who become, by virtue of their reflexively circulating discourse, a social entity."[22] Crucially, Warner argues that a public is not a given, preexisting social entity. Rather, it is a form of discursive address that hopes to bring a social collective into being—precisely the form of subjunctive address that del Mundo employs at the beginning of his monograph.

The form of address that imagines a public and, in so doing, hopes to constitute a real audience of participants in the social world, is both subjunctive and specific. (A grammatical mood, the word *subjunctive* refers to something imagined or considered possible, a longed-for potentiality.) The feeling of being bound in a shared social world with others is created by the circulation of discourse.[23] While printed texts were key to the emergence of the modern notion of the public, contemporary "publics are increasingly organized around visual or audio texts."[24] In responding to the discursive hailing of a specific public, we identify as participants who belong, however briefly, to the commons it envisions. To take a few everyday examples—an ad for the next season of a TV show, a sign announcing the availability of vegan food, a trailer for the opening of a film festival, a hashtag thread for a protest march—all these public messages in a media-saturated world are addressed to unfamiliar recipients. But if one or more of these messages commands my attention or arouses my interest, then I become, however briefly, a member of that particular public to which other strangers also belong.

Similarly, through its director, cast, genre, style, marketing, distribution, and exhibition, a film addresses the audience it hopes to reach. In practice, media audiences are both virtual and real. Media industry scholars Timothy Havens and Amanda Lotz make a distinction between the "constructed audience" imagined by creators and industry players "in the process of making a media product" and the "real audience," which "doesn't enter into the equation until after the product has been created." The constructed audience, "based on decision-makers' perceptions" of reception dynamics, is imaginary prior to the actual audiences constituted by reception and circulation.[25] Like the risky enterprise of making a movie in the hopes of finding an audience, Philippine audiovisual archival advocacy must address a public vitally interested in media preservation as though it already exists; public advocacy for archives speaks to a simultaneously virtual and real public that already cares. A kind of optimism subtends the dreaming/imagining/creating of an archival public, one that proceeds through a disavowal of its own subjunctive mode: "Public speech contends with the necessity of addressing its public as already existing real persons."[26]

Warner acknowledges that his scholarship is imbricated in processes of bringing queer counterpublics into being.[27] As he puts it, "Writing to a public helps to make a world, insofar as the object of address is brought into being partly by postulating and characterizing it."[28] His self-reflexivity allows me to recognize what I am attempting in this book. In writing about the precarious afterlives of older works of Philippine cinema, I participate in ongoing efforts to bring a public committed to audiovisual archiving into being. In part, this book has traced the degree to which a public for Philippine film archives—users, advocates, stakeholders, and supporters—has only haltingly emerged; as such, it is one of many constellated attempts to enlarge the circle of involved participants attentive to Philippine cinema's archival condition. No single discourse creates a public since it is a broad and ongoing sphere of encounter and interaction.[29] Given this, my work takes its place in a growing ambit of circulation that projects the vital stakes of archival access and film preservation to a wider social world.

PEPOT ARTISTA: CINEPHILIC ARCHIVEOLOGY

I approach del Mundo's film *Pepot Artista* (Pepot superstar; 2005) as an archiveological work whose subject is the cinematic archive from which it borrows. By "archiveology," Catherine Russell refers to a "media art practice" characterized by "the reuse, recycling, appropriation, and borrowing of archival material."[30] In deploying archiveological formal tactics, the film audaciously imagines an archival public for Philippine cinema, "projecting the field of argument" as it "postulates a world."[31] While I have likened Philippine archiving to a riverine system that connects formal institutions to informal collections and hybridizes their practices, the concept of archiveology allows me to shift gears. From the perspective of archiveology, archives might also be construed as a reservoir of cinematic fragments rife for remixing in the service of imagining an archival public. By extracting visual and audial quotations from their original contexts and creating new meanings through montage, found footage films have the potential to offer a counterarchive. As Russell underscores: "In archiveology, film clips are compiled and ordered according to a system and arrangement other than that for which they were originally made. In this sense, the collection serves as a new archive."[32]

In *Pepot Artista*, archiveology addresses a public pleasurably engaged in and critically attentive to Philippine cinema's archival condition. The low-budget digital independent film *Pepot Artista* gleans a handful of moments from an increasingly forgotten reservoir of the nation's cinematic past, thus leveraging what Thomas Elsaesser calls cinephilia's capacity to bring a "crisis of memory . . . mediated by technologies of recording, storage and retrieval" into sharp focus.[33] In the grim pre-NFAP era, with a national film archive nowhere in sight, *Pepot Artista* playfully imagined a public that roots for archival film preservation (figure E.1). Like *Iskalawags* in the previous chapter, *Pepot Artista* is a fictive and deeply nos-

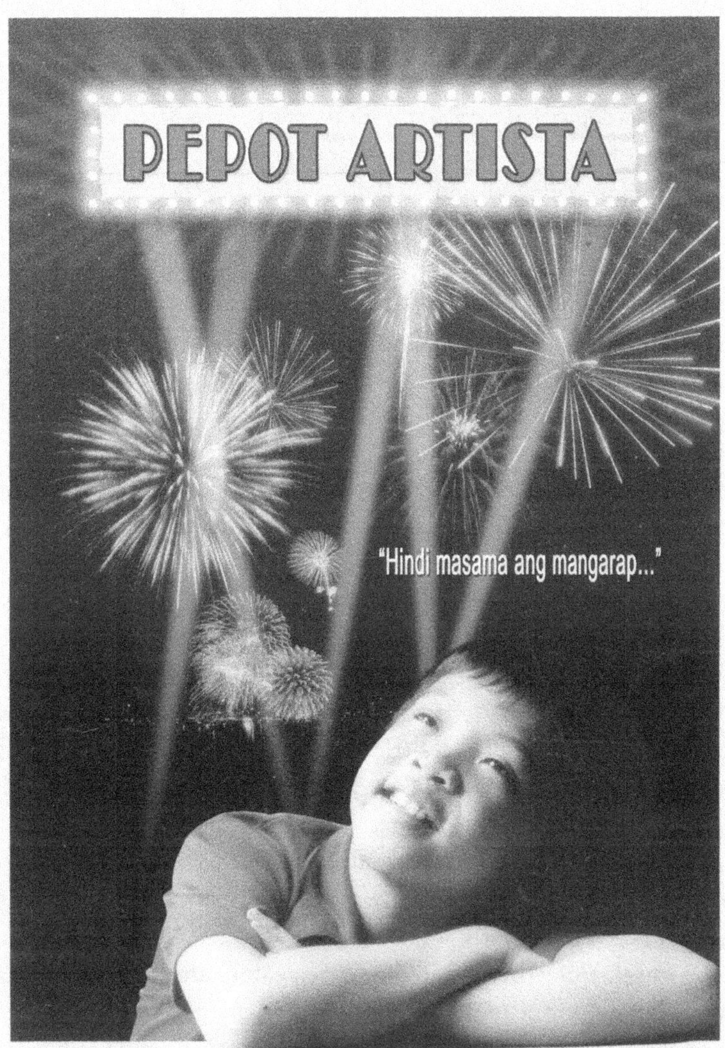

E.1 Poster for *Pepot Artista* (Pepot superstar; dir. Clodualdo del Mundo Jr., 2005). The tagline reads: "There's no harm in dreaming." Courtesy of Marti Magsanoc and Archivo 1984 Gallery.

talgic archive, forged by a filmmaker's personal cinephilic memory, that is projected onto the public sphere. While it cannot preserve in toto the films it excerpts, *Pepot Artista*'s archiveology enacts the survival of older cinephilic pleasures.

Archival footage is central to the film's appeal. Excerpts from *Alas, Hari, at Sota* (Ace, king, and jack; 1971), starring Fernando Poe Jr. (known as FPJ and lionized by Video 48 and *Iskalawags*); fragments of the Nora Aunor teen romance *Lollipops and Roses* (1971); and snippets of the Golden Age classic *Biyaya ng Lupa* (Blessings of the land; dir. Manuel Silos, 1959) address knowing film buffs while offering cinematic pedagogy for moviegoers who have never seen these films. *Pepot Artista*'s contagious cinephilia can evoke a longing for films one has never seen, initiating spectators into the archive's popular pleasures. This, in fact, is the important work *Pepot Artista* does for my own teaching of Philippine cinema.

Set a decade earlier than *T-Bird at Ako*, *Pepot Artista* re-creates the movie-mad culture of the early 1970s, a milieu dominated by the superstardom of Nora Aunor (affectionately referred to as "Guy" by her fans) and Tirso Cruz III (nicknamed "Pip" by his devotees), who were romantically linked both on- and off-screen.[34] The child protagonist Pepot (Elijah Castillo) is the impoverished moviegoer-as-dreamer. The tagline for the movie poster reads: "There's no harm in dreaming" (*Hindi masama ang mangarap*) (see figure E.1). A little boy who sells *komiks* (comic book–sized movie magazines) on the street, Pepot dreams of emulating his screen idols: action king FPJ and teen icons Guy and Pip.

Pepot's story in the 1970s is recounted by the retrospective voice-over narration of a present-day movie writer, later implicitly revealed to be the adult Pepot in the early aughts. As the Narrator (Noni Buencamino) achieves his lifelong dream of telling Pepot's story, the film's three-tiered structure, built on the motif of cinephilic dreaming, is laid bare. Pepot's dream of superstardom and the Narrator's dream of recounting Pepot's tale parallel filmmaker-historian del Mundo's off-screen archival aspirations. As such, it is the cinematic companion text to del Mundo's monograph *Dreaming of a National Audio-Visual Archive*, which drew attention to Philippine cinema's archive crisis a year before the film's release (figure E.2).

Pepot Artista vivifies the historically specific pleasures of watching Tagalog cinema in Manila movie theaters in the 1970s. The young Pepot worships at the feet of his screen idols within a now-eclipsed exhibition context as he and other fans avidly consume a projected film in a crowded movie theater. In *Pepot Artista*, the materiality of media history is memo-

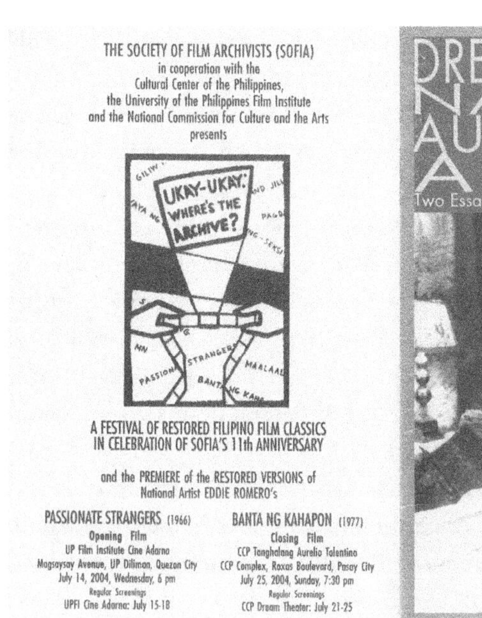

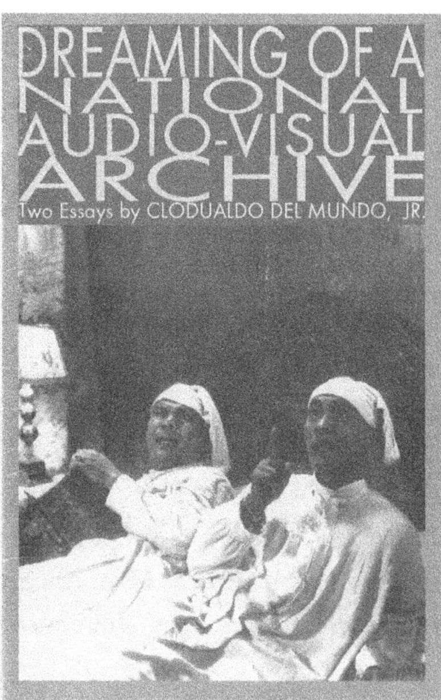

E.2 Front and back covers of Clodualdo del Mundo Jr.'s monograph *Dreaming of a National Audio-Visual Archive*, published by SOFIA in 2004, a year before the release of *Pepot Artista*. Author's collection.

rialized in shots of film reels delivered by bicycle courier to the Bellevue, an Art Deco–inspired single-screen theater in Paco, Manila. Pepot takes his seat alongside other rowdy-yet-rapt popular audience members eating *inihaw na mais* (grilled corn on the cob) in darkness, illuminated only by the beam of a 35mm film projector. In other scenes, he wanders among the poorly paid artisans who create gigantic, hand-painted billboards for the latest movie releases, star vehicles adapted from serials published in the *komiks* hawked by young Pepot when he is not in school.

As a low-budget production financed with 500,000 pesos in grant money from the Cinemalaya Independent Film Festival, *Pepot Artista* won Cinemalaya's inaugural Best Picture prize in 2005 and went on to a one-week theatrical run at a single movie house in Metro Manila, the Promenade Theater in the posh suburb of Greenhills.[35] Though never commercially released on DVD, *Pepot Artista* circulated through two subscription-based video-on-demand (SVOD) services: the Hawaii-based AsiaPacificFilms.tv, which partnered with Alexander Street Press in 2012, and Iflix, first launched in the Philippines and Malaysia in 2015.[36]

As a work of archiveological research, *Pepot Artista* is institutionally reliant on the various archives credited in the film's acknowledgments—LVN Pictures, Sampaguita Pictures, Premiere Productions, and especially ABS-CBN Film Archives, where del Mundo screened vintage Tagalog films he would eventually excerpt. In a hybrid role that combined scholar, filmmaker, cinephile, and fan, del Mundo sourced archival footage on analog Betacam video from the ABS-CBN Film Archives.[37] He then digitally edited these together with original footage shot on mini-DV using a Panasonic DVX-100.[38] In this way, *Pepot Artista* enacts archiveological cinephilia via analog videotapes accessed by the filmmaker in an institutional archive, in contrast to the bootlegged Betamax tapes prominent in *Iskalawags*' story world.

Indeed, much of Philippine cinema's archival afterlife was rescued and still resides on analog video. According to a 2013 NFAP report, the bulk of its collection at that point consisted of fifty-three hundred videotapes, the majority of which were on U-matic and Betacam formats.[39] Video is prominent in Philippine cinema's archival afterlives because, as Lucas Hilderbrand observes, "the politics of video have, from the beginning, been a politics of access."[40] However, Marita Sturken also cautions that analog video was never intended to be an archival medium. Video was designed to allow consumer recording of television's simultaneous transmission, offering the immediate pleasure of instant replay.[41] Ironically, Filipino photochemical cinema was migrated to analog video formats because the latter were newer and more accessible to nonprofessionals than nitrate, acetate, and polyester film; in the long run, however, video has proved less durable than those older formats and carriers.[42]

Pepot Artista was materially recombinant in terms of the analog and digital formats, carriers, and platforms involved in its preproduction, production, postproduction, and distribution phases (researched on Betacam, recorded on mini-DV, digitally edited using computer software, and streamed online through SVOD). Its institutional support was likewise hybridized. The CCP is prominent in the institutional scaffolding that supported the publication of *Dreaming*, the SOFIA monograph for which *Pepot Artista* serves as a kind of companion film, since the CCP also hosts the Cinemalaya festival at which *Pepot Artista* premiered. The personal-institutional context for *Pepot Artista* as a work of archival advocacy thus encompasses corporate divisions (the ABS-CBN-Film Archive), government agencies (the CCP), and a nongovernmental organization (SOFIA), with key figures linking various projects and organizations to one another

(CCP's Vicky Belarmino and ABS-CBN's Mary del Pilar, like del Mundo, are prime movers at SOFIA). As a screenwriter for the New Cinema masterwork *Maynila sa Kuko ng Liwanag*, an emeritus film professor, and a former president of SOFIA, del Mundo had a level of access to industry figures and formal archives well beyond that of the nonacademic film buffs his movie lionizes. This is not to criticize the film or its director but simply to call attention to *Pepot Artista*'s material and institutional underpinnings. The indie film showcases a filmmaker-historian-advocate's use of cinephilic archiveology in the service of a public-facing advocacy, a point to which I would like at last to return.

STYLE AND THE IMAGINED PUBLIC

Warner emphasizes that the simultaneously "subjunctive" (i.e., potential) and "autotelic" (i.e., self-creating) quality of the public means that addressing a public requires "political confidence," which not all marginal groups or causes can muster.[43] If the local film audience fervently coveted by independent and alternative filmmakers in the Philippines has proved elusive, then confidence in the actual or potential existence of a public committed to safeguarding the nation's audiovisual archives is even harder to summon. Public discourses that advocate for archival film preservation circulate more narrowly and less often than domestically produced mainstream and indie films. (By contrast, think of Hollywood blockbusters' confident address to global audiences, despite the prevailing understanding of media industries as risk industries.) This is what makes *Pepot Artista* so arresting: its unshakable confidence in the existence of a cinephilic public that can be persuaded to advocate for archives. Combining an over-the-top style with winking allusions and archival excerpts, *Pepot Artista* hails a very particular archival public—imagined yet potentially self-actualizing—with an audacity equal to its young protagonist's faith in his own future superstardom.

Style is usually understood as purely a matter of form, referring primarily to film techniques, genre conventions, and/or auteurist signatures. Yet film style is also a tactic of public address that delineates a work's intended audience and path of circulation. Style as a means of addressing a public must "concretize the world in which discourse circulates, . . . offer its members direct and active membership through language, . . . [and] place strangers on a shared footing."[44] *Pepot Artista* exemplifies the use of a stylistic register that eschews a universally legible aesthetic language (an impossible goal, at any rate) in favor of defining the specific audience the work seeks to address, a social world of Filipino film lovers that the movie believes to already be out there.

The cinematic style used by the movie *Pepot Artista* to hail and constitute an archival public deploys a range of political, literary, cultural, and cinematic allusions. The tense economic and political milieu of the 1970s is evoked through a subplot in which Pepot's father, a low-income worker who hopes to work in Saudi Arabia, is deceived by an illegal recruiter for overseas labor. In another scene, Pepot is framed in the foreground while a wall in the background is vandalized with anti-Marcos graffiti that reads, "Marcos *Tuta*," a reference to the militant student movement's critique of the Marcos dictatorship as a puppet of US imperialism.

The film's literary allusions take place against this political backdrop. Pepot and his elementary school classmates mount a failed production of *Florante at Laura* (Florante and Laura), a nineteenth-century epic poem by Tagalog poet laureate Francisco Balagtas. The poem's iconic opening lines, uttered by its suffering hero Florante ("*Sa loob at labas ng bayan kong sawi* . . . " [Both inside and outside my hapless nation . . .]), who bewails his captivity while bound to a tree, are conventionally interpreted as an allegorical reference to Philippine suffering under Spanish colonial rule. Underscored by the film's final intertitle, and repeated by various characters in an audition, this dialogue motif anchors the film's closure when it is quoted a final time by an adult Pepot as the present-day Narrator. The Narrator's concluding voice-over reframes young Pepot as a kind of contemporary Florante, an Everyman (or "Every Fan") figure whose dreams of becoming a famous actor or singer are an antidote to despair and poverty. Alongside its citation of high Tagalog literature, the film also foregrounds allusions to popular culture, especially the lowbrow *komiks* that fostered a movie-mad fan culture after the demise of the studio system.[45]

Through a plethora of cinematic references encoded in dialogue, cameos, and archival footage, the film repeatedly posits an audience of cinephiles, pop culture aficionados, and literati on the other side of its public address. An early scene features a roll call of Pepot's schoolmates, whose names are all thinly disguised references to famous figures from Philippine literature, music, theater, and film. "Jose Rizalino," Pepot's full name, alludes to nineteenth-century novelist and national hero Jose Rizal. Puns and cameos presume an audience of cultural insiders knowledgeable about Philippine history, culture, and popular cinema: mainstream director

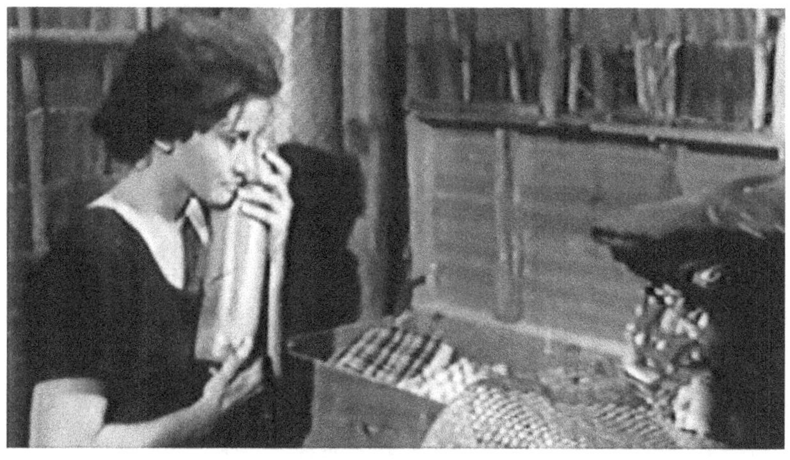

E.3 *Pepot Artista* features several archiveological excerpts, such as this scene from *Biyaya ng Lupa* (Blessings of the land; dir. Manuel Silos, 1959). Film still.

Jose Javier Reyes and avant-garde animator Roxlee shoot a movie on location in Pepot's neighborhood; movie actors Joel Torre, Boots Anson-Roa, Ricky Davao, and talk show host Butch Francisco are featured in scenes leading up to an audition at ABS-CBN; and local musicians Yoyoy Villame and Lourd de Veyra are seen busking and drinking, respectively, a short distance from Pepot's home.

Pepot Artista's most striking use of style to hail an archival public involves archiveological quotations from Filipino film history. Pepot and his pals emulate FPJ's action movie masculinity, punctuated by excerpts from *Alas, Hari, at Sota*. (Years later, the Cebuano boys in *Iskalawags* would take FPJ's *Asedillo* as their gender template.) When Pepot begs his overdramatizing mother (herself a former movie extra) for money to buy clothes for an audition, she responds anachronistically by reaching for an *alkansya*, a hollow bamboo container for storing one's savings. Pepot's mother (Rio Locsin) is reenacting a poignant scene from the 1959 film *Biyaya ng Lupa*, in which a conscientious mother's lifetime savings for each of her children—amounting to small heaps of coins—are hidden in individual bamboo *alkansya* bearing their names (figure E.3). To underscore the allusion, an excerpt of the original melodramatic scene from Manuel Silos's film is intercut with Pepot's conversation with his mother.

Other memorable moments of *Pepot Artista*'s archiveology involve the camp antics of teen heartthrobs Nora Aunor and Tirso Cruz III, who

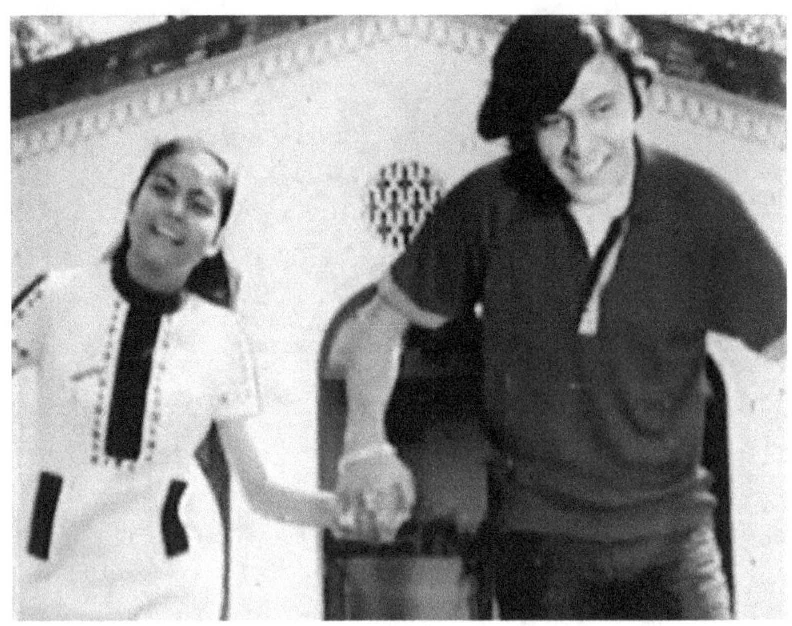

E.4 *Pepot Artista* quotes archival footage featuring Nora Aunor and Tirso Cruz III from the 1971 romantic teen musical *Guy and Pip* (dir. German Moreno). Film still.

jump into a pool fully clothed in groovy bell-bottom ensembles while holding hands (figure E.4).[46] Antiquated capers and love scenes from *Guy and Pip* and *Lollipops and Roses*, revisited through the faded yet saturated look of deteriorating color footage, spark cinephilic memories for viewers familiar with these stars and films while provoking imagined nostalgia on the part of moviegoers unfamiliar with yet charmed by these excerpts. A work of archiveological pedagogy dense with political, literary, and cinematic allusions, *Pepot Artista* is often tonally uneven, especially in inexplicably zany scenes stuffed with zealously delivered yet illegible allusions.[47] For all its lack of polish, however, the film's winking allusions to canonical literature and intermedial popular culture (*komiks*, radio hits, film, and television) forge a uniquely cinephilic-and-archival idiom.

In deploying a stylistic vernacular that continually references Philippine history and revisits the delights of the cinematic archive, *Pepot Artista* is suffused with an ambition to constitute a particular public, one that grasps the significance of audiovisual archives to the larger project of cultural nationalism. Through its cinephilic intertextuality and buoyant style, the film hopes to hail and constitute an audience of archivally aware film buffs. This optimistic ambition explains the recurring motif of characters breaking the fourth wall to direct their jokes to a (very particular type of) viewer. The diegetic protagonists are addressing extrafilmic audiences familiar with Philippine cinema, culture, and history, moviegoers who might be awakened to the gratifications of the archive. *Pepot Artista* introduces a film buff's personal archive of affectively charged cinematic memories into paths of public circulation. Its inside jokes and cinephilic archiveology fold the old into the new, enacting the survival of nearly forgotten cinephilic pleasures, even as the aging source films fade from public circulation.

AN ARCHIVAL COUNTERPUBLIC?

Self-recognition is a necessary, but not sufficient, condition for an archival public to coalesce. To self-identify as a member of a shared social world is one thing; to act in concert with others to achieve a common end is quite another. This much is conveyed by Warner, who emphasizes that publics are agentive: "Publics act historically. They are said to rise up, to speak, to reject false promises, to demand answers, to change sovereigns, to support troops, to give mandates for change, to be satisfied, to scrutinize public conduct, to take role models, to deride counterfeits." The capacity of collective entities to become social movements that "acquire agency in relation to the state," and thus "enter the temporality of politics," is a salient feature of what Warner calls a counterpublic.[48]

Pepot Artista's confident cinephilic address notwithstanding, an engaged counterpublic that scrutinizes Philippine government officials' management of film archives, demands answers when state film collections teeter on the brink of collapse, or opposes the government's destabilization of a major corporate audiovisual archive, has historically failed to emerge. A counterpublic entails durative collective involvements in "the hope of transforming, not just policy, but the space of public life itself."[49] Given this collective-agentive dimension, no one film or monograph can call a Philippine archival counterpublic into being; that is beyond even Pepot's dreaming.

At a September 2020 SOFIA microlearning session on the topic of Philippine film history, both speakers and organizers seemed baffled by a question posed by a participant: "How can ordinary citizens help with the archiving of our movies?"[50] This query struck me as somewhat expected, given the webinar's large turnout of about a hundred people, many of whom seemed to be "ordinary interested moviegoers" (as the webinar put it) rather than professional archivists. The question was only gradually met with answers about what individual film buffs might do: bring possible candidates for film restoration to SOFIA's attention, organize their own personal audiovisual collections, or strive to learn more about the history of Philippine cinema. Strikingly, no possibilities relating to collective advocacy for audiovisual archiving, whether via social media campaigns or legislative lobbying, were broached, nor did SOFIA leadership discuss the many structural changes to cultural policy that its own members have proposed over the decades. This moment—when seasoned archive advocates were at a loss to answer a version of the question "Where do we go from here?"—remains with me as a missed opportunity to collectively imagine an archival counterpublic. It is symptomatic of the painful truth that one must look outside Philippine history for effective examples of public advocacy for media archiving.

One instructive historical precedent involves the efforts of a vigilant archival counterpublic that successfully pressured the Australian government to secure the NFSA's institutional autonomy in 2008. As Ray Edmondson recounts, the archive's stakeholders organized themselves as the Archive Forum in 2004 to petition the Australian prime minister for the NFSA's independence from the administrative umbrella of memory institutions. In 2006, the last lobbying document for the NFSA's statutory authority was sent to Parliament, representing the collective stance of fifteen hundred professionals and academics. The final passage of the NFSA Act in 2008 was accomplished through the political support of the Labor Party and the vigilant efforts of a broad-based stakeholder advocacy.[51] Edmondson emphasizes that public support for audiovisual archiving in Australia was decades in the making, going back to a widely publicized 1981 campaign called the "Last Film Search," a "treasure hunt for old films" that "captured the national imagination and brought the work of the NFA [National Film Archive] to broad public notice."[52] The NFSA's struggle to achieve legislated institutional autonomy and stability is a resonant one in the Philippine archival context, since the NFSA has been a close regional collaborator with the PIA, CCP, SOFIA, and SEAPAVAA since the 1990s.

In contrast, the closure, imperilment, or volatility of various state and corporate film archives in the Philippines—the FAP, which collapsed in 1986; the PIA-MPD, which closed in 2004; the uncertain future of the ABS-CBN Film Archives following the conglomerate's 2020 franchise denial; and ongoing legislative lobbies to secure the institutional autonomy of a national audiovisual archive—have historically failed to call forth an archival counterpublic of sufficient magnitude to insulate these archives from political vicissitude. Edmondson expounds on the usual composition of stakeholders for cultural memory institutions: those who utilize the collection or provide its content; "government, media professional associations and advocates championing philosophical or public policy issues"; as well as "staff, volunteers and advisers, commentators, [and] professional bodies and associations" such as UNESCO.[53]

If a large bloc of stakeholders in audiovisual archiving has failed to coalesce, it may be because the Philippines' anarchival history has resulted in relatively few users being able to access these archives for their purposes, whether personal, commercial, scholarly, or professional. Paul Grant puts it forcefully: "An archive without engagement by both memory workers and the public is a crypt."[54] In the absence of ready access to formal state or corporate archives, "ordinary moviegoers" interested in historical Philippine films turn to online video-sharing platforms, personal or informal collections, and academic libraries. Few would think to approach the NFAP/PFA, ABS-CBN, CCP, or MOWELFUND, since a layperson with a general interest in Philippine cinema might not be granted access to these collections, given the gatekeeping processes of formal archives.

In chapter 2, I referred to this as the chicken-and-egg problem arising from Philippine cinema's anarchival condition: wide public support to campaign for legislative security, ample funding, autonomous governance, and a permanent home for a national audiovisual archive cannot be achieved without first giving the public straightforward, reliable access to its holdings. Lacking established, enduring archives, few stakeholders can be mobilized to press for an archive that endures. No archival counterpublic without readily accessible archives: if this hunch holds true, then broad access is the necessary precondition for archival autonomy and longevity. If recognized as an immediate priority for audiovisual memory collections, access might eventually pave the way for long-term public awareness and support for Philippine cinema's embattled archives.

NOTES

INTRODUCTION. KEYWORDS FOR PHILIPPINE CINEMA'S ARCHIVAL AFTERLIVES

1 *Ibong Adarna* was written and directed by Vicente Salumbides, with Manuel Conde serving as technical supervisor.

2 Del Mundo, *Dreaming*, 4–5.

3 Walters-Johnston, email to author.

4 The First Golden Age of Philippine cinema refers to critically acclaimed films made at the height of the studio system, especially during the 1940s and 1950s. David, "Second Golden Age," 2.

In an essay in the unpublished *Philippine Audiovisual Archives Collections: An Inventory*, the only comprehensive national inventory of its kind, Junio writes with frustration about the Philippines' archival condition: "From 1919, the year when *Dalagang Bukid* [Country maiden] was produced . . . to the present, we have a national output of, more or less, 8,000 feature films. . . . Inevitably you ask: *Where are these films*? I daresay 65% is GONE! Of the 350+ pre-war (i.e., World War II) films alone, we have less than 10 titles preserved in the original format. As a matter of interest, the only existing nitrate film—LVN's *Ibong Adarna* (1941)—is now in a freezer waiting to be copied to safety film." Junio, "Movie in My Mind," 7; emphasis in original.

5 The Library of Congress does hold nitrate copies of early colonial films made during the American occupation of the Philippines. See del Mundo, *Native Resistance*; and Deocampo, *Film*.

6 Julie Galino started her career with LVN Pictures, Inc., in 1990, working in the sales and postproduction departments. She began supervising the LVN Film Archives in 2002; when LVN closed its laboratory operations in 2005, she stayed on as administrative and finance officer while handling its film and memorabilia collection. Galino joined ABS-CBN Film Archives and Restoration in 2011 and is the current head of the Film Archives.

7 Galino, personal interview with author. Confirming Junio's account, Galino recalled that the nitrate dupe negative of *Ibong Adarna* was frozen and subsequently thawed in an ordinary freezer at LVN prior to the 2005

restoration, in consultation with archivists at the National Film and Sound Archive of Australia (NFSA). Galino, phone interview with author.

8 I address this idea in a different way elsewhere: "This latency of historical experience, the noncoincidence of historical event with a calendrical index, forcefully attests to a temporality that exceeds linear ordering." B. C. Lim, *Translating Time*, 185.

9 I am grateful to an anonymous reader for Duke University Press for the turn of phrase "wishful misremembering."

10 Takemoto, "Looking for Jiro Onuma," 248, 264.

11 According to ABS-CBN's film restoration head, Leo Katigbak, more than eight thousand Philippine movies were made on film between 1919 and the shift to digital cinema in 2012. While "a little over half survived in all formats," only "two thousand have been documented to have surviving film copies." Katigbak, "Ganito Tayo Noon."

12 The five surviving Filipino full-length feature films from the prewar period are *Zamboanga* (dir. Eduardo de Castro, 1937); *Tunay Na Ina* (True mother; dir. Octavio Silos, 1939); *Giliw Ko* (My dear; dir. Carlos Vander Tolosa, 1939); *Pakiusap* (Lover's plea; dir. Octavio Silos, 1940); and *Ibong Adarna* (Adarna bird; dir. Vicente Salumbides, 1941). See Junio, "Movie in My Mind," 7–8; del Mundo, *Native Resistance*, 7–8; and Deocampo, "Zamboanga."

In 2009, archival sleuthing by cinephile-archivists Teddy Co and Martin Magsanoc established that footage from two Filipino silent films from 1931, *Moro Pirates* (dir. Jose Nepomuceno) and *Princess Tarhata* (director unknown), had been reedited as a single film and released in the US market under the title *Brides of Sulu* in 1934. See San Diego, "Archivists Reclaim."

13 Deocampo, *Films from a "Lost" Cinema*. According to Paul Grant, only four predigital Visayan films survive. Grant, email to author. See chapter 6, note 12.

14 Patino, "From Colonial Policy," 52. Old film prints were also used for the flared section of toy horns (*torotot*) used in New Year's celebrations. Katigbak, "Ganito Tayo Noon."

15 See Pierce, *Survival of American Silent Feature*; and Edmondson and Pike, *Australia's Lost Films*.

16 Grant and Anissimov, *Lilas*, 18. Deocampo reflects: "If I (as [a] film historian) were to only consider films and their physical presence as [the] basis for writing a history of early Philippine cinema, then the five prewar films you mentioned would have made my job as [a] film historian impossible. In addition to films, . . . paratextual documents (film catalogues, reviews, posters, advertisements, show bills, interviews, biographies, scripts, and other ephemera—all contained in archival holdings) [are] equally significant sources of 'knowledge' about a country's cinema and its history." Deocampo, email to author.

17 Bruno, *Streetwalking on a Ruined Map*, 153.

18 *Audiovisual* is an inclusive term for moving images and recorded sound across a range of media, formats, and *carriers* (the physical objects, such as vinyl records, nitrocellulose film, videotapes, DVDs or Blu-ray discs, on which audiovisual *content* is stored). *Film*, used in a narrow technical sense, denotes negative or positive film strips coated with light-sensitive emulsion, used either in still photography or in photochemical (analog) cinema (Edmondson, *Audiovisual Archiving*, 19–20). Historically, many types of film have dominated motion picture production: e.g., nitrate (or nitrocellulose, aka celluloid), cellulose acetate (aka "safety" film), and polyester film. While Dan Streible argues for a strictly materialist and historically rigorous use of the term *film* that excludes digital movies and refers only to "strips of transparent material coated with light-sensitive emulsion" (Streible, "Moving Image History," 228), other audiovisual archivists adopt a more expansive and flexible usage of the term to refer to "moving images in general as well as particular types of works, such as feature films, regardless of carrier" (Edmondson, *Audiovisual Archiving*, 21).

This book focuses on film archives that collect photochemical cinema on film strips, while recognizing that film in a more capacious sense has been broadcast on television, watched on videotape, and circulated digitally. In practice, film archives are hybrid in terms of media formats and carriers and in their institutional structures, which may overlap with those of other memory institutions, such as libraries and museums. My use of *film archive* follows from the names of key entities in this study, such as the NFAP/PFA. While actual collections may contain a range of audiovisual media, the prominence of "film" in their organizational descriptors indicates that film (in both materialist and popular senses of the term) remains central to the mandate and priorities of these institutions.

19 Referred to only as the "Film Archive" or "Film Archives" in Marcos's Executive Order 640-A, its first director general, Ernie de Pedro, referred to the agency as the Film Archives of the Philippines with the acronym NFAP (despite the lack of "National" in its designation) in his 1986 report (De Pedro, "Overview of the Film Archives"; F. E. Marcos, Executive Order No. 640-A). In this book, I refer to the 1980s Film Archives as the FAP to distinguish it from the NFAP reestablished by the FDCP in 2011.

20 SOFIA was incorporated on June 27, 1993, the same year that the ASEAN Conference-Workshop on Film Retrieval, Restoration, and Archiving was held in Manila. Its eight founding members personified the commitment and support of the state institutions and private entities they worked for: Agustin "Hammy" Sotto (CCP); Belina "Bel" Capul and Mary del Pilar (PIA); Annella Mendoza (UP Film Center); Josephine "Jo" Atienza; Ricky Orellana and Violeta Velasco (MOWELFUND); and Renato "Sonny" San Miguel. Mendoza, "Seven Years of the Society of Film Archivists," 1.

21 In reestablishing the NFAP in 2011, Briccio Santos became the first FDCP chair to act on the FDCP's weak archival mandate. Early in his term, tensions between the fledgling NFAP and the SOFIA-led advocacy movement were sparked by Administrative Order 26 signed by President Benigno Aquino III, which required all government entities and private parties to deposit copies of their audiovisual collections to the NFAP (B. S. Aquino III, Administrative Order No. 26). Lacking clear policies on acquisition and copyright, the administrative order generated skepticism among archivists from both state and private entities who interpreted this as a nonconsultative, top-down move on the part of the FDCP and the NFAP.

22 The FDCP's archival mandate reads: "to ensure the establishment of a film archive in order to conserve and protect film negatives and/or prints as part of the nation's historical, cultural, and artistic heritage." Congress of the Philippines, Republic Act No. 9167.

23 By 2020, four years after Duterte's appointment of Mary Liza Diño as chair of the FDCP, the PFA had seen increased turnover of leadership and staff positions and had restored fewer films than the prior NFAP. By her own admission, Diño "had no prior knowledge about film archiving" at the time of her appointment (Diño-Seguerra, "Vision for FDCP's Philippine Film Archive"). Many of the film restorations touted as PFA accomplishments in Diño's 2020 article had actually been undertaken by the NFAP under the prior FDCP chair.

The local archive community was critical of the PFA's infrequent film restorations and lack of publications during the three-year period commemorating the Centennial of Philippine Cinema (2018–20) under Diño's FDCP tenure (Co, email to author, August 24, 2020). Stakeholders noted that the PFA did not provide updates about the status of their deposited collections or inform them of the potential impact of the PFA's planned move to a new structure in Intramuros on their collections (Orellana, Skype interview with author).

In July 2022, the newly elected president, Ferdinand "Bongbong" Marcos Jr., appointed former actor Tirso S. Cruz III as the chair of the FDCP, *Rappler*, "Tirso Cruz III Officially Assumes Position."

24 Patino, "From Colonial Policy," 44.

25 Unrealized proposals for a permanent national audiovisual repository date back to a 1981 UNESCO report (Roads, "Manila National Film Centre"). In August 2020, the PFA announced that plans to construct an archive building in the historic district of Intramuros, Manila, had been delayed by the pandemic (Diño-Seguerra, "Vision for FDCP's Philippine Film Archive").

26 B. C. Lim, "Analysis and Recommendations."

27 Chapter 2 examines the closure of various state entities' film collections.

28 Derrida, *Archive Fever*, 10–12.

29 Derrida, *Archive Fever*, 19.

30 Lippit, *Atomic Light*, 8–9, 12, 33.

31 Kumar, *National Film Archives*, 16. *Deferral* here means that films' degradation, while inevitable, can be delayed; under ideal conditions, films can last for over a century or more. Edmondson, *Audiovisual Archiving*, 53–54.

32 Usai, *Death of Cinema*, 113–15; Edmondson, *Audiovisual Archiving*, v. Ray Edmondson is the founding president of SEAPAVAA and former deputy director and now curator emeritus of the NFSA. On film and audiovisual preservation as a historically mutable and socially structured practice, see Frick, *Saving Cinema*, 6; and Gracy, *Film Preservation*, 22.

33 The conflicts, debates, and aspirations encoded in historical processes of self-naming were foregrounded in a September 2020 Cinema Sala virtual roundtable that posed the polemical question, "Are We Filipinx?," for which I served as moderator and opening speaker.

34 Rodríguez, *Forced Passages*, 1–2.

35 Mojares, "Formation of Filipino Nationality," 12–13, 26.

36 Lobato, *Shadow Economies of Cinema*, 10.

37 My discussion of formal and informal archives is inspired by Lobato, who argues that today's global film culture combines the formal distribution pipelines of media conglomerates with other informal routes through which movies reach consumers. In a transnational context dominated by "shadow economies of cinema" that are largely "unmeasured, unregulated, and extra-legal" (Lobato, *Shadow Economies of Cinema*, 1), we might also speak of "shadow archives" or informal archival conduits (e.g., video stores, microcuratorial projects, pop-up community screenings, personal sharing, and outright piracy) with which formal institutional repositories are entangled.

38 Rafael, "Preface to the Philippine Edition," xi–xii.

39 Rafael, "Sovereign Trickster."

40 On martial law in Mindanao, see Gotinga, "After 2 and a Half Years." On the Anti-Terrorism Act of 2020, see McCarthy, "Why Rights Groups Worry." On the abrogation of the defense agreement, see Llaneta, "UP Protests against Threat"; and Talabong, "Duterte Gov't Ends 1989 Deal."

41 See Dulay et al., "Continuity, History, and Identity."

42 The ECP was created via presidential decree (Executive Order No. 770) in 1982 and was abolished by Marcos in 1985. The FDCP, established in 2002 via Republic Act 9167, inherits several of the ECP's functions. See F. E. Marcos, Executive Order No. 770; F. E. Marcos, Executive Order No. 1051; Congress of the Philippines, Republic Act No. 9167.

43 Constitutional Commission, 1987 Constitution of the Republic of the Philippines, Art. VII, Sec. 16, as clarified by Reyes, email to author.

44 Campos, *End of National Cinema*, 278; Villarama, "Current Film Distribution Trends," 104.

45 The FDCP is charged with the growth of the commercial film industry through production incentives, film festivals, and the development of both domestic and foreign markets for Philippine cinema. Congress of the Philippines, Republic Act No. 9167.

46 Olgado and Roque, "Position Paper on House Bill No. 2404"; Lim, Olgado, and Roque, "Position Paper on the Interrelated House Bills"; Lim, Olgado, and Roque, "Position Paper on the Substitute Bill."

47 Brown, "Crippled Cinema," 264–65.

48 Brown, "Crippled Cinema," 286–87.

49 Villarama, "Current Film Distribution Trends," 100.

50 Edmondson, "National Film and Sound Archive," 362.

51 On self-theorizing, see Caldwell, "Cultures of Production," 199–201.

52 Abad, "Timeline"; Gutierrez, "Philippine Congress Officially Shuts Down." Hard hit by the closure in 2020, the ABS-CBN Film Archives was initially concerned not only about ongoing restoration projects but also about the safety of the archive's vaults and holdings, especially given a threatened government takeover of the network complex, a move that recalls an earlier historical precedent: the Marcos dictatorship's seizure of all media outlets upon the declaration of martial law in 1972, resulting in the destruction of "the master copies of all programs" produced by ABS-CBN's radio and television network prior to martial law. Avendaño, "Final Cut"; see also M. O. Lim, "ABS-CBN Shutdown."

Leo Katigbak, head of ABS-CBN Film Restoration, summed up the impact of the franchise denial on the ABS-CBN Film Archives. By August 31, 2020, the archives staff were reduced from fourteen to five workers; and DVD releases and full digital restorations (which are collaboratively outsourced to domestic and international partners) were halted due to budget restrictions. Katigbak, "Ganito Tayo Noon"; Katigbak, email to author.

53 Del Mundo, qtd. in Chua, "Hard Work of Saving."

54 In 1997, Bel Capul described SOFIA as a "professional association of AV [audiovisual] archive practitioners composed of middle level managers coming from different institutions with AV archive holdings." When the Philippines hosted the first SEAPAVAA conference in 1996, Philippine president Fidel Ramos formally recognized SOFIA as the "lead coordinating body" spearheading the establishment of a National Film Archive. Capul, "Annex I."

55 Allyson Field cautions against reifying the value and authority of surviving films. Field, *Uplift Cinema*, 25.

56 On "gray literature," see Gitelman, *Paper Knowledge*, 115–16.

57 Edmondson, "National Film and Sound Archive," 8–9, 81.

58 Gitelman, *Paper Knowledge*, 19.

59 Gitelman, *Paper Knowledge*, 4–5.

60 The former head of the Film Archives of the ABS-CBN Corporation until her retirement in 2019, Mary del Pilar is a SOFIA cofounder. A SOFIA past president and member of its Board of Trustees, she was head of the PIA-MPD Film Laboratory from 1991 to 2000. In addition to having served as Executive Council member of the NCCA Committee on Cinema, she served as SEAPAVAA treasurer and chair of its Technical Committee from 1996 to 2000.

Vicky Belarmino is a past president of SOFIA and a cultural officer and film archivist of the CCP's Film, Broadcast, and New Media Production and Exhibition Department. She serves as festival coordinator for the Cinemalaya Philippine Independent film festival. She was an Executive Council member of the NCCA Committee on Cinema (2004–10) and also served as an officer and Executive Council member of SEAPAVAA (2008–13). Her mentors include two premier historians of Philippine film, scholars Agustin "Hammi" Sotto (at SOFIA) and Nicanor Tiongson (at CCP), exemplifying the strong links between academia and archiving in the careers of SOFIA prime movers.

Edmondson notes the unique value of personal papers accumulated by cultural workers and institutional insiders, "which could not have been separately assembled by any other researcher" (Edmondson, "National Film and Sound Archive," 377). On the role of SEAPAVAA and other archives in shaping "the formation of a regional conception of Asian cinema," see O. Khoo, *Asian Cinema*, chap. 6.

61 The career of Bel Capul, a SOFIA cofounder, bridged the Marcos and post-EDSA eras of film archiving, given her work at the Communications Research Office of the NMPC from 1979 to 1985 and her years at the PIA-MPD from 1986 to 2004, a period that coincides with the heyday of the PIA's film restoration and preservation efforts. In the 1990s, as head of the PIA-MPD, Capul trained film laboratory technicians in restoration processes, thus paving the way for the establishment of SOFIA. As a SOFIA member and past president (1996–98), Capul supervised several film restorations and spearheaded the restoration of *Tunay Na Ina*, one of the earliest surviving Filipino films. She went on to serve as president of SEAPAVAA (2002–8) and chair of UNESCO's Memory of the World Marketing Subcommittee in 2009. She retired from the PIA in 2017.

Vicky Bejerano is a PIA staff member whose career spans the transition from the defunct MPD to the current MISD; like Capul, she embodies much of these units' institutional memory. From 1991 to 2003, Bejerano worked as a chemist and sensitometrist at the MPD's Film Lab. From 2009 onward, she was the sole employee of the PIA Archives Unit under the MISD.

62 Gitelman, *Paper Knowledge*, 84–85.

63 Gitelman, *Paper Knowledge*, 3.

64 Harding, "Rethinking Standpoint Epistemology," 57.

65 Haraway, "Situated Knowledges," 187–88.

66 Haraway, "Situated Knowledges," 191.

67 In this book, all translations from Filipino and Taglish (a mixture of Tagalog-based Filipino and English) into English are my own, with the exception of quoted English subtitles for Filipino films.

68 Haraway, "Situated Knowledges," 190–91.

69 Haraway, "Situated Knowledges," 189.

70 Schwartz and Cook, "Archives, Records, and Power," 1, 9, 12.

71 On patriarchal conceptions of the archivist as the "handmaiden" to the historian, see Cook, "Archive(s) Is a Foreign Country," 608–9; and Cook, "Evidence, Memory, Identity, and Community," 107. T. R. Schellenberg's influential archival theory is explored in Cook, "Evidence, Memory, Identity, and Community."

72 Harding, "Rethinking Standpoint Epistemology," 60–61; Trouillot, *Silencing the Past*, xix.

73 See Fossati, *From Grain to Pixel*. The establishment of the graduate Moving Image Archiving and Preservation (MIAP) program at New York University in 2004 was key to this shift.

74 Cook, "Archive(s) Is a Foreign Country," 614–15.

75 Edmondson, *Audiovisual Archiving*, 82.

76 See the journal issue titled "Cinema and the Archives in the Philippines," *Plaridel* 15, no. 2 (2018).

77 Trouillot, *Silencing the Past*, 19–21, 151–52.

78 Comaroff and Comaroff, *Theory from the South*, 6–7.

79 Haraway, "Situated Knowledges," 187.

80 Kathryn Pyne Addelson notes: "The academic disciplines are constructed to preserve themselves, their bailiwicks, and the careers and authority of their members." Addelson, "Knower/Doers and Their Moral Problems," 273.

81 Said, *Representations of the Intellectual*, 76–77.

82 Barthes, *Roland Barthes by Roland Barthes*, 52.

83 Alexis Tioseco's letter was first published in *Rogue* in July 2008. Tioseco, "Letter I Would Love."

84 Trouillot, *Silencing the Past*, 19–20.

85 Cook, "Archive(s) Is a Foreign Country," 629–31.

86 Parikka, "Archival Media Theory," 1–2.

87 Parikka, "Archival Media Theory," 16.

88 Steedman, *Dust*, 69.

89 Gracy, *Film Preservation*, 1–2, 57.

90 Gracy, *Film Preservation*, 17–19; Houston, *Keepers of the Frame*.

91 Harris, *Archives and Justice*, 121–22.

92 Carolyn Steedman speaks of "the constraints which . . . are made by the documents themselves: what they permit you to write, the permissions they offer." Steedman, *Dust*, x–xi.

93 Derrida, *Archive Fever*, 11–12.

94 Frick, *Saving Cinema*, 13–14.

95 Derrida, *Archive Fever*, 1–3.

96 In a conference paper, Deocampo cites a *Manila Times* editorial from 1917 urging the establishment of a National Film Archive. Deocampo, "Propaganda Influenced Concept."

97 Salumbides, *Motion Pictures in the Philippines*, 10–11.

98 Pinga, letter from Film Institute of the Philippines.

99 Under Diosdado Macapagal's presidency, Republic Act 4165 created the National Commission on Culture in 1964; film was not listed among the country's various arts. In the Marcos era, Republic Act 4846 did not include cinema as a cultural property in need of preservation, nor was cinema mentioned among the seven arts worthy of state support at the 1966 CCP groundbreaking ceremonies, "Alay at Pamana." Congress of the Philippines, Republic Act No. 4165; Congress of the Philippines, Republic Act No. 4846; "Appendix B: Program for the Ceremonies."

100 Pinga, "Looking at Our Film Institute," 4.

101 BNFI, "BNFI/UNESCO/CAPREFIL Final Report," 4–6.

102 B. Lumbera, "Approaches to the Filipino Film," 96, 99.

103 The impulse to go beyond mourning was inspired by an undergraduate student in my "Time and Cinema" course in spring 2017. During my lecture on the loss of indexicality due to the shift from analog to digital media, the student asked: "I get it, but what are we mourning?"

104 Stoler, *Along the Archival Grain*, 10.

105 Fossati, *From Grain to Pixel*, 48.

106 Willems, "Beyond Normative Dewesternization," 7.

107 Cassano, *Southern Thought and Other Essays*, 1.

108 Trouillot, *Silencing the Past*, 26–27.

109 Stoler, *Along the Archival Grain*, 3.

110 Steedman, *Dust*, 81.

111 "There is a double nothingness in the writing of history and in the analysis of it: it is about something that never did happen in the way it comes to be represented (the happening exists in the telling or the text); and it is made out of materials that aren't there, in an archive or anywhere else." Steedman, *Dust*, 154.

112 Field, *Uplift Cinema*, x–xi.

113 Field, *Uplift Cinema*, 23–27.

114 See Salumbides, *Motion Pictures in the Philippines*, 11; del Mundo, *Dreaming*, 4; B. Lumbera, "Approaches to the Filipino Film," 96; Deocampo, *Lost Films of Asia*.

115 Grant and Anissimov, *Lilas*, 9–10.

116 Trouillot, *Silencing the Past*, 55.

117 Edmondson advises cultural workers in memory institutions to be aware of their own institutional histories, but the Philippines' anarchival conditions make his counsel difficult to operationalize. Edmondson, *Audiovisual Archiving*, 76.

118 See Edmondson, "You Only Live Once."

119 Trouillot, *Silencing the Past*, 55.

120 Schwartz and Cook, "Archives, Records, and Power," 13.

121 Harris, *Archives and Justice*, 89, 103.

122 Cook, "Evidence, Memory, Identity, and Community," 101–2.

123 Cook, "Archive(s) Is a Foreign Country," 606.

124 Del Mundo, *Dreaming*, 14.

125 Derrida, *Archive Fever*, 3. Harris discusses archival appraisal as a political operationalization of Derridean consignation: "Appraisal brings into sharpest focus the power [of consignation] wielded by archivists. . . . Which stories will be consigned to the archive and which will not." Harris, *Archives and Justice*, 104.

126 Trouillot, *Silencing the Past*, 23–24.

127 Velasco, PIA Circular No. 1; Velasco, PIA Circular No. 3; Velasco, PIA Circular No. 4; Velasco, PIA Special Order No. 195.

128 Edmondson, *Audiovisual Archiving*, 52.

129 National Film Archives of the Philippines [hereafter NFAP], Film Inspection and Status Report; NFAP, email to author. The NFAP's film inspection and status report is made with reference to Jean-Louis Bigourdan's four-part classification of the condition of cellulose acetate films. *Good or Fair* refers to "films [that] are not decaying, or are just starting to decay," and "can last several centuries in proper storage," while *actively decaying* means that "film may decay at a fast pace depending on storage conditions" but "can last a century in cold storage" (Bigourdan, "Vinegar Syndrome," 1–2). According to Belarmino, "The prints at the time we opened the cans were in pretty good condition. The vinegar smell was not too pronounced, the prints were clean, no fungus, and the winding was not too tight, so it was easy to unroll and put in the projector." Belarmino, email to author.

130 Espiritu, *Passionate Revolutions*, 20.

131 Joaquin, "Marcos '70," 195.

132 E. Garcia, "Open Letter to Militant," 9.

133 Rafael, "Patronage, Pornography, and Youth," 155.

134 Within his first 100 days in power, Bongbong Marcos's administration shrank the budgets for the Philippines' national cultural and historical agencies. Announced in August 2022 and adopted on December 5 of that year, the *National Expenditure Program*'s 2023 allocations for

the National Historical Commission of the Philippines (NHCP) and the National Archives of the Philippines (NAP) were slashed by 27.26 percent and 25.27 percent in comparison to the previous year, respectively; the National Library of the Philippines' (NLP) budget was cut by 22.64 percent, while the National Commission for Arts and Culture (NCCA) faced the steepest cutbacks, at 83.9 percent. Department of Budget and Management, *National Expenditure Program*.

135 An especially important source was Jose Lacaba's 1982 book *Days of Disquiet, Nights of Rage*.

136 Amid a paucity of cinematic images, the First Quarter Storm bequeaths a soundtrack of activist songs and rallying cries. The enduring protest chant "*Makibaka, huwag matakot*!" (Struggle on, do not be afraid!) is one example of seventies activism's sonic legacy.

137 During the Diliman Commune of February 1971, students at UP Diliman erected barricades to stop the police and Philippine Constabulary from entering the campus to disperse student protesters. What began as a "peaceful solidarity strike with jeepney drivers over an oil price hike" became an "explosion of unrest" that lasted longer than a week as students occupied the campus and blocked accessways with furniture, objects, and their own bodies. More than eighteen students were arrested, and at least one student was killed. See Abad, "Lookback."

138 Letter to author [Re: Conditions for Research Access], September 9, 2014.

139 B. C. Lim, letter to Secretary of Information Herminio "Sonny" Coloma.

140 I later gathered that the motivation behind the PIA's bureaucratic stonewalling of my September 2014 research request was a matter of internal politics. What should have been a pro forma procedure (PIA Secretary General Oquineña's initialing of the research contract and fee waiver for the digitization of access copies) was delayed by what the director general's chief of staff called "internal issues." The contract had been previously approved by a higher authority, cabinet member Herminio "Sonny" Coloma, secretary of communications. This was apparently viewed as sidestepping the PIA secretary general's office, since my request had not gone through the "proper channels." B. C. Lim, letter to Secretary of Information Herminio "Sonny" Coloma; Avendaño, phone conversation with author.

141 The Wikipedia definition more or less accords with Jeff Martin's definition of kinescopes as "film recordings made of a broadcast directly from a television screen." Martin, "Dawn of Tape," 46.

142 Frick, *Saving Cinema*, 6.

143 I am grateful to Dan Bustillo's feedback on an earlier draft for sparking this insight.

144 Belarmino, email to author.

145 Steyerl, "In Defense of the Poor Image."

146 Goldgel-Carballo, "Reappropriation of Poverty," 114. See also G. C. Khoo, "Just-Do-It-(Yourself)," on the DIY sensibility of Malaysian independent cinema.

147 While my discussion of "making do" draws primarily on anarchival Philippine conditions and global South cultural production, there are also certain parallels with Michel de Certeau's notion of "making do" to refer to creative "styles of action" or "ways of operating" within constrained circumstances in order to achieve "unexpected results." Certeau focuses, however, on consumer practices, not cultural production or archival work-arounds. Certeau, *Practice of Everyday Life*, 30.

148 G. Lumbera, Zoom interview with author.

149 Ricky Orellana is the current director of the MOWELFUND Film Institute. A SOFIA cofounder and vice president, Orellana served as secretary general of SEAPAVAA from 2017 to 2019.

150 Orellana, Skype interview with author.

151 According to Leo Enticknap, telecine (the electronic capture of film for conversion to an analog television signal for broadcast) has tended to be conflated with digital frame-by-frame scanning of films. Enticknap, *Film Restoration*, 139–40. This might help explain why Belarmino likened the digital migration of 16mm films to kinescoping.

152 Del Mundo, *Dreaming*, 8–9.

153 At various public lectures in which I discussed tactics of making do, some audiences understandably referred to these as DIY or do-it-yourself practices. However, in contrast to dictionary definitions of DIY as work done by nonprofessionals who lack the relevant qualifications, making do is deployed by professionals due to a dearth of funding and institutional support, not for want of training or expertise. In response to an earlier draft of this book, Bono Olgado remarked that professional archivists were being forced by circumstances to embrace amateurism; I am grateful to him for this insight.

154 For example, as chapter 2 details, leftovers of the FAP and the LVN Pictures' Film Archives eventually ended up at the PIA-MPD before it, in turn, closed in 2004, its oddments turned over to the NFAP from 2013 to 2015.

155 Bruno, *Streetwalking on a Ruined Map*, 3, 13, 16.

156 Bruno, *Streetwalking on a Ruined Map*, 149–50.

157 *Merriam-Webster*, s.v. "afterlife (*n.*)," accessed May 5, 2018, http://www.merriam-webster.com/dictionary/app.

158 Fossati, *From Grain to Pixel*, 13–17.

159 Fossati, *From Grain to Pixel*, 13–14. Fossati defines the "archival life of film" as "the life of film once it has entered the archive, from selection to preservation, from restoration to exhibition and digitization." Fossati, *From Grain to Pixel*, 23.

160 Famously, the controversial digital "restoration" of Georges Melies's 1902 *A Trip to the Moon* by Lobster Films came at the cost of destroying the hand-tinted nitrate source, sparking a debate on the ethics of destruction as preservation. See Sperb, *Flickers of Film,* 71–88; Bonnard, "Melies' Voyage Restoration."

161 Lippit, *Atomic Light*, 9.

162 Dulay et al., "Continuity, History, and Identity," 93–94.

163 Harris, *Archives and Justice*, 290–91.

164 Stein, "Manila's Angels," 49, 51.

165 As explored in chapter 3, a significant number of LVN Pictures' films survive in private hands, housed at the ABS-CBN Film Archives, together with a collection of studio memorabilia.

166 Ranada, "After ABS-CBN Decision, Duterte 'Happy.'"

167 Arondekar, *For the Record*, 1.

168 See Dinshaw, "Got Medieval?"; Rohy, "Ahistorical"; Yue, "Queer Asian Cinema"; Chiang and Wong, "Asia Is Burning"; and Chiang, Henry, and Leung, "Trans-in-Asia, Asia-in-Trans."

169 Campos, *End of National Cinema,* 280.

170 Zafra, "Building an Audience," 77.

171 Cvetkovich, *Archive of Feelings*, 7–8.

172 Cvetkovich, *Archive of Feelings*, 8.

173 Co, personal interview with author. Teddy Co was instrumental in the recovery and repatriation of the "lost films" of Gerardo de Leon, Manuel Conde, and Nonoy Marcelo, among others. A SOFIA member, he cofounded and curated for the Cinema Rehiyon Film Festival. From 2017 to 2019, he served as the commissioner of the arts for the NCCA and chair of the NCCA's Committee on Cinema.

174 In *Camera Lucida*, Barthes describes the *punctum* as the "wound," "sting," or "prick" of time; if some photographs strike us with force and poignancy, it is because they attest "that has-been." Barthes, *Camera Lucida*, 26–27, 77.

175 Cvetkovich writes of her "conviction that the study of the present transforms historical methods." While reconstructing the recent history of gay and lesbian activism during the AIDS crisis, Cvetkovich realized "how perilously close to being lost even the recent past is" due to "resistance and neglect." Cvetkovich, *Archive of Feelings*, 10.

176 Orellana, Skype interview with author.

177 Camus, *Myth of Sisyphus*, 75–76.

178 Camus, *Myth of Sisyphus*, 5–6.

179 Camus, *Myth of Sisyphus*, 11–12, 15, 20.

180 Camus, *Myth of Sisyphus*, 39.

181 Camus, *Myth of Sisyphus*, 59.

182 Povinelli, *Economies of Abandonment*.

183 Camus, *Myth of Sisyphus*, 3.

184 Camus, *Myth of Sisyphus*, 82–83.

185 Camus, *Myth of Sisyphus*, 81–82.

186 Tioseco, "Letter I Would Love."

187 Warner, *Publics and Counterpublics*.

188 Conrad, "Analog, the Sequel," 28.

189 Usai, *Silent Cinema*, xiv.

190 Although *Ibong Adarna* has been screened on the cable channel Cinema One and on Facebook, it has not been commercially released on DVD. Katigbak, "Ganito Tayo Noon"; Katigbak, email to author.

191 Del Mundo, *Native Resistance*, 69–73, 79–80, 87.

192 Del Mundo, *Native Resistance*, 80.

193 The film's art director, Richard Abelardo, known for his special effects cinematography and credited for his process shots on *Ibong Adarna*, worked in various Hollywood studios, including Warner Bros., in the 1930s. Deocampo, *Film*, 357–58.

194 Thomas N. Headland and Janet Headland note that human rights abuses against the Agta Negritos of the Philippines are rooted in "racial and ethnic prejudices" and "competitive exclusion" over scarce resources like agricultural land. See Headland and Headland, "Limitation of Human Rights," 79.

195 *Ibong Adarna*'s depiction of the indigenous *negrito/a* couple recalls the American practice of "blacking up" white performers with makeup, greasepaint, or burnt cork. As such, the couple's brief appearance alludes to the visual conventions of blackface minstrelsy, an entertainment form with roots in the eighteenth and nineteenth centuries whose legacy continues to be felt in twentieth-century and twenty-first-century media. As Lott's influential analysis underscores, blackface theatrical traditions encode "white racial dread" and a simultaneous fascination with and ridicule of black bodies (Lott, *Blackface Minstrelsy*, 4–6). Similarly, Nicholas Sammond defines blackface minstrelsy as "a white performance of imagined blackness" that stages a "relationship between imagined blackness and imagined whiteness." Sammond, *Birth of an Industry*, 5–11.

196 Deocampo, *Film*, 190–91.

197 Isleta, "Letter and Project Proposal from Honesto M. Isleta."

198 Del Mundo, *Native Resistance*, 79–82. The colorful plumage was "digitally handpainted" for ABS-CBN's 2019 version. Katigbak, "Ganito Tayo Noon."

199 Hilderbrand, *Inherent Vice*, 12.

200 A faculty member of the UP School of Library and Information Studies, Olgado served as the inaugural director for the NFAP and, later, its senior consultant (2012–14). He was a member of the SEAPAVAA Executive Council (2014–20) and cochair of the International Outreach Committee of the Association of Moving Image Archivists (AMIA) (2012–15).

201 Olgado, email to author, 2018.

202 Hilderbrand, *Inherent Vice,* 15.

203 Appadurai, *Social Life of Things*; Appadurai, "Consumption, Duration, and History."

204 Usai, *Silent Cinema*, 12.

205 Usai, *Silent Cinema*, 16.

206 Edmondson, *Audiovisual Archiving*, 47, 56, 59.

207 Slide, *Nitrate Won't Wait*, 1.

208 Habib, "Ruin, Archive," 132.

209 As Rumesh Kumar observes, "nitrate film has acquired a Benjaminian aura over the last few decades, having become a significant artefact—not unlike a museum object—even in instances when it might have historically only been a projection copy, especially if it is the only surviving one." Kumar, "National Film Archives,"16.

210 Usai, *Silent Cinema*, 12–13.

211 National Film and Sound Archive of Australia, "Base Polymers."

212 In his reading of *Lyrical Nitrate* (Peter Delpeut, 1991), Andre Habib observes: "The film archive is a strange tomb, characterized by what it lacks, and slowly decomposing." Habib, "Ruin, Archive," 122.

213 Bazin, "Ontology of the Photographic Image," 4–5.

214 Rosen, *Change Mummified*, 28.

215 Usai, *Death of Cinema*, 67.

216 Usai ends *The Death of Cinema* with a sardonic faux epistolary exchange between the publisher and a reader, all of which, one gathers, was penned by the author himself. Usai, *Death of Cinema*, 111–29.

CHAPTER 1. A TALE OF THREE BUILDINGS

A shorter version of this chapter appeared previously as "A Tale of Three Buildings: The National Film Archive, Marcos Cultural Policy, and Anarchival Temporality," in *Beauty and Brutality: Manila and Its Global Discontents* (2003), edited by Martin F. Manalansan IV, Robert Diaz, and Rolando B. Tolentino. Used by permission of Temple University Press.

1 L. J. Cruz, "Politicians Take to the Air"; Nakpil, "Audio-visual Politics."

2 The blurry areas of figure 1.2 are an indexical trace of the archival research context through which I encountered this source. At the time of my 2009 research trip to the Rizal Library at the Ateneo de Manila University, only low-cost photocopying by a staff member (not scanning) was available. The blurring may have been present in the newsprint original or introduced by the photocopying process (most photocopiers in Manila universities at the time used powder toners).

3 Rama, "Now Showing."

4 Polotan, "Ginupit ng Tadhana"; Cristobal, "Ill-Fated Tadhana"; Joaquin, "Press Discovers the Cinema." A propaganda war between Marcos's Nacionalista Party and the opposing Liberal Party raged on film and television a month and a half before the elections. The young Ferdinand Marcos, his father, and two other persons were charged with the murder of Ilocos Norte Representative-Elect Julio Nalundasan, the victorious opponent of Ferdinand Marcos's father in the 1935 elections for assemblyman of Ilocos Norte. Ferdinand Marcos was convicted by the Court of First Instance but later exonerated by the Supreme Court. According to the Liberal Party, the Nalundasan murder was "glorified" and "justified" in *Iginuhit ng Tadhana*. Although *Iginuhit* was initially banned, the Supreme Court lifted the ban on the film's exhibition fifty-two days before the presidential election. In response, the Liberal Party declared a nationwide commemoration of the Nalundasan case, beginning with a television episode of *The Inside Story* that detailed the political killing. Rama, "Now Showing."

5 Cristobal, "Marcos in Miranda"; Aspiras, "Marcos."

6 Joaquin, "Image of Imelda," 44.

7 Sebastiampillai, "Love Teams," 59–60.

8 Signed on September 22, 1972, the day after Proclamation 1081 imposed a state of martial law, Marcos's first letter of instruction directed the press and defense secretaries to seize all privately owned newspapers, magazines, and radio and television outlets to "prevent [their] use . . . [for] propaganda purposes against the government" (F. E. Marcos, Letter of Instruction No. 1). The forcible seizure of all nongovernment media outlets signaled Marcos's desire to commandeer oligarchically controlled media for his own purposes.

9 Joaquin, "Imelda in Malacañang."

10 Lopez, "Who Says?," 7.

11 The coinage *edifice complex* has been attributed to Rafael Salas, a former executive secretary in the Marcos administration (Sicat, *Cesar Virata*, 417–18). The Marcoses' architectural mania has historical roots in the American colonial administration's deployment of infrastructure for ideological ends from the 1910s to the 1930s. The oldest cultural memory institutions in the Philippines—today's National Museum of the Philippines, National Archives of the Philippines, and National Library of the Philippines—were founded in the Spanish colonial era and restructured under American rule. Bernadette Patino describes the American consolidation of a putatively Filipino heritage via an architecturally oriented heritage policy as "a means to control the development of national identity in its new colony." Patino, "From Colonial Policy," 48–49, 68.

12 Imelda Marcos qtd. in Nolledo, "Human Settlement for the Tao," 38. After the conjugal dictatorship of Ferdinand and Imelda Marcos was ousted from power in February 1986, Imelda Marcos faced several trials for racketeering and corruption in the United States and the Philippines. She has nonetheless enjoyed an extensive political career post-EDSA, having been elected as a Member of the Philippine House of Representatives for Leyte, her home province, in 1992, and in Ilocos Norte's 2nd District, her late husband's home province, from 2010 to 2019.

13 It has been noted that 1965, President Ferdinand Marcos's first year in office, coincided with the advent of nationalist student demonstrations in that decade. A. C. Cruz, "Natural History," 20.

14 Joaquin, "Before the Blow," 372; Lico, *Edifice Complex,* 66–67.

15 Lico, *Edifice Complex,* 50–54, 85.

16 F. E. Marcos, Executive Order No. 640-A.

17 B. S. Aquino Jr., *Garrison State in the Make*, 218–19.

18 Fernandez, "Mass Culture and Cultural Policy," 492–93.

19 *Korea Herald*, "Marcos' Daughter Takes Part."

20 Benedicto, "Queer Space in the Ruins," 27. In another inscription of its queer afterlife, *The Amazing Show* housed at the Manila Film Center is the backdrop for Eduardo Roy Jr.'s film *Quick Change* (2013), a social realist depiction of Manila's *bakla* transgender community. By June 2019, the dilapidated Manila Film Center was under renovation. *The Amazing Show* went on hiatus during the COVID-19 pandemic.

21 I. Marcos, "Sanctuary of the Filipino Soul," 31. See also Lico, *Edifice Complex*, 102.

22 In our April 15, 2021, and June 7, 2021, position papers on various national film archives bills being deliberated by the Philippine House of Representatives, my coauthors, Benedict Olgado and Rose Roque, and I recommended that the scope of the proposed agency be widened from film archiving to audiovisual archiving and that this envisioned institution be named the Philippine Audiovisual Archives. Sadly, a consolidated bill did not come to fruition during that congressional session.

23 Borer, "From Collective Memory," 96.

24 Edmondson, *Audiovisual Archiving*, 30.

25 Edmondson, "National Film and Sound Archive," 152.

26 Derrida, *Archive Fever*, 2–3.

27 Abramson et al., "Introduction," vii.

28 Many articles anthologized in *Governing by Design* "address failures, points in the historical record when projects went unrealized. They suggest that plans, schemes, books, journals, objects, buildings, and technologies often emerge less from pure intentionality as out of negotiation with the radical indeterminacy of a given situation." Abramson et al., "Introduction," xi.

29 Stoler, *Along the Archival Grain*, 20.

30 Quotation from Sterne, "Cultural Policy Studies," 59–60, 70.

31 On film's exclusion from founding state cultural policies, see Congress of the Philippines, Republic Act No. 4165; Congress of the Philippines, Republic Act No. 4846. For film decrees from the late Marcos era, cf. Ferdinand Marcos's Executive Orders 640-A and 770, signed into law in 1981 and 1982, respectively.

32 Fernandez, "Mass Culture and Cultural Policy," 492.

33 F. E. Marcos, Executive Order No. 640-A; F. E. Marcos, Executive Order No. 770; F. E. Marcos, Executive Order No. 1051.

34 Tiongson, "Filipino Film in the Decade," xx–xxiii; Salazar, "Philippines' Marcos Orders Review"; M. V. Giron, "Trial Begins"; *Village Voice*, "Only One Oppressor."

35 M. V. Giron, "New Bill Proposing an End"; M. V. Giron, "Marcos Plucks Censor Thorn."

36 On the institutional disarray that engulfed the FAP upon the dissolution of the ECP, see de Pedro, "Overview of the Film Archives," 22.

37 *Variety*, "Archives Shift to Snippers Hit."

38 Patino, "From Colonial Policy," 42, 45, 55, 58.

39 De Pedro, "Overview of the Film Archives." At a roundtable discussion for the Philippine Cinema Heritage Summit convened by the NFAP in 2013, de Pedro claimed to have kept the FAP partially afloat until 1989 through a patchwork of funding from four European agencies. National Film Archives of the Philippines, Transcript of Roundtable Discussion.

40 F. E. Marcos, Executive Order No. 1051; de Pedro, "Overview of the Film Archives," 2–3; F. E. Marcos, Presidential Decree No. 1986.

41 Schmelter was interviewed by Jasmine Trice at the Southeast Asian Cinemas Research Network Symposium, Archives, Activism, Aesthetics, on March 16, 2018, at the Centre for Contemporary Arts in Glasgow. My thanks to SEACRN co-organizer Philippa Lovatt for providing me with a video recording of this interview. As director of the Goethe-Institut Manila, Schmelter was instrumental in the collaborative institutional network that fostered the flourishing of experimental and avant-garde cinema in the Philippines in the late 1980s and early 1990s. Deocampo, *Cine*, 25.

42 Over a conference dinner on March 15, 2018, Schmelter told me that the FAP collection had been flooded. See also de Pedro's remarks at the Philippine Cinema Heritage Summit roundtable. National Film Archives of the Philippines, Transcript of Roundtable Discussion.

43 Patino, "From Colonial Policy," 59.

44 Joaquin, "Press Discovers the Cinema," 5.

45 Celoza, *Ferdinand Marcos and the Philippines*, 87.

46 Victor Ordoñez, "The Neglect of the Past," a background paper on the Presidential Commission on Culture and the Arts, qtd. in Fernandez, "Mass Culture and Cultural Policy," 495.

47 F. E. Marcos, Executive Order No. 30.

48 Imelda Marcos, qtd. in Nolledo, "(First) Lady of the House," 8.

49 On "matters of art and culture" as "women's work," see Fernandez, "Mass Culture and Cultural Policy," 492–93.

50 Baluyut, *Institutions and Icons of Patronage*, 13; Maramag, *Cultural Center of the Philippines*, 9.

51 Coseteng, "Imelda Project," 16–17.

52 Polites, *Architecture of Leandro Locsin*, 9–13.

53 Lico, *Edifice Complex*, 49–50.

54 Coseteng, "Imelda Project," 16–17.

55 Baluyut, *Institutions and Icons of Patronage*, 14–15; see, for instance, Senator Benigno Aquino's acrid critique of the CCP project (B. S. Aquino Jr., *Garrison State in the Make*, 218).

56 Baluyut, *Institutions and Icons of Patronage*, 11.

57 F. E. Marcos, Executive Order No. 640-A; F. E. Marcos, Executive Order No. 770; F. E. Marcos, Executive Order No. 1051.

58 Constantino, "People's Culture," 26–27.

59 Baluyut, *Institutions and Icons of Patronage*, 35.

60 Tiongson, "Winds of Change," 30.

61 "Statement of the YCC Film Desk."

62 Philippine Information Agency and Society of Film Archivists, Consultation Meeting; Mendoza, "Seven Years of the Society," 1.

63 Aguilar, "Political Conjuncture and Scholarly Disjunctures," 22; Dulay et al., "Continuity, History, and Identity," 93–94.

64 Whaley, "Philippines Ex-President Is Arrested."

65 De Dios, *Analysis*, 22.

66 De Dios, *Analysis*, 34.

67 De Dios, *Analysis*, 12; Bello, Kinely, and Elinson, *Development Debacle*, 14.

68 *Daily Express*, "Gov't Takes Over Film Center Work"; *Daily Express*, "First Lady."

69 *Bulletin Today*, "Film Center's Sixth Floor Falls."

70 *Daily Express*, "Gov't Takes Over Film Center Work."

71 Stein, "Manila's Angels," 48.

72 To take one example, the first half of a *Bulletin Today* news article reports on the tragic deaths of workers while the second half, in press-release style, shifts to an enumeration of government film initiatives that would be housed at the Manila Film Center. *Bulletin Today*, "Film Center's Sixth Floor Falls."

73 *Daily Express*, "First Lady."

74 Benigno and Zapanta, "'Instant' Film Center," 13.

75 Tatad, "MIFF Passes," 8.

76 Lopez, "Who Says?," 7.

77 Benigno and Zapanta, "'Instant' Film Center," 12–13.

78 *Business Day*, "Film Center Collapses; *Daily Express*, "First Lady."

79 Lacaba, "Misadventures in the Dream Trade," 17.

80 For the censorship exemption, see F. E. Marcos, Executive Order No. 770. Arguing for a nuanced consideration of *bomba*, David points out that several sexploitation films exhibited at the Manila Film Center articulated powerful social critique within unexpected registers of "social decadence" and "protofeminist consciousness." David, "Cultural Policy Experience," 55, 57.

81 Stein, "Manila's Angels," 54.

82 Stein, "Manila's Angels," 54.

83 F. E. Marcos, Executive Order No. 868; F. E. Marcos, Executive Order No. 1051.

84 David, "Cultural Policy Experience," 53, 55–56.

85 Stein, "Manila's Angels," 49, 51.

86 Roads, "Manila National Film Centre."

87 Certeau, *Practice of Everyday Life*, 117–18.

88 Stein, "Manila's Angels," 48–49.

89 *Korea Herald*, "Marcos' Daughter Takes Part."

90 Sheringham, "Archiving," 10–14.

91 Lacaba, "Misadventures in the Dream Trade," 17.

92 F. E. Marcos, Executive Order No. 1051.

93 De Pedro, "Overview of the Film Archives," 2–3.

94 Mendoza, "Audio-Visual Archiving," 4.

95 Mendoza, "Seven Years of the Society," 7.

96 Nizette and Petherbridge, "Assessment of Potential Sites," 1–3.

97 Leandro V. Locsin Partners, Architects, "Architectural Design Concept."

98 Borer, "From Collective Memory," 96–97.

99 Edmondson, "Notes on Sustainability," 25.

100 Steedman has explored both the powerful appeal and the inherent limitations of Derrida's exploration of the archive as a "capacious metaphor." Though stemming initially from a consideration of the *arkhe* in Greek slave society, the archive in Derrida's *Archive Fever* expands to include media-historical transformation (entertaining the question of "the future of the archive, as the register, ledger and letter are replaced by email and the computer file"). In such a deployment, "archive" expands to become a "portmanteau term" "strap[ping] together" diverse types of "modern repository" and including "the whole of modern technology, its storage,

retrieval, and communication." Steedman, *Dust*, 4. For quotations from Stoler, see her *Along the Archival Grain*, 32.

101 Grant, "Presenting Cebuano Cinema," 212.

102 Deleuze, *Bergsonism*, 15.

103 B. C. Lim, *Translating Time*, 100.

104 Borges, "Library of Babel," 112–14.

105 Borges, "Library of Babel," 115.

106 Borges, "Library of Babel," 116.

107 Lippit, *Atomic Light*, 8, 10 (italics added).

108 Lippit, *Atomic Light*, 11.

109 "Undefined and forged in ash, the shadow archive, an 'archive of the virtual,' as Derrida calls it, erupts from the feverish imagination of a *mal d'archive*, an archive illness and desire that *burns with a passion*. An archive sickness in the sense of lovesickness, the secret archive burns with a longing and fever that nurtures the irreducible distance." Lippit, *Atomic Light*, 10.

110 Joaquin, "Woman of the Year," 123, 127.

111 Lico, *Edifice Complex*, 50–53, 107–8, 115.

112 This is Benigno and Zapanta's paraphrase of Manila Film Center architect Froilan Hong's account. Benigno and Zapanta, "'Instant' Film Center," 13.

113 Ferdinand Marcos was nearing the end of his second and final presidential term, per the 1935 Constitution, when he invoked a constitutional provision to declare martial law in Proclamation 1081, officially dated September 21, 1972 (F. E. Marcos, Proclamation No. 1081). Martial law was essentially the imposition of a "constitutional dictatorship" (Joaquin, "Before the Blow," 378). Marcos's televised announcement that the Philippines had been placed under martial law aired at 7:00 p.m. on September 23, in the wake of several high-profile bombings in Manila and a staged ambush of Secretary of Defense Juan Ponce Enrile. This spate of state-orchestrated violence, allegedly the work of communists, provided Marcos with a pretext for the imposition of martial law. *Official Gazette of the Philippines*, Declaration of Martial Law.

114 B. Anderson, "Cacique Democracy in the Philippines," 18.

115 Though martial law was officially terminated via Marcos's Proclamation 2045 in 1981, key aspects of it remained in effect until the dictatorship was deposed in 1986 (e.g., provisions for military suppression of "violence, insurrection, rebellion, and subversion" as well as the suspension of the writ of habeas corpus). I thank my partner, Joya Escobar, for pointing out that the martial law years were a form of "borrowed time" that may have something to do with the feverish pace of Imeldific temporality.

116 Derrida, *Archive Fever*, 29, 33, 36.

CHAPTER 2. SILENCE, PERSEVERANCE, AND SURVIVAL IN STATE-RUN PHILIPPINE FILM ARCHIVES

A previous version of this chapter, "Fragility, Perseverance, and Survival in State-Run Philippine Archives," appeared in *Plaridel* 15, no. 2 (December 2018): 1–40, published by the University of the Philippines College of Mass Communication, https://www.plarideljournal.org/. Used by permission.

1 Schwartz and Cook, "Archives, Records, and Power," 5, 9.

2 Edmondson, *Audiovisual Archiving*, 10, 74.

3 Velasco, PIA Circular No. 1; Velasco, PIA Circular No. 3; Velasco, PIA Circular No. 4; Velasco, PIA Special Order No. 195.

4 Edmondson underscores the "need for archival practice to be guided by an explicit policy so that decisions are policy-based rather than arbitrary." Edmondson, *Audiovisual Archiving*, 63–64.

My research access requests for documents relating to the closure of the MPD and the creation of the MISD were approved by Herminio "Sonny" Coloma, secretary of the Presidential Communications Operations Office from 2010 to 2016 (Coloma, letter to author, October 14, 2015). In the course of my research, I encountered no archival policy documents relating to the decision to close down the MPD.

5 My research visits to the MISD Film Vault, which housed what remained of the former MPD's film collection, occurred during the PIA's turnover of the majority of its film holdings to the revived NFAP from 2013 to 2015.

6 Given that "heat and humidity are major contributors to the problem of vinegar syndrome" (Bigourdan, "Vinegar Syndrome," 4), the absence of temperature and humidity controls in the context of the tropical Philippine climate likely hastened the demise of the defunct MPD's film collection.

7 C. C. Aquino, Executive Order No. 100.

8 For example, LVN's first sound film, *Giliw Ko* (My beloved) from 1939, was collaboratively restored in 1998 by the PIA and the NFSA with the support of LVN, SOFIA, and SEAPAVAA. The Australian government gifted the restored film to the Philippines to commemorate the centennial of Philippine independence. Paras, "Return of a Golden Oldie."

9 Edmondson's PhD thesis recounts the NFSA's history from 1935 to 2008, analyzing the institution's struggle to define its identity, assure "good governance," and achieve institutional autonomy from various umbrella organizations: first, the National Library of Australia, from which it separated in 1984, and later the Australian Film Commission, with which it first merged in 2003 and from which it subsequently separated upon achieving "statutory status" and the passage of the NFSA Act of 2008. Edmondson traces a controversial and at times bitter history in which "questions about personal and institutional ethics, public officials' duty

of care, managerial and financial competence, and the role of public activism, emerge repeatedly." Edmondson, "National Film and Sound Archive," vi–vii, 3.

10 Edmondson, "National Film and Sound Archive," 374.

11 On public policy as an arena of conflict, see Addelson, "Knower/Doers," 276–79; on awareness, advocacy, support and political will, see Edmondson, *Audiovisual Archiving*, 33.

12 Edmondson, "National Film and Sound Archive," 5.

13 Edmondson, "National Film and Sound Archive," 6.

14 Trouillot, *Silencing the Past*, 53–54.

15 Harris, *Archives and Justice*, 124.

16 Leguiab, "Fade Out," 12.

17 Created circa 1952, the NMPC predated the Marcos regime but was placed at the forefront of Marcos era media production after the 1972 declaration of martial law, when state media production was consolidated under its auspices. Capul, personal interview with author; *Official Gazette of the Republic of the Philippines*, Presidential Communications Reforms.

18 The PIA absorbed the assets of both the Office of Media Affairs (OMA) and the NMPC, which had previously been merged under NMPC director Gregorio Cendaña in 1980. The Aquino administration ordered the turnover of the OMA-NMPC's considerable assets to the PIA, except for Marcos era radio and television units like the Bureau of Broadcast Services, Channel 4, and Channel 9 (the Marharlika Broadcasting System). C. C. Aquino, Executive Order No. 100; Capul, personal interview with author; *Official Gazette of the Republic of the Philippines*, "Presidential Communications Reforms"; Tuazon, "Government Media."

19 De Pedro, "Overview of the Film Archives."

20 Philippine Information Agency Management Information System Division [hereafter PIA-MISD], Status of MTRCB Film Archives and Library Division.

21 The memorandum of agreement between the MTRCB and the PIA notes that although the MTRCB was tasked with film preservation under Executive Order No. 1051, its Film Archives and Library Division was incapable of maintaining a film collection due to its meager budget. The PIA, as a government agency that both preserved and restored films and maintained a film collection under the MPD, agreed to accept the MTRCB films. Both the MTRCB and the PIA agreed to "protect ownership, copyright, storage/preservation, [and] access" to the films and to collaborate on the joint maintenance and preservation of these materials (Movie and Television Review and Classification Board and Philippine Information Agency [hereafter MTRCB-PIA], Memorandum of Agreement). The joint agreement left the duration of this arrangement unspecified. MTRCB-PIA, Memorandum of Agreement; MTRCB-PIA, Annex A.

22 Movie and Television Review and Classification Board and Movie Workers Welfare Fund [hereafter MTRCB-MOWELFUND], Memorandum of Agreement; MTRCB-MOWELFUND, Annex A. For the PIA's adoption of "streamlining and cost-cutting measures," see Velasco, letter to MTRCB chairwoman Ma. Consoliza P. Laguardia.

23 The MTRCB holdings in MOWELFUND's care were acquired by the NFAP in May 2012. "Acquired from Mowelfund Audiovisual Archives, the MTRCB Collection consists of 35mm prints of full length features, trailers, trims and cuts. Notable titles in the collection are *Minsa'y Isang Gamu-gamo* [Once a Moth] by Lupita Kashiwara, *Sakada* by Behn Cervantes, and *Olongapo: The Great American Dream* by Chito Roño" (NFAP, *NFAP Annual Report 2011–2012*, 5, 11). An NFAP inventory of the MOWELFUND collection lists the elements for 713 film titles in a variety of gauges (8mm, Super 8mm, 16mm, 35mm, and quarter inch/open reel). NFAP, MOWELFUND (NFAP Inventory).

24 The acronym LVN is based on the surnames of the company's three founders: Narcisa Buencamino Vda. de Leon, Carmen Villongco, and Eleuterio Navoa.

25 Del Mundo, *Dreaming*, 16–17.

26 Sotto, letter to PIA undersecretary Honesto Isleta.

27 Capul, letter to SOFIA president Clodualdo "Doy" del Mundo.

28 Capul, letter to SOFIA president Clodualdo "Doy" del Mundo; Capul, letter to LVN Pictures general manager Nenita Eraña; Eraña, letter to PIA-MISD staff director Belina Capul.

29 Olgado, Letter from NFAP Head Benedict Salazar Olgado to PIA Director-General Jose Mari Oquiñena.

30 B. S. Aquino III, "Administrative Order No. 26."

31 Coloma, Re: Transfer of Audio-visual Collections of PIA to NFAP; NFAP, List of PIA Film Titles as Deposited/Transferred; NFAP, NFAP Inventory List: Inventory of PIA Film Collections; NFAP, Inventory List—NFAP; NFAP, NFAP (PIA) Initial Inventory of 3rd Batch; Philippine Information Agency and Film Development Council of the Philippines [hereafter PIA-FDCP], Annex A; PIA-FDCP, Memorandum of Agreement.

32 Leguiab, "Fade Out," 11.

33 Capul, personal interview with author.

34 Leguiab, "Fade Out," 12.

35 Leguiab, "Fade Out," 12–13.

36 Leguiab, "Fade Out," 13.

37 To wit: electoral fraud in the 2004 presidential elections; payoffs from *jueteng* gambling syndicates; kickbacks from telecommunications deals (NBN-ZTE); and fiscal malfeasance at the Philippine Amusement and Gaming Corporation and the Philippine Charity Sweepstakes Office. Ar-

rested on corruption charges in 2012 under the presidential administration of Noynoy Aquino, Arroyo was cleared of charges under the Supreme Court during the Duterte presidency. Mangahas, "Gloria Gets Richer Fastest"; Whaley, "Philippines Ex-President Is Arrested"; Whaley, "Philippines Clears Gloria Macapagal Arroyo."

38 The MISD is charged with several responsibilities, quoted (in Velasco, PIA Circular No. 4) as follows:

- Automated collection, organization, storage and retrieval of management-oriented data/information,
- On-line retrieval and selective dissemination of data information for institutional decision making, and
- Operation of the PIA Library and integration of all PIA document collections in print, film, video, photo, and slides. Velasco, PIA Circular No. 4.

39 Velasco, PIA Circular No. 1.

40 Aragones, email to PIA-MISD Library and Archives section head Maria Victoria Bejerano.

41 Trouillot, *Silencing the Past*, 48–49 (italics added).

42 Leguiab, "Fade Out," 11.

43 Caldwell, "Cultures of Production," 199.

44 Caldwell, "Cultures of Production," 201–3.

45 The following figures are cited by *Tinig* under the subheading "Income Indicators":

> In the three-year time frame used by the [*MPD* Review] Committee, it was found that the film laboratory had a decreasing annual income in transactions with the private sector. *MPD* earned P729,522 in 2001, P727,836 in 2002 and P357,431 in 2003. . . .
>
> . . . It is interesting to note that there is actually an increase in the annual inter-agency trust receipts in the three-year time frame used by the Committee. The annual average inter-agency trust receipt of [P3,857,215] is broken down into the following: P623,821 in 2001, P1,877,952 in 2002 and a high of P9,069,873 in 2003. Leguiab, "Fade Out," 11–12.

46 Leguiab, "Fade Out," 11–12.

47 Capul, personal interview with author. Capul's Taglish syntax was characteristically elliptical, but "they" here appears to refer to officials at the highest management level of the PIA.

48 Leguiab, "Fade Out," 11–12.

49 Leguiab, "Fade Out," 12.

50 PIA Special Order No. 195, which reassigns personnel of the defunct MPD to other divisions, reads: "It is understood that all positions to be vacated by compulsory retirees under [the] Motion Picture Division will

be reclassified/collapsed in order to create new positions for the Management Information System Division." Velasco, PIA Special Order No. 195.

51 Leguiab, "Fade Out," 13.

52 Capul, personal interview with author.

53 Edmondson, *Audiovisual Archiving*, 26.

54 Leguiab, "Fade Out," 12 (italics added).

55 Leguiab, "Fade Out," 11.

56 Leguiab, "Fade Out," 13.

57 Edmondson, "National Film and Sound Archive," 375.

58 Capul, personal interview with author.

59 Edmondson, "Notes on Sustainability," 25; Edmondson, *Audiovisual Archiving*, 36.

60 Velasco, PIA Circular No. 4.

61 United Nations Educational, Scientific, and Cultural Organization, "Report by the Director-General," 2.

62 Philippine Atmospheric, Geophysical and Astronomical Services Administration, "Climate of the Philippines."

63 Edmondson, *Audiovisual Archiving*, 46.

64 Bejerano, personal interview with author.

65 According to the NFAP, between August 22, 2013, and May 15, 2016, the total number of film elements turned over by the PIA to the NFAP was as follows: 4,341 identified films on celluloid; 93 unidentified films. The total number of cans containing the films on celluloid and sound on magnetic tape turned over was 7,247 (Patino, email to Benedict "Bono" Olgado). In 2017, the PIA donated additional audiovisual materials and motion picture equipment to the NFAP-FDCP as follows: "130 units (843 pieces) of functional and non-functional motion picture processing equipment and supplies, 33 titles of videotapes, and 10 titles (292 rolls) of films formerly held by the defunct Motion Picture Division." Gaje, memorandum to PIA director-general Harold E. Clavite.

66 Steyerl notes that whereas "the production of culture was [once] considered a task of the state," the decline of "non-commercial" films in government archives points to the reduced importance of state-sponsored media production under neoliberalism. Steyerl, "In Defense," 6.

67 Gracy, *Film Preservation*, 37, 183–84, 216.

68 Fossati, *From Grain to Pixel*, 13–17.

69 Edmondson, *Audiovisual Archiving*, vi.

70 Capul's Taglish remarks are as follows: "*Sabi niya*, [and he was] very clear, since I was fighting for [film] preservation [under the MPD], '*E, kung ang* government *nga hindi inaasikaso 'yan*, why do you push for it?' *Sabi ko, 'sino ba ang* government? It's people who are on top and who can do something." Capul, personal interview with author.

71 "In that sense I agree with you that remiss *ang* government in terms of appreciating that [the importance of film preservation] . . . market forces are *talagang* market forces, *mga* business-minded *'yan. Pero dapat nakikita talaga ng* government *'yan* [the public interest in film preservation] *tapos nagkaroon ng* intervention. *Parang 'yan ang mahina pa, mahina ngayon o wala. Lalo na, papalit-palit ang* head of . . . *yung mga* leadership *sa* [government] organization *na* passing-by *sila*." Capul, personal interview with author.

72 Mendoza, Draft Elements for a Master Plan.

73 B. C. Lim, "Analysis and Recommendations," 27; Olgado and Roque, "Position Paper on House Bill No. 2404"; Lim, Olgado, and Roque, "Position Paper on the Interrelated House Bills."

74 Edmondson, *Audiovisual Archiving*, 5.

75 Edmondson, *Audiovisual Archiving*, 49–51.

76 Duterte's 2017 appointment of a nonlibrarian, Cesar Gilbert Adriano, to the post of director for the National Library of the Philippines led outraged librarians to criticize the president for disregarding the Anti-Graft and Corrupt Practices Act by "knowingly approving a benefit in favor of an unqualified individual." Evangelista, "The Librarians."

77 Edmondson, "National Film and Sound Archive," 326.

78 Sotto, "Annex H," 1–2.

79 Edmondson, "National Film and Sound Archive," 46.

80 Edmondson, "National Film and Sound Archive," 238–39.

81 B. Anderson, "Cacique Democracy in the Philippines," 18–23.

82 I regard the shot of Mariveles as an Imeldific image. In her speech at the CCP in 1969, Imelda interprets Mount Mariveles's resemblance to a sleeping goddess, seen from Manila Bay, as an image of the "First Filipina." I. Marcos, "Sanctuary of the Filipino Soul."

83 Olgado, personal interview with author, 2017.

84 Usai, *Silent Cinema*, 14.

85 I presented an early draft of this chapter during a keynote at the Graduate Student Conference of the University of Southern California's Cinema and Media Studies program on October 20, 2017. I am grateful for the audience's engaged responses, which prompted me to think about this film in relation to Chion's exploration of the *acousmêtre*.

86 Chion, *Voice in Cinema*, 18–19.

87 Chion notes that the film experience can also be unintentionally acousmatized during reception. Chion, *Voice in Cinema*, 19.

88 Lippit, *Atomic Light*, 31–32, 95.

89 Lippit, *Atomic Light*, 31–32.

90 Olgado, email to author, 2017.

91 Usai, *Silent Cinema*, 39.

92 Steyerl, "In Defense."

93 Steyerl, "In Defense."
94 Edmondson, *Audiovisual Archiving*, 17.
95 Kumar, "National Film Archives," 36.
96 Edmondson, "National Film and Sound Archive," 356 (italics added).
97 Cvetkovich, "Public Feelings," 460, 467.
98 Povinelli, *Economies of Abandonment*, 110–12.
99 Povinelli, *Economies of Abandonment*, 115 (italics added).
100 Povinelli, *Economies of Abandonment*, 112–16.
101 Povinelli, *Economies of Abandonment*, 103.
102 Edmondson, "National Film and Sound Archive," 356.
103 Povinelli, *Economies of Abandonment*, 115, 119.
104 Povinelli, *Economies of Abandonment*, 118–19 (italics added).
105 Povinelli, *Economies of Abandonment*, 130 (italics added).
106 On enduring under reduced conditions of life, see Povinelli, *Economies of Abandonment*, 128.
107 The two PIA archivists' feedback and approval of an earlier version of this chapter, published in the journal *Plaridel,* were emailed to me in 2018. (Bejerano, email to author, February 15, 2018; Capul, email to author.) By the time I finalized this book in 2023, Capul had passed away, but Bejerano gave her feedback and approval of this chapter. Bejerano, email to author, July 18, 2023.
108 Edmondson, "You Only Live Once," 175–83.
109 Bejerano and Capul, personal interview and feedback meeting with author.

CHAPTER 3. PRIVATIZATION AND THE ABS-CBN FILM ARCHIVES

1 Avendaño, "Final Cut"; ABS-CBN Film archives, "ABS-CBN Inventories as of March 2018: Restored Titles." My thanks to Julie Galino for sharing the latter inventory with me.
2 Since the NFAP/PFA did not respond to my January 2018 email request for a list of completed restorations, what follows is an approximate list of eighteen film titles restored by the NFAP and the PFA in collaboration with various domestic and international partners as of 2020. The below list is based on the *NFAP Annual Report 2011–2012* as well as newspaper reportage and PFA press releases on NFAP/PFA restorations. Alzona, "NFAP Looks to Restore"; *Philippine Star*, "Insiang Returns"; Provincial Government of Iloilo, "First Hiligaynon Movie Returns Home"; San Diego, "Genghis Khan, Lost and Found"; Diño-Seguerra, "Vision for FDCP's Philippine Film Archive"; Manila Bulletin Entertainment, "Sagip Pelikula and FDCP." The majority of the restorations were completed during the term of FDCP chair Briccio Santos. Years refer to original release and subsequent restoration.

Genghis Khan (dir. Manuel Conde, 1950/2012)
Maynila sa Mga Kuko ng Liwanag (Manila in the claws of neon; dir. Lino Brocka, 1975/2013)
On My Way to Consciousness, I Reached China (dir. Henry Francia, 1968/2013)
Tronong Puti (White throne; dir. Roxlee, 1984/2013)
Sa Maynila (In Manila; dir. Mike Alcazaren, Jo Atienza, and Ricky Orellana, 1991/2013)
A Portrait of the Artist as a Filipino (dir. Lamberto Avellana, 1965/2015)
Insiang (dir. Lino Brocka, 1976/2015)
Ginauhaw Ako, Ginagutom Ako (I am thirsty, I am hungry; dir. Quirino Baterna and Leonardo Q. Belen, 1977/2016)
Batang West Side (West Side Avenue; dir. Lav Diaz, 2001/2016)
Noli me Tangere (Touch me not; dir. Gerardo de Leon, 1961/2016)
White Slavery (dir. Lino Brocka, 1985/2016)
Damortis (dir. Briccio Santos, 1986/2016)
Pagdating sa Dulo (At the end; dir. Ishmael Bernal, 1971/2016)
Zamboanga (dir. Eduardo de Castro, 1937/2017)
Brutal (dir. Marilou Diaz-Abaya, 1980/2019)
Manila by Night (dir. Ishmael Bernal, 1980/2019)
Dalagang Ilocana (Ilocana maiden; dir. Olive La Torre, 1954 (restoration begun 2020; completed 2022)
Maalaala mo Kaya (Do you remember; dir. Mar S. Torres, 1954; restoration begun 2020)

3 Patino, "From Colonial Policy," 44–46.
4 Gracy, *Film Preservation*, 6–7.
5 Napoli, "Media Economics," 164–65, 167.
6 Edmondson, "National Film and Sound Archive," 109.
7 Edmondson, *Audiovisual Archiving*, 44–46, 54–55.
8 For ABS-CBN's corporate structure, see ABS-CBN Corporate: Businesses, Corporate Structure, Business Segments; ABS-CBN Corporate: Our Organization. According to Manet Dayrit of Central Digital Lab, the postproduction facility with which ABS-CBN collaborates, restoration projects have not resulted in significant profits even for ABS-CBN: "They're not getting a return on investments on this. They know that it's not the monetary returns that's important, but it's preserving our heritage" (Dayrit, qtd. in M. Cruz, "Devastating Effects"). According to ABS-CBN Film Archives head Leo Katigbak, the corporate outlay for digital film restorations is between 1 and 10 million pesos. Beyond their enormous expense, restorations are labor-intensive, requiring digital frame-by-frame restoration of an average of 130,000 frames per ninety-minute film. Katigbak, qtd. in Avendaño, "Final Cut."
9 Edmondson, *Audiovisual Archiving*, 33–35.

10 Schnabel, "Fast Facts."

11 Gutierrez, "Philippine Congress Officially Shuts Down."

12 Abad, "Timeline."

13 In 2016, Rodrigo Duterte ordered a controversial hero's burial for the late dictator Ferdinand Marcos at the Libingan ng Mga Bayani (Heroes' Cemetery). However, the Duterte-Marcos alliance soured in 2021 when Duterte refused to support Bongbong Marcos's presidential candidacy, calling him a "weak leader" and imputing drug use (Gavilan, "Timeline"; Buan, "Duterte Rejects Alliance with Lakas"). In May 2022, Duterte's daughter, Sara Zimmerman Duterte, ran for the vice presidency alongside Bongbong Marcos, who ran for president. Their combined ticket won that year's national elections, but the alliance between the two political dynasties remained strained. Wee and Elemia, "Marcos-Duterte Ticket Won."

14 Abad, "Timeline."

15 Gutierrez, "Philippine Congress Officially Shuts Down"; see also Cepeda, "Makabayan Bloc Wants House Plenary"; Abad, "Timeline"; Buan, "During Pandemic, Supreme Court Favors Duterte"; Buan, "Killed and Shuttered ABS-CBN."

16 Galino, email to author, March 27, 2018; Galino, email to author, July 31, 2018.

17 San Diego, "Inside the Kapamilya Film Vaults."

18 In 2008, Clodualdo del Mundo Jr. wrote: "Honestly, the ABS-CBN Film Archive is our de facto national film archive. It now houses the LVN collection . . . , the FPJ collection, and virtually all the films produced by Regal, RVQ, and other companies. Moreover, it operates as a real archive should because researchers are allowed to access its collection!" Del Mundo, "Quest for a National Film Archive."

19 Avendaño, "Final Cut."

20 A screenshot of this message, circulating among Filipino chat groups and attributed to Leo Katigbak, was emailed to me by Patrick Campos on July 18, 2020. Campos, Email to author.

21 M. Cruz, "Devastating Effects."

22 Katigbak, "Ganito Tayo Noon."

23 Katigbak, email to author.

24 Katigbak, "Ganito Tayo Noon." Leo Katigbak notes that while several other Philippine entities and companies undertake film restoration (the FDCP, FPJ Productions, and Viva Films), ABS-CBN's output puts it at the forefront of the field.

25 De Vera, "4.5 Million Pinoys Jobless."

26 IBON Foundation, "14 Charts."

27 Eugenio Lopez III held the title of chairman emeritus until his resignation in 2020. As of 2023, Martin L. Lopez and Augusto Almeda-Lopez

served as chairman and vice-chairman of ABS-CBN, respectively. See ABS-CBN Corporate: Our Leadership.

28 Godinez, "Privatization and Deregulation," 265.

29 Bordwell, Thompson, and Smith, *Film Art*, 42. In 2005, ABS-CBN acquired cable rights (twenty-five years) and online rights (eight years) for 102 film titles produced by LVN Film Studios. In addition to these LVN films, LVN memorabilia (costumes and props) are also housed at the ABS-CBN Film Archives. Galino, email to author, March 27, 2018.

30 Schatz, "Studio System and Conglomerate Hollywood," 26–27.

31 Larkin, *Signal and Noise*, 3–4.

32 Del Pilar's and Galino's own professional transitions from the state-run PIA film library to ABS-CBN (in the 1990s, in del Pilar's case) and from LVN to ABS-CBN (in the 2000s, in Galino's case) register larger shifts toward privatization in the balance of the Philippine archival world.

33 Edmondson, "Notes on Sustainability," 25.

34 Del Pilar, personal interview with author.

35 *Graphic*, "ABS-CBN Launches the Era of Total Professionalism."

36 McCoy, "Rent-Seeking Families," 460–506. Fernando Lopez was a three-term vice president, serving one term under President Quirino and two terms under President Marcos.

37 McCoy, "Rent-Seeking Families," 513–16; Sioson–San Juan, *Pinoy Television*, 205.

38 Sioson–San Juan, *Pinoy Television*, 64–66, 202–4; McCoy, "Rent-Seeking Families," 494; *Graphic*, "ABS-CBN Launches the Era of Total Professionalism."

39 Sioson–San Juan, *Pinoy Television*, 54, 203.

40 McCoy, "Rent-Seeking Families," 494–95.

41 Doronila, "Media," 197.

42 McCoy, "Preface," xvii–xviii.

43 Doronila, "Media," 198; Sioson–San Juan, *Pinoy Television*, 71.

44 McCoy, "Rent-Seeking Families," 452.

45 Sioson–San Juan, *Pinoy Television*, 204.

46 McCoy, "Rent-Seeking Families," 458–59, 480, 508.

47 McCoy, "'Anarchy of Families,'" 7.

48 McCoy, "Preface," xii.

49 Hau, *Elites and Ilustrados*, 1, 3.

50 McCoy, "'Anarchy of Families,'" 10–11, 31.

51 McCoy, "'Anarchy of Families,'" 12. Given that pervasive rent-seeking has characterized other Asian nations such as South Korea, Japan, Indonesia, Malaysia, and Thailand, McCoy wondered why these countries were more successful in creating the conditions for economic growth than the Philippines. McCoy speculated that rent-seeking has been particularly pernicious in the Philippines because of its combination of

frequent elections (occasions for elites to "extract concessions from the executive") and lack of export-led industrialization that would otherwise have exposed oligarchic family corporations to market discipline (McCoy, "Preface," xiv–xv). In the two decades since McCoy's analysis was published, Philippine economic trends have shifted dramatically. As Hau noted in 2017, "The country's economic advantage is now also seen to lie in its supply of English-speaking, educated Filipinos who perform business-outsourcing services for American and other companies abroad. This labor-exporting and service-sector-based developmental path pursued by the Philippines remains largely beyond the purview of the new economic growth theory, which has not developed models to analyze the role of the service sector nor the implications of the increased blurring between service and manufacturing." Hau, *Elites and Ilustrados*, 10.

52 McCoy, "Rent-Seeking Families," 495.

53 McCoy, "Rent-Seeking Families," 442, 445.

54 *Graphic*, "ABS-CBN Launches the Era of Total Professionalism."

55 McCoy, "Rent-Seeking Families," 507.

56 McCoy, "Rent-Seeking Families," 509.

57 Sioson–San Juan, *Pinoy Television*, 97, 105–6.

58 McCoy, "Rent-Seeking Families," 510–12; Sioson–San Juan, *Pinoy Television*, 13.

59 On parallels between Ferdinand Marcos and Ninoy Aquino, see Hau, *Elites and Ilustrados*, 204–5; on similarities between Marcos and Eugenio Lopez Sr., see McCoy, "Rent-Seeking Families," 430.

60 B. Anderson, "Cacique Democracy," 20–21.

61 Ressa, "In the Crosshairs of History." Convicted of cyber libel in June 2020, Nobel laureate Maria Ressa is the CEO and founder of *Rappler*, which, like ABS-CBN and *Philippine Inquirer*, published extensive coverage of Duterte's drug war.

62 Millard O. Lim observes that Duterte "was able to get rid of his enemy without extraordinary measures because fortuitous circumstances allowed him to use the law—R.A. 3846 [the Radio Control Law of 1963, which prohibits radio and TV broadcast operation in the absence of a congressional franchise] and an expired R.A. 7966 [ABS-CBN's lapsed legislative franchise from 1995]—as a weapon against his enemy." M. O. Lim, "ABS-CBN Shutdown."

63 Duterte, qtd. in Ranada, "After ABS-CBN Decision."

64 Elemia, "Big Comeback"; ABS-CBN News, "ABS-CBN Shutdown."

65 Rappler.com, "Cultural Vacuum."

66 Elemia, "Isabela Governor Bemoans ABS-CBN."

67 Kerkvliet and Mojares, "Themes in the Transition," 1.

68 See Hau, *Elites and Ilustrados*, 165–223.

69 Sioson–San Juan, *Pinoy Television*, 205.

70 Alliance of Artists for the Creation of a Ministry of Culture, qtd. in Fernandez, "Mass Culture and Cultural Policy," 494.

71 Fernandez, "Paths of Policy," 31.

72 Fernandez, "Paths of Policy," 35.

73 I owe this insight to Carol Hau's feedback on an earlier draft.

74 See, for example, the opening caveats of Executive Order 100 creating the PIA. C. C. Aquino, Executive Order No. 100.

75 *Hollywood Reporter*, "Philippines' President Aquino Sets Up Film Agency Task Force"; M. V. Giron, "Aquino to Keep Marcos," 1, 93.

76 C. C. Aquino, Memorandum Order No. 2; C. C. Aquino, Memorandum Order No. 274.

77 C. C. Aquino, Memorandum Order No. 274.

78 M. V. Giron, "Aquino to Keep Marcos," 35.

79 Tiongson "Filipino Film in the Decade," xvii–xviii.

80 Tiongson, "Filipino Film in the Decade," xviii.

81 Tiongson, "Filipino Film Industry," 45.

82 Though incomplete, the twenty-three-page copy of the report that I perused at the PIA-MISD Film Archives was officially stamped as received at 3:33 p.m. on May 23, 1986, by the Office of the Senate Secretary for Legislation.

83 Qtd. in de Pedro, "Overview of the Film Archives," 7. I have not been able to find a copy of the task force's report.

84 According to de Pedro's report, "The National Film Collection has over 2,140 titles, with only 384 Filipino films and 34 foreign films so far inspected and certified as to their completeness. . . . This Collection includes the earliest film in the NFAP collection: 'Escenas Callejeras' (1897), a silent documentary ascribed to the film pioneer Antonio Ramos [and] over 30 documentaries from 1897 to 1927." De Pedro notes, however, that over 400 black-and-white films donated by Sampaguita Studio to the FAP in 1985 were "completely gone" due to irreversible deterioration. De Pedro, "Overview of the Film Archives," 11.

85 De Pedro, "Overview of the Film Archives," 9.

86 De Pedro, "Overview of the Film Archives," 10.

87 F. E. Marcos, Executive Order No. 640-A; F. E. Marcos, Executive Order No. 770.

88 F. E. Marcos, Executive Order No. 1051.

89 M. V. Giron, "New Bill Proposing an End"; M. V. Giron, "Marcos Plucks Censor Thorn."

90 F. E. Marcos, Presidential Decree No. 1986.

91 PIA-MISD, Status of MTRCB Film Archives and Library Division.

92 De Pedro, "Overview of the Film Archives," 2–3. As previously mentioned in note 19 of the introduction, de Pedro referred to the Film

Archives of the Philippines as the "NFAP," despite the lack of the word *national* in the archives' official name.

93 De Pedro, "Overview of the Film Archives," 23.

94 Based on the NFAP transcript of the second roundtable discussion held during the 2013 Philippine Heritage Summit (convened by the NFAP on January 25, 2013), former FAP director-general Ernie de Pedro claimed to have kept the FAP afloat until 1989 through a combination of foreign aid and racetrack bets (NFAP, Transcript of Roundtable Discussion, 8). While these recollections are difficult to substantiate, the kernel of his remarks refers to the institutional demise of the FAP during Cory Aquino's presidency. Throughout this book I refer to 1986 as the year of the FAP's effective death, since the cessation of government funding meant it would no longer qualify as a state-run national film archive, despite the ingenious stratagems de Pedro claims to have employed until 1989.

95 De Pedro, "Overview of the Film Archives," 12. According to de Pedro, the FAP managed a computerized database for the Asia-Pacific Cooperation in Film and Video Exchange, a collaborative project involving the Asia Broadcasting Union, UNESCO, and various archives in Malaysia, India, and the Philippines (14).

96 De Pedro, "Overview of the Film Archives," 1.

97 C. C. Aquino, "State of the Nation Address."

98 C. C. Aquino, qtd. in Godinez, "Privatization and Deregulation," 267.

99 Godinez, "Privatization and Deregulation," 265, 266, 268.

100 Godinez, " Privatization and Deregulation," 283–84.

101 Del Pilar, personal interview with author.

102 David, "Second Golden Age"; see also David, *Fields of Vision.*

103 Tiongson, "Filipino Film Industry," 30.

104 David, "Second Golden Age."

105 David, "Second Golden Age," 14–15.

106 Tiongson urged the Aquino government to end onerous taxation and relaunch specific ECP mechanisms: tax rebates and the production of winning screenplays (Tiongson, "Filipino Film Industry," 32–33, 57–58). While these policy recommendations were never adopted, the latter (funding support for the production of top screenplays) is an ECP era mechanism that was revived in the 2000s by the Cinemalaya Independent Film Festival, which has played a major role in the emergence of digital independent filmmaking in the Philippines.

107 David, "Second Golden Age," 15.

108 Tiongson, "Filipino Film Industry," 32.

109 Estrada, Executive Order No. 323.

110 PMO-ABS-CBN, Deed of Absolute Sale for the film "Himala," 1–2. Though I was only able to peruse the deed of sale for the film *Himala*, I assume

that the rights to each of the three other ECP films auctioned by the PMO were sold to ABS-CBN through a similarly worded contract.

111 Godinez, "Privatization and Deregulation," 266.

112 PMO-ABS-CBN, Deed of Absolute Sale for the film "Himala," 3.

113 Gracy, *Film Preservation*, 210.

114 Gracy, *Film Preservation*, 6–7, 27.

115 Gracy, *Film Preservation*, 93.

116 Larkin, *Signal and Noise*, 3.

117 Larkin, *Signal and Noise*, 4.

CHAPTER 4. QUEER ANACHRONISMS AND TEMPORALITIES OF RESTORATION

Epigraphs: Leo Katigbak, qtd. in Orosa, "ABS-CBN Restores T-Bird," and in San Diego, "'T-Bird at Ako.'"

1 Dumaual, "'Miracle' behind 'Himala' HD Restoration." Katigbak estimates that restorations cost anywhere between 500,000 to 100 million pesos (US$10,000 to US$2 million). While these costs may or may not be recouped on a per film basis, he notes that Sagip Pelikula overall is "practically breaking even" in the context of the total cost of restorations. Katigbak, "Ganito Tayo Noon."

2 Katigbak, quoted in San Diego, "Restoring 'Himala.'" Katigbak's remark refers to the Criterion Collection as a multiplatform distributor of restored canonical works of world cinema accompanied by special features and original supplements.

3 For critical analyses of *Himala*, see B. C. Lim, "Cult Fiction"; B. C. Lim, "Fandom, Consumption, and Collectivity"; Tadiar, *Fantasy-Production*.

4 The DVD version of a "Digitally Restored & Remastered" *T-Bird at Ako* was released by Star Home Video in 2015. An earlier unrestored version of *T-Bird at Ako* was released on DVD by Paragon Home Video in 2008. Currently, Blu-ray is not a widely distributed commercial format in the Philippines. DVD is the carrier on which ABS-CBN's restored titles have been commercially distributed (in addition to broadcast, cable, and online platforms).

5 Orosa, "ABS-CBN Restores T-Bird." Katigbak defines a classic film along four vectors: awards and recognition; historical significance; box office performance and audience impact; and the ability to offer a "cultural snapshot" of an era. Katigbak, "Ganito Tayo Noon."

6 Orosa, "ABS-CBN Restores T-Bird."

7 As Laura Mulvey observes of DVD rereleases, "This new life (movies reissued and restored, new modes of consumption) also transforms the way in which old films are consumed." Mulvey, *Death 24× a Second*, 21.

8 Arondekar, *For the Record*, 4.

9 Chiang and Wong, "Asia Is Burning," 122.

10 Chiang, Henry, and Leung, "Trans-in-Asia, Asia-in-Trans," 299–300.

11 According to an online filmography posted by a fan identified only as "@ffv," Nora Aunor and Vilma Santos costarred in a total of four films: *T-Bird at Ako*, *Ikaw ay Akin*, *Young Love* (dir. Tony Cayado, 1970), and *Pinagbuklod ng Pag-ibig* (Bound by love; dir. Leonardo L. Garcia, 1978). @ffy, "Filmography: T-Bird at Ako (1982)," November 17, 2009, https://starforallseasons.com/2009/11/17/filmography-t-bird-at-ako-1982/.

12 I. Cruz, "T-Bird at Ako (1982)."

13 Zafra, "T-Bird at Ako."

14 *T-Bird at Ako*'s many allusions to both stars' filmographies confirm its address to fans and movie buffs: the title and lyrics of the movie's theme song, "*Hiwaga ng Pag-ibig*" (Miracle of love), advert to Nora Aunor's multiawarded film, *Himala*; Sabel's dance number and the name of a character in the opening courtroom scene refer to two critically acclaimed Vilma Santos films, *Burlesk Queen* (dir. Celso Ad. Castillo, 1977) and *Rubia Servios* (dir. Lino Brocka, 1978).

15 On Noranian fandom, see Tadiar, *Fantasy-Production*, 332; B. C. Lim, "Fandom, Consumption, and Collectivity," 181. I explore the untranslatability of *bakla* elsewhere: "Bakla is no mere Filipino synonym for the English word gay. . . . *Bakla* messily conflates concepts that are usually kept distinct in transnational LGBTQ vocabularies, collapsing same-sex desire (homosexuality), gender expression (male femininity), gender nonconformity with assigned sex (trans identifications)," and the stigmatization endured by many queers. B. C. Lim, "Queer Aswang Transmedia," 184.

16 Nora's best-known love team partner was Tirso Cruz III, while Vilma's was Edgar Mortiz.

17 Sebastiampillai, "Love Teams," 86–87.

18 Sebastiampillai, "Love Teams," 103, 120.

19 Print advertisement for *T-Bird at Ako*, accessed August 1, 2018, https://starforallseasons.com/.

20 The studio era of Philippine filmmaking stretched from roughly 1936 to 1961, with a hiatus from 1941 to 1945 due to World War II. The middle to late 1960s ushered in the excesses of poststudio era filmmaking in the Philippines: quickie filmmaking financed by inexperienced producers; films of poor technical quality and low prestige in comparison with big studio productions; and the unprecedented power of freelance stars like Nora Aunor and Vilma Santos who were able to command inflated talent fees unheard of in the days of studio contracts for stars. Lacaba, "Movies, Critics," 176; Celino, "Busiest Stars of 1965," 38–39.

21 White, *Uninvited*, 31–32.

22 White, *Uninvited*, 30.

23 White, *Uninvited*, 41.

24 Castle, *Apparitional Lesbian*, 1, 3.

25 *Eat Bulaga!* host Vic Sotto is shown holding a microphone at the left margin of the frame.

26 Zafra, "T-Bird at Ako."

27 Demafeliz, "Pearly Shells," 66.

28 Tiongson, "Si Kristo, Ronnie Poe," 12–14.

29 B. C. Lim, "Sharon's Noranian Turn," 320–27.

30 Thoreson, "Realizing Rights in Manila," 550.

31 Constable, "Sexuality and Discipline," 550–52.

32 In their critique of conflations between gender neutrality, sexual orientation, and trans subjectivity, Vidal-Ortiz and Martínez note that the genderqueer or nonbinary folx referenced by the term *Latinx* are not by default lesbian, gay, or bisexual. Moreover, not all transgender persons adopt nonbinary or gender-fluid identities; in some cases, binary genders can reinforce a trans person's transitioning desires and identity of choice. Vidal-Ortiz and Martínez, "Latinx Thoughts," 389.

33 Guno, "'Filipinx,' 'Pinxy'"; Toledo, "Filipino or Filipinx?"

34 On September 26, 2020, I served as the moderator and opening speaker for "Are We Filipinx?: A Cinema Sala Couch Talk," which brought together panelists from Metro Manila, Cotabato City, Los Angeles, and Hawaii and was livestreamed to a transnational audience via Zoom. The other roundtable participants were filmmaker Marie Jamora (founder of Cinema Sala); journalist Dino-Ray Ramos; Bangsamoro-based writer Marrian Pio Roda Ching; documentary filmmaker PJ Raval; actress and transgender activist Rain Valdez; and author and scholar Laurel Flores Fantauzzo.

35 Mabalon, *Little Manila*, 20. See also Ching, "Is the Filipino Language?"

36 I am grateful to Dan Bustillo for pointing me to scholarship on the term *Latinx*. *Filipinx* is preceded and inspired by *Latinx*, a term that first came into use around 2004 by US and European queer millennials in an online world. Two crucial differences have emerged between *Latinx* and *Filipinx*. First, *Filipinx* remains a nationally delimited rather than hemispheric term; in contrast, *Latinx* is a pan-ethnic term that exceeds national boundaries (Milian, "Extremely Latin, xoxo," 124). Second, the *x* in *Latinx* marks an allegiance with and appropriation of indigeneity, alluding to the ancient Nahuatl word *Mexicano* in opposition to the Spanish colonial term *Mejico*. (Milian, "Extremely Latin, xoxo," 127). In contrast, the *x* in *Filipinx* does not designate *lumad* or indigenous non-Christian, non-Muslim cultures in the Philippines.

37 Rafael, "Patronage, Pornography, and Youth"; Muñoz, "Feeling Brown, Feeling Down." At least 10 percent of the total Philippine population

participates in the migrant labor economy as OFWs. San Juan, "Overseas Filipino Workers," 99.

38 See Yue, "Queer Asian Cinema"; and S.-H. Lim, *Celluloid Comrades.*

39 Spot.ph, "Revisiting the Lesbian-Themed Classic" (italics added). Spot.ph is a self-described "One-Stop Urban Lifestyle Guide to the Best of Manila."

40 Thoreson, "Realizing Rights in Manila," 557.

41 Halperin, *One Hundred Years of Homosexuality.*

42 Halperin, *How to Do the History*, 2–3.

43 Rohy, "Ahistorical," 61–63, 65.

44 Dinshaw, "Got Medieval?," 203.

45 In a 2012 essay, Thoreson writes: "For low-income respondents to a survey on sexuality and poverty . . . gender and sexuality were frequently conflated and analytically undifferentiated. When asked about their sexuality (*sekswalidad*), respondents variously self-identified as gay, male, bisexual, homosexual, lesbian, ladyboy, *bakla*, female, transgender, shemale, lesbian/tomboy, girl, and third sex. When asked to identify their gender (*kasarian*), respondents identified as male, female, gay, *bakla*, girl, ladyboy, *bading*, bisexual, homosexual, Third Sex, billy boy, masculine, single, lesbian, boy, 'male and female,' and 'unsure.' The conflation of gender and sexuality in each response hints at a framework considerably more flexible than the one brokers [of transnational, middle-class LGBT activist organizations] themselves employ." Thoreson, "Realizing Rights in Manila," 548.

46 Fajardo, "Queering and Transing," 125–27.

47 Rodriguez, qtd. in Fajardo, "Queering and Transing," 127.

48 Fajardo, "Queering and Transing," 128–29.

49 Serano, "Julia Serano's Trans, Gender, Sexuality."

50 Constable, "Sexuality and Discipline," 551.

51 Fajardo, "Transportation," 409.

52 Fajardo, "Queering and Transing," 125–27

53 J. Tan, "Beijing Meets Hawai'i," 144–46.

54 Thoreson, "Realizing Rights in Manila," 530–31.

55 Fajardo, "Transportation," 405, 413.

56 Freeman, *Time Binds*, xiii (italics added).

57 The prominence of English and Taglish in certain scenes connotes class and educational privilege on the part of specific characters like the prosecutor. In contrast, Maxie, Sabel, and Rubia all speak primarily in Filipino.

58 As Thoreson notes, contemporary human rights discourse retains a primarily antistatist inflection in the Philippines, which can occlude socioeconomic, everyday concerns such as homelessness and forms of mistreatment routinely endured by queer *pinoys*, especially impoverished ones, that would be "virtually impossible to redress through law." Thoreson, "Realizing Rights in Manila," 537.

59 Zafra, "T-Bird at Ako." Screenwriter Ilagan's purported conflict with director Zialcita over *T-Bird at Ako*'s heteronormative ending recalls Andrea Weiss's discussion of similar tensions between *Queen Christina* (1933). According to Weiss, director Rouben Mamoulian's directorial intent was disrupted by the queer performance of star Greta Garbo and the insertion of a "lesbian joke" in the script by Garbo's rumored lover, screenwriter Salka Viertel. These parallels suggest the possibility that a larger structural dynamic between heteronormative directors and queer performers/writers may be at work. Weiss, *Vampires and Violets*, 36–38.

60 Gomez, "Danny Zialcita."

61 See the Philippine Commission on Women's policy brief urging the repeal of *destierro* as enshrined in Article 247 of the Revised Penal Code (Philippine Commission on Women, "Upholding the Right to Life"). In January 2020, the Philippine Supreme Court dismissed "with finality" a petition to reconsider its September 2019 denial of same-sex marriage. Herrera, "Rundown on the History."

62 Fajardo, "Transportation," 404–5.

63 Cantor, "To Conform or Not," 97.

64 Weiss, *Vampires and Violets*, 33.

65 Mulvey, *Death 24× a Second*, 31.

66 Diaz, "Queer Love and Urban Intimacies," 2.

67 Diaz, "Queer Love and Urban Intimacies," 3.

68 Espiritu, *Passionate Revolutions*, 1–6.

69 Frontality, or "the positioning of figures so that they face the viewer," functions to direct the spectator's gaze. Bordwell, Thompson, and Smith, *Film Art*, G3, 151–52.

70 Weiss, *Vampires and Violets*, 30.

71 Bautista, "Nora Had an Affair."

72 Maglipon, Pingol, and Paredes, "Nora Superstar," 118.

73 Maglipon, Pingol, and Paredes, "Nora Superstar," 118.

74 ABS-CBN Entertainment, "Nora Confesses She Had a Crush."

75 White, *Uninvited*, 33.

76 Maglipon, Pingol, and Paredes, "Nora Superstar," 120.

77 Maglipon, Pingol, and Paredes, "Nora Superstar," 120. Interview questions were typically given in English, while Aunor's answers were quoted in Filipino, which I have translated here.

78 "As [UP film professor Libay Linsangan] Cantor stressed, . . . 'coming out is not part of our culture—of course, not in a bad way. We just know that that person's gay.'" (Cantor, qtd. in Thoreson, "Realizing Rights in Manila," 550). In contrast to the post-Stonewall North American model of coming out and leaving the biological family behind, Audrey Yue notes that queer Asian films emphasize practices of partial coming out, "reticence," "constant negotiation," and remaining within but also "reconfiguring"

the blood family (Yue, "Queer Asian Cinema," 148). For a critique of the rhetoric of "coming out of the closet," see S.-H. Lim, *Celluloid Comrades*, 51–52.)

79 White, *Uninvited*, 31.

80 Weiss, *Vampires and Violets*, 33.

81 White, *Uninvited*, 32, 47.

82 Mulvey, "Visual Pleasure and Narrative Cinema," 19, 25. See also Metz, "From 'The Imaginary Signifier,'" 806–7.

83 White, *Uninvited*, 37.

84 White, *Uninvited*, 36.

85 I am punning here on Mulvey's characterization of classical Hollywood cinema as "an illusion *cut to the measure* of [patriarchal] desire." Mulvey, "Visual Pleasure and Narrative Cinema," 25 (italics added).

86 Spot.ph, "Revisiting the Lesbian-Themed Classic."

87 Spot.ph, "Revisiting the Lesbian-Themed Classic."

88 Mulvey, *Death 24× a Second*, 28.

89 Mulvey, *Death 24× a Second*, 8.

90 Mulvey, *Death 24× a Second*, 170–71.

91 See chapter 3, note 2.

92 Del Pilar, personal interview with author.

93 "Restoration Advocacy Campaign Vignettes" are included in the DVD bonus features for *T-Bird at Ako*. Brief clips of restored New Cinema masterpieces—*Ganito Kami Noon*; *Oro, Plata, Mata*; and *Himala*—are prominent in these celebrity-hosted plugs.

94 Gracy, *Film Preservation*, 93.

95 In addition to restoring *Himala* and *Oro, Plata, Mata*, both ECP films, ABS-CBN had also restored and rereleased nine other New Cinema films by 2018:

    Ganito Kami Noon, Paano Kayo Ngayon (As we were; dir. Eddie Romero, 1976)
    Tatlong Taong Walang Diyos (Three years without God; dir. Mario O'Hara, 1976)
    Ikaw ay Akin (You are mine; dir. Ishmael Bernal, 1978)
    Kakabakaba ka ba (Will your heart beat faster?; dir. Mike de Leon, 1980)
    Kasal (Marriage; dir. Laurice Guillen, 1980)
    Langis at Tubig (Oil and water; dir. Danny Zialcita, 1980)
    Moral (Morals; dir. Marilou Diaz-Abaya, 1982)
    Cain at Abel (Cain and Abel; dir. Lino Brocka, 1982)
    Karnal (Carnal; dir. Marilou-Diaz Abaya, 1983)

96 ABS-CBN Film Archives, "ABS-CBN Inventories."

97 I would have wanted to expand my discussion of film authorship beyond directors and to explore the question of sexual and ethnic minoritarian-

ism (not only gender diversity) in my analysis of restoration priorities. Unfortunately, data on above and below the line film workers in the Philippines are not comprehensively recorded, nor are issues of ethnicity and sexuality trackable beyond anecdotal knowledge.

98 The women directors with the largest number of restored films are Star Cinema stalwarts Cathy Garcia Molina, Joyce Bernal, Olivia Lamasan, and Rory Quintos, in descending order; between eight and ten of these directors' films have been restored by ABS-CBN. Other female directors who have had between one and five titles restored by ABS-CBN are, in descending order, Laurice Guillen, Marilou Diaz Abaya, Mae Czarina Cruz, and Veronica Velasco. Abaya and Guillen are also the only female filmmakers included among the auteurs of the Philippine New Cinema. ABS-CBN Film Archives, "ABS-CBN Inventories."

99 By 2018, ABS-CBN had restored only three other movies featuring explicit LGBTQ+ representation (2.6 percent of its output): *Moral* (dir. Marilou Diaz-Abaya, 1982), *Ang Lalaki Sa Buhay ni Selya* (The man in Selya's life; dir. Carlitos Siguion Reyna, 1998), and *In My Life* (dir. Olivia Lamasan, 2009).

100 San Diego, "'T-Bird at Ako.'"

101 Marchetti, "Subcultural Studies," 413.

102 Hebdige, *Subculture*, 92–93.

103 Drake, "Distribution and Marketing," 64.

104 C. Anderson, *Long Tail.*

105 McDonald, "From Online Video Store," 205.

106 Bordwell, Thompson, and Smith, *Film Art*, 42.

107 Drake, "Distribution and Marketing," 77.

108 Orosa, "ABS-CBN Restores T-Bird."

109 Orosa, "ABS-CBN Restores T-Bird."

CHAPTER 5. INFORMAL ARCHIVING IN A RIVERINE SYSTEM

1 Merv Espina notes that the Kalampag Tracking Agency, the curatorial screening program he cofounded with Shireen Seno, has often been interpellated as an archive. Espina, email to author, March 5, 2020.

In addition, many scholars have argued for understanding video rental stores as film archives or informal film schools (see, for instance, Greenberg, *From Betamax to Blockbuster*, 107–8; Herbert, *Videoland*, 88; Wilken, "Video Stores," 1). Daniel Herbert, for example, notes the proximity of video stores to archives, museums, and open-stack libraries (Herbert, *Videoland*, 57). Herbert also notes that the video store clerk "functions as both media archivist and librarian" (Herbert, *Videoland*, 80). Similarly, Kathleen Williams understands the video store clerk as a curatorial figure (Williams, "Internet Killed the Video Store," 199).

2 Statista Research Department, "Penetration Rate of Video Streaming (SVOD)"; Stoll, "Ranking of Countries."

3 For 2022 population data, see World Bank, "Population Total—Philippines."

4 For an analysis of how Netflix's algorithmic personalization and recommendations system (PRS) functions to "govern" the audience tastes it purports to reflect, see Arnold, "Netflix and the Myth of Choice/Participation/Autonomy." For a critique of Netflix's genres and microgenres as forms of "hidden advertising," see Smith-Rowsey, "Imaginative Indices and Deceptive Domains."

5 The Video 48 blog can be accessed at http://video48.blogspot.com/.

6 Pamaran, "Video 48, the Last Rental." See also Snow, "Video 48 Is the Last Rental Store."

7 Baldoza, "Simon Santos."

8 Pamaran, "Video 48, the Last Rental."

9 Straw, "Embedded Memories," 3. For Will Straw, the internet as an immediately accessible, data-based high-storage platform can revitalize outmoded forms by imbuing them with new significance and cultural worth.

10 Pamaran, "Video 48, the Last Rental."

11 See David James's discussion of similar domestic and paradomestic screenings in the Los Angeles avant-garde film scene. James, *Most Typical Avant-Garde*, 213.

12 Espina, email to author, June 23, 2020.

13 Seno and Espina, "Kalampag Tracking Agency," 245.

14 Seno and Espina, personal interview with author.

15 Seno and Espina, "Kalampag Tracking Agency," 246.

16 Seno and Espina, personal interview with author.

17 The characteristically intimate scale of alternative film scenes poses distinct archival problems that Espina and Seno are well positioned to address. As archivists who specialize in experimental cinema note, "The world of experimental filmmaking remains small and depends on personal relationships between artists, archivists and scholars, and no machine of professionally produced public relation[s] material that has now turned into an archival resource supports and promotes it." Groschke, Koerber, and Meiller, "Who Is Going to Look?," 129.

18 Walter Benjamin writes that the "inveterate collector" turns a "deaf ear to all reminders from the everyday world of legality," such as prompts to return long-overdue books. This suggests that legality and collecting have long been at cross-purposes, even in an earlier era of purely tangible, tactile media collections. Benjamin, "Unpacking My Library," 62–63.

19 Espina, email to author, June 20, 2020; Espina, email to author, June 23, 2020; Espina, email to author, June 24, 2020; Masters, "Manila's Oldest Artist-Run Space."

20 Santos, post on Video 48's Facebook page.

21 Teddy Co responded to Santos's Facebook announcement: "In the absence of a proper government film archive for several decades, Video 48 was the de facto Repository for Philippine Cinema, along with Casa Grande Vintage Filipino Cinema, ABS-CBN Film Archives, and FPJ Productions. It is alarming that the government film agencies only have humid film storage bodegas, with their film collections slowly rotting away. Video 48 will be remembered for keeping the flame of our memories of Philippine cinema alive." Co, comment on Simon Santos's July 1, 2020, Facebook post.

22 Santos, email to author. The Optical Media Board's requirement bordered on the absurd, since Video 48 had long since outlived the companies that supplied the obsolete home video formats (Betamax, VHS, and VCD among them) archived in Santos's store.

23 My amateur understanding of river ecosystems derives from Rutledge et al., "Understanding Rivers"; National Geographic Society, "River"; and Cummins and Wilzbach, "Rivers and Streams."

24 Lobato, *Shadow Economies of Cinema*, 16.

25 Lapniten, "'River Will Bleed Red.'"

26 Cummins and Wilzbach, "Rivers and Streams."

27 My personal collection began in the early 1990s with Betamax and VHS tapes acquired in video stores in Manila, New York, and New Jersey during my first teaching job in Quezon City and my subsequent postgraduate training in New York City. My collection grew to include commercial VCDs and DVDs purchased in Manila shopping malls and via online US retailers catering to overseas Filipino consumers, such as kabayancentral .com. Most recently, I have relied on MPEG and M4V movie files ripped from various sources (commercial VCDs and DVDs, tapes and discs obtained from archives or libraries, or shared by collectors, students, colleagues, and filmmakers). These are stored on a variety of carriers, from DVDs to external firewire and USB drives and online cloud storage services.

28 In the North American context, Klinger notes that the 1970s and 1980s saw the peak of personal 8mm and 16mm film collecting. Klinger, "Contemporary Cinephile," 57.

29 Hilderbrand, *Inherent Vice*, 10. As Joshua Neves and Bhaskar Sarkar emphasize, writing responsibly about Asian video cultures demands a shift away from the idealized naturalization of high-bandwidth digital experiences rooted in the perspectives of the global North, which privilege "speed, reliability, ubiquity, access, participation, innovating, and convergence" in ways that cannot be presumed in the global South. Neves and Sarkar, "Introduction," 6.

30 I recall that from around 2006 onward, LVN and Sampaguita—both former major film production companies in the studio era—offered the

small-scale, largely unpublicized distribution of a limited selection of their own vintage films. Migrated from unrestored, often deteriorating film prints to VHS tapes (and, later, to VCDs and DVDs), these copies could be ordered directly from these studios whether through personal archival contacts or via advanced order from retailers like kabayancentral .com.

31 Deocampo, *Short Film*, 52–53.

32 Hilderbrand, "Cinematic Promiscuity," 215.

33 Co, personal interview with author.

34 Klinger, "Contemporary Cinephile," 88.

35 I first encountered the Kalampag Tracking Agency's screening program at the March 2018 Glasgow Short Film Festival, in conjunction with a Southeast Asian Cinemas Research Network Symposium. For a list of Kalampag's screenings, see Shireen Seno's blog, "The Kalampag Tracking Agency," accessed July 15, 2023, https://shireenseno.tumblr.com/post /97270782783/the-kalampag-tracking-agency..

36 Klinger, "Contemporary Cinephile," 56, 82, 88–89. Klinger notes that high-end collectors coexist with "shadow collectors who pursue fringe titles and frequently engage in 'illicit' practices, such as dubbing films illegally from prerecorded tapes or buying bootleg titles, to form their libraries." Klinger, "Contemporary Cinephile," 63.

37 "In fact, the store's records show that Brocka actually returned a tape that he borrowed a day before his untimely death [in 1991]." Pamaran, "Video 48, the Last Rental."

38 On the video store as both a "consumption junction" and a space of "sociability," see Greenberg, *From Betamax to Blockbuster*, 114.

39 Bonus features on DVD extras contribute to a marketing rhetoric of exclusivity, scarcity, and insider knowledge through "'making-of' documentar[ies] with behind-the-scenes explanations" and trivia (Klinger, "Contemporary Cinephile," 68–70). Addressing a mainstream consumer through a rhetoric of "insider-ness" is also at work in ABS-CBN's promotional rhetoric around older Filipino "classics" that have been digitally restored or remastered, supplemented with paratextual bonus material.

40 Seno and Espina, personal interview with author. Russel Belk notes that collections sometimes begin with "inherited 'seed' objects or an intact 'starter collection' that primed the adoption of a collector role." Belk, "Collectors and Collecting," 318.

41 Acland, "Introduction," xx–xxiii.

42 Acland, "Introduction," xx.

43 Benjamin, "Unpacking My Library," 61.

44 Henning writes, "If the torn or trodden photograph lying in the street speaks of a tragedy or a broken relationships, and the photo album found in a house clearance sale, of a forgotten and unmourned life, then the

collector becomes a loving, if surrogate, mourner." Henning, "New Lamps for Old," 62.

45 Belk reflects, "In the sense that nations are also collectors of art and artefacts, concern with loss of national pride results in efforts to repatriate such objects when they are in the hands of other nations and to prevent further loss of national heritage in this way." Belk, "Collectors and Collecting," 322.

46 Del Mundo, *Dreaming of a National*, 16.

47 Belk, "Collectors and Collecting," 320; J. Davis, "Going Analog," 231.

48 Seno and Espina, personal interview with author; Espina, email to author, March 5, 2020.

49 Perusing both the display shelves and hard copy lists of Video 48's catalog in 2019, I found very few nonfiction films; moreover, with the exception of a few titles directed by Raya Martin, I encountered no other avant-garde or experimental shorts.

50 Herbert, *Videoland*, 85, 90, 93. In the North American context, Herbert observes that the legendary reputation of video meccas does not equate to economic profitability, since such a store "lives more in the virtual space of people's memories and imaginations than it does in their daily activities; . . . this virtual prominence threatens the store's continued existence in material space." Herbert, *Videoland*, 100.

51 Greenberg, *From Betamax to Blockbuster*, 6–7

52 Kathleen Williams notes that by the time "Blockbuster Video announced the widespread closure of its U.S. stores in late 2013 . . . video stores had been in decline for the last decade." However, as a major multinational franchise, Blockbuster's closure "seemed to signal the death of video stores entirely." Williams, "Internet Killed the Video Store," 195.

53 Herbert, *Videoland*, 3, 7, 11.

54 While Amazon and Netflix are the best-known examples of long tail economics, Kevin McDonald notes that video rental businesses were already operationalizing long tail strategies well before the ascendancy of internet companies. McDonald, "From Online Video Store," 205–6.

55 Serreng, personal interview with author. I am grateful to video clerk Emely Serreng for agreeing to be interviewed during my August 2019 visit and for subsequently emailing me permission to refer to her by name in this chapter. Serreng, email to author.

56 Herbert, *Videoland*, 95.

57 Video 48's owner, Simon Santos, is the son of renowned painter, illustrator, and comics artist Mauro "Malang" Santos. That the building was family owned helped Video 48 survive the downturn of the video rental business; the West Gallery on the second floor of the same building was owned by a Santos sibling. Video 48's video clerk Emely Serreng was a second-generation family employee whose father was a gallery staff member under Santos's father. Serreng, personal interview with author.

58 A lifelong FPJ fan, Santos recalls that his movie collection began with clippings of the star's photos and promotional materials, many of which he shares on another blog that pays tribute to the star. Video 48, "FPJ," accessed July 15, 2023, http://fpj-daking.blogspot.com/. See also Baldoza, "Simon Santos"; Pamaran, "Video 48, the Last Rental."

59 Greenberg, *From Betamax to Blockbuster*, 14; Herbert, *Videoland*, 6, 50–51.

60 Herbert, *Videoland*, 58.

61 Herbert, *Videoland*, 55–57.

62 Conventionally, video stores display empty cases, their spines and cover art serving as advertisements for the films themselves. Greenberg, *From Betamax to Blockbuster*, 86–87.

63 Possibly reflecting the historical importance of softcore *bomba* films to the history of Tagalog cinema in the seventies and eighties, sexploitation titles are integrated within the main Filipiniana collection, in contrast to the US practice of separately shelving adult films in a back room of the video store.

64 Mulvey, "Some Reflections," 190.

65 Williams, "Internet Killed the Video Store," 207.

66 Klinger, "Contemporary Cinephile," 57–60.

67 Davis and Yeh, "VCD as Programmatic Technology," 228, 239.

68 Hu, "Chinese Re-makings of Pirated VCDs," 208, 223. See also Wang, "Piracy and the DVD/VCD Market."

69 Deocampo, *Short Film*, 3, 11.

70 Deocampo, *Short Film*, 97.

71 Del Mundo, "Film Industry Is Dead!"; see also Campos, *End of National Cinema*, 245–46.

72 De Guzman, "Philippine Experimental Film Practice," 57, 63.

73 Deocampo, *Short Film*, 101; see also Deocampo, "Into the Light," 26.

74 Deocampo, *Short Film*, viii, 3, 97.

75 Trice, *City of Screens*, 8–29.

76 Roxlee, "Roxlee's 12 Commandments."

77 Seno and Espina, personal interview with author.

78 Knight, "Archiving, Distribution, and Experimental Moving Image Histories," 66.

79 Knight, "Archiving, Distribution, and Experimental Moving Image Histories," 78.

80 Seno and Espina, personal interview with author.

81 Seno and Espina, "Kalampag Tracking Agency," 248.

82 Groschke, Koerber, and Meiller, "Who Is Going to Look?," 129.

83 Groschke, Koerber, and Meiller, "Who Is Going to Look?," 133.

84 De Guzman, "Philippine Experimental Film Practice," 63.

85 For archival principles of *context linkage* and *fixity*, see Edmondson, *Audiovisual Archiving*, 52, 57.

86 Seno and Espina, "Kalampag Tracking Agency," 246.

87 Powers, "A DIY Come-On," 73.

88 Groschke, Koerber, and Meiller, "Who Is Going to Look?," 132.

89 Espina reflects, "For the older works especially, these [exchanges between filmmakers at Kalampag screenings] were rare opportunities to illuminate actual histories. Simple things people take for granted, such as date or medium and other such clerical errors, were pointed out. These details are important and would have otherwise gone unnoticed for such errors have been published and republished in what little actual documentation they were mentioned in." Seno and Espina, "Kalampag Tracking Agency," 246–47.

90 Baumgärtel, "Sine-Kino-Connection," 17.

91 Roxlee, "Roxlee's 12 Commandments."

92 Deocampo, *Short Film*; de Guzman, "Philippine Experimental Film Practice"; and Baumgärtel, "Sine-Kino-Connection," are notable exceptions.

93 Espina, email to author, June 20, 2020.

94 Deocampo, *Short Film*, 22–23, 98.

95 De Guzman, "Philippine Experimental Film Practice," 57, 60–62.

96 Deocampo, *Short Film*, 21–22, 103.

97 Espina, email to author, June 20, 2020. This was also mentioned in Seno and Espina, personal interview with author.

98 Orellana comments on the "dirty sound" ensuing from some of these make-do transfers: "This could [have] been avoided if we had the connector to connect the camera and the sound [output] of the projector. The audio of the projector should have been patched directly to the camera. In the absence of the connector, what was captured was the image projected on the wall, [while] the camera microphone picked up ambient sound during the transfer. [In MOWELFUND,] we are careful, in the absence of the connector, so we don't talk during the transfer, but the mechanical sound of the projector is captured. But Roxlee was OK with running commentary or joking; they sometimes didn't know that it was captured. He wasn't particular about that and sometimes he even liked that those sounds were captured."

Orellana recalls that some of the earliest examples of make-do transfers were conducted for the Independent Film and Video Festival held in Cubao in 1986 using "a Super 8mm projector and a bulky U-matic video camera directly patched to a U-matic recorder"; other analog-to-digital transfer processes evolved in later decades. Orellana, Skype interview with author.

99 This process was discussed in the introduction to this book.

100 Seno and Espina, personal interview with author.

101 Seno and Espina, personal interview with author.

102 James, *Most Typical Avant-Garde*, 17.

103 The Movie Workers Welfare Foundation, or MOWELFUND Foundation, was first organized in 1974; its film production and training unit, the MOWELFUND Film Institute, was subsequently established in 1979, acquiring "an impressive line-up of filmmaking equipment—from 35 mm to super-8 and video," funded by "the income generated through the holding of the annual Metro Manila Film Festival." Deocampo, *Short Film*, 32–33.

The attendees at the Sine-Kino workshops included acclaimed experimental filmmakers, pioneering audiovisual archivists, and cinephilic collectors. See Baumgärtel "Sine-Kino-Connection," 9–10.

Filmmaker and collector Cesar Hernando writes that the Goethe-Institut's workshops were "free of charge or by invitation. The result of these workshops is a flowering of experimental films during the period. To make experimental films without sponsorships is next to impossible and very expensive." Hernando, "Appendix 1," 66; see also Baumgärtel, "Sine-Kino-Connection"; Deocampo, "Into the Light."

104 Baumgärtel, "Sine-Kino-Connection," 8.

105 Janetzko, "Experimental Film Productions," 57; Orellana, Skype interview with author. Deocampo notes, "Dr. Schmelter became the kind godfather of the country's alternative cinema. He arrived at the most exciting of times when the country convulsed with anti-Marcos radicalism." Deocampo, "Into the Light," 25.

106 See Janetzko, "Experimental Film Productions"; Deocampo, "Into the Light," 24–25.

107 Orellana, Skype interview with author. Although Orellana was not a participant in that particular Janetzko workshop, he was a frequent workshop visitor who "pitched in" on some of the films, for example, by hand-drawing special effects directly onto the film strip for Louie Quirino and Donna Sales's *The Girl from Bikini Island* (1990).

108 Seno and Espina, "Kalampag Tracking Agency," 252. This was also touched on in Seno and Espina, personal interview with author.

109 James, *Most Typical Avant-Garde*, 16, 18.

110 Co, email to author, August 24, 2020; Janetzko, "Sine-Kino-Connection," 58.

111 Janetzko writes that various resources in Manila were enabling conditions for his workshops: "1) the presence of a local and experienced partner in film-education and production: the Mowelfund Film Institute; 2) the existence of a state-owned local film laboratory at the Philippine Information Agency (PIA), which strongly supported the workshop; 3) a mixture of participants ranging from beginners to those with some experience in independent film production including a few [who] already had some experience in experimental film; and finally 4) an environment that guaranteed freedom of expression (in contrast, due to strict censorship

regulations, only about half of the films of the same program could be shown in Singapore and Malaysia)." Janetzko, "Sine-Kino-Connection," 57.

112 Orellana notes that several of the films produced in Janetzko's collage-focused optical printing workshop used found footage from the same filmic sources (cf. Leyran's *Bugtong*, Regiben Romana's *Pilipinas* [1990], and Cesar Hernando's *Kalawang* [Rust] [1990]; the latter is also included in Kalampag's screening program). Orellana clarifies: "At the time, copyright was not a big issue, since they were outtakes and outcuts. An outtake is a 'no good' take, the takes you didn't use. [In contrast,] outcuts are trimmings from the take you did use, what was on the cutting room floor and eventually dumped in the garbage." Orellana, Skype interview with author.

113 James, *Most Typical Avant-Garde*, 18.

114 The biography of films as commodities resonates with Arjun Appadurai's meditation on "the social life of things," the disparate temporalities of capitalism and the "paths," "diversions," and "restrictions" that disrupt the expected flow of commodities. Appadurai, *Social Life of Things*, 17–25.

115 Fossati, *From Grain to Pixel*, 21. On their analog-to-digital transfer processes, see Espina, email to author, June 20, 2020.

116 Seno and Espina, "Kalampag Tracking Agency," 247.

117 Seno and Espina, "Kalampag Tracking Agency," 247.

118 Seno and Espina, personal interview with author.

119 Seno and Espina, personal interview with author.

120 Seno and Espina, personal interview with author.

121 Seno and Espina, personal interview with author.

122 Constrained by a budget that covered only Lumbera's and Harn's bus fare from Manila to Balete, Batangas, Lumbera asked his mother to approach the school about shooting the film there. Credited as "momyger" (a neologism combining "mommy" and "manager") in the film's end credits, Lumbera's mother (Susan J. Lumbera) asked the school kids and their teacher to participate in the film as a favor. In return, the production provided them with juice packs during the shoot as a small token of gratitude. When the film eventually won recognition at the CCP's Twenty-Third Alternative Film and Video competition in 2011 (Gawad CCP Para sa Alternatibong Pelikula at Video), Tito & Tito used their prize money to purchase an electric fan for the kids' classroom. G. Lumbera, emails to author, August 12, 2020; G. Lumbera, Zoom interview with author. This interview was conducted primarily in Filipino and Taglish.

123 Lumbera credits his brother for the original concept for *Class Picture*, since it was his brother who pointed out this puzzling aspect of class photographs. G. Lumbera, Zoom interview with author.

124 G. Lumbera, Zoom interview with author. The ISO rating, as determined by the International Organization for Standardization, refers to

photochemical film's sensitivity to light as a guide to correct exposure; digital still cameras are also assigned ISO ratings.

125 *Class Picture*'s sepia images of faceless students and their lone teacher recall Bill Morrison's compilation film *Decasia* (2002), which features deteriorated nitrate footage of what appear to be faceless children of color under the tutelage of nuns in a colonial schoolyard.

126 Seno and Espina, personal interview with author.

127 G. Lumbera, Zoom interview with author.

128 My translation of Lumbera's original Taglish remarks. G. Lumbera, Zoom interview with author.

129 G. Lumbera, Zoom interview with author.

130 G. Lumbera, Zoom interview with author.

131 Powers, "A DIY Come-On," 75.

132 G. Lumbera, email to author, August 19, 2020.

133 G. Lumbera, Zoom interview with author.

134 Lobato, *Shadow Economies of Cinema*, 4, 19.

135 Lobato, *Shadow Economies of Cinema*, 4.

136 Lobato, *Shadow Economies of Cinema*, 1.

137 Serreng, personal interview with author. Manila's film and television companies were longtime patrons of Video 48. During my two-hour weekday visit to Video 48 in August 2019, clients no longer rented media titles but rather routinely purchased inexpensive digital copies. The only other customer was a courier picking up a title for Tuko Film Productions, a prolific independent production outfit with ties to other Ortigas-owned media production, distribution, and exhibition companies, such as TBA studios and Cinema 76, a microcinema venue.

138 Lobato, *Shadow Economies of Cinema*, 41.

139 Lobato, *Shadow Economies of Cinema*, 51, 91.

140 Lobato, *Shadow Economies of Cinema*, 73–74. See also Krapp, "Hollywood's Piracy Problem."

141 Tolentino, "Piracy Regulation," 2. Laikwan Pang writes, "International copyright laws are major and powerful tools that perpetuate and reinforce the historically constructed uneven distribution of global wealth, as the developed world has become home to the intellectual property owners, while the developing world houses the users." Pang, "Piracy/Privacy," 111.

142 Lobato, *Shadow Economies of Cinema*, 89; Tran, "Piracy on the Ground," 51.

143 Baumgärtel, "Media Piracy," 13.

144 Tolentino, "Piracy Regulation," 2, 18–19.

145 Deligero, Skype interview with author, April 26, 2019.

146 Neves and Sarkar, "Introduction," 2, 8.

147 Liang, "Porous Legalities," 8, 10.

148 Herbert, *Videoland,* 3. In the United States, the rental giant Blockbuster Video began its decline in 2004 and declared bankruptcy in 2010. See McDonald, "From Online Video Store," 203–7.

149 Writing in the context of the United States, Greenberg explains that "according to the 'first sale' doctrine, retailers who purchased a movie on videotape and rented it to customers were not legally required to give the movie's makers a cut of their rental profits" (Greenberg, *From Betamax to Blockbuster*, 84). In the Philippines, Section 177.3 of the Intellectual Property Code stipulates that "the possessor of a lawful copy may only distribute the work without liability for violation of the copyright proprietor's distribution right but may not reproduce it or create a derivative work from it" (International Association for the Protection of Intellectual Property [AIPPI] Philippines et al., "Exhaustion Issues in Copyright Law"). In effect, the first sale doctrine mandates that a video store is allowed to sell or rent out the legal copy that it purchased, but it is not allowed to make more copies of it for commercial purposes outside of fair use.

150 Serreng, personal interview with author.

151 Serreng, personal interview with author.

152 Trice, *City of Screens*, 80. A premier "shopping and leisure district in the pre-mall era," Quiapo was an upscale movie theater district from the 1950s to the 1970s (Tolentino, "Piracy Regulation," 13). By 2004, however, Quiapo was the "most notorious" of all Metro Manila markets for pirated audiovisual discs (Baumgärtel, "Media Piracy," 11). The Philippine state has engaged in an explicit "racialization of media piracy" in its campaigns against Muslim Filipino DVD vendors, who are an ethnic minority in Catholic-majority Philippines. Tolentino, "Piracy Regulation," 1, 5.

153 Seno and Espina, personal interview with author.

154 Espina, email to author, March 5, 2020.

155 Straw, "Embedded Memories," 7.

156 Sarkar, "Media Piracy and the Terrorist," 359.

CHAPTER 6. BINISAYA

1 Trouillot, *Silencing the Past*, 55.

2 Throughout this book and in keeping with colloquial usage, I use *Manila* as shorthand for the National Capital Region (NCR), also known as Metro Manila. The National Capital Region consists of one municipality and sixteen cities, the City of Manila among them.

3 K. R. Tan, "Constituting Filmic and Linguistic Heritage," 148. On the variety of Philippine languages, see K. R. Tan, "Creating Ripples in Philippine Cinema," 37. As Teddy Co put it in a SOFIA lecture marking

the centennial of Philippine cinema, "In the first eighty years, Philippine cinema was a Tagalog cinema; but in the last twenty years, from 2000 onward until the present, Philippine cinema has branched out across the archipelago to include so many forms of filmmaking: full-length films, short films, student films, science films, video art, and so on. It's a very exciting period." Co, "Reconfiguring Philippine Cinema."

4 Grant, "Presenting Cebuano Cinema," 208.

5 National Assembly, Commonwealth Act No. 184; Quezon, Executive Order No. 134; E. S. Giron, "Tagalog Lurches On," 15. See B. C. Lim, "Sharon's Noranian Turn," 337–42, for a discussion of the national language wars of the 1960s and 1970s in relation to Philippine cinema.

6 Rafael, "Taglish, or the Phantom Power," 169; N. Tan, "What the PH Constitutions Say." English is designated an official language in the 1935, 1973, and 1987 Constitutions of the Philippines; it was excised in the 1943 Constitution under the Japanese occupation. For a discussion of the conflicted history of English in the Philippines, see D. Cruz, *Transpacific Femininities*, 13–14.

7 Del Mundo, "Philippine Cinema," 30–31, 40.

8 Co, "In Search of Philippine Regional Cinema," 18.

9 Deocampo, *Films from a "Lost" Cinema*, 3.

10 Grant, "Ang Pelikulang Binisaya," 73.

11 Deocampo, *Films from a "Lost" Cinema*, 12–34.

12 The four earliest surviving Visayan titles are *Badlis sa kinabuhi* (Destiny; dir. Leroy Salvador, 1969); *Aliyana ang engkantada* (Aliyana the enchantress; dir. Eugene Labella, 1974); *Ang Manok ni San Pedro* (St. Peter's rooster; dir. Joe Macachor, 1977); and *Matud Nila* (They said; dir. Leroy Salvador, 1991). Grant, email to author.

13 Grant, "Cinema Becoming Regional."

14 Grant, "Ang Pelikulang Binisaya," 75.

15 On the role of geography and the "city's presence" in cinema, see James, *Most Typical Avant-Garde*, 16, 18. Vernacular cinemas challenge Manila's privileged geocinematic centrality as the city whose spatiality is foregrounded by mainstream Tagalog movies. As explained by Teddy Co, "The Philippine movie industry has always been centered in Manila. All the major production companies, film distributors, processing laboratories, and post-production facilities are virtually clustered in the urban areas of Metro Manila. As such, the films produced cannot help but carry a strong Manila flavor, even if they have been shot in other parts of the country." Co, "In Search of Philippine Regional Cinema," 17.

16 Campos, "Binisaya, a New Generation," 215.

17 Campos, "Binisaya, a New Generation," 214–17. The 2011 Binisaya festival was co-organized by Anissimov via Sinekultura, an educational screening

program at the University of San Carlos Talamban. Grant has collaborated on two of Deligero's films, the short *Babylon* (2017) and the feature *A Short History of a Few Bad Things* (2018), for which Grant received story and screenwriter credits, respectively.

18 Campos, "Binisaya, a New Generation," 215; Groyon, "Cinemarehiyon 2009," 185. In addition to regional film festivals, academic institutions have emerged as the new hubs of vernacular filmmaking in regions outside Metro Manila. Groyon, "Cinemarehiyon 2009," 179–80, 194–95.

19 Deligero, email to author, March 9, 2021.

20 Deligero, email to author, March 9, 2021.

21 Caldwell, "Cultures of Production," 199–201.

22 Grant and Anissimov, *Lilas*, 9–10. The turn toward paracinematic ephemera extends beyond Binisaya film scholarship to other historiographies of Philippine cinema. See Deocampo, email to author.

23 Trouillot, *Silencing the Past*, 58.

24 Campos, "Small Film, Global Collections," 31; Grant, "Cinema Becoming Regional."

25 Grant, "Cinema Becoming Regional" (italics added).

26 Grant and Anissimov, *Lilas*, 15.

27 Higson, "Concept of National Cinema," 37–44.

28 Brown, "Crippled Cinema?," 267–68.

29 Grant and Anissimov, *Lilas*, 19.

30 Grant and Anissimov, *Lilas*, 19.

31 Deocampo, *Films from a "Lost" Cinema*, 13; Co, "In Search of Philippine Regional Cinema," 18.

32 Grant and Anissimov, *Lilas*, 21. See also K. Tan, "Constituting Filmic and Linguistic Heritage," 142–48, 160.

33 Groyon, "Cinemarehiyon 2009," 177–80, 195. Teddy Co, one of the prime movers of the Cinema Rehiyon film festival (a flagship project of the NCCA National Committee on Cinema, for which Co served as vice-head), self-reflexively critiqued the first two years of Cinema Rehiyon in 2009 and 2010. The festival's theme for both those years, "Alternatibo: Films from the Other Philippines," marginalized the very films Cinema Rehiyon purported to foreground. "Both festivals were held at the CCP in Manila, . . . a *Manila-centric* venue wherein the regional films were described as *the other*. . . . The idea was problematic already, and didn't sit well with some regional filmmakers. The implication here was that the *other* Philippines wasn't the true or real Philippines." Co, "Ten Years of Cinema Rehiyon."

34 Campos, "Topos, Historia, Islas," 161.

35 *Captive culture* is National Artist Resil Mojares's term for the "concentration" of "intellectual activity, political and administrative control, and economic and cultural policymaking" in Manila. Co's championing

of regional cinemas is inspired by Mojares's call to develop "alternative counter-centers" to Manila's hegemony. Mojares, "Decentralizing Culture," 90; Co, "In Search of Philippine Regional Cinema," 20.

36 Campos, "Binisaya, a New Generation," 218.

37 Grant, "Cebu's Black Sheep of God," 106.

38 Grant, "Cebu's Black Sheep of God," 103.

39 In *Shooting Iskalawags in Camotes* (dir. Neil Briones, 2013), Deligero reflects: "I don't know whether *Iskalawags* has a genre. All our movies don't have a genre."

40 My thanks to Keith Deligero for sharing *Shooting Iskalawags in Camotes* with me on Vimeo (https://vimeo.com/118051217/62eab20fd4). I am also grateful to Adonis Jurado and Joya Escobar for their help in translating and transcribing Deligero's remarks in *Shooting Iskalawags in Camotes* from Cebuano; I rely on their translation in addition to the documentary's English subtitles for my discussion.

41 My thanks to Erik Tuban for generously providing me with an English translation of his unpublished story "Kapayas," originally written in Cebuano. Tuban, "Kapayas."

42 Erik Tuban, author of the source story "Ang Kapayas," appears as the adult Intoy in *Iskalawags*. Osorio is credited as the film's producer, co-screenwriter, assistant director, and subtitler; Zuasola as co-screenwriter and production designer; and Briones as cinematographer and colorist. Deligero had multiple roles as director, co-screenwriter, director of photography, cinematographer, and voice actor for Intoy's voice-over narration. Briones, Deligero, and Osorio also worked as camera operators.

43 Deligero, interviewed in *Shooting Iskalawags in Camotes*.

44 Deligero, Skype interview with author and her undergraduate students.

45 The Visayan word *malinawon* means "peaceful."

46 With small exceptions, character exposition and nonchronological storytelling in *Iskalawags* are largely faithful to Tuban's source story, "Kapayas."

47 Deligero, Skype interview with author and her undergraduate students.

48 The "Hoy Valderama" scene in *Iskalawags* expands on a brief episode in "Kapayas" where the kids playact an action film scene in which a hero named Valderama is surrounded by enemies.

49 My thanks to Patrick Campos for helping me identify *Iskalawags*' allusions to specific Tagalog action movies.

50 Banayo, "Kapag Puno na Ang Salop."

51 Deligero, Zoom interview with author.

52 Deligero, Zoom interview with author.

53 Deligero, Skype interview with author and her undergraduate students. For a discussion of bootleg video cultures in North America, see Hilderbrand, *Inherent Vice*.

54 Deligero, Skype interview with author and her undergraduate students.

55 Deligero, Skype interview with author and her undergraduate students. In another conversation, Deligero credits the Philippines' digital indie filmmaking boom to piracy, since most indie filmmakers regularly watch pirated films, listen to illicitly downloaded music, and edit their films on unlicensed software. Deligero reflects that piracy enabled his own informal cinematic education, allowing him to see otherwise inaccessible films, and speculates that bootlegged media was likewise a vital influence on other Philippine filmmakers. Deligero, Skype interview with author.

56 Deligero, Skype interview with author.

57 Deligero, Skype interview with author and her undergraduate students.

58 Deligero, Skype interview with author.

59 Deligero, Skype interview with author.

60 The monthlong annual celebration of Tagalog-based Filipino as the national language was established by Proclamation 1041, a 1997 presidential decree by Fidel V. Ramos.

61 The Rice Pledge was introduced via Proclamation 494 by President Benigno Aquino III in 2012. See B. S. Aquino, Proclamation No. 494; Department of Agriculture, Philippine Rice Research Institute, "President Aquino Proclaims 2013 as National Year of Rice."

62 Deligero recalls that Liklik's Rice Pledge "was improvised, it was not part of the script. When we were shooting, I discovered that this was a new thing that the kids are required to do, to train them not to waste rice." The director added the scene because it fit in with other scenes of oration, "the delivery of language to the public." Deligero, Skype interview with author and her undergraduate students.

63 There is no explicit spatial setting in Tuban's short story "Kapayas," but according to Deligero, Tuban had the province of Negros Oriental in mind. Deligero, Zoom interview with author.

64 F. E. Marcos, Proclamation No. 1374.

65 Deligero wryly observes, "There goes Bulldog, rehearsing, talking to nobody. . . . He was just wearing slippers and a *barong*." Deligero, Skype interview with author and her undergraduate students.

66 Deligero, Skype interview with author and her undergraduate students.

67 Deligero, Skype interview with author and her undergraduate students.

68 Campos, *End of National Cinema*, 279–81; Zafra, "Building an Audience," 68–69.

69 Campos, "Binisaya, a New Generation," 219.

70 Deligero, qtd. in Grant, "Cebu's Black Sheep of God," 109.

71 *A Short History of* BINISAYA (Archipelago, 2020), https://vimeo.com/383804036. In that video, Deligero explains that the Binisaya movement originated as a small, filmmaker-organized "group exhibit" at an art gallery in Cebu City, featuring three short films, all made in 2009: *Uwan Init*

Pista Sa Langit (Sun showers on Earth, a feast in heaven), codirected by Deligero and Zuasola; Zuasola's *Mga Damgo* (Dreams); and de los Reyes's *Yawyaw* (Murmur). According to the *Philippine Star,* the first Binisaya exhibition was held on October 30, 2009, at Turtle's Nest Book Café and Art Gallery in Cebu City (*Philippine Star*, "Cinemarehiyon"). *A Short History of BINISAYA*, https://vimeo.com/383804036.

72 *A Short History of BINISAYA*.

73 Deligero, qtd. in Campos, "Binisaya, a New Generation," 217.

74 Deligero, Skype interview with author and her undergraduate students.

75 Deligero, qtd. in Campos, "Binisaya, a New Generation," 215.

76 Chawdhury, qtd. in Campos, "Binisaya, a New Generation," 219.

77 Grant, "Presenting Cebuano Cinema," 211–12.

78 Deligero, Skype interview with author and her undergraduate students.

79 Deligero, qtd. in Campos, "Binisaya, a New Generation," 215.

80 Trice, *City of Screens*, 21.

81 Deligero, qtd. in Campos, "Binisaya, a New Generation," 215.

82 Deligero, qtd. in Campos, "Binisaya, a New Generation," 219.

83 Deligero, Zoom interview with author.

84 Sing, "STOP/10."

85 Deligero, Zoom interview with author.

86 Deligero, Zoom interview with author.

87 *Shooting Iskalawags in Camotes*; Deligero, email to author, February 18, 2021.

88 Deligero, Zoom interview with author.

89 K. R. Tan, email to author.

90 Deligero, Zoom interview with author.

91 The two kids are briefly seen in *Binisaya sa San Francisco*, a YouTube video documenting the 2012 Binisaya screening in San Francisco, Camotes Islands (https://www.youtube.com/watch?v=52FPqEqKaow&list=PLBD06E5CF11B33FC5&index=15).

92 Deligero, Zoom interview with author.

93 Deligero speaks of "the challenge we face in our Binisaya screenings. It's hard to show local audiences movies about themselves because these are movies about what they already know. They think, 'Why should I watch what I live every day?'" He reflects that realistic stories about Cebuano life can become "challenging and boring" for local audiences because they lack escapist pleasure. Deligero, email to author, February 18, 2021.

94 *Shooting Iskalawags in Camotes.*

95 Deligero, email to author, February 18, 2021.

96 Deligero, Zoom interview with author.

97 Deligero, Zoom interview with author.

98 Deligero, Zoom interview with author.

99 Deligero, Zoom interview with author.

100 Deligero, Zoom interview with author.

101 Deligero, Zoom interview with author.

102 Deligero, Skype interview with author and her undergraduate students.

103 This is the author's English translation of a line from Tolentino's paper for a 2008 Cinemalaya film congress. The Filipino original reads: "*Ang indie films ay mga pelikulang naghahanap ng audience.*" Tolentino, "Mga Leksyon Mula sa Political Film Collectives" (Lessons for indie cinema from political film collectives).

104 This is the author's English translation of Tolentino's Filipino original, which reads: "*Ipalabas ito sa mga lugar na walang lubos na akses sa indie films pero may demand para sa alternatibong kwento ng panlipunang buhay.*" Tolentino, "Mga Leksyon Mula sa Political Film Collectives" (Lessons for indie cinema from political film collectives).

105 Chawdhury, qtd. in Campos, "Binisaya, a New Generation," 219.

106 Campos, *End of National Cinema*, 218.

107 Belarmino, Zoom interview with author.

108 Villarama, "Current Film Distribution Trends," 101.

109 In an interview for the Singapore-based blog *SINdie*, Deligero wryly muses: "I'm not very comfortable using the term 'independent,' [since] from what I've learned every film is very 'dependent' on a certain budget regardless of how big or small it is. It will also be dependent on the people you make the film with. So maybe I'm more into 'dependent' filmmaking [laughs]." Deligero qtd. in Sing, "STOP/10."

110 Deligero, Zoom interview with author.

111 For a discussion of the fallout from a 2009 dispute between the FDCP, a Cebuano theater chain, and the city government of Cebu, see Grant, "Ang Pelikulang Binisaya," 78–81; Grant and Anissimov, *Lilas*, 29.

112 K. R. Tan, "Constituting Filmic and Linguistic Heritage," 154–55.

113 Villarama, "Current Film Distribution Trends," 101.

114 K. R. Tan, "Constituting Filmic and Linguistic Heritage," 154–56.

115 K. R. Tan, "Creating Ripples in Philippine Cinema," 41.

116 Villarama, "Current Film Distribution Trends," 102.

117 My thanks to Keith Deligero for giving me access to *Iskalawags*, *Shooting Iskalawags in Camotes*, and *A Short History of BINISAYA* on VimeoPro; these titles have never been commercially released outside of cable broadcasts. I am grateful to Patrick Campos for facilitating my email introduction to Deligero.

118 K. R. Tan "Constituting Filmic and Linguistic Heritage," 156–58. As previously mentioned, the reduction or elimination of the amusement tax is a long-running demand that has been voiced by several generations of film scholars and industry advocates. See Tiongson, "Filipino Film Industry," 45; Villarama, "Current Film Distribution Trends," 105.

119 K. R. Tan, "Constituting Filmic and Linguistic Heritage," 154–58.

120 Campos, "Small Film, Global Collections," 30; see also Villarama, "Current Film Distribution Trends," 100.

121 Villarama, "Current Film Distribution Trends," 102.

122 Tiongson, "Rise of the Philippine New Wave," 14.

123 Mendoza, qtd. in Baumgärtel, "Inexpensive Film Should Start," 163.

124 Deligero, Skype interview with author and her undergraduate students.

125 Tuban, "Kapayas."

126 Deligero, Skype interview with author and her undergraduate students.

127 Tuban, "Kapayas."

128 Deligero, *A Short History of* BINISAYA.

129 Deligero continued with an analogy: "It's like you go to the coast to buy fresh fish from the fishermen, with no agent and no middleman, so that the fishermen can benefit. [*Kana ganing muadto ka sa coast para magpalit ng isda sa mga mangingisda. Ana siya ka* fresh, *na walay* agent, *walay* middle man *nga maka*-benefit *ang* fishermen.] That's the future of Philippine cinema." Binisaya 2020 closing ceremony, accessed March 7, 2021, https://www.youtube.com/watch?v=Pyjn6_08TCE&list=PLQmm54mwdx5ZRyv4lxHAYCFQXymziY8Kh&index=3.

130 Deligero, Zoom interview with author.

131 Deocampo, *Films from a "Lost" Cinema.*

132 K. R. Tan, "Constituting Filmic and Linguistic Heritage," 145–46.

133 K. R. Tan, "Creating Ripples in Philippine Cinema," 43.

134 Deocampo, *Films from a "Lost" Cinema.*

135 Deligero, qtd. in Campos, "Binisaya, a New Generation," 220.

136 Deligero, Zoom interview with author.

137 Trice, *City of Screens*, 11, 18–19, 21.

138 Trice, *City of Screens*, 38, 113–14.

139 Deligero, Zoom interview with author.

EPILOGUE. OF AUDIENCES AND ARCHIVAL PUBLICS

The analysis of *Pepot Artista* in this chapter draws on an earlier version in a different form, "Pepot and the Archive: Cinephilia and the Archive Crisis of Philippine Cinema," a short essay that appeared in *Flow* 12, no. 3 (July 2, 2010), https://www.flowjournal.org/.

1 Lacaba, "Notes on Bakya," 117. Lacaba's essay was originally published in the *Philippines Free Press* on January 31, 1970.

2 Espiritu "National Allegory," 48, 52. Patrick Campos writes: "Protectionism, of course, is not a real option in the current . . . state of affairs, given the 'free' trade agreements by which the Philippine economy is bound. As such, the liberalization of film imports, especially of American movies,

perpetuates cultural imperialism and the continued exportation of profit to foreign producers without clear returns for Philippine cinema." Campos, *End of National Cinema*, 278.

3 Daroy, "Main Currents," 58.

4 Brocka, "Philippine Movies," 260–61. Brocka's essay was originally published in *Manila Review* in October 1974.

5 Tioseco writes, "I wish we focused our attention more on audience education, development, and literacy than on dumbing down films to pander to them." Tioseco, "Letter I Would Love."

6 Brocka, "Philippine Movies," 261.

7 On *indie cinema*, see Campos, *End of National Cinema*, 221–35. The oxymoronic label "maindie" refers to indie film productions that aspire to broad mainstream success and commercial profitability. ABS-CBN News, "'Maindie' Movies Combine Edge, Relevance."

8 Campos, *End of National Cinema*, 277.

9 Zafra, "Building an Audience," 71.

10 Drawing on urban studies, Trice characterizes Metro Manila as a "revanchist city," that is, a city that is punitive toward the impoverished majority of its denizens. An analog to Manila as a revanchist city is the shopping mall multiplex, which Trice sees as a revanchist cinema that attempts to exclude undesirable, nonbourgeois audiences. Trice, *City of Screens*, chap. 1.

11 Campos, *End of National Cinema*, 279–81. Similarly, Jessica Zafra describes Cinemalaya's niche market as composed of "college and high school students, young professionals, members of the arts and film sector, and expatriates." Zafra, "Building an Audience," 68–69.

12 Trice, *City of Screens*, 124–38.

13 Q and A Zoom discussion for B. C. Lim, "Informal Archival Flows: Kalampag Tracking Agency and Video 48."

14 Deligero, Zoom interview with author.

15 Usai, *Silent Cinema*, vii–viii.

16 Del Mundo, *Dreaming of a National*. Around the same period that del Mundo was writing, the Digital Cinema Initiative (DCI), established by major Hollywood players in 2002, issued joint technical specifications for digital cinema in 2005 and revised them in 2007. The DCI's specifications inaugurated a gradual but decisive shift in archival film practice worldwide. In the Philippines and elsewhere, more and more restored films would be encrypted for distribution as a Digital Cinema Package (DCP). Fossati, *From Grain to Pixel*, 57–59.

17 Del Mundo, *Dreaming of a National*, 3.

18 This was a high-profile international collaboration between the NFAP/FDCP, Martin Scorsese's World Cinema Project, the Cineteca di Bologna/L'Immagine Ritrovata Laboratory, and local stakeholders (LVN,

Cinema Artist Philippines, and Mike de Leon), with funding from the Qatar-based Doha Film Institute. Asian Film Archive, "Restored: Manila in the Claws of Light," accessed March 14, 2021, https://www.asianfilmarchive.org/event-calendar/restored-manila-in-the-claws-of-light-maynila-sa-mga-kuko-ng-liwanag-1975/.

19 ABS-CBN Film Archives, "ABS-CBN Inventories."

20 Patino, "From Colonial Policy," 42–44, 61–62.

21 Warner, *Publics and Counterpublics*, 8. Warner argues that the understanding of oneself as a member of specific publics happens constantly. At the same time, however, the idea of the public goes largely unrecognized as a "fictional" type of "social imaginary." Warner, *Publics and Counterpublics*, 12.

22 Warner, *Publics and Counterpublics*, 11–12.

23 "All discourse or performance addressed to a public must characterize the world in which it attempts to circulate, projecting for that world a concrete and livable shape, and attempting to realize that world through address" (Warner, "Publics and Counterpublics," 81). Warner's discussion recalls Michel Foucault's analysis of the rules and enunciative modalities that regulate discursive formations. Above all I am reminded of Foucault's concept of discourse as not so much the expression of a unified subjectivity but a "field of regularity" in which various positions of a dispersed subject can be located. Foucault, *Archeology of Knowledge*, 38, 53–55.

24 See Warner, *Publics and Counterpublics*, 16, 51.

25 Havens and Lotz, *Understanding Media Industries*, 113.

26 Warner, "Publics and Counterpublics," 82.

27 Warner, *Publics and Counterpublics*, 17–18.

28 Warner, "Publics and Counterpublics," 64.

29 Warner, "Publics and Counterpublics," 62.

30 Russell, *Archiveology*, 1.

31 Warner, "Publics and Counterpublics," 63–64.

32 Russell, *Archiveology*, 27.

33 Elsaesser, "Cinephilia," 40.

34 As in *T-Bird at Ako*, queer valences underwrite *Pepot Artista*, which exemplifies a campy mode of temporal drag similar to that theorized by Elizabeth Freeman in *Time Binds*. A queer reading of *Pepot Artista* is explored in B. C. Lim, "Pepot and the Archive."

35 Campos, *End of National Cinema*, 222. According to the Bangko Sentral of the Philippines (BSP) database, the US dollar to Philippine foreign exchange rate in July 2005 (when *Pepot Artista* was released) averaged 56.1 pesos to the dollar. The film's seed grant of 500,000 pesos would have amounted to less than US$9,000, not adjusted for inflation.

36 Del Mundo, email to author. While Alexander Street allowed US viewers to access *Pepot Artista*, Iflix made the movie available to audiences in

the Philippines. "Asia Pacific Films Joins Forces with Alexander Street Press," *Alexander Street*, October 31, 2012, https://alexanderstreet.com/content/asia-pacific-films-joins-forces-alexander-street-press; and Iflix, "Watch Cinemalaya Classics on Iflix," Facebook post dated July 30, 2019, https://www.facebook.com/iflixPH/photos/a.737328119713663/2354273178019141/?type=3.

37 Betacam is a half-inch professional analog videocassette carrier introduced by Sony in 1982.

38 Del Mundo, email to author.

39 NFAP, *NFAP Annual Report 2011–2012*, 8–9. U-matic is a three-quarter-inch videocassette format first marketed by Sony in 1971; a high-band broadcast U-matic format was introduced in the 1980s. The Library of Congress has significant U-matic holdings for access copies and proofs of copyright.

40 Hilderbrand, "Cinematic Promiscuity," 214.

41 Sturken, "Paradox in the Evolution," 103–5, 120–21.

42 In archives, Betamax, VHS, and three-quarter-inch U-matic tapes, as well as their respective (commercially unavailable) playback technologies, are analog media artifacts as carefully preserved as celluloid. During a visit to the archives of the MOWELFUND Institute in 2005, I vividly recall seeing a roomful of old audiovisual equipment that had been cannibalized for parts to keep a single U-matic videocassette deck in working condition. In subsequent years, however, MOWELFUND either donated or sold its remaining U-matic players and outsourced the migration of titles in that format to the FDCP or other postproduction companies such as Central Digital Lab. Orellana, Skype interview with author.

43 Warner, "Publics and Counterpublics," 50, 52, 82.

44 Warner, "Publics and Counterpublics," 77.

45 *Pepot*'s emphases on fandom and the devoted following surrounding star Nora Aunor recall a short documentary film also directed by del Mundo, *Superfan* (2009), about Armando "Mandy" Diaz Jr., Nora Aunor's best-known fan.

46 Tirso Cruz III was appointed FDCP chair by President Bongbong Marcos in July 2022; the Philippine Film Archive (PFA) is a division of the FDCP. Thus, in an unforeseen coincidence, Cruz, featured in the archiveological film *Pepot Artista* in 2005, seventeen years later became the government official in charge of the national film archive.

47 *Pepot Artista*'s broad humor causes some of its jokes to fall flat. A puzzling, possibly offensive sound motif underscores one character's disability: creaking nondiegetic noises on the soundtrack punctuate the idiosyncratic sign language the family uses to communicate with Pepot's deaf older brother, Juancho (Jian Pascual).

48 Warner, "Publics and Counterpublics," 88–89.

49 Warner, "Publics and Counterpublics," 89.
50 Society of Filipino Archivists for Film, SOFIA Microlearning Series.
51 Edmondson, "National Film and Sound Archive," 236–48.
52 Edmondson, "National Film and Sound Archive," 105.
53 Edmondson, "National Film and Sound Archive," 47.
54 Grant, "Presenting Cebuano Cinema," 212.

BIBLIOGRAPHY

Abad, Michelle. "Lookback: The Diliman Commune of 1971." *Rappler*, February 1, 2021. https://www.rappler.com/newsbreak/iq/lookback-what-happened-up-diliman-commune-1971.

Abad, Michelle. "Timeline: Duterte against ABS-CBN's Franchise Renewal." *Rappler*, January 17, 2020. https://rappler.com/newsbreak/iq/timeline-duterte-against-abs-cbn-franchise-renewal.

Abramson, Daniel, Arindam Dutta, Timothy Hude, and Jonathan Massey for Aggregate. "Introduction." In Aggregate, *Governing by Design: Architecture, Economy, and Politics in the Twentieth Century*, pp. vii–xvi. Pittsburgh: University of Pittsburgh Press, 2012.

ABS-CBN Corporate: Businesses, Corporate Structure, Business Segments. Accessed July 30, 2018. http://corporate.abs-cbn.com/businesses.

ABS-CBN Corporate: Our Leadership. Accessed July 14, 2023. http://corporate.abs-cbn.com/about-us/our-leadership.

ABS-CBN Corporate: Our Organization. Accessed July 30, 2018. http://corporate.abs-cbn.com/about-us/organization.

ABS-CBN Entertainment. "Nora Confesses She Had a Crush on Vilma." February 22, 2015. https://www.youtube.com/watch?v=qv54nGo20Ak&feature=youtu.be.

ABS-CBN Film Archives. "ABS-CBN Inventories as of March 2018: Restored Titles." Accessed via email from Julie Galino, March 27, 2018.

ABS-CBN News. "ABS-CBN Shutdown, 3 Years Later." May 5, 2023. https://news.abs-cbn.com/spotlight/05/05/23/abs-cbn-shutdown-3-years-later.

ABS-CBN News. "'Maindie' Movies Combine Edge, Relevance." August 12, 2012. https://news.abs-cbn.com/lifestyle/08/22/12/'maindie'-movies-combine-edge-relevance.

Acland, Charles. "Introduction." In Acland, *Residual Media*, xiii–xxvii.

Acland, Charles, ed. *Residual Media*. Minneapolis: University of Minnesota Press, 2007.

Addelson, Kathryn Pyne. "Knower/Doers and Their Moral Problems." In *Feminist Epistemologies*, edited by Linda Alcoff and Elizabeth Potter, 265–94. New York: Routledge, 1993.

Aguilar, Filomeno V. "Political Conjuncture and Scholarly Disjunctures: Reflections on Studies of the Philippine State under Marcos." *Philippine Studies: Historical and Ethnographic Viewpoints* 67, no. 1 (2019): 3–30.

Alvarez, Pantaleon D., et al. House Bill 6595. An Act Recognizing the Civil Partnership of Couples, Providing for Their Rights and Obligations. Seventeenth Congress, Republic of the Philippines House of Representatives. October 10, 2017. https://issuances-library.senate.gov.ph/bills/house-bill-no-6595–17th-congress-republic.

Alzona, Rodel. "NFAP Looks to Restore 10 Classic Filipino Films This Year Using Swedish Technology." *Business Mirror*, June 18, 2016. https://businessmirror.com.ph/nfap-looks-to-restore-10-classic-filipino-films-this-year-using-swedish-technology/.

Anderson, Benedict. "Cacique Democracy in the Philippines: Origins and Dreams." In *Discrepant Histories: Translocal Essays on Filipino Cultures*, edited by Vicente L. Rafael, 3–47. Philadelphia: Temple University Press, 1995.

Anderson, Chris. *The Long Tail: Why the Future of Business Is Selling Less of More.* New York: Hyperion, 2006.

Appadurai, Arjun, ed. *The Social Life of Things: Commodities in Cultural Perspective.* Cambridge: Cambridge University Press, 1986.

Appadurai, Arjun. "Consumption, Duration, and History." In *Streams of Cultural Capital: Transnational Cultural Studies*, edited by David Palumbo-Liu and Hans Ulrich Gumbrecht, 23–45. Stanford, CA: Stanford University Press, 1997.

"Appendix B: Program for the Ceremonies, Alay at Pamana, April 17, 1966." In Baluyut, *Institutions and Icons of Patronage*, 97–99.

Aquino, Benigno S., Jr. *A Garrison State in the Make and Other Speeches.* Makati, Philippines: Benigno S. Aquino, Jr. Foundation, 1985.

Aquino, Benigno S., III. Administrative Order No. 26: "Prescribing the Rules on the Deposit of Copies of Films and Other Audio-Visuals to the National Film Archive of the Philippines." *Official Gazette*, April 17, 2012. http://www.officialgazette.gov.ph/2012/04/17/administrative-order-no-26-s-2012/.

Aquino, Benigno S., III. Proclamation No. 494: "Declaring the Year 2013 as the National Year of Rice and Directing the Department of Agriculture to Lead Its Celebration." *Official Gazette*, October 18, 2012. https://www.officialgazette.gov.ph/2012/10/18/proclamation-no-494-s-2012/.

Aquino, Corazon C. Executive Order No. 100: "Creating the Philippine Information Agency." *Official Gazette*, December 24, 1986. http://www.officialgazette.gov.ph/1986/12/24/executive-order-no-100-s-1986/.

Aquino, Corazon C. Memorandum Order No. 2: "Creating a Task Force to Oversee and to Take Charge of All Film-Related Government Agencies." March 5, 1986. http://www.gov.ph/1986/03/05/memorandum-order-no-2-s-1986/.

Aquino, Corazon C. Memorandum Order No. 274: "Providing for the Composition of the Task Force to Oversee and Take Charge of All Film-Related

Government Agencies Created under Memorandum No. 2, Series of 1986, and Clarifying Its Duties and Functions." *Official Gazette*, January 9, 1990. http://www.officialgazette.gov.ph/1990/01/09/memorandum-order-no-274-s-1990/.

Aquino, Corazon C. "State of the Nation Address 1988: Corazon Aquino." Inquirer.net, July 7, 2015. http://sona.inquirer.net/113/state-of-the-nation-address-1988-corazon-aquino/.

Aragones, Liberty D. Email to PIA-MISD Library and Archives section head Maria Victoria Bejerano, Re: Request for a copy of issuance, re: MPD dissolution, April 12, 2017. Forwarded to author by Maria Victoria Bejerano on May 29, 2017.

Arnold, Sarah. "Netflix and the Myth of Choice/Participation/Autonomy." In McDonald and Smith-Rowsey, *The Netflix Effect*, 49–62.

Arondekar, Anjali. *For the Record: On Sexuality and the Colonial Archive in India*. Durham, NC: Duke University Press, 2009.

ASEAN Seminar on Film and Video Archive Management. Report on Asean Seminar on Film and Video Archive Management. May 8–June 3, 1995.

Aspiras, Jose D. "Marcos: 'Destined by Fate.'" *Examiner*, October 31, 1965.

Avendaño, Christine O. "Final Cut: Film 'Rescue' Unit among Casualties of ABS-CBN Shutdown." *Philippine Daily Inquirer*, July 19, 2020.

Avendaño, Winifred. Phone conversation with author, November 24, 2014.

Baldoza, Jonathan. "Simon Santos: The Man behind a Film Haven." *Rappler*, May 22, 2012. https://www.rappler.com/life-and-style/5712-movies-simon-santos-the-man-behind-a-haven.

Baluyut, Pearlie Rose S. *Institutions and Icons of Patronage: Arts and Culture in the Philippines during the Marcos Years, 1965–1986*. Manila: University of Santo Tomas Publishing House, 2012.

Banayo, Lito. "Kapag Puno na Ang Salop: The President Has Had Enough." *Manila Standard*, November 21, 2018.

Barthes, Roland. *Camera Lucida: Reflections on Photography*. Translated by Richard Howard. New York: Hill and Wang, 1981.

Barthes, Roland. *Roland Barthes by Roland Barthes*. Translated by Richard Howard. Berkeley: University of California Press, 1977.

Baumgärtel, Tilman. "An Inexpensive Film Should Start with an Inexpensive Story: Interview with Brilliante Mendoza and Armando Bing Lao." In *Southeast Asian Independent Cinema: Essays, Documents, Interviews*, edited by Tilman Baumgärtel, 155–70. Hong Kong: Hong Kong University Press, 2012.

Baumgärtel, Tilman, ed. *Kinosine: Philippine-German Cinema Relations*. Manila: Goethe-Institut Philippenen, 2007. http://www.goethe.de/ins/ph/pro/ksi/kinosine.pdf?wt_sc=kinosine.

Baumgärtel, Tilman. "Media Piracy: An Introduction." In *A Reader on International Media Piracy: Pirate Essays*, edited by Tilman Baumgärtel, 9–23. Amsterdam: Amsterdam University Press, 2015.

Baumgärtel, Tilman. "The Sine-Kino-Connection: Philippine-German Cinema Relations." In Baumgärtel, *Kinosine*, 8–18.

Bautista, Mario. "Nora Had an Affair with a Lesbian Named Portia Ilagan?" *Showbiz Portal,* January 2011. http://www.showbiz-portal.com/2011/01/nora-aunor-had-affair-with-lesbian.html.

Bazin, André. "The Ontology of the Photographic Image." *Film Quarterly* 13, no. 4 (Summer 1960): 4–9.

Bejerano, Maria Victoria. Email to author, Fwd: Letter to NFAP for Bliss Lim's book publication project, March 24, 2017.

Bejerano, Maria Victoria. Email to author, Re: Draft of book chapter on PIA, July 18, 2023.

Bejerano, Maria Victoria. Email to author, Re: Revised article and documents requested, February 15, 2018.

Bejerano, Maria Victoria. Personal interview with author, Philippine Information Agency, Quezon City, Philippines, September 9, 2014.

Bejerano, Maria Victoria, and Belina Capul. Personal interview and feedback meeting with author, Management Information Systems Division, Philippine Information Agency, Quezon City, Philippines, February 8, 2018.

Belarmino, Victoria. Email to author, Re: Research query, March 7, 2017.

Belarmino, Victoria. Zoom interview with author, February 22, 2021.

Belk, Russell W. "Collectors and Collecting." In *Interpreting Objects and Collections*, edited by Susan M. Pearce, 317–26. London: Routledge, 1994.

Bello, Walden, David Kinely, and Elaine Elinson. *Development Debacle: The World Bank in the Philippines.* San Francisco: Institute for Food and Development Policy, 1982.

Benedicto, Bobby. "Queer Space in the Ruins of Dictatorship Architecture." *Social Text* 31, no. 4 (Winter 2013): 25–47.

Benedicto, Bobby. *Under Bright Lights: Gay Manila and the Global Scene.* Minneapolis: University of Minnesota Press, 2014.

Benigno, Nena C., and P. A. Zapanta. "The 'Instant' Film Center." *Weekend,* February 21, 1982.

Benjamin, Walter. "A Short History of Photography." Translated by Phil Patton. *Artforum* 15, no. 6 (February 1977): 46–51.

Benjamin, Walter. "Unpacking My Library: A Talk about Book Collecting." In *Illuminations,* edited and with an introduction by Hannah Arendt, 59–68. 1968. Reprint, New York: Schocken Books, 1985.

Besser, Howard. "Digital Preservation of Moving Image Material?" *Moving Image* 1, no. 2 (Fall 2001): 39–55.

Bigourdan, Jean-Louis. "Vinegar Syndrome: An Action Plan." In *The Vinegar Syndrome: Prevention, Remedies and the Use of New Technologies—A Handbook*, 1–7. Bologna, Italy: GAMMA Group, 2000. Accessed October 8, 2017. http://www.imagepermanenceinstitute.org/sub_pages/action-plan.pdf.

BNFI [Bureau of National and Foreign Information] et al. "BNFI/UNESCO/CAPREFIL Final Report: First Conference Cataloguing and Preservation of Filipino Films." Unpublished typescript. August 31, 1977. Margaret Herrick Library, Los Angeles.

Bonnard, Martin. "Melies' Voyage Restoration: Or, The Risk of Being Stuck in the Digital Reconstruction." *Moving Image* 16, no. 1 (Spring 2016): 139–47.

Bordwell, David. *Pandora's Digital Box: Films, Files, and the Future of Movies.* Madison, WI: Irvington Way Institute Press, 2012.

Bordwell, David, Kristin Thompson, and Jeff Smith. *Film Art: An Introduction.* 11th ed. New York: McGraw Hill, 2017.

Borer, Michael Ian. "From Collective Memory to Collective Imagination: Time, Place, and Urban Redevelopment." *Symbolic Interaction* 33, no. 1 (Winter 2010): 96–114.

Borges, Jorge Luis. "The Library of Babel." In *Collected Fictions*, translated by Andrew Hurley, 112–18. New York: Penguin, 1998.

Bozak, Nadia. "Salvage Ethnography and the Exoticisation of Decay in Peter Delpeut's Lyrical Nitrate and Bill Morrison's Decasia." In *Beyond the Screen: Institutions, Networks and Publics of Early Cinema*, edited by Marta Braun, Charlie Keil, Rob King, Paul Moore, and Louis Pelletier, 200–206. New Barnet, UK: John Libbey, 2012.

Brocka, Lino. "Philippine Movies: Some Problems and Prospects" (1974). In *Readings in Philippine Cinema*, edited by Rafael Guerrero, 259–62. Manila: Experimental Cinema of the Philippines, 1983.

Brown, Matthew H. "The Crippled Cinema of a Crippled Nation? Preliminary Notes on Nollywood and the Nigerian State." In *Auteuring Nollywood: Critical Perspectives on "The Figurine,"* edited by Adeshina Afolayan, 257–97. Ibadan, Nigeria: Ibadan University Press, 2014.

Bruno, Giuliana. *Streetwalking on a Ruined Map: Cultural Theory and the Films of Elvira Notari.* Princeton, NJ: Princeton University Press, 1993.

Buan, Lian. "During Pandemic, Supreme Court Favors Duterte Twice and Makes Others Wait." *Rappler*, August 10, 2020. https://rappler.com/newsbreak/in-depth/supreme-court-pandemic-performance-track-record.

Buan, Lian. "Duterte Rejects Alliance with Lakas Because 'Marcos Is a Weak Leader.'" *Rappler*, November 19, 2021. https://www.rappler.com/nation/elections/duterte-speech-november-18-bongbong-marcos-weak-leader/.

Buan, Lian. "Killed and Shuttered ABS-CBN Gets No Help from Supreme Court." *Rappler*, August 25, 2020. https://rappler.com/nation/supreme-court-junks-abs-cbn-petition-ntc-moot.

Bulletin Today. "Film Center's Sixth Floor Falls; At Least 3 Dead." November 18, 1981.

Business Day. "Film Center Collapses; 20 Workers Feared Dead." November 18, 1981.

Butler, Judith. "Gender Is Burning: Questions of Appropriation and Subversion." In *Dangerous Liaisons: Gender, Nation, and Postcolonial Perspectives*, edited by Anne McClintock, Aamir Mufti, and Ella Shohat, 381–95. Minneapolis: University of Minnesota Press, 1997.

Butler, Judith. *Gender Trouble: Feminism and the Subversion of Identity*. New York: Routledge, 1999.

Cabato, Regine. "The State of Culture under Duterte." *CNN Philippines*, August 3, 2017. http://cnnphilippines.com/life/culture/arts/2017/08/03/the-state-of-culture-under-duterte-katrina-stuart-santiago.html.

Caldwell, John T. "Cultures of Production: Studying Industry's Deep Texts, Reflexive Rituals, and Managed Self-Disclosures." In *Media Industries, History, Theory, and Method*, edited by Jennifer Holt and Alisa Perren, 199–212. Malden, MA: Wiley-Blackwell, 2009.

Campos, Patrick F. "Binisaya, a New Generation of Cebuano Filmmakers: An Interview with Keith Deligero and Ara Chawdhury." *Plaridel: A Philippine Journal of Communication, Media, and Society* 14, no. 1 (January–June 2017): 213–20.

Campos, Patrick F. "Early Cinema History and the Emergence of 'Filipino' Film." *Plaridel: A Philippine Journal of Communication, Media, and Society* 10, no. 1 (February 2013): 82–88.

Campos, Patrick F. Email to Author, July 18, 2020.

Campos, Patrick F. *The End of National Cinema: Filipino Film at the Turn of the Century*. Diliman, Quezon City: University of the Philippines Press, 2016.

Campos, Patrick F. "Small Film, Global Collections." In Japan Foundation, Manila, *Art Archive 02*, 28–35. Manila: Japan Foundation, Manila, 2019.

Campos, Patrick F. "Topos, Historia, Islas: Film Islands and Regional Cinemas." *Journal of Cinema and Media Studies* 60, no. 3 (Spring 2021): 163–68.

Camus, Albert. *The Myth of Sisyphus and Other Essays*. Translated by Justin O'Brian. New York: Knopf, 1955.

Canlas, Jomar. "ABS-CBN Lays Off 4,000 Workers." *Manila Times*, September 1, 2020. https://www.manilatimes.net/2020/09/01/news/national/abs-cbn-lays-off-4000-workers/762021/.

Cantor, Libay Linsangan. "To Conform or Not to Conform, That Is the Gender-Queer Question: Re-examining the Lesbian Identity in Bernal's 'Manila by Night.'" *Kritika Kultura* 19 (2012): 90–114.

Capul, Belina. "Annex 1: Toward a National Film Archive for the Philippines." Paper presented at the Workshop/Consultative Meeting on the Development Plan for AV Archiving in the Region: The ASEAN Catalogue of Film and Television Productions. Quezon City, Philippines, December 1–5, 1997.

Capul, Belina. Email to author, Re: Revised article and documents requested, February 19, 2018.

Capul, Belina. "Evolving a National Focus Point for AV Archiving." Unpublished conference paper, 2000. Personal papers of Victoria Belarmino and Mary del Pilar.

Capul, Belina. Letter to LVN Pictures general manager Nenita Eraña, May 9, 2007. Dilimon, Quezon City, (PIA–MISD) Archive.
Capul, Belina. Letter to SOFIA president Clodualdo "Doy" del Mundo, November 30, 2004. Dilimon, Quezon City, PIA–MISD Archive.
Capul, Belina. Personal interview with author, Philippine Information Agency, Quezon City, Philippines, August 12, 2014.
Cassano, Franco. *Southern Thought and Other Essays on the Mediterranean*. New York: Fordham University Press, 2012.
Castle, Terry. *The Apparitional Lesbian: Female Homosexuality and Modern Culture*. New York: Columbia University Press, 1993.
Celino, Ross F. "Busiest Stars of 1965." *Weekly Graphic*, January 5, 1966.
Celoza, Albert F. *Ferdinand Marcos and the Philippines: The Political Economy of Authoritarianism*. Westport, CT: Praeger, 1997.
Cepeda, Mara. "Makabayan Bloc Wants House Plenary to Vote on ABS-CBN Franchise." *Rappler*, July 22, 2020. https://www.rappler.com/nation/makabayan-wants-house-plenary-vote-abs-cbn-franchise.
Certeau, Michel de. *The Practice of Everyday Life*. Translated by Steven Rendall. Berkeley: University of California Press, 1984.
Chiang, Howard, Todd A. Henry, and Helen Hok-Sze Leung. "Trans-in-Asia, Asia-in-Trans." *TSQ: Transgender Studies Quarterly* 5, no. 3 (2018): 298–310. https://doi.org/10.1215/23289252-6900682.
Chiang, Howard, and Alvin K. Wong. "Asia Is Burning: Queer Asia as Critique." *TSQ: Transgender Studies Quarterly* 58, no. 2 (2017): 121–26. https://doi.org/10.1080/14735784.2017.1294839.
Ching, Marrian Pio Roda. "Is the Filipino Language Even as Gender-Neutral as We Think It Is?" *CNN Philippines*, June 29, 2020. https://www.cnn.ph/life/culture/2020/6/29/filipinx-gender-neutral.html.
Chion, Michel. *The Voice in Cinema*. Translated by Claudia Gorbman. New York: Columbia University Press, 1999.
Chua, Zsarlene B. "The Hard Work of Saving Philippine Cinema's Gems." *Business World*, January 5, 2017. http://bworldonline.com/the-hard-work-of-saving-philippine-cinemas-gems/.
Co, Teddy. Comment on Simon Santos's July 1, 2020, post on Video 48's Facebook page. July 1, 2020. https://www.facebook.com/philippinecinema/.
Co, Teddy. Email to author, Re: Research query re regional cinemas, August 24, 2020.
Co, Teddy. Email to author, Re: Research query re regional cinemas, September 3, 2020.
Co, Teddy. Email to author, Re: Surviving films, March 15, 2021.
Co, Teddy. "In Search of Philippine Regional Cinema." *Movement* 2, no. 1 (1987): 17–20.
Co, Teddy. Personal interview with author, Santa Mesa Heights, Quezon City, Philippines, September 30, 2012.

Co, Teddy. "Reconfiguring Philippine Cinema: Conversations on the First Hundred Years of Philippine Cinema." Lecture for SOFIA Microlearning Series (Session 2). Zoom webinar. September 11, 2020.

Co, Teddy. "Ten Years of Cinema Rehiyon." In *2018 Cinema Rehiyon [Festival] Catalog*, 11–13. Quezon City, Philippines: Dakila, 2018.

Coloma, Herminio. Letter to author, October 14, 2015.

Coloma, Herminio [as Sonny Coloma]. Letter to author, Re: Conditions for research access, September 9, 2014.

Coloma, Herminio. Re: Transfer of Audio-visual Collections of PIA to NFAP. Memorandum from PCOO Secretary Herminio "Sonny" Coloma. May 23, 2013.

Comaroff, Jean, and John Comaroff. *Theory from the South: Or, How Euro-America Is Evolving toward Africa*. Boulder, CO: Paradigm, 2012.

Congress of the Philippines. Republic Act No. 4165: "An Act Creating the National Commission on Culture and Providing Funds Therefor." Lawphil.net, August 4, 1964. https://www.lawphil.net/statutes/repacts/ra1964/ra_4165_1964.html.

Congress of the Philippines. Republic Act No. 4846: "An Act to Repeal Act Numbered Thirty Eight Hundred Seventy-Four, and to Provide for the Protection and Preservation of Philippine Cultural Properties." Lawphil.net, June 18, 1966. https://www.lawphil.net/statutes/repacts/ra1966/ra_4846_1966.html.

Congress of the Philippines. Republic Act No. 9167: "An Act Creating the Film Development Council of the Philippines, Defining Its Powers and Functions, Appropriating Funds Therefor, and for Other Purposes." Lawphil.net, June 7, 2002. https://www.lawphil.net/statutes/repacts/ra2002/ra_9167_2002.html.

Conrad, Suzanna. "Analog, the Sequel: An Analysis of Current Film Archiving Practice and Hesitance to Embrace Digital Preservation." *Archival Issues* 34, no. 1 (2012): 27–43.

Constable, Nicole. "Sexuality and Discipline among Filipina Domestic Workers in Hong Kong." *American Ethnologist* 24, no. 3 (August 1997): 539–58.

Constantino, Renato. "A People's Culture Not a Seepage from Above—Not a Return to the Past: Our Language, a Case of Enforced Stagnation." *Graphic*, February 19, 1969.

Constitutional Commission. 1987 Constitution of the Republic of the Philippines. *Official Gazette*, February 2, 1987. https://www.officialgazette.gov.ph/constitutions/1987-constitution/.

Cook, Terry. "The Archive(s) Is a Foreign Country: Historians, Archivists and the Changing Archival Landscape." *American Archivist* 74, no. 2 (Fall–Winter 2011): 600–632.

Cook, Terry. "Evidence, Memory, Identity, and Community." *Archival Science* 13 (2013): 95–120.

Coseteng, Alice M. L. "The Imelda Project." *Weekly Graphic*, April 13, 1966.
Cristobal, Adrian E. "The Ill-Fated Tadhana." *Weekly Graphic*, September 15, 1965.
Cristobal, Adrian E. "Marcos in Miranda." *Weekly Graphic*, August 11, 1965.
Cruz, Andres Cristobal. "A Natural History of Our Nationalist Demonstrations." *Graphic*, February 9, 1966.
Cruz, Denise. *Transpacific Femininities: The Making of the Modern Filipina*. Durham, NC: Duke University Press, 2012.
Cruz, Isagani. "T-Bird at Ako (1982)." *Parade*, September 22, 1982. www.oocities.org/pinoymovies/tbirdatako.html.
Cruz, Lorenzo J. "Politicians Take to the Air." *Weekly Graphic*, July 28, 1965.
Cruz, Marinel. "Devastating Effects of ABS-CBN's Film Restoration and Archives Group Shutdown." *Philippine Daily Inquirer*, July 23, 2020. https://entertainment.inquirer.net/384429/devastating-effects-of-abs-cbns-film-restoration-and-archives-group-shutdown.
Cummins, Kenneth W., and Margaret A. Wilzbach. "Rivers and Streams: Ecosystem Dynamics and Integrating Paradigms." In *Encyclopedia of Ecology*, edited by Brian Fath, 2:579–93. Amsterdam: Elsevier, 2019.
Cvetkovich, Ann. *An Archive of Feelings: Trauma, Sexuality, and Lesbian Public Cultures*. Durham, NC: Duke University Press, 2003.
Cvetkovich, Ann. "Public Feelings." *South Atlantic Quarterly* 106, no. 3 (Summer 2007): 459–68.
Czach, Liz. "Cinephilia, Stars, and Film Festivals." *Cinema Journal* 49, no. 2 (Winter 2010): 139–45.
Daily Express. "First Lady: Filmfest to Go on as Scheduled." November 20, 1981.
Daily Express. "Gov't Takes Over Film Center Work; Toll Now 8." November 19, 1981.
Daroy, Petronilo Bn. "Main Currents in the Filipino Cinema." In *The Urian Anthology, 1970–1979: Selected Essays on Tradition and Innovation in the Filipino Cinema of the 1970s by the Manunuri ng Pelikulang Pilipino*, edited by Nicanor G. Tiongson, 48–61. Manila: M. L. Morato, 1983.
David, Joel. "A Cultural Policy Experience in Philippine Cinema." In *Wages of Cinema: Film in Philippine Perspective*, 48–61. Diliman, Quezon City: University of the Philippines Press, 1998.
David, Joel. *Fields of Vision: Critical Applications in Recent Philippine Cinema*. Quezon City, Philippines: Ateneo de Manila University Press, 1995.
David, Joel. "A Second Golden Age (An Informal History)." In *The National Pastime: Contemporary Philippine Cinema*, 1–17. Manila: Anvil, 1990.
Davis, Darrell William, and Emilie Yueh-yu Yeh. "VCD as Programmatic Technology: Japanese Television Drama in Hong Kong." In *Feeling Asian Modernities: Transnational Consumption of Japanese TV Dramas*, edited by Koichi Iwabuchi, 227–47. Hong Kong: Hong Kong University Press, 2004.

Davis, John. "Going Analog: Vinylphiles and the Consumption of the 'Obsolete' Vinyl Record." In Acland, *Residual Media*, 222–36.

De Dios, Emmanuel, ed. *An Analysis of the Philippine Economic Crisis: A Workshop Report*. Quezon City: University of the Philippines Press, 1984.

de Guzman, Anna Marie G. "Philippine Experimental Film Practice: Influences and Directions through the Films of Roxlee." *Plaridel: A Philippine Journal of Communication, Media, and Society* 1, no. 1 (February 2004): 57–64.

Deleuze, Gilles. *Bergsonism*. Translated by Hugh Tomlinson and Barbara Habberjam. New York: Zone Books, 1991.

Deligero, Keith. Email to author, Re: Research queries about *Iskalawags*, February 18, 2021.

Deligero, Keith. Email to author, Re: Updates, March 9, 2021.

Deligero, Keith. Skype interview with author, April 26, 2019.

Deligero, Keith. Skype interview with author and her undergraduate students in Film and Media Studies 160: Filipino Indie Cinema, University of California, Irvine, May 1, 2019.

Deligero, Keith. Zoom interview with author, March 5, 2021.

del Mundo, Clodualdo, Jr. *Dreaming of a National Audio-Visual Archive*. Manila: Society of Film Archivists, 2004.

del Mundo, Clodualdo, Jr. Email to author, July 25, 2018.

del Mundo, Clodualdo, Jr. "The Film Industry Is Dead! Long Live Philippine Cinema!" *Sanghaya*, December 31, 2002. http://sanghaya.net.ph/welcome/2002/12/31/the-film-industry-is-dead-long-live-philippine-cinema/.

del Mundo, Clodualdo, Jr. *Native Resistance: Philippine Cinema and Colonialism, 1898–1941*. Manila: De La Salle University Press, 1998.

del Mundo, Clodualdo, Jr. "Philippine Cinema: An Historical Overview." *Asian Cinema* 10, no. 2 (March 1999): 29–66.

del Mundo, Clodualdo Jr. "Quest for a National Film Archive Continues." *Philippine Daily Inquirer*, July 4, 2008. http://showbizandstyle.inquirer.net/entertainment/entertainment/view/20080704-146505/Quest-for-a-national-film-archive-continues.

del Pilar, Mary. Personal interview with author, ABS-CBN Eugenio Lopez Jr. Communications Center Building, Quezon City, Philippines, March 9, 2018.

Demafeliz, Jorge. "Pearly Shells." In *Si Nora Aunor Sa Mga Noranian: Mga Paggunita at Pagtatapat*, edited by Nestor De Guzman, 66. Quezon City: Milflores Publishing, 2005.

Deocampo, Nick. *Cine: Spanish Influences on Early Cinema in the Philippines*. Pasig, Philippines: Anvil, 2007.

Deocampo, Nick. Email to author, Re: Comments on your abstract, July 16, 2020.

Deocampo, Nick. *Film: American Influences on Philippine Cinema.* Manila: Anvil, 2011.

Deocampo, Nick. *Films from a "Lost" Cinema: A Brief History of Cebuano Films.* Manila: National Commission for Culture and the Arts (NCCA), 2005.

Deocampo, Nick. "Into the Light: Philippine Alternative Cinema and the *Neuer Deutscher Film*." In Baumgärtel, *Kinosine*, 20–29.

Deocampo, Nick, ed. *Lost Films of Asia.* Pasig City, Philippines: Anvil, 2006.

Deocampo, Nick. "The Propaganda Influenced Concept of 'National Cinema' during the Japanese Occupation." Paper presented at the Sandaan: Philippine Cinema Centennial Conference, University of the Philippines Film Institute, Quezon City, Philippines, September 14, 2017.

Deocampo, Nick. *Short Film: Emergence of a New Philippine Cinema.* Edited by Alfred A. Yuson. Manila: Communication Foundation for Asia, 1985.

Deocampo, Nick. "Zamboanga: 'Lost' Philippine-Made Film Discovered in U.S. Archive." Special Edition, *Movement* (Feb. 2004): 2–7.

Department of Agriculture, Philippine Rice Research Institute. "President Aquino Proclaims 2013 as National Year of Rice." *Official Gazette*, November 8, 2012. https://www.officialgazette.gov.ph/2012/11/08/president-aquino-proclaims-2013-as-national-year-of-rice/.

Department of Budget and Management, Republic of the Philippines. *National Expenditure Program Volume III FY 2023.* August 22, 2022. https://www.dbm.gov.ph/index.php/budgetdocuments/2023/national-expenditure-program-fy-2023/373-budget-documents/2023/2346national-expenditure-program-volume-iii-fy-2023.

de Pedro, Ernie A. "Overview of the Film Archives." Report for Hon. Joker C. Arroyo, Executive Secretary, from Ernie A. de Pedro, Director-General, Film Archives of the Philippines. May 22, 1986. Diliman, Quezon City, PIA-MISD Archive.

Derrida, Jacques. *Archive Fever: A Freudian Impression.* Chicago: University of Chicago Press, 1996.

De Vega, Guillermo C. *Film and Freedom: Movie Censorship in the Philippines.* Manila: Vega, 1975.

De Vera, Ben O. "4.5 Million Pinoys Jobless in 2020." *Philippine Inquirer*, December 4, 2020. https://newsinfo.inquirer.net/1367928/4–5m-pinoys-jobless-in-2020.

Diaz, Robert G. "Queer Love and Urban Intimacies in Martial Law Manila." *Plaridel: A Philippine Journal of Communication, Media, and Society* 9, no. 2 (August 2012): 1–19.

Diño-Seguerra, Liza. "The Vision for FDCP's Philippine Film Archive." *Manila Times*, August 9, 2020. https://www.manilatimes.net/2020/08/09/the-sunday-times/arts-awake/the-vision-for-fdcps-philippine-film-archive/752670.

Dinshaw, Carolyn. "Got Medieval?" *Journal of the History of Sexuality* 10, no. 2 (April 2001): 202–12.

Doronila, Amando. "The Media." In *The Philippines after Marcos*, edited by R. J. May and Francisco Nemenzo, 194–206. London: Croom Helm, 1985.

Drake, Philip. "Distribution and Marketing in Contemporary Hollywood." In *The Contemporary Hollywood Film Industry*, edited by Paul McDonald and Janet Wasko, 63–82. Malden, MA: Blackwell, 2008.

Dulay, Dean, Allan Hicken, Anil Menon, and Ronald Homes. "Continuity, History, and Identity: Why Bongbong Marcos Won the 2022 Philippine Presidential Election." *Pacific Affairs* 96, no. 1 (March 2023): 85–104.

Dumaual, Miguel. "The 'Miracle' behind 'Himala' HD Restoration." ABS-CBN News, November 7, 2012. http://news.abs-cbn.com/lifestyle/11/07/12/miracle-behind-himala-hd-restoration.

Edmondson, Ray. *Audiovisual Archiving: Philosophy and Principles.* 3rd ed. Paris: UNESCO, 2016.

Edmondson, Ray. "National Film and Sound Archive: The Quest for Identity." PhD diss., University of Canberra, 2011.

Edmondson, Ray. "Notes on Sustainability." In *2013 Philippine Cinema Heritage Summit: A Report*, 24–25. Manila: National Film Archives of the Philippines, 2013.

Edmondson, Ray. "You Only Live Once: On Being a Troublemaking Professional." *Moving Image* 2, no. 1 (Spring 2002): 175–84.

Edmondson, Ray, and Andrew Pike. *Australia's Lost Films.* Canberra: National Library of Australia, 1982.

Egan, Kate. "The Celebration of a 'Proper Product': Exploring the Residual Collectible through the 'Video Nasty.'" In Acland, *Residual Media*, 200–221.

Elemia, Camille. "The Big Comeback: How ABS-CBN Pulled off Its Return to Free TV." *Rappler*, October 28, 2020. https://www.rappler.com/newsbreak/in-depth/how-abs-cbn-pulled-off-return-to-free-tv-zoe.

Elemia, Camille. "Isabela Governor Bemoans ABS-CBN News Absence amid Massive Flooding." *Rappler*, November 16, 2020. https://www.rappler.com/nation/isabela-governor-albano-bemoans-abs-cbn-news-absence-flooding.

Elsaesser, Thomas. "Cinephilia or the Uses of Disenchantment." In *Cinephilia: Movies, Love and Memory*, edited by Marijke de Valck and Malte Hagener, 27–44. Amsterdam: Amsterdam University Press, 2005.

Enticknap, Leo. *Film Restoration: The Culture and Science of Audiovisual Heritage.* Basingstoke, UK: Palgrave Macmillan, 2013.

Eraña, Nieva Paz L. Letter to PIA-MISD Staff Director Belina Capul, November 24, 2008. Diliman, Quezon City, PIA-MISD Archive.

Espina, Merv. Email to author, Re: Research query, March 5, 2020.

Espina, Merv. Email to author, Re: Research query, June 20, 2020.

Espina, Merv. Email to author, Re: Research query, June 23, 2020.

Espina, Merv. Email to author, Re: Research query, June 24, 2020.
Espina, Merv. Email to author, Re: Research query, June 25, 2020.
Espiritu, Talitha. "National Allegory, Modernization, and the Cinematic Patrimony of the Marcos Regime." In *Popular Culture in Asia: Memory, City, Celebrity*, edited by Lorna Fitzsimmons and John A. Lent, 43–64. Basingstoke, UK: Palgrave Macmillan, 2013.
Espiritu, Talitha. *Passionate Revolutions: The Media and the Rise and Fall of the Marcos Regime*. Athens: Ohio State University Press, 2017.
Estrada, Joseph Ejercito. Executive Order No. 323: "Constituting an Inter-Agency Privatization Council and Creating a Privatization and Management Office (PMO) under the Department of Finance for the Continuing Privatization of Government Assets and Corporations." Privatization and Management Office, Government of the Philippines, December 6, 2000. http://www.pmo.gov.ph/eo323.pdf.
Evangelista, Patricia. "The Librarians: A Rappler Profile." *Rappler*, February 23, 2018. https://www.rappler.com/newsbreak/rich-media/196642-national-library-philippines-librarians-cesar-gilbert-adriano.
Fajardo, Kale Bantigue. "Queering and Transing the Great Lakes: Filipino/a Tomboy Masculinities and Manhoods across Waters." *GLQ: A Journal of Lesbian and Gay Studies* 20, nos. 1–2 (2014): 115–40.
Fajardo, Kale Bantigue. "Transportation: Translating Filipino and Filipino American Tomboy Masculinities through Global Migration and Seafaring." *GLQ: A Journal of Lesbian and Gay Studies* 14, nos. 2–3 (2008): 403–24.
Fernandez, Doreen G. "Mass Culture and Cultural Policy: The Philippine Experience." *Philippine Studies* 37, no. 4 (1989): 488–502.
Fernandez, Doreen G. "Paths of Policy." *Midweek*, May 18, 1988.
Field, Allyson Nadia. *Uplift Cinema: The Emergence of African American Film and the Possibility of Black Modernity*. Durham, NC: Duke University Press, 2015.
Film Heritage Foundation. "Preserving Our Film Heritage." Accessed April 26, 2023. http://filmheritagefoundation.co.in/preserving-our-film-heritage/.
Fossati, Giovanna. *From Grain to Pixel: The Archival Life of Film in Transition*. Amsterdam: Amsterdam University Press, 2009.
Foucault, Michel. *The Archeology of Knowledge and the Discourse on Language*. Translated by A. M. Sheridan Smith. New York: Pantheon Books, 1972.
Freeman, Elizabeth. "Packing History, Count(Er)Ing Generations." *New Literary History* 31, no. 4 (Autumn 2000): 727–44.
Freeman, Elizabeth. *Time Binds: Queer Temporalities, Queer Histories*. Durham, NC: Duke University Press, 2010.
Frick, Caroline. *Saving Cinema: The Politics of Preservation*. New York: Oxford University Press, 2011.

Gaje, Virgilio M. Memorandum to PIA director-general Harold E. Clavite. Inventory listing of the remaining audiovisual materials and equipment for deposit and/or transfer to NFAP. May 30, 2017. Diliman, Quezon City, PIA-MPD Archive.

Galino, Julie. Email to author, Re: Phone call re Ibong Adarna?, March 27, 2018.

Galino, Julie. Email to author, Re: Research query on when ABS-CBN Archive was founded, July 31, 2018.

Galino, Julie. Personal interview with author, ABS-CBN Eugenio Lopez Jr. Communications Center Building, Quezon City, Philippines, March 9, 2018.

Galino, Julie. Phone interview with author, March 5, 2018.

Garcia, Ed. "An Open Letter to Militant Young Christians on the Challenges of the '70s in the Philippines." *Now*, February 28, 1970.

Garcia, J. Neil. "Male Homosexuality in the Philippines: A Short History," *International Institute for Asian Studies Newsletter* 35 (2004): 13.

Gavilan, Jodesz. "Timeline: The Marcos Burial Controversy." *Rappler*, November 18, 2016. https://www.rappler.com/newsbreak/iq/151667-timeline-ferdinand-marcos-burial-controversy/.

Giron, Eric S. "Tagalog Lurches On." *Mirror*, August 7, 1965.

Giron, Marietta V. "Aquino to Keep Marcos Pic Law." *Variety*, April 2, 1986.

Giron, Marietta V. "Marcos Plucks Censor Thorn after Filipino Trade Tirade." *Variety*, October 16, 1985.

Giron, Marietta V. "New Bill Proposing an End to Pic Censorship Stirring Up Philippines." *Variety*, March 27, 1985.

Giron, Marietta V. "Trial Begins for Filipino Film Directors." *Variety*, February 6, 1985.

Gitelman, Lisa. *Paper Knowledge: Toward a Media History of Documents.* Durham, NC: Duke University Press, 2014.

Godinez, Zinnia F. "Privatization and Deregulation in the Philippines: An Option Package Worth Pursuing?" *ASEAN Economic Bulletin* 5, no. 3 (March 1989): 259–89.

Goldgel-Carballo, Victor. "The Reappropriation of Poverty and the Art of 'Making Do' in Contemporary Argentine Cultural Production." *Global South* 8, no. 1 (2014): 112–27.

Gomez, Jerome. "Danny Zialcita: The Entertainer." *Metro Him*, July–August 2008. http://news.abs-cbn.com/focus/03/12/13/remembering-danny-zialcita.

Gotinga, J. C. "After 2 and a Half Years, Martial Law Ends in Mindanao." *Rappler*, December 31, 2019. https://rappler.com/nation/martial-law-mindanao-ends-december-31–2019.

Gotinga, J. C. "Unlawful for Government to Seize ABS-CBN Properties—Senators." Rappler.com, July 24, 2020. https://rappler.com/nation/senators-say-unlawful-government-seize-abs-cbn-properties.

Gracy, Karen F. *Film Preservation: Competing Definitions of Value, Use, and Practice.* Chicago: Society of American Archivists, 2007.

Grant, Paul Douglas. "Ang Pelikulang Binisaya: Cebuano Film and the Search for a Regional Cinematic Heritage." *Film International* 11, nos. 3–4 (2013): 73–83.

Grant, Paul Douglas. "Cebu's Black Sheep of God: Interview with Keith Deligero." *Film International* 11, nos. 3–4 (2013): 103–9.

Grant, Paul. "Cinema Becoming Regional, Unbecoming Cinema." *La Furia Umana*, no. 23 (2015). http://www.lafuriaumana.it/index.php/56-archive/lfu-23/345-paul-grant-cinema-becoming-regional-unbecoming-cinema.

Grant, Paul Douglas. Email to author, Re: Surviving films, March 15, 2021.

Grant, Paul. "Presenting Cebuano Cinema at the MEMORY International Film Heritage Festival." *Plaridel: A Philippine Journal of Communication, Media, and Society* 15, no. 2 (December 2018): 207–13.

Grant, Paul, and Misha Boris Anissimov. *Lilas: An Illustrated History of the Golden Ages of Cebuano Cinema.* Cebu, Philippines: University of San Carlos Press, 2016.

Graphic. "ABS-CBN Launches the Era of Total Professionalism in Philippine Broadcasting." ABS-CBN Inaugural Supplement, December 18, 1968.

Greenberg, Joshua M. *From Betamax to Blockbuster: Video Stores and the Invention of Movies on Video.* Cambridge, MA: MIT Press, 2008.

Groschke, Annette, Martin Koerber, and Daniel Meiller. "Who Is Going to Look at That? Experiences, Possibilities, and Pitfalls of Keeping Experimental Film in a Mid-Sized Film Archive." *Moving Image* 12, no. 1 (Spring 2012): 128–35.

Groyon, Vicente. "Cinemarehiyon 2009." In *A Reader in Philippine Film History and Criticism*, edited by Jonathan Chua, Rosario Cruz-Lucero, and Rolando B. Tolentino, 177–96. Diliman, Quezon City: University of the Philippines Press, 2014.

Guno, Niña V. "'Filipinx,' 'Pinxy' among New Nonbinary Words in Online Dictionary." *Philippine Inquirer*, September 7, 2020. https://newsinfo.inquirer.net/1332278/filipinx-pinxy-among-new-nonbinary-words-in-online-dictionary.

Gutierrez, Jason. "Philippine Congress Officially Shuts Down Leading Broadcaster." *New York Times*, July 10, 2020. https://www.nytimes.com/2020/07/10/world/asia/philippines-congress-media-duterte-abs-cbn.html.

Habib, Andre. "Ruin, Archive, and the Time of Cinema: Peter Delpeut's Lyrical Nitrate." *SubStance* 35, no. 2 (2006): 120–39.

Halperin, David M. *How to Do the History of Homosexuality.* Chicago: University of Chicago Press, 1992.

Halperin, David M. *One Hundred Years of Homosexuality and Other Essays on Greek Love.* New York: Routledge, 1990.

Haraway, Donna. "Situated Knowledges: The Science Question in Feminism and the Privilege of Partial Perspective." In *Simians, Cyborgs, and Women*, 183–201. New York: Routledge, 1991.

Harding, Sandra. "Rethinking Standpoint Epistemology: What Is 'Strong Objectivity'?" In *Feminist Epistemologies*, edited by Linda Alcoff and Elizabeth Potter, 49–82. New York: Routledge, 1993.

Harris, Verne. *Archives and Justice: A South African Perspective*. Chicago: Society of American Archivists, 2007.

Hau, Caroline S. *Elites and Ilustrados in Philippine Culture*. Quezon City: Ateneo de Manila University Press, 2017.

Havens, Timothy, and Amanda D. Lotz. *Understanding Media Industries*. New York: Oxford University Press, 2017.

Headland, Thomas N., and Janet D. Headland. "Limitation of Human Rights, Land Exclusion, and Tribal Extinction: The Agta Negritos of the Philippines." *Human Organization* 56, no. 1 (1997): 79–90.

Heath, Stephen. "Questions of Property: Film and Nationhood." *Cinetracts* 1, no. 4 (Spring–Summer 1978): 2–11.

Hebdige, Dick. *Subculture: The Meaning of Style*. London: Routledge, 1979.

Henning, Michelle. "New Lamps for Old: Photography, Obsolescence, and Social Change." In Acland, *Residual Media*, 48–65.

Herbert, Daniel. *Videoland: Movie Culture at the American Video Store*. Berkeley: University of California Press, 2014.

Hernando, Cesar. "Appendix 1: Philippine Experimental Cinema—Timeline." *Plaridel: A Philippine Journal of Communication, Media, and Society* 1, no. 1 (February 2004): 65–66.

Herrera, Felix. "A Rundown on the History of Same-Sex Marriage in the Philippines." *Esquire Philippines*, January 7, 2020. https://www.esquiremag.ph/politics/news/same-sex-marriage-in-the-philippines-a2292-20200107.

Higson, Andrew. "The Concept of National Cinema." *Screen* 30, no. 4 (1989): 36–46.

Hilderbrand, Lucas. "Cinematic Promiscuity: Cinephilia after Videophilia." *Framework* 50, nos. 1–2 (Spring–Fall 2009): 214–17.

Hilderbrand, Lucas. *Inherent Vice: Bootleg Histories of Videotape and Copyright*. Durham, NC: Duke University Press, 2009.

Hollywood Reporter. "Philippines' President Aquino Sets up Film Agency Task Force." March 25, 1986.

Houston, Penelope. *Keepers of the Frame: The Film Archives*. London: British Film Institute, 1994.

Hu, Kelly. "Chinese Re-makings of Pirated VCDs of Japanese TV Dramas." In *Feeling Asian Modernities: Transnational Consumption of Japanese TV Dramas*, edited by Koichi Iwabuchi, 205–26. Hong Kong: Hong Kong University Press, 2004.

IBON Foundation. "14 Charts: What the Government Has Done to Our Pandemic Economy." *Ibon*, February 10, 2021. https://www.ibon.org/14-charts-what-the-government-has-done-to-our-pandemic-economy/.

International Association for the Protection of Intellectual Property (AIPPI) Philippines, Del Rosario & Del Rosario, Giselle Angelica C. Munoz, and Ma. Alice E. Adao. "Exhaustion Issues in Copyright Law." May 15, 2014. https://aippi.org/wp-content/uploads/committees/240/GR240philippines.pdf.

Isleta, Honesto M. "Letter and Project Proposal from Honesto M. Isleta, Press Undersecretary, Philippine Information Agency Officer-in-Charge, to Jaime Laya, Chairman of the Board, National Commission for Culture and the Arts." September 8, 1997. Personal papers of Victoria Belarmino and Mary del Pilar.

James, David E. *The Most Typical Avant-Garde: History and Geography of Minor Cinemas in Los Angeles*. Berkeley: University of California Press, 2005.

Janetzko, Christoph. "Experimental Film Productions in the Philippines." In Baumgärtel, *Kinosine*, 56–61.

Japan Foundation, Manila, ed. *Art Archive 02: A Collection of Essays on Philippine Contemporary Literature and Film*. Manila: Japan Foundation, Manila, 2019. https://drive.google.com/file/d/1gDexwhajYQ6Rjtd2koH_byefia3Rnzzk/view.

Joaquin, Nick. "Before the Blow: Ninoy's Senate Years." In B. S. Aquino, *A Garrison State in the Make and Other Speeches*, 355–90.

Joaquin, Nick [as Quijano de Manila]. "Image of Imelda." *Philippines Free Press*, January 23, 1965.

Joaquin, Nick [as Quijano de Manila]. "Imelda in Malacañang." *Philippines Free Press*, May 28, 1966.

Joaquin, Nick [as Quijano de Manila]. "Marcos '70." In *Reportage on the Marcoses: 1964–1970*, 194–209. Manila: National Media Production Center, 1979.

Joaquin, Nick [as Quijano de Manila]. "The Press Discovers the Cinema." *Philippines Free Press*, September 18, 1965.

Joaquin, Nick [as Quijano de Manila]. "Woman of the Year." In *Reportage on the Marcoses: 1964–1970*, 122–32. Manila: National Media Production Center, 1979.

Junio, Arnulfo. "The Movie in My Mind: A Film Archivist's Reflection." In NCCA Committee on Archives and SOFIA (Proponents), *Philippine Audiovisual Archives Collections: An Inventory*, 2003.

Katigbak, Leo. Email to author, Re: Follow-up questions on Sagip Pelikula, January 27, 2022.

Katigbak, Leo. "Ganito Tayo Noon . . . Sagip Pelikula: Restoring Our Cinematic Heritage." Zoom webinar, January 27, 2022.

Kerkvliet, Benedict J., and Resil B. Mojares. "Themes in the Transition from Marcos to Aquino: An Introduction." In *From Marcos to Aquino: Local*

Perspectives on Political Transition in the Philippines, edited by Benedict J. Kerkvliet and Resil B. Mojares, 1–12. Quezon City, Philippines: Ateneo de Manila Press, 1991.

Khoo, Gaik Cheng. "Just-Do-It-(Yourself): Independent Filmmaking in Malaysia." *Inter-Asia Cultural Studies* 8, no. 2 (2007): 227–47.

Khoo, Olivia. *Asian Cinema: A Regional View*. Edinburgh: Edinburgh University Press, 2021.

Klinger, Barbara. "The Contemporary Cinephile: Film Collecting after the VCR." In *Beyond the Multiplex: Cinema, New Technologies, and the Home*, 54–90. University of California Press, 2006.

Knight, Julia. "Archiving, Distribution, and Experimental Moving Image Histories." *Moving Image* 12, no. 1 (Spring 2012): 65–86.

Korea Herald. "Marcos' Daughter Takes Part in Rites to Appease Spirits." July 21, 1982.

Krapp, Peter. "Hollywood's Piracy Problem." *The Conversation*, February 17, 2016. https://theconversation.com/hollywoods-piracy-problem-53786.

Kumar, Ramesh. "National Film Archives: Policies, Practices, and Histories: A Study of the National Film Archive of India, EYE Film Institute Netherlands, and the National Film and Sound Archive, Australia." PhD diss., New York University, 2016.

Lacaba, Jose F. *Days of Disquiet, Nights of Rage: The First Quarter Storm and Related Events*. 1982. New edition, Pasig, Philippines: Anvil, 2003.

Lacaba, Jose F. "Misadventures in the Dream Trade." *Mr. & Ms. Magazine*, February 2, 1982.

Lacaba, Jose. "Movies, Critics, and the Bakya Crowd." In *Readings in Philippine Cinema*, edited by Rafael Ma Guerrero, 175–81. Manila: Experimental Cinema of the Philippines, 1983.

Lacaba, Jose. "Notes on Bakya." In *Readings in Philippine Cinema*, edited by Rafael Guerrero, 117–23. Manila: Experimental Cinema of the Philippines, 1983.

Lapniten, Karlston. "'The River Will Bleed Red': Indigenous Filipinos Face Down Dam Projects." *Mongabay*, February 26, 2021. https://news.mongabay.com/2021/02/the-river-will-bleed-red-indigenous-filipinos-face-down-dam-projects/.

Larkin, Brian. *Signal and Noise: Media Infrastructure, and Urban Culture in Nigeria*. Durham, NC: Duke University Press, 2008.

Leandro V. Locsin Partners, Architects. "Architectural Design Concept." In *2013 Philippine Cinema Heritage Summit: A Report*, 10–12. Manila: National Film Archives of the Philippines, 2013.

Lefebvre, Henri. *The Production of Space*. Translated by Donald Nicholson-Smith. Oxford: Basil Blackwell, 1991.

Leguiab, Jefferson P. "Fade Out: Motion Pictures Division, Fade In: Management Information System Division." *Tinig* [Philippine Information Agency (PIA) newsletter] 2, no. 2 (2004): 11–13.

Leng, Tan Bee. "Preserving Our National Audio-Visual Heritage." *AV Archives Bulletin, Official Quarterly Newsletter of the Southeast Asia-Pacific Audio-Visual Archive Association (SEAPAVAA)* 1, no. 1 (1996): 11.

Liang, Lawrence. "Porous Legalities and Avenues of Participation." In *Sarai Reader 2005: Bare Acts*, 6–17. Delhi: Centre for the Study of Developing Societies, 2005. http://archive.sarai.net/files/original/8d57bfa1bcb57c80a7af903363c07282.pdf.

Lico, Gerard. *Edifice Complex: Power, Myth, and Marcos State Architecture*. Quezon City, Philippines: Ateneo de Manila University Press, 2003.

Lim, Bliss Cua. "Analysis and Recommendations in the Wake of the 2013 Philippine Cinema Heritage Summit." In *2013 Philippine Cinema Heritage Summit: A Report*, 26–32. Manila: National Film Archives of the Philippines, 2013.

Lim, Bliss Cua. "A Brief History of Archival Advocacy for Philippine Cinema." In *2013 Philippine Cinema Heritage Summit: A Report*, 14–20. Manila: National Film Archives of the Philippines, 2013.

Lim, Bliss Cua. "Cult Fiction: *Himala* and Bakya Temporality." *Spectator* 24, no. 2 (Fall 2004): 61–72.

Lim, Bliss Cua. "Fandom, Consumption, and Collectivity in the Philippine New Cinema: Nora and the Noranians." In *The Precarious Self: Women and the Media in Asia*, edited by Youna Kim, 179–203. Basingstoke, UK: Palgrave Macmillan, 2012.

Lim, Bliss Cua. "Informal Archival Flows: Kalampag Tracking Agency and Video 48." Lecture for SOFIA Microlearning Series (Session 5). Zoom webinar. February 26, 2021.

Lim, Bliss Cua. Letter to Secretary of Information Herminio "Sonny" Coloma, September 8, 2014.

Lim, Bliss Cua. "Pepot and the Archive: Cinephilia and the Archive Crisis of Philippine Cinema." *Flow* 12, no. 3 (July 2, 2010). https://www.flowjournal.org/2010/07/pepotem-and-the-archive/.

Lim, Bliss Cua. "Queer Aswang Transmedia: Folklore as Camp." *Kritika Kultura* 24 (2015): 178–225.

Lim, Bliss Cua. "Sharon's Noranian Turn: Stardom, Embodiment, and Language in Philippine Cinema." *Discourse* 31, no. 3 (Fall 2009): 318–58.

Lim, Bliss Cua. *Translating Time: Cinema, the Fantastic, and Temporal Critique*. Durham, NC: Duke University Press, 2009.

Lim, Bliss Cua, Benedict S. Olgado, and Rose Roque. "A Position Paper on the Interrelated House Bills (1745, 2320, 4332, 8171, and 8924) regarding the Creation of the National Film Archive of the Philippines." April 15, 2021. Addressed to Christopher V. P. De Venecia, Chair, Special Committee on Creative Industry and Performing Arts, Eighteenth Congress, Republic of the Philippines House of Representatives. Published in Bliss Cua Lim, Benedict S. Olgado, and Rose Roque, "Toward an Autonomous Philippine Audiovisual Archives," *Pelikula: A Journal of Philippine Cinema* 6

(2021): 228–39. https://58686479-5e42-4048-b1f7-e91523ee7fbc.filesusr.com/ugd/e760e1_f7948d3e3bfb4429a47f4ab7dec1f979.pdf.

Lim, Bliss Cua, Benedict S. Olgado, and Rose Roque. "A Position Paper on the Substitute Bill for the Interrelated House Bills (1745, 2320, 4332, 8171, and 8924) regarding the Creation of the National Film Archive of the Philippines." June 7, 2021. Addressed to Cristal L. Bagatsing, Chairperson, Joint Technical Working Group, and Christopher V. P. De Venecia, Chairperson, Special Committee on Creative Industry and Performing Arts, Eighteenth Congress, Republic of the Philippines House of Representatives. Published in Bliss Cua Lim, Benedict S. Olgado, and Rose Roque, "Toward an Autonomous Philippine Audiovisual Archives," *Pelikula: A Journal of Philippine Cinema* 6 (2021): 228–39. https://58686479-5e42-4048-b1f7-e91523ee7fbc.filesusr.com/ugd/e760e1_f7948d3e3bfb4429a47f4ab7dec1f979.pdf.

Lim, Millard O. "ABS-CBN Shutdown: 1972 and 2020." *Business World*, July 13, 2020. https://www.bworldonline.com/abs-cbn-shutdown-1972-and-2020/.

Lim, Song-Hwee. *Celluloid Comrades: Representations of Male Homosexuality in Contemporary Chinese Cinemas.* Honolulu: University of Hawaii Press, 2006.

Lippit, Akira Mizuta. *Atomic Light (Shadow Optics).* Minneapolis: University of Minnesota Press, 2005.

Llaneta, Celeste Ann Castillo. "UP Protests against Threat to Academic Freedom." *University of the Philippines News*, January 21, 2021. https://up.edu.ph/up-protests-against-threat-to-academic-freedom/.

Lobato, Ramon. *Shadow Economies of Cinema: Mapping Informal Film Distribution.* London: Palgrave Macmillan on behalf of the British Film Institute, 2012.

Lopez, Salvador P. "Who Says Rome Can't Be Built in a Day?" *Mr. & Ms. Magazine*, February 16, 1982.

Lott, Eric. *Love and Theft: Blackface Minstrelsy and the American Working Class.* New York: Oxford University Press, 2013.

Lumbera, Bienvenido. "Approaches to the Filipino Film." In *The Urian Anthology 1970–1979*, edited by Nicanor G. Tiongson, 94–101. Manila: Manuel L. Morato, 1983.

Lumbera, Gym. Email to author, Re: Class picture, August 12, 2020.

Lumbera, Gym. Email to author, Re: Class picture, August 19, 2020.

Lumbera, Gym. Zoom interview with author, August 12, 2020.

Mabalon, Dawn Bohulano. *Little Manila Is in the Heart: The Making of the Filipina/o American Community in Stockton, California.* Durham, NC: Duke University Press, 2013.

Macapagal, Diosdado. "Appendix A: [August 4, 1964] Republic Act 4165: An Act Creating the National Commission on Culture and Providing Funds Therefor." In Baluyut, *Institutions and Icons of Patronage*, 92–96.

Maglipon, Jo-Ann Q., Anna Pingol, and Andrew A. Paredes. "Nora Superstar." *Yes!*, October 2011.

Manalansan, Martin. *Global Divas: Filipino Gay Men in the Diaspora*. Quezon City, Philippines: Ateneo de Manila University Press, 2006.

Mangahas, Malou. "Gloria Gets Richer Fastest, Beats Cory, Ramos, Erap." Philippine Center for Investigative Journalism. 2009, http://pcij.org/stories/gloria-gets-richer-fastest-beats-cory-ramos-erap/.

Manila Bulletin Entertainment. "Sagip Pelikula and FDCP to Screen Restored PH Film Classics at MET." *Manila Bulletin*, February 18, 2022. https://mb.com.ph/2022/2/18/sagip-pelikula-and-fdcp-to-screen-restored-ph-film-classics-at-met.

Maramag, Ileana, ed. *Cultural Center of the Philippines*. Manila: Cultural Center of the Philippines, ca. 1970. University of California Southern Regional Library Facility, Los Angeles.

Marchetti, Gina. "Subcultural Studies and the Film Audience: Rethinking the Film Viewing Context." In *The Cult Film Reader*, edited by Ernest Mathijs and Xavier Mendik, 403–18. Maidenhead, UK: Open University Press/McGraw-Hill Education, 2008.

Marcos, Ferdinand E. "Appendix V: [June 18, 1966] Republic Act No. 4846, an Act to Repeal Act Numbered 3874, and to Provide for the Protection and Preservation of Philippine Cultural Properties." In Baluyut, *Institutions and Icons of Patronage*, 147–52.

Marcos, Ferdinand E. Executive Order No. 30: "Creating the Cultural Center of the Philippines." *Official Gazette*, June 25, 1966. http://www.officialgazette.gov.ph/1966/06/25/executive-order-no-30-s-1966/.

Marcos, Ferdinand E. Executive Order No. 640-A: "Prescribing Guidelines to Promote and Enhance the Preservation, Growth, and Development of the Motion Picture Art and Science in the Philippines." *Official Gazette*, January 5, 1981. http://www.officialgazette.gov.ph/1981/01/05/executive-order-no-640-a-s-1981/.

Marcos, Ferdinand E. Executive Order No. 770: "Creation of the Experimental Cinema of the Philippines and Placing the Film Archives under the Umbrella Organization of the ECP." Lawphil.net, January 29, 1982. https://www.lawphil.net/executive/execord/eo1982/eo_770_1982.html.

Marcos, Ferdinand E. Executive Order No. 868: "Reorganizing the Board of Review for Motion Pictures and Television Created under Republic Act No. 3060, as Renamed and Reconstituted under Executive Orders Nos. 585, 745 and 757, and Expanding Its Functions, Powers and Duties." Lawphil.net, February 1, 1983. https://www.lawphil.net/executive/execord/eo1983/eo_868_1983.html.

Marcos, Ferdinand E. Executive Order No. 1051: "Abolition of the Defunct Experimental Cinema of the Philippines and the Transfer of the Functions and Personnel of the Film Archives to the Board of Review for Motion Pictures and Television." *Official Gazette*, August 8, 1985. http://www.officialgazette.gov.ph/1985/08/08/executive-order-no-1051-s-1985/.

Marcos, Ferdinand E. Letter of Instruction No. 1: "Prevention of the Use of Privately Owned Media Facilities and Communications." *Official Gazette*, September 21, 1972. http://www.officialgazette.gov.ph/1972/09/22/letter-of-instruction-no-1-s-1972/.

Marcos, Ferdinand E. Presidential Decree No. 1986: "Creating the Movie and Television Review and Classification Board." Lawphil.net, October 5, 1985. https://www.lawphil.net/statutes/presdecs/pd1985/pd_1986_1985.html.

Marcos, Ferdinand E. Proclamation No. 1081: "Proclaiming a State of Martial Law in the Philippines." *Official Gazette*, September 21, 1972. http://www.officialgazette.gov.ph/1972/09/21/proclamation-no-1081/.

Marcos, Ferdinand E. Proclamation No. 1374: "Declaring the Period from May 5 to 11, 1975, as Barong Filipino Week." *Official Gazette*, January 17, 1975. https://www.officialgazette.gov.ph/1975/01/17/proclamation-no-1374-s-1975/.

Marcos, Ferdinand E. Proclamation No. 2045: "Proclaiming the Termination of the State of Martial Law throughout the Philippines." *Official Gazette*, January 17, 1981. http://www.officialgazette.gov.ph/1981/01/17/proclamation-no-2045-s-1981/.

Marcos, Imelda. "Sanctuary of the Filipino Soul." In Maramag, *Cultural Center of the Philippines*, 31–33.

Martin, Jeff. "The Dawn of Tape: Transmission Device as Preservation Medium." *Moving Image* 5, no. 1 (Spring 2005): 45–66.

Masters, HG. "Manila's Oldest Artist-Run Space Damaged in Fire." *ArtAsiaPacific Magazine*, June 4, 2020. http://www.artasiapacific.com/News/ManilasOldestArtistRunSpaceDamagedInFire.

McCarthy, Julie. "Why Rights Groups Worry about the Philippines' New Anti-terrorism Law." NPR, July 21, 2020. https://www.npr.org/2020/07/21/893019057/why-rights-groups-worry-about-the-philippines-new-anti-terrorism-law.

McCoy, Alfred W. "'An Anarchy of Families': The Historiography of State and Family in the Philippines." In McCoy, *An Anarchy of Families*, 1–32.

McCoy, Alfred W., ed. *An Anarchy of Families: State and Family in the Philippines*. Quezon City, Philippines: Ateneo de Manila University Press, 1994.

McCoy, Alfred W. "Preface." In McCoy, *An Anarchy of Families*, xi–xxx.

McCoy, Alfred W. "Rent-Seeking Families and the Philippine State: A History of the Lopez Family." In McCoy, *An Anarchy of Families*, 429–536.

McDonald, Kevin. "From Online Video Store to Global Internet TV Network." In McDonald and Smith-Rowsey, *The Netflix Effect*, 203–18.

McDonald, Kevin, and Daniel Smith-Rowsey, eds. *The Netflix Effect: Technology and Entertainment in the 21st Century*. New York: Bloomsbury, 2016.

Mendoza, Annella M., ed. "Audio-Visual Archiving: Frequently Asked Questions." *Society of Film Archivists (SOFIA) Newsletter* 1, no. 1 (August 1999): 4–5. Personal papers of Victoria Belarmino and Mary del Pilar.

Mendoza, Annella M. Draft Elements for a Master Plan to Save the Philippines' Film Heritage. June 29 1994. Personal papers of Victoria Belarmino and Mary del Pilar.

Mendoza, Annella M., ed. "Seven Years of the Society of Film Archivists." *Society of Film Archivists (SOFIA) Newsletter* 1, no. 1 (August 1999): 1, 7. Personal papers of Victoria Belarmino and Mary del Pilar.

Metz, Christian. "From 'The Imaginary Signifier.'" In *Film Theory and Criticism: Introductory Readings*, 5th ed., edited by Leo Braudy and Marshall Cohen, 800–817. New York: Oxford University Press, 1999.

Milian, Claudia. "Extremely Latin, XOXO: Notes on LatinX." *Cultural Dynamics* 29, no. 3 (October 4, 2017): 121–40. https://doi.org/10.1177/0921374017727850.

Mojares, Resil B. "Decentralizing Culture in the Philippines." *Solidarity*, nos. 108–9 (1986): 89–93.

Mojares, Resil B. "The Formation of Filipino Nationality under U.S. Colonial Rule." *Philippine Quarterly of Culture and Society* 34, no. 1 (March 2006): 11–32.

Movie and Television Review and Classification Board and Movie Workers Welfare Fund. Annex A: List of Films to Be Deposited at the Cultural Center of the Philippines; List of Films to Be Deposited at the University of the Philippines Film Center. 2005. Diliman, Quezon City, PIA-MISD Archive.

Movie and Television Review and Classification Board and Movie Workers Welfare Fund. Memorandum of Agreement. 2005. Diliman, Quezon City, PIA-MISD Archive.

Movie and Television Review and Classification Board and Philippine Information Agency. Annex A: Films Transferred to the PIA. September 27, 1999. Diliman, Quezon City, PIA-MISD Archive.

Movie and Television Review and Classification Board and Philippine Information Agency. Memorandum of Agreement. October 6, 1999. Diliman, Quezon City, PIA-MISD Archive.

Mulvey, Laura. *Death 24× a Second: Stillness and the Moving Image*. London: Reaktion Books, 2006.

Mulvey, Laura. "Some Reflections on the Cinephilia Question." *Framework* 50, nos. 1–2 (Spring and Fall 2009): 190–93.

Mulvey, Laura. "Visual Pleasure and Narrative Cinema." In *Visual and Other Pleasures*, 14–26. Bloomington: Indiana University Press, 1989.

Muñoz, José Esteban. "Feeling Brown, Feeling Down: Latina Affect, the Performativity of Race, and the Depressive Position." *Signs* 31, no. 3 (Spring 2006): 675–88.

Nadilo, Sebastian. "The Cinemalaya Film Festival Announced Changes for 2015 and 2016." *Film Focus*, March 19, 2015. http://filmfocus-en.blogspot.com/2015/03/the-cinemalaya-film-festival-announced.html.

Nakpil, Carmen Guerrero. "Audio-visual Politics." *Weekly Graphic*, September 15, 1965.

Napoli, Philip M. "Media Economics and the Study of Media Industries." In *Media Industries, History, Theory, and Method*, edited by Jennifer Holt and Alisa Perren, 161–71. Malden, MA: Wiley-Blackwell, 2009.

National Assembly. Commonwealth Act No. 184: "An Act to Establish a National Language Institute and Define Its Powers and Duties." *Official Gazette*, November 13, 1936. https://www.officialgazette.gov.ph/1936/11/13/commonwealth-act-no-184/.

National Film and Sound Archive of Australia. "Base Polymers." *Preservation Guide*. Accessed April 26, 2023. https://www.nfsa.gov.au/preservation/guide/handbook/base-polymers.

National Film Archives of the Philippines. Email to author, Re: Condition of PIA martial law films. October 11, 2017.

National Film Archives of the Philippines. Film Inspection and Status Report, PIA Collection. March 24, 2017. Email forward to author from Maria Victoria Bejerano, Fwd: Letter to NFAP for Bliss Lim's book publication project, March 24, 2017.

National Film Archives of the Philippines. Inventory List—NFAP. December 23, 2014. Personal papers of Benedict "Bono" Olgado.

National Film Archives of the Philippines. List of PIA Film Titles as Deposited/Transferred to FDCP-NFAP. August 22, 2013. Diliman, Quezon City, PIA-MISD Archive.

National Film Archives of the Philippines. MOWELFUND (NFAP Inventory). February 20, 2018. Email forwarded to author by Benedict "Bono" Olgado, February 21, 2018.

National Film Archives of the Philippines. *NFAP Annual Report 2011–2012*. May 2, 2013. https://issuu.com/nfap/docs/nfap_annualreport_20112012.

National Film Archives of the Philippines. NFAP Inventory List: Inventory of PIA Film Collections. November 27–December 1, 2014. Personal papers of Benedict "Bono" Olgado.

National Film Archives of the Philippines. NFAP (PIA) Initial Inventory of 3rd Batch (16 and 35 mm) Film Inventory. April 28, 2015. Personal papers of Benedict "Bono" Olgado.

National Film Archives of the Philippines. Transcript of Roundtable Discussion 2, 2013 Philippine Heritage Summit, convened January 25, 2013, by the NFAP.

National Geographic Society. "River." Resource Library, Encyclopedic Entry. July 30, 3029. https://www.nationalgeographic.org/encyclopedia/river/.

National Media Production Center, Office of the President, and the Department of National Defense, producers. *From a Season of Strife* [motion picture], 1972.

Neves, Joshua, and Bhaskar Sarkar. "Introduction." In *Asian Video Cultures: In the Penumbra of the Global*, edited by Joshua Neves and Bhaskar Sarkar, 1–32. Durham, NC: Duke University Press, 2017.

Nizette, Mark, and Guy Petherbridge. Assessment of Potential Sites for a Philippines National Audio Visual Archives Facility. July 1996. Film, Broadcast, and New Media Production and Exhibition Department of the Cultural Center of the Philippines (CCP).

Nocon, Ramon. "Finally, a National Film Archive." *Philippine Daily Inquirer*, October 27, 2011. http://entertainment.inquirer.net/18699/finally-a-national-film-archive.

Nolledo, Wilfrido D. "The (First) Lady of the House." *Focus Philippines*, June 30, 1979.

Nolledo, Wilfrido D. "A Human Settlement for the Tao." *Focus Philippines*, June 23, 1979.

Official Gazette of the Republic of the Philippines. "Declaration of Martial Law." Accessed July 28, 2015. http://www.gov.ph/featured/declaration-of-martial-law/fm-declaresmartial-law/.

Official Gazette of the Republic of the Philippines. "Presidential Communications Reforms." Accessed January 13, 2018. http://www.officialgazette.gov.ph/featured/presidential-communications/.

Olgado, Benedict Salazar. Email to author, Re: *Ibong Adarna* reel 2, March 4, 2018.

Olgado, Benedict Salazar. Email to author, Re: Inspection results, September 20, 2017.

Olgado, Benedict Salazar. Letter from NFAP Head Benedict Salazar Olgado to Film Development Council of the Philippines Chair Briccio Santos, Re: Resignation from the FDCP, December 23, 2013.

Olgado, Benedict Salazar. Letter from NFAP Head Benedict Salazar Olgado to PIA Director-General Jose Mari Oquiñena, Re: Request for transfer of key heritage Filipino feature films currently at the Philippine Information Agency archives, February 19, 2013. Diliman, Quezon City, PIA-MISD Archive.

Olgado, Benedict Salazar. Personal interview with author, Diliman, Quezon City, August 18, 2016.

Olgado, Benedict Salazar. Personal interview with author, September 28, 2017.

Olgado, Benedict Salazar. Videoconference interview with author, May 8, 2017.

Olgado, Benedict S., and Rose Roque. "A Position Paper on House Bill No. 2404, an Act Creating the National Film Archive to Be Managed by the Film Development Council, and Appropriating Funds Therefor." May 17, 2017. Addressed to Antonio L. Tinio, Chairperson, Committee on Public Information, Seventeenth Congress, Republic of the Philippines House of Representatives.

Orellana, Ricky. Skype interview with author, August 26, 2020.

Orosa, Rosalinda L. "ABS-CBN Restores T-Bird at Ako." *Philippine Star*, March 8, 2015. https://www.philstar.com/entertainment/2015/03/08/1431215/abs-cbn-restores-t-bird-ako.

Pamaran, Maan D'Asis. "Video 48, the Last Rental Shop in Manila, Keeps a Bygone Era Alive." *Esquire Philippines*, December 18, 2017. https://www.esquiremag.ph/long-reads/features/the-last-video-rental-shop-in-manila-a1664-20171208-lfrm2.

Pang, Laikwan. "Piracy/Privacy: The Despair of Cinema and Collectivity in China," *boundary 2* 31, no. 3 (Fall 2004): 101–24.

Paras, Wilhelmina. "Return of a Golden Oldie." *Asiaweek*, December 4, 1998. http://edition.cnn.com/ASIANOW/asiaweek/98/1204/feat4.html.

Parikka, Jussi. "Archival Media Theory: An Introduction to Wolfgang Ernst's Media Archeology." In Wolfgang Ernst, *Digital Memory and the Archive*, edited by Jussi Parikka, 1–22. Minneapolis: University of Minnesota Press, 2013.

Patino, Bernadette. Email to Benedict "Bono" Olgado, Re: Data analysis request from Bliss, PIA-NFAP turnover, May 9, 2017. Email copied to author by Benedict "Bono" Olgado and Bernadette Patino.

Patino, Bernadette Rose Alba. "From Colonial Policy to National Treasure: Tracing the Making of Audiovisual Heritage in the Philippines." *Plaridel: A Philippine Journal of Communication, Media, and Society* 15, no. 2 (December 2018): 41–70.

Philippine Atmospheric, Geophysical and Astronomical Services Administration. "Climate of the Philippines." Accessed July 18, 2023. https://www.pagasa.dost.gov.ph/information/climate-philippines.

Philippine Commission on Women. "Upholding the Right to Life and Security of Spouses and Daughters: Repealing Article 247 of the Revised Penal Code." Policy Brief No. 10. March 19, 2020. https://pcw.gov.ph/upholding-the-right-to-life-and-security-of-spouses-and-daughters-repealing-article-247-of-the-revised-penal-code/.

Philippine Information Agency and Film Development Council of the Philippines. Annex A: Inventory of Deposited Materials from PIA to NFAP. September 23, 2013. Diliman, Quezon City, PIA-MISD Archive.

Philippine Information Agency and Film Development Council of the Philippines. Memorandum of Agreement. August 23, 2013. Diliman, Quezon City, PIA-MISD Archive.

Philippine Information Agency and Society of Film Archivists. Consultation Meeting Establishing the National Film/Video Archive Facility, Annotated Agenda. 1997. Personal papers of Victoria Belarmino and Mary del Pilar.

Philippine Information Agency Management Information System Division. Status of MTRCB Film Archives and Library Division. June 1999. Diliman, Quezon City, PIA-MISD Archive.

Philippine Star. "Cinemarehiyon: Binisaya Film Festival." August 2, 2012. https://www.philstar.com/cebu-entertainment/2012/08/02/834119/cinemarehiyon-binisaya-film-festival.

Philippine Star. "Insiang Returns to 53rd New York Film Festival." August 27, 2015. https://www.philstar.com/entertainment/2015/08/27/1492533/insiang-returns-53rd-new-york-film-festival.

Pierce, David. *The Survival of American Silent Feature Films: 1912–1929*. Washington DC: Council on Library and Information Resources and Library of Congress, 2013.

Pinga, Ben G. Letter from Film Institute of the Philippines, Inc., September 3, 1981. Margaret Herrick Library, Los Angeles.

Pinga, Ben G. "Looking at Our Film Institute." *Cinema Philippines*, July–September (1968): 4–9. Margaret Herrick Library, Los Angeles.

Pinga, Ben G. "Report on Screen Education." Unpublished typescript. Film Institute of the Philippines. ca. 1956. Margaret Herrick Library, Los Angeles.

Polites, Nicholas. *The Architecture of Leandro Locsin*. New York: Weatherhill, 1977.

Polotan, Kerima. "Ginupit ng Tadhana [Censored by Destiny]." *Philippines Free Press*, September 11, 1965.

Povinelli, Elizabeth A. *Economies of Abandonment: Social Belonging and Endurance in Late Liberalism*. Durham, NC: Duke University Press, 2011.

Powers, John. "A DIY Come-On: A History of Optical Printing in Avant-Garde Cinema." *Cinema Journal* 57, no. 4 (Summer 2018): 71–95.

Privatization and Management Office (PMO) and ABS-CBN Broadcasting Corporation. Deed of Absolute Sale for the film "Himala." June 21, 2001. Signed by Renato B. Valdecantos, Chief Privatization Officer, PMO; Eugenio L. Lopez III, Chairman and CEO, ABS-CBN; Socorro V. Vidanes, Senior-Vice President for Television, ABS-CBN; and Leonardo P. Katigbak, Vice-President for Acquisitions and Archives, ABS-CBN. Diliman, Quezon City, ABS-CBN Film Archives.

Provincial Government of Iloilo. "First Hiligaynon Movie Returns Home." Province of Iloilo website, June 21, 2016. http://www.iloilo.gov.ph/culture-and-history-tourism-travel/first-hiligaynon-movie-returns-home.

Quezon, Manuel L. Executive Order No. 134: "Proclaiming the National Language of the Philippines Based on the 'Tagalog' Language." *Official Gazette*, December 30, 1937. https://www.officialgazette.gov.ph/1937/12/30/executive-order-no-134-s-1937/.

Rafael, Vicente L. "Patronage, Pornography, and Youth: Ideology and Spectatorship during the Early Marcos Years." In *White Love and Other Events in Filipino History*, 122–61. Quezon City, Philippines: Ateneo de Manila University Press, 2000.

Rafael, Vicente L. "Preface to the Philippine Edition." In *White Love and Other Events in Filipino History,* xi–xiv. Quezon City, Philippines: Ateneo de Manila University Press, 2000.

Rafael, Vicente L. "The Sovereign Trickster." *Journal of Asian Studies* 78, no. 1 (2019): 141–66.

Rafael, Vicente L. "Taglish, or the Phantom Power of the Lingua Franca." In *White Love and Other Events in Filipino History*, 162–89. Durham, NC: Duke University Press, 2000.

Rafael, Vicente L. *White Love and Other Events in Filipino History*. Quezon City, Philippines: Ateneo de Manila University Press, 2000.

Rama, Napoleon G. "Now Showing: A Double-Trouble Program." *Philippines Free Press*, September 25, 1965.

Ramos, Christia Marie. "Sotto Sees No Senate Objection to Bill Declaring Marcos Birthday a Local Holiday." *Philippine Inquirer*, September 3, 2020. https://newsinfo.inquirer.net/1330711/sotto-sees-no-senate-objection-to-bill-declaring-marcos-birthday-a-local-holiday.

Ramos, Fidel V. Proklamasyon Blg. 1041. Nagpapahayag Ng Taunang Pagdiriwang Tuwing Agosto 1–31 Bilang Buwan Ng Wikang Pambansa [Declaring the Annual Celebration of National Language Month, from August 1–31]. *Official Gazette*, July 15, 1997. https://www.officialgazette.gov.ph/1997/07/15/proklamasyon-blg-1041-s-1997–2/.

Ranada, Pia. "After ABS-CBN Decision, Duterte 'Happy' He 'Dismantled' Philippine Oligarchy." *Rappler*, July 14, 2020. https://rappler.com/nation/duterte-happy-dismantled-philippine-oligarchy.

Rappler.com. "Cultural Vacuum: How ABS-CBN's Shutdown Affects Media Culture." *Rappler*, September 1, 2020. https://www.rappler.com/hustle/work/rolando-tolentino-media-culture-effects-abs-cbn-shutdown.

Rappler.com. "Marcos Buried at Libingan ng Mga Bayani." *Rappler*, November 19, 2016. https://rappler.com/nation/ferdinand-marcos-heroes-burial.

Rappler.com. "Tirso Cruz III Officially Assumes Position as FDCP Chair." *Rappler*, July 22, 2022. https://www.rappler.com/entertainment/celebrities/tirso-cruz-iii-officially-assumes-position-fdcp-chair/.

Ressa, Maria A. "In the Crosshairs of History: The Lopez Family." *Rappler*, July 25, 2020. https://www.rappler.com/video/rappler-talk-video/interview-lopez-family-crosshairs-history-chita-taylor-berta-feliciano.

Reyes, Oliver. Email to author, Re: Presidential appointments for government agencies, May 21, 2021.

Roads, Christopher. "The Manila National Film Centre." Report Prepared for the Government of the Philippines by the United Nations Educational, Scientific and Cultural Organization (UNESCO). Paris, 1981. https://unesdoc.unesco.org/ark:/48223/pf0000047235.

Rodríguez, Dylan. *Forced Passages: Imprisoned Radical Intellectuals and the U.S. Prison Regime*. Minneapolis: University of Minnesota Press, 2006.

Rohy, Valerie. "Ahistorical." *GLQ: A Journal of Lesbian and Gay Studies* 12, no. 1 (2006): 61–83.

Rony, Fatimah Tobing. *The Third Eye: Race, Cinema, and Ethnographic Spectacle.* Durham, NC: Duke University Press, 1996.

Rosen, Philip. *Change Mummified: Cinema, Historicity, Theory.* Minneapolis: University of Minnesota Press, 2001.

Roxlee. "Roxlee's 12 Commandments for Independent Filmmakers." *Philippine Daily Inquirer*, December 13, 2011. https://entertainment.inquirer.net/24005/roxlee%E2%80%99s-12-commandments-for-independent-filmmakers.

Russell, Catherine. *Archiveology: Walter Benjamin and Archival Film Practices.* Durham NC: Duke University Press, 2018.

Rutledge, Kim, Melissa McDaniel, Santani Teng, Hilary Hall, Tara Ramroop, Erin Sprout, Jeff Hunt, Diane Boudreau, and Hilary Costa. "Understanding Rivers." National Geographic Resource Library, March 14, 2011, https://www.nationalgeographic.org/article/understanding-rivers/?utm_source=BibblioRCM_Row.

Said, Edward. *Representations of the Intellectual: The 1993 Reith Lectures.* New York: Pantheon Books, 1994.

Salazar, Oskar. "Philippines' Marcos Orders Review of Exec. Order 868." *Hollywood Reporter*, February 22, 1983.

Salumbides, Vicente. *Motion Pictures in the Philippines.* Manila?: n.p. 1952.

Sammond, Nicholas. *Birth of an Industry: Blackface Minstrelsy and the Rise of American Animation.* Durham, NC: Duke University Press, 2015.

San Diego, Bayani, Jr. "Archivists Reclaim 2 Silent PH Films 'Pirated' by US." *Philippine Daily Inquirer*, August 26, 2011. http://entertainment.inquirer.net/11043/archivists-reclaim-2-silent-ph-films-'pirated'-by-us-film-fest-opens-friday.

San Diego, Bayani, Jr. "Cinemalaya 'Loses' Cojuanco." *Philippine Inquirer*, January 25, 2014. https://entertainment.inquirer.net/131455/cinemalaya-loses-cojuangco.

San Diego, Bayani, Jr. "Genghis Khan, Lost and Found." *Philippine Daily Inquirer*, September 2, 2012. http://entertainment.inquirer.net/56568/genghis-khan-lost-and-found.

San Diego, Bayani, Jr. "Inside the Kapamilya Film Vaults." *Philippine Daily Inquirer*, September 12, 2010. http://showbizandstyle.inquirer.net/entertainment/entertainment/view/20100912-291865/Inside-the-Kapamilya-film-vaults.

San Diego, Bayani, Jr. "Restoring 'Himala.'" *Philippine Daily Inquirer*, August 5, 2012. http://entertainment.inquirer.net/52959/restoring-himala.

San Diego, Bayani, Jr. "Restoring 'Portrait,' the Work of 3 National Artists." *Philippine Daily Inquirer*, March 29, 2015. http://entertainment.inquirer.net/166833/restoring-portrait-the-work-of-3-national-artists.

San Diego, Bayani, Jr. "'T-Bird at Ako' in UP Diliman." *Philippine Daily Inquirer*, February 16, 2015. http://entertainment.inquirer.net/163205/t-bird-at-ako-in-up-diliman.

San Juan, E., Jr. "Overseas Filipino Workers: The Making of an Asian-Pacific Diaspora." *Global South* 3, no. 2 (2009): 99–129.

Santos, Simon. Email to author, Re: SOFIA talk on February 26, March 4, 2021.

Santos, Simon. Post on Video 48's Facebook page. July 1, 2020. https://www.facebook.com/philippinecinema/.

Sarkar, Bhaskar. "Media Piracy and the Terrorist Boogeyman: Speculative Potentiations." *positions: asia critique* 24, no. 2 (2016): 344–68.

Schatz, Tom. "The Studio System and Conglomerate Hollywood." In *The Contemporary Hollywood Film Industry*, edited by Paul McDonald and Janet Wasko, 13–42. Malden, MA: Blackwell, 2008.

Schmelter, Uwe. Interview with Jasmine Trice, Southeast Asian Cinemas Research Network Symposium: "Archives, Activism, Aesthetics." March 16, 2018. Centre for Contemporary Arts, Glasgow.

Schnabel, Chris. "Fast Facts: What You Should Know about ABS-CBN." *Rappler*, July 5, 2017. https://www.rappler.com/business/fast-facts-abs-cbn-corporation-lopez.

Schwartz, Joan M., and Terry Cook. "Archives, Records, and Power: The Making of Modern Memory." *Archival Science* 2 (March 2002): 1–19.

Sebastiampillai, Chrishandra. "Love Teams in 1970s Philippine Cinema." PhD diss., Monash University Institute of Graduate Research, Malaysia, 2019.

Seno, Shireen, and Merv Espina. "The Kalampag Tracking Agency." In *Arkipel Grand Illusion: 3rd Jakarta International Documentary and Experimental Film Festival Catalogue*, 245–61. Jakarta: Forum Lenteng, 2015.

Seno, Shireen, and Merv Espina. Personal interview with author, Green Papaya, Quezon City, Philippines, March 28, 2018.

Serano, Julia. "Julia Serano's Trans, Gender, Sexuality, and Activism Glossary." Accessed July 18, 2023. http://www.juliaserano.com/terminology.html.

Serreng, Emely. Email to author, Re: SOFIA talk on Feb. 26, March 4, 2021.

Serreng, Emely. Personal interview with author. Video 48, Quezon City, Philippines, August 23, 2019.

Sheringham, Michael. "Archiving." In *Restless Cities*, edited by Matthew Beaumont and Gregory Dart, 1–17. London: Verso, 2010.

Sicat, Gerardo P. *Cesar Virata: Life and Times through Four Decades of Philippine Economic History*. Diliman, Quezon City: University of the Philippines Press, 2014.

Sing, Jeremy. "STOP10: Keith Deligero and Breaking Down 'Babylon.'" *Sindie*, August 2018. https://www.sindie.sg/2018/08/stop10-keith-deligero-and-breaking-down.html.

Sioson–San Juan, Thelma, ed. *Pinoy Television: The Story of ABS-CBN*. Quezon City, Philippines: ABS-CBN Broadcasting, 1999.

Slide, Anthony. *Nitrate Won't Wait: A History of Film Preservation in the United States.* Jefferson, NC: McFarland, 2000.

Smith-Rowsey, Daniel. "Imaginative Indices and Deceptive Domains." In McDonald and Smith-Rowsey, *The Netflix Effect*, 63–79.

Snow, Juan. "Video 48 Is the Last Rental Store in Manila." *Good News Pilipinas*, December 14, 2017. https://www.goodnewspilipinas.com/video-48-is-the-last-rental-store-in-manila/.

Society of Filipino Archivists for Film. "Reconfiguring Philippine Cinema: Conversations on the First Hundred Years of Philippine Cinema." SOFIA Microlearning Series (Session 2). Zoom webinar. September 11, 2020.

Sotto, Agustin. "Annex H: SOFIA (Society of Film Archivists)–PHILIPPINES." Paper presented at the Workshop/Consultative Meeting on the Development Plan for AV Archiving in the Region: The ASEAN Catalogue of Film and Television Productions, December 1–5, 1997, Quezon City, Philippines.

Sotto, Agustin. Letter to PIA undersecretary Honesto Isleta, September 19, 1994. Diliman, Quezon City, PIA-MISD Archive.

Sperb, Jason. *Flickers of Film: Nostalgia in the Time of Digital Cinema.* New Brunswick, NJ: Rutgers University Press, 2016.

Spot.ph. "Revisiting the Lesbian-Themed Classic *T-Bird at Ako*." *Spot*, April 20, 2014. https://www.spot.ph/entertainment/56209/revisiting-the-lesbian-themed-classic-t-bird-at-ako.

Star Home Video. *T-Bird at Ako* and *Ikaw ay Akin*. ABS-CBN Film Restoration Presents. Digitally restored and remastered. 2016. Color, 114 min. and 125 min., respectively. In Tagalog with English subtitles.

"Statement of the YCC Film Desk on the Disqualification of Emerson Reyes' Entry from the Eighth Cinemalaya Independent Film Festival." Young Critics Circle Film Desk, August 3, 2012. https://yccfilmdesk.wordpress.com/tag/cinemalaya-controversy/.

Statista Research Department. "Penetration rate of the video streaming (SVOD) market in the Philippines from 2017 to 2027." Statista.com, June 28, 2023. https://www.statista.com/forecasts/1258016/video-streaming-svod-penetration-rate-philippines.

Steedman, Carolyn. *Dust: The Archive and Cultural History.* New Brunswick, NJ: Rutgers University Press, 2002.

Stein, Elliott. "Manila's Angels." *Film Comment* 9, no. 5 (September–October 1983): 48–55.

Sterne, Jonathan. "Cultural Policy Studies and the Problem of Political Representation." *Communication Review* 5 (2002): 59–89.

Steyerl, Hito. "In Defense of the Poor Image." *e-flux* 10 (November 2009). http://www.e-flux.com/journal/10/61362/in-defense-of-the-poor-image/.

Stoler, Ann Laura *Along the Archival Grain: Epistemic Anxieties and Colonial Common Sense.* Princeton, NJ: Princeton University Press, 2009.

Stoll, Julia. "Ranking of Countries with the Highest Penetration Rate of Subscription Video-on-Demand (SVOD) Services Worldwide in 2023." Statista.com, July 11, 2023. https://www.statista.com/statistics/813698/svod-reach-by-country/.

Straw, Will. "Embedded Memories." In Acland, *Residual Media*, 3–15.

Streible, Dan. "Moving Image History and the *F*-Word; or, 'Digital Film' is an Oxymoron." *Film History* 25, nos. 1–2 (2013): 227–35.

Sturken, Marita. "Paradox in the Evolution of an Art Form: Great Expectations and the Making of a History." In *Illuminating Video: An Essential Guide To Video Art*, edited by Doug Hall and Sally Jo Fifer, 101–21. New York: Aperture in association with the Bay Area Video Coalition, 1990.

Tadiar, Nefertiti Xina M. *Fantasy-Production: Sexual Economies and Other Philippine Consequences for the New World Order*. Quezon City, Philippines: Ateneo de Manila University Press, 2004.

Takemoto, Tina. "Looking for Jiro Onuma: A Queer Meditation on the Incarceration of Japanese Americans during World War II." *GLQ: A Journal of Lesbian and Gay Studies* 20, no. 3 (2014): 241–75.

Talabong, Rambo. "Duterte Gov't Ends 1989 Deal Barring Troops from UP." *Rappler*, January 18, 2021. https://www.rappler.com/nation/duterte-government-ends-department-national-defense-university-philippines-accord-january-2021.

Tan, Jia. "Beijing Meets Hawai'i: Reflections on Ku'er, Indigeneity, and Queer Theory." *GLQ: A Journal of Lesbian and Gay Studies* 23, no. 1 (2017): 137–50.

Tan, Katrina Ross. "Constituting Filmic and Linguistic Heritage: The Case of Filipino Regional Films." In *Citizens, Civil Society, and Heritage-Making in Asia*, edited by Hsin-Huang Michael Hsiao, Hui Yew-Foong, and Philippe Peycamed, 137–63. Singapore: ISEAS Publishing with Institute of Sociology, Academia Sinica, and International Institute for Asian Studies, 2017.

Tan, Katrina Ross. "Creating Ripples in Philippine Cinema: The Rise of Regional Cinema." In Japan Foundation, Manila, *Art Archive 02*, 37–43.

Tan, Katrina Ross. Email to author, Re: Chapter on Binisaya and *Iskalawags*, March 12, 2021.

Tan, Nigel. "What the PH Constitutions Say about the National Language." *Rappler*, August 7, 2014. https://www.rappler.com/newsbreak/iq/national-language-philippine-constitutions.

Tatad, Francisco S. "The MIFF Passes." *Mr. & Ms. Magazine*, February 16, 1982.

Thoreson, Ryan. "Philippine Supreme Court Considers Same-Sex Marriage." *Human Rights Watch*, June 19, 2018. https://www.hrw.org/news/2018/06/19/philippine-supreme-court-considers-same-sex-marriage.

Thoreson, Ryan Richard. "Realizing Rights in Manila: Brokers and the Mediation of Sexual Politics in Manila." *GLQ: A Journal of Lesbian and Gay Studies* 18, no. 4 (2012): 529–63.

Tiongson, Nicanor G. "The Filipino Film Industry." *East-West Film Journal* 6, no. 2 (1992): 23–61.

Tiongson, Nicanor G. "The Filipino Film in the Decade of the 1980s." In *The Urian Anthology 1980–1989*, edited by Nicanor G. Tiongson, xvi–xxxv. Manila: Antonio P. Tuvera, 2001.

Tiongson, Nicanor G. "The Rise of the Philippine New Wave Indie Film, 2000–2009." In *The Urian Anthology, 2000–2009*, edited by Nicanor G. Tiongson, 2–45. Quezon City: University of the Philippines Press, 2013.

Tiongson, Nicanor G. "Si Kristo, Ronnie Poe, at Iba Pang 'Idolo': Apat Na Pagpapahalaga Sa Dula at Pelikulang Pilipino" [Of Christ, Ronnie Po, and other 'idols': four values in Philippine theater and film]. *Sagisag* 4, no. 9 (September 1979): 12–18.

Tiongson, Nicanor G. "The Winds of Change: 1986–1994." In *Genesis: Cultural Center of the Philippines 40th Anniversary Commemorative Issue*, edited by Doreen G. Yu, 28–39. Manila: Cultural Center of the Philippines, 2010.

Tioseco, Alexis. "The Letter I Would Love to Read to You in Person." *Rogue*, July 2008. https://www.nangmagazine.com/ten-years-after/alexis-tioseco.

Tioseco, Alexis. "Wishful Thinking for Philippine Cinema." *Philippine Free Press*, December 13, 2008. https://alexistioseco.wordpress.com/2009/03/15/wishful-thinking-for-philippine-cinema/.

Toledo, John. "Filipino or Filipinx?" *Philippine Inquirer*, September 15, 2020. https://opinion.inquirer.net/133571/filipino-or-filipinx.

Tolentino, Rolando B. "Mga Leksyon Mula sa Political Film Collectives sa Indie Cinema" [Lessons for indie cinema from political film collectives]. Paper presented at the Fourth Cinemalaya Film Congress of Independent Films, Cultural Center of the Philippines (CCP), Manila, July 8, 2008. https://rolandotolentino.wordpress.com/tag/cinemalaya/.

Tolentino, Rolando B. "Piracy Regulation and the Filipino's Historical Response to Globalization." *Social Science Diliman: A Philippine Journal of Society and Change* 5, nos. 1–2 (2009): 1–25.

Tolentino, Rolando, and O. J. Jacinto. "Cultural Vacuum: How ABS-CBN's Shutdown Affects Media Culture." *Rappler*, September 1, 2020. https://www.rappler.com/hustle/work/rolando-tolentino-media-culture-effects-abs-cbn-shutdown.

Tran, Tony. "Piracy on the Ground: How Informal Media Distribution and Access Influences the Film Experience in Contemporary Hanoi, Vietnam." In Baumgärtel, *Reader on International Media Piracy*, 51–80.

Trice, Jasmine Nadua. *City of Screens: Imagining Audiences in Manila's Alternative Film Culture*. Durham, NC: Duke University Press, 2021.

Trouillot, Michel-Rolph. *Silencing the Past: Power and the Production of History*. Boston: Beacon Press, 1995.

Tuazon, Ramon R. "Government Media: Rewriting Their Image and Role." National Commission for Culture and the Arts, Republic of the Philippines, 2015. http://ncca.gov.ph/subcommissions/subcommission-on-cultural

-disseminationscd/communication/government-media-rewriting-their-image-and-role/.

Tuban, Erik. "Kapayas." [Papaya]. Unpublished short story. English translation by Erik Tuban. November 17, 2013. Shared with author via Messenger [Facebook], March 9, 2021.

Ty, Leon O. "Her Husband's Best Campaigner." *Examiner*, December 5, 1965.

Ty, Leon O. "The People's Choice." *Examiner*, November 21, 1965.

United Nations Educational, Scientific, and Cultural Organization. "Report by the Director-General on the Implications of the Proclamation of a World Day for Audiovisual Heritage." September 1, 2006, http://unesdoc.unesco.org/images/0014/001469/146936e.pdf.

Usai, Paolo Cherchi. *The Death of Cinema: History, Cultural Memory, and the Digital Dark Age*. London: British Film Institute, 2001.

Usai, Paolo Cherchi. *Silent Cinema: An Introduction*. London: British Film Institute, 2000.

Variety. "Archives Shift to Snippers Hit." October 16, 1983.

Velasco, Renato S. Letter to MTRCB chairwoman Ma. Consoliza P. Laguardia, November 2, 2004. Diliman, Quezon City, PIA-MISD Archive.

Velasco, Renato S. PIA Circular No. 1: "Review Committee for Motion Pictures Division." March 8, 2004. Diliman, Quezon City, PIA-MISD Archive.

Velasco, Renato S. PIA Circular No. 3: "Implementation of the MPD-Related Management Committee Decisions by the MPD Review Committee." April 26, 2004. Diliman, Quezon City, PIA-MISD Archive.

Velasco, Renato S. PIA Circular No. 4: "Management Information System Division (MISD)." April 29, 2004. Diliman, Quezon City, PIA-MISD Archive.

Velasco, Renato S. PIA Special Order No. 195. July 15, 2004. Diliman, Quezon City, PIA-MISD Archive.

Vidal-Ortiz, Salvador, and Juliana Martínez. "Latinx Thoughts: Latinidad with an X." *Latino Studies* 16 (2018): 384–95.

Video 48 on Facebook. July 1, 2020. https://www.facebook.com/Video-48-108377235916862.

Village Voice. "Only One Oppressor." November 15, 1983.

Villarama, Baby Ruth. "Current Film Distribution Trends in the Philippines." In Japan Foundation, Manila, *Art Archive 02*, 98–105.

Walters-Johnston, Josie. Email to author, Re: Query re Ibong Adarna, March 5, 2018.

Wang, Shujen. "Piracy and the DVD/VCD Market: Contradictions and Paradoxes." In *Art, Politics, and Commerce in Chinese Cinema*, edited by Ying Zhu and Stanley Rosen, 71–83. Hong Kong: Hong Kong University Press, 2010.

Warner, Michael. *Publics and Counterpublics*. New York: Zone, 2005.

Warner, Michael. "Publics and Counterpublics." *Public Culture* 14, no. 1 (2002): 49–90.

Wee, Sui-Lee, and Camille Elemia. "The Marcos-Duterte Ticket Won. Can This Philippine Alliance Last?" *New York Times,* January 10, 2023. https://www.nytimes.com/2023/01/10/world/asia/philippines-marcos-duterte.html.

Weiss, Andrea. *Vampires and Violets: Lesbians in Cinema.* London: Jonathan Cape, 1992.

Whaley, Floyd. "Philippines Clears Gloria Macapagal Arroyo, Ex-President, of Graft Charges." *New York Times,* July 19, 2016. https://www.nytimes.com/2016/07/20/world/asia/philippines-gloria-arroyo-corruption-dismissed.html.

Whaley, Floyd. "Philippines Ex-President Is Arrested in Hospital on New Charges." *New York Times,* October 4, 2012. http://www.nytimes.com/2012/10/05/world/asia/philippines-ex-president-arrested-in-hospital-on-new-charges.html.

White, Patricia. "Lesbian Minor Cinema." *Screen* 49, no. 4 (Winter 2008): 410–25.

White, Patricia. *Uninvited: Classical Hollywood Cinema and Lesbian Representability.* Bloomington: Indiana University Press, 1999.

Wilken, Rowan. "Video Stores, Media Technologies, and Memory." *Media Fields Journal* 1 (2010): 1–9.

Willems, Wendy. "Beyond Normative Dewesternization: Examining Media Culture from the Vantage Point of the Global South." *Global South* 8, no. 1 (2014): 7–23.

Williams, Kathleen. "Internet Killed the Video Store: Video Stores, Cultural Memory, Nostalgia, and Fandom." In *Everybody Hurts: Transitions, Endings, and Resurrections in Fan Cultures,* edited by Rebecca Williams, 195–207. Iowa City: University of Iowa Press, 2018.

World Bank. "Population, Total—Philippines." Accessed July 15, 2023. https://data.worldbank.org/indicator/SP.POP.TOTL?locations=PH.

Yue, Audrey. "Queer Asian Cinema and Media Studies: From Hybridity to Critical Regionality." *Cinema Journal* 53, no. 2 (Winter 2014): 145–51.

Zafra, Jessica. "Building an Audience for Indie Cinema." In *Making Waves: 10 Years of Cinemalaya,* edited by Clodualdo del Mundo Jr., 66–77. Manila: Cultural Center of the Philippines and Anvil, 2014.

Zafra, Jessica. "T-Bird at Ako: Nora Aunor and Vilma Santos Get Bi-curious." *Interaksyon,* November 17, 2009. https://starforallseasons.com/2009/11/17/filmography-t-bird-at-ako-1982/.

INDEX

Page numbers in *italics* refer to figures.

www.ingramcontent.com/pod-product-compliance
Lightning Source LLC
LaVergne TN
LVHW010557100826
845148LV00014B/2743

* 9 7 8 1 4 7 8 0 2 5 7 3 3 *